Economic Transformation in Central Europe: A Progress Report

Economic Transformation in Central Europe: A Progress Report

Edited by
Richard Portes

© European Communities 1993

British Library Cataloguing in Publication Data
A CIP record for this book is available from the British Library

Centre for Economic Policy Research
25–28 Old Burlington Street, London W1X 1LB
ISBN 1-898128-00-6

Office for Official Publications of the European Communities
2 rue Mercier, L-2985 Luxembourg
ISBN 92-826-5680-2   Catalogue number: CM-78-93-289-EN-C

Typeset by Philip Armstrong
Printed in Great Britain by Butler & Tanner Ltd, Frome, Somerset

Contents

Tables

Figures

Preface

In December 1991 the European Commission requested the Centre for Economic Policy Research to launch a study of the process of Central Europe's economic transformation in its social and political context, as seen by economists from the region themselves. The aim was to achieve a balanced presentation of issues that are often controversial by commissioning two papers with different perspectives on each country. Each paper was the subject of a detailed commentary by an expert from the European Community: David Begg (Birkbeck College, University of London, and CEPR) for the CSFR; Gérard Roland (Université Libre de Bruxelles and CEPR) for Hungary; and Daniel Cohen (CEPREMAP and ENS, Paris, and CEPR) for Poland. The papers were discussed in a meeting with the Commission's services in Brussels and then revised extensively.

The project has benefited from the active involvement of the Commission's services, notably Jérôme Vignon and Paul Löser of the Forward Studies Unit, and Joan Pearce and Rutger Wissels of the Directorate-General for Economic and Financial Affairs. CEPR is pleased, too, to issue this volume in a joint imprint with the Commission. We believe it should command the attention of both policy-makers and analysts as an up-to-date assessment of the difficult but ultimately positive and rewarding process of economic transformation in which we in the European Community have so great a stake.

I am grateful to Liz Paton for copy-editing the papers and to CEPR staff, in particular our Publications Manager, David Guthrie.

Richard Portes

4 March 1993

Contributors

László Antal, *Kopint-Datorg Institute for Economic and Market Research and Informatics, Budapest*

Stanislaw Gomulka, *London School of Economics*

Valtr Komárek, *Institute for Forecasting, Prague*

Kálmán Mizsei, *Institute for World Economics, Budapest, and Institute for East-West Studies, New York*

Domenico Mario Nuti, *Commission of the European Communities*

Richard Portes, *CEPR and Birkbeck College (University of London)*

Werner Riecke, *National Bank of Hungary*

Dariusz K Rosati, *UN Economic Commission for Europe, Geneva*

Jan Svejnar, *Center for Economic Research and Graduate Education, Prague, and University of Pittsburgh*

1   Central Europe: the way forward

Domenico Mario Nuti and Richard Portes

1   Introduction and Summary

The 1989 revolutions in Central and Eastern Europe (CEE) started a progressive and irreversible move towards political pluralism and parliamentary democracy, private enterprise, and a market economy open to international trade and investment. A 'third way' was briefly discussed, but there was no blueprint for a coherent, stable model 'in between' state socialism with central planning and capitalism with markets. The many failed reform programmes from the mid-1950s onwards in CEE discredited all models of 'market socialism', and little attention was paid to the recent achievements of Chinese reforms. The economic transformation of CEE has been based on the propositions that the market is necessary to organize production and exchange, and private ownership is necessary to motivate economic agents.

The transformation was made harder by major inherited problems: macroeconomic imbalances; deep distortions of prices; equally distorted behavioural patterns of managers, workers, and consumers; and a capital stock inappropriate to domestic and foreign demand, to current technological possibilities, and to environmental protection. Thus systemic change was accompanied by macroeconomic stabilization programmes supported by international solidarity and by efforts to restructure institutions as well as productive capacities.

This complex process has progressed at different speeds in the various countries and sectors. The starting positions were different, and so have been the achievements to date. These are set out and analysed in the papers on the CSFR, Hungary and Poland that were prepared for this project. In general, stabilization has been relatively fast and successful, and prices were rapidly freed from administrative control. Institutional transformation has been slower than initially expected, especially because of political and technical delays to privatization. There has been a dynamic development of new small-scale private enterprise, mainly in services, but restructuring of state industry has hardly begun. Despite the world economic recession, exports to the West have grown rapidly.

1.1   East Germany

East Germany implemented instant macroeconomic stabilization through currency replacement and Federal takeover of external debt. Systemic change there came through the extension to the East of long-standing, well-functioning Western institutions and administration. Privatization and restructuring were facilitated by the relatively large number of domestic potential investors and entrepreneurs, as well as massive subsidies from the Federal budget. Membership of the European Community was automatically achieved; unification was a concomitant, priceless bonus.

Economic recovery in East Germany might have been faster, however, if the new institutional structure had initially been simpler, less sophisticated and less demanding than that of the West. Restitution of property to former (now Western) owners has created great uncertainty and delays and has thereby inhibited investment. The steep rise of real wages has made much previously existing capacity uneconomic and has also discouraged new investment, despite a wide range of investment subsidies. And the shortage of managers even in Germany suggests how scarce a resource they are throughout the region; it also might justify a more active structural policy by the Treuhandanstalt. The cost of transformation, much larger than expected, was borne not only by the people but also by the financial markets. But German circumstances were unique and cannot be replicated elsewhere in CEE.

1.2   *Stabilization, Liberalization and Systemic Transformation in the Visegrad Countries*

This project has focused on the three Central European countries (now four, after the split of Czechoslovakia) connected by the Visegrad Treaty, which led in January 1993 to an agreement to create a free trade area among them. The Polish stabilization and transformation programme of January 1990 provided a shock therapy prototype for the rest of the region. Hungary, though burdened with a heavy external debt, had a much better internal macroeconomic balance and did not need Polish-style stabilization, but it intensified price and trade liberalization along similar lines in 1990-1. The CSFR was favoured by an even better macroeconomic point of departure, but this was offset by harder tasks of institutional change (no private sector, high degree of monopolization) and industrial restructuring (away from metallurgy, armaments and machine-building).

On the whole, stabilization has been successful. The initial jump in the price level was greater than expected in both Poland and the CSFR, and significant inflation has persisted in Poland, but the rate has come down markedly rather than taking off into hyperinflation. This was mainly because of a large improvement in the state budget, but after some time the fiscal position has tended to deteriorate. The initial strong improvement of the balance of payments was also partly transitory.

Liberalization, too, has been a success. Prices were freed, markets have definitively replaced administrative allocation for goods and services, and microeconomic imbalances have been mainly eliminated in producer goods as well as consumer goods markets (contrast the sequel to price liberalization in Russia). The remaining 'coordination failures' are in foreign trade with former CMEA partners (of which more below). But goods markets are the easiest. There are signs of progress in labour markets, but that needs institution-building as well as the creation of housing markets, which is also difficult. Capital markets are the slowest to develop and require even more activist policies by the authorities.

In general, and not surprisingly, the systemic transformation has been more gradual than stabilization and liberalization. Hungary had been engaged in that process for some time, and the difference is clear, although that advantage has not notably speeded up privatization in Hungary relative to the CSFR and Poland. Nevertheless, in all three a monolithic banking system has yielded to a multi-level system of central and commercial banks; there are nascent financial markets; there has been some privatization of state assets as well as the creation of many new small private firms; and all have opened dramatically to foreign trade, which has been sharply redirected from East to West, in particular the European Community. The detailed results of stabilization, liberalization and institutional transformation are set out in the country papers.

1.3   The Depression

Bad news accompanies the good news. All countries have seen a large, protracted fall in national income, industrial output, investment and living standards; large-scale unemployment is following. Whatever the contribution of measurement errors, we do not doubt the depth of the depression, and we devote Section 2 to a discussion of the causes of the fall in output and its persistence. This will help us to interpret the lessons of the past three years and their implications both for policy choices elsewhere in the region and for current policy decisions in the Central European countries.

There were hidden unemployment, hidden inflation, activities generating negative value added, and substantial environmental damage. But the depression is not merely a result of making these visible, nor a necessary consequence of macroeconomic stabilization. The distortions were exceptionally large, pervasive and deep-rooted, and the shock of liberalization was bound to disorient expectations and create coordination problems. Yet the bigger the initial distortions, the greater the scope for quick improvement through reallocation of resources to more efficient uses. The breakdown of intra-CMEA trade, and particularly of trade with the former Soviet Union, has hurt badly: a loss of markets and often of essential intermediate inputs, and a deterioration of the terms of trade. But this has been partly self-inflicted, and policies could have mitigated rather than exaggerated it.

To some extent the depression has been due to specific features of stabilization measures and reform policies, such as: the high transitional costs of freeing trade ahead of structural change; initial overshooting of credit squeezes; currency under- and overvaluation; delays in privatization; and neglect meanwhile of the still large state sector.

All these factors either have once-for-all effects that should have been absorbed by now or are rectifiable by policy changes, which we discuss in section 4. Thus one could expect the decline to come to an end in 1993, at least for these 'early starters'. In fact the decline of output has slowed down; in Poland industrial production has begun to recover; in Hungary and the Czech Republic there have been signs of bottoming out; but recovery without the resumption of investment has fragile foundations, and unemployment will continue to rise for some time.

1.4   International Aspects

The international community has played a leading role in assisting the economies of CEE, with loans from the IMF, the World Bank, the EC, the EBRD and the EIB; funds backing exchange-rate stability and convertibility; emergency aid, grants, guarantees and technical assistance. The Community's PHARE programme, promptly initiated in mid-1989 for Hungary and Poland, has been extended to the other countries of the region.

The economic achievements of the Visegrad three/four have been matched by closer political as well as economic ties with the European Community, through the association agreements ('Europe Agreements') signed in December 1991. These have established an ongoing political dialogue which is to be formalized through 'Association Councils'. They aim at implementing a free trade area (except for agriculture) in two successive five-year stages, with rapid initial progress except for the 'sensitive' products that represent 35–45% of these countries' exports to the Community. There are provisions intended to bring about 'approximation of laws' by the associating countries to Community norms in important areas such as competition policy. The agreements record the intention of the Eastern countries to progress towards Community membership but express no commitment to this from the EC. The Edinburgh Council has now asserted such an intention.

The progress of the CSFR has been hindered by the split between the Czech and Slovak republics. Although nationalism and national disintegration have characterized many Eastern countries, Czech and Slovak separation appears to have been amicable. It does, however, create complex and difficult economic problems, ranging from currency arrangements to banking, financial and supply relationships which were not resolved before the January 1993 split.

1.5 Problems and Solutions

Everywhere new problems have also emerged, which can be eased by international resources and technical assistance but cannot be resolved without determined government action with popular support in the countries concerned. Indeed, there is a strong case for making international assistance more tightly conditional on domestic commitment to tackle these problems.

First, there is a widespread fiscal crisis. On the revenue side, taxes on profits of state enterprises were a major source, and they have fallen sharply with the output and profitability of those firms and the shift of some of them into the private sector, which normally does not pay at the same rate (whether because of tax privileges, avoidance or evasion). Introducing value added taxation takes time. The black and grey economy of the past may have been a source of flexibility and of entrepreneurs, but it also leaves a legacy of weak tax morality.

On the expenditure side, unemployment and often overgenerous social welfare provisions are costly (e.g. retirement at 60 for men and 55 for women in Hungary; pensions indexed to 'statistical' 1988-9 wage levels in Poland; accelerated retirement). Debt service is also a heavy fiscal burden in Hungary. The tax system and its administration must be modernized, and budgetary discipline must be strengthened. This is essential in countries with limited domestic financial markets and access to international finance, where therefore deficits entail monetary expansion and crowd out investment. Legislative bodies must be educated to take a more responsible role in the control of expenditure and the passage of budgets that meet both domestic and international obligations.

Second, there is a widespread failure of enterprise debtors to make scheduled payments of principal and interest to creditors, both banks and other enterprises. Financial stability is threatened, and the price mechanism cannot work properly. The normal process of exit in a market economy is suspended, and the disproportionate share of bank credit in effect going to refinancing of incumbents impedes entry. It is therefore necessary to recapitalize the banks; to put loss-making state-owned enterprises that may be 'too big to fail' on explicit, strictly cash-limited fiscal subsidies; and as part of the preparation for privatization, to 'mark to market' the debts (as well as the physical assets) of the state enterprises. Only then will it be possible to enforce liquidation and bankruptcy procedures. And when commercial banks have more freedom and room for manoeuvre, they will need more and better trained personnel; and they will require more sophisticated supervision by the central banks, which must rapidly develop their expertise in both regulation and monetary policy.

Third, it is necessary to reverse the 'state desertion' that, in the name of *laissez-faire*, has left adrift the enterprises that are still in the state sector – as most are. Privatization is moving slowly – even the voucher scheme of free distribution in the CSFR was nowhere near comprehensive and has not yet brought actual transfer of control for those firms to which it applies (in Slovakia the process will now slow down); and voucher privatization sacrifices scarce budgetary revenue. The political resistance to privatization that has made the process so slow may even increase as unemployment rises. There are also strong arguments for breaking up the big firms before privatizing them.

Meanwhile, the state firms are operating under weak, often perverse incentives and no central guidance. The growth of the small-scale new private firms cannot substitute for restructuring the large state firms in industry, and it is now evident that the market cannot do that job without guidance. Thus there is a need to work out and implement conscious industrial policies, with help from abroad; to 'commercialize' immediately all state enterprises that do not yet have proper legal frameworks; to give appropriate incentives to managers that stop the decapitalization of the state firms and induce them to reorganize and seek new markets; and to accelerate privatization with a wide menu of methods adapted to the political, economic and industrial circumstances.

Fourth, there is a clear danger of wage-push inflation in some countries. The distribution of income has shifted markedly away from industrial workers (and farmers); there are understandable disillusionment and impatience, pent-up aspirations for the fruits of the new era; and widespread populist tendencies. It would be unfortunate indeed if rising unemployment were the only source of wage discipline. Hungary appears to have had for some time an informal social pact that has brought a fall in real wages and in inflation. In Poland, Enterprise Pacts now seek to obtain the same result, so far with little success. Either such agreements or more formal arrangements may be necessary to give legitimacy to necessary austerity policies that will otherwise be avoided by weak governments and fragmented parliaments. Modern trade unions have a responsibility here and in the development and implementation of the social safety net.

Fifth, after decades of high but misdirected capital accumulation, there is now underinvestment. The restructuring of existing capacities, the development of public sector infrastructure, and the resumption of economic growth all require higher investment. Domestic savings levels are substantial, but they are not being channelled effectively into investment: budget deficits swallow up a large part, and domestic financial intermediation cannot deal properly with the remainder. Without further cuts in living standards, higher investment requires a greater flow from abroad, including debt restructuring and relief. But private foreign direct investment has so far been disappointing. Public international funds can partly fill the gap, but the Central European countries must themselves do much more to create the legal framework, incentives, domestic economic environment, and credible, stable policies that will bring higher levels of foreign investment.

Sixth, the opening of trade with the West – with convertibility, low tariffs, and few quantitative restrictions – was too abrupt. Despite the initial, protective devaluations in Poland and the CSFR, many important industrial branches became vulnerable. And it will be politically impossible to keep the real exchange rate at a level that gives these countries Third World wages. Nor is that justified. It may be too late to bring in significant tariffs, but import surcharges can give more time to adjust and are also a useful source of budgetary revenue.

1.6 The Regional Dimension

Meanwhile, regional integration could be very helpful. Moves towards a free trade area in Central Europe should be strongly encouraged; and though delayed, it is still urgent to create a functioning payments (settlements) system between them and former Soviet Union countries, which is a realistic and badly needed mechanism to keep trade going. (A payments union is unrealistic and probably unworkable.) Harmonization on the same standards (the Europe Agreements) will indirectly bring some regional harmonization, but this should be pursued directly as well. The implementation of the Visegrad free trade area will restore competitiveness in intra-regional trade that had been eroded by the Europe Agreements.

There is much to be done in integrating the physical infrastructure of the region: telecommunications and transport, energy, and environmental protection. Overall, a regional strategy for services could help to overcome the tremendous weaknesses inherited from the past that limit, for example, the development of the immense potential for tourism. Cross-border integration of financial services could also help to promote trade and cross-border investment within the region – geographical proximity should bring a much higher level of both trade and investment than has yet been attained.

1.7 The Political Underpinning of Economic Transformation

Progress along the lines sketched above will still leave deep social and political problems. The political system (constitutions), the 'political classes', and the institutions of civil society are all still weak. Poland's parliament is fragmented and its governments correspondingly unstable. Though reasonable minimum threshold vote percentages have avoided this in the CSFR and Hungary, each has serious political difficulties – Czech and Slovak nationalism (which in the latter case has potentially serious ramifications); in Hungary, unpopularity of the governing party and an internal challenge to its leadership from the extreme right. The 'expectations gap' creates political pressure for social expenditure, and economic activity itself is still not fully depoliticized – as we see in the 'clientism' manifested by the Hungarian government. Administrative capacities are weak throughout the region, and the press is not always vigorous and fully independent.

Most importantly, governments need successes. Growth, once resumed, should be able to feed itself, justifying the more optimistic predictions of acceleration in the second half of this decade. In the 'good equilibrium', skilled labour does not migrate, productivity rises, and so do their wages; investment comes in, expectations become more confident, and the rate of return to further investment rises. But this virtuous circle is not yet in motion and will not by any means be automatic. Sensible policies must promote it.

2   Causes of the Fall in Output

Here we confront the big puzzle: why has output fallen so quickly and sharply in Central and Eastern Europe (CEE), and why has the fall persisted?

It is truly a puzzle and a difficult one. Although central planning was not totally devoid of virtues – at least by comparison with disorganized markets with poor incentives – it was very inefficient in a conventional sense: it yielded an allocation far inside the production–utility–possibility frontier. In principle, it should have been possible to move towards that frontier with reallocations that made everybody better off. The puzzle is why, instead, the switch to market allocation in Central and Eastern Europe appears to have reduced output a lot and made most people worse off.

2.1   Neither the 'J-curve' nor 'Creative Destruction'

A common rationalization of the depression is the 'J-curve hypothesis': that an initial phase of sharp contraction is unavoidable in the transition, the inevitable cost of restructuring and cutting back the public sector. The original J-curve story about the effects of devaluation on the trade balance rests on the distinction between short- and long-run elasticities and is empirically testable. The analogy with economic transformation, however, is not a serious 'hypothesis', except in the trivial sense that it 'predicts' that output will eventually turn up. It simply restates the problem. In any case, what we have now still looks like an 'L-curve'. The lag is too long.

Such a deep contraction and its persistence were not predicted. That may reflect either misunderstanding of the microfoundations or unforeseen external shocks. But there is a good case for the cock-up hypothesis: that those devising policies and forecasting their outcomes simply got the policies wrong. Alternatively, they may have foreseen the outcomes but believed nevertheless that the policies were the best feasible, and hence put a gloss on the consequences to minimize political opposition.

The fall in output has not been accompanied by radical restructuring. Despite initial labour reserves in the enterprises, unemployment has not risen as much as output has fallen. There have been few bankruptcies (though they have become significant in Hungary since mid-1992). This has hindered resource reallocation and worsened the downturn of output. Tight macro policies have hit investment and have thereby also impaired restructuring. We are not observing Schumpeterian 'creative destruction'. Much of the lost output was not in negative value-added activities, and many of these continue. Moreover, the desirable Schumpeterian process is the result of innovation, investment and competition, which are notably lacking in the transformation of Eastern Europe.

We now turn to the substantive explanations that have been proposed for the decline in output.

2.2 Measurement Errors

Under central planning managers had incentives to overstate production targets and were forced to report fulfilment of those plans even if actual production was less. And now the private sector is under-reported. Moreover, measured output is not closely related to welfare – quality and composition and availability are all up.

(1) We should be somewhat sceptical about massaging the data repeatedly. The October 1991 version of the Berg and Sachs paper on Poland published in *Economic Policy* 14 (April 1992) estimated the fall in Polish consumption in 1990 at 7.3% and that in GDP (expenditure measure) at 7.7%. The final version revised these to 4.8% and 4.9% respectively. (World Bank data show 14.7% and 11.9%.)

(2) We should also recall that under central planning, there were incentives to under-report output in some circumstances. The 'ratchet effect' penalized excessively good performance by raising the following period's plan correspondingly; and to get more inputs in period $(t + 1)$, managers wanted to show unfavourable input–output coefficients in period t. The balance of incentives to over- and under-report depended on the precise lag structure and parameters of plan–performance–bonus relationships.

(3) The increase in private sector output is primarily in services. No one is seriously claiming that Poland is like Northern Italy, with many little manufacturing firms tucked away, all highly productive and escaping taxes. These countries do need some transfer of labour into services, but perhaps more of it should come from agriculture than from industry; do we want them eventually to look more like Germany or the US?

(4) Although the level of private sector output may be under-recorded, it is significantly less under-recorded now than it was before it was legalized

and encouraged. Thus its growth must be over-recorded, as previously illegal or unrecorded activities surface.

(5) The consumer surplus resulting from better access to markets is never recorded in national income accounting and there is no reason why it should be here, especially in view of the parallel unrecorded welfare decrease due to unemployment and generalized insecurity.

(6) Consider the 'unwanted output' argument more carefully. 'Unwanted' must refer to demand, and thus to price: the 'true' or 'world market' price of these goods is very low. In the extreme, 'unwanted output' is production generating negative value added at world prices. In that case, stopping it should show GDP *up* at world prices. So is this just a measurement problem? No, because in many cases the value-subtracting activities had appeared profitable because they were supported by other sectors, such as underpriced primary product or intermediate good output. The switch to world market prices should raise measured value added in those sectors. The question then arises whether the market has worked: whether it is eliminating the unwanted, value-subtracting production or whether the contraction is more random, less rational. Unfortunately, recent research suggests the latter.

2.3   Macroeconomic Stabilization

There has undoubtedly been a strong negative demand shock resulting from macro policies. Even Czechoslovakia implemented macroeconomic tightening in the IMF programme begun in January 1991, although there was no serious macro imbalance at the outset. But why tighten, then?

(1) In the CSFR as elsewhere, some policy-makers started with exaggerated notions of excess demand, the monetary overhang, and the virtues of the 'free-market' exchange rate. They therefore overestimated the extent of devaluation required.

(2) The excessive devaluation gave an unnecessarily large inflationary shock, which then did indeed require severely restrictive policies to stop the propagation of inflation.

(3) Macroeconomic policy was therefore much too tight in the CSFR (which could also have borrowed abroad to cushion the shock of transformation). In Poland, the initial devaluation caused a fall in the real money supply; the combination of nominal targeting and unexpectedly high inflation made the fall greater than intended, but no corrective action was taken for months.

(4) A credit squeeze cannot really restrict many firms which can effectively force their banks or suppliers to lend, so for a given degree of required macro tightness the squeeze has to go further and differentially hits the small firms and the private sector.

(5) But we must definitively reject the rationalization that macroeconomic stabilization must have a substantial though temporary cost in terms of lost output. This is simply false. Survey papers from the World Bank and the IMF covering over a dozen major LDC stabilization efforts show that hyperinflation has been stopped almost instantaneously with no major output costs, while stabilization programmes in chronic-inflation countries have resulted in an initial expansion followed by a later recession. So either CEE is very different or policies have done something wrong – or indeed, policies were wrong because those guiding them did not realize that CEE is very different.

(6) Thus the restrictive macroeconomic policies overshot, at least for the short run. But a further rationalization contends that a deep recession was necessary to stabilize in the medium run. The fundamental objective is to contain the growth of wages. There was virtually no unemployment in these economies; a substantial fall in output was therefore necessary to reduce the 'excessive' employment. The output fall was brought about by restricting demand; and this had to go very far, since even when output fell, firms hoarded labour (productivity fell) since there were inadequate incentives to maintain profitability (no privatization). We find this argument unacceptable on several grounds. First, the evidence is not yet clear on the relative roles in the decline of output played by the cut in aggregate demand, shifts in the composition of demand, and negative supply shocks. Second, to the extent that a rise in unemployment was required, there was ample scope to create it through policies that would force firms to release the many disguised unemployed (surplus labour) and to eliminate negative value added activities; relying on aggregate demand restriction that would bring deep cuts in useful output was clearly much costlier. Third, there was and is a role for incomes policies in restraining wage growth.

2.4 Foreign Trade

The demand and terms of trade shocks, coming primarily from the former Soviet Union (FSU), clearly played a major role. But we should not forget that the trade breakdown was partly self-inflicted, at the initiative of the CEE countries; they knew the shift to world market prices and the disintegration of CMEA were coming; and they made little effort to mitigate the shock. Moreover, some who use this as a rationale for the contraction in output also tell us that this trade was undesirable anyway, that the exports to FSU in particular were the output from the dinosaur firms that ought to go as soon as possible.

2.5   Microfoundations

Inadequate microfoundations and lack of structural reforms have had substantial macroeconomic effects. Here we include property rights, lending discipline, managerial motivation, and much else. These, in our view, are the key factors behind the lack of supply response ('supply inertia'). They reflect the *differentia specifica* of the formerly planned economies that were neglected in the macroeconomic policy programmes.

All these explanations doubtless have some role. There is certainly no acceptable monocausal interpretation. Moreover, there may be different primary causes for the initial contraction and for its subsequent persistence.

3   Lessons from the Experience of Central Europe

What lessons do we draw from the experience of the CSFR, Hungary and Poland? The main issue is not 'Big Bang' versus gradualism – rather, it is sequencing and priorities, although some policies have simply been wrong.

3.1   Gradualism or Shock Therapy

The range of available alternatives between gradualism and shock therapy is narrower than is often thought. On the one hand, several key steps in stabilization and reform should be nearly simultaneous. There can be no reason to postpone the move to market clearing prices, a uniform exchange rate, decentralized foreign trade, legalization of private property and enterprise, the beginning of privatization, while raising interest rates from perfunctory levels and cutting product subsidies, inflationary budget deficits, and automatic credits to loss-making firms. Moreover, some degree of shock therapy is necessary if the authorities cannot credibly precommit themselves to follow a consistent gradualist programme – in those circumstances, gradualism will be a recipe for continuing subsidies, rent-seeking, and avoidance of serious restructuring. On the other hand, institution-building can only be gradual, because it is a time-consuming process.

The difference between Hungarian gradualism and shock therapy elsewhere has been overplayed. East Germany offers the only example of true 'global shock therapy'. It was not necessary to have done it that way, but the political choice was made to import the entire programme – including a new currency – and implement it simultaneously. The disadvantages of this approach are now clear in the precipitous fall of output since July 1990, high and rising unemployment, and huge financial transfers required from the West. Even those transfers, as well as massive administrative and technical assistance, have not yet been sufficient to banish the spectre of a German Mezzogiorno. Perhaps the global shock would have worked if the East had not also imported the West's high wage rates, or if there were no demands for restitution of nationalized properties to their previous owners; but perhaps such an abrupt and comprehensive set of socioeconomic changes simply cannot be absorbed properly.

This is an extreme case. It is unlikely to be replicated elsewhere (except Korea), and it does not determine the choice between 'gradualism' and a 'Big Bang'. Evidently the initial conditions determine some decisions: if the economy is sliding into hyperinflation, a full stabilization package may appear urgent. Yet its chances of lasting success may be slim if a sound tax base cannot be created quickly; or if supply will not respond to a more stable macroeconomic environment. It may then seem that even the full stabilization bang, perhaps including currency convertibility, will not be sufficient as an initial step.

One can indeed argue that it is necessary to do almost everything simultaneously, because it is well known in economics that everything depends on everything else. That is what we learn from general equilibrium theory. Dynamics is difficult, the more so when the outcome depends on the path chosen as well as the speed; the easiest strategy, it may seem, is just to ignore the path and jump quickly.

But it may be impossible to jump far enough to get all the way across the crevasse. The hypothesis that 'Big Bang' is the most effective road is not testable, simply because it is administratively, institutionally and probably politically infeasible to implement all the required reforms at once, except in the German model. It is always possible, however, to blame the failure of any programme on what it left out or implemented inadequately. Thus the negative results of the Polish package are attributed to the delay of privatization, since without it large firms did not have the incentive to respond to the new environment. Yet one might say that the preoccupation with macroeconomic issues even after the stabilization itself drew attention and momentum away from privatization.

The initial conditions did not put forward many candidates for a gradualist approach. East Germany was clearly one. Czechoslovakia did take its time, in so far as nothing was really decided until after the elections of May 1990, and then the programme was not implemented until January 1991, with fairly extensive preparations. But then it was introduced as a sharp, general discontinuity. In view of circumstances elsewhere, Hungary appears to be the only feasible example of gradualism. And that has been the choice of the government elected in April 1990, although the opposition would probably have tried much faster implementation of a comprehensive blueprint.

Hungary's history is special. Even there, the switch of the target model from reformed socialism to capitalism was fairly sudden and roughly coincidental with the 1989 revolutions in the other countries. Shock macroeconomic stabilization was not undertaken because it was not needed. And Hungary benefited not so much from a more gradualist approach as such but from an early start and from proper sequencing. For example, first financial markets for bonds were introduced in 1985, then the banking system was reformed in 1987, then markets for shares were established in 1989, ahead of privatization. The only gradualist element distinctive to Hungary is its approach towards convertibility, achieved only *de facto* but still not formally adopted. This delay seems not to have deterred foreign investment.

For other East European countries and those of the former Soviet Union, there may be a necessary 'minimum bang'. But in some cases no feasible set of measures is likely to be sufficient to achieve stabilization without unsustainable output falls. In such circumstances it might be wise not to play for high stakes with an ambitious stabilization programme, but rather to focus on sectors like agriculture and energy which may be fairly independent of the macroeconomy. Meanwhile, one can pursue the somewhat more limited goal of implementing a set of measures necessary to establish a 'regime change' – a definitive and irreversible exit from the socialist planned economy, sufficient to change expectations. This has now been achieved in all the countries of Central Europe, and perhaps Bulgaria and Romania as well.

3.2   Convertibility and Opening the Economy

In external policy, the move to currency convertibility should come as soon as it is at all feasible. In addition to reinforcing the move to openness and the credibility of policy, convertibility helps to import competition and a new equilibrium price structure.

Hungarian postponement of convertibility is not simply dilatory but the direct consequence of Hungary's honourable but costly refusal to seek a reduction of its external debt burden. This policy has helped to bring new loans and foreign direct investment, and for Hungary to raise the question of debt relief now would jeopardize that achievement. But the burden of debt service is heavy, especially its domestic fiscal consequences. If Western governments were to offer debt relief in exchange for the early formal offer of convertibility, there could be gains all around.

Elsewhere, the feasibility of convertibility must be judged case by case. Of course a sufficient devaluation of the nominal exchange rate will eliminate excess demand for foreign exchange, but that may give a real exchange rate so low as to be unsustainable and indeed undesirable. In every case, going to convertibility must be accompanied by a sensible exchange-rate policy: do not devalue excessively; peg initially; then go to a crawling peg or tablita. Some of the output loss in Poland and the CSFR is due, directly or indirectly, to violation of one or more of those principles. Excessive initial devaluation exaggerates the price level shock, and this requires overly restrictive monetary policies to stop the propagation of inflation. Inflexible adherence to a nominal exchange rate peg may result in wide swings of the real exchange rate.

Excessively abrupt opening of the economy has unwisely and unnecessarily exaggerated the initial shock. Convertibility, decentralization of formerly centrally planned foreign trade transactions, opening of the economy – all these can be achieved and yield great benefits without instant free trade. A significant fraction of manufacturing activity may generate negative value added at world market prices. Yet many unprofitable firms do add value, and therefore potentially consumable output and net exports. Instant unrestricted free trade may put them out of business as well, and the resources may then remain idle and produce no value added. Tariffs may temporarily safeguard some efficiently produced output and employment. Here is a feasible opportunity for carefully judged gradualism.

There is a *prima facie* case for initial tariff protection – for senile even more than for infant industries. Indeed, the case is also that some of the apparently senile industries and firms could in fact adjust, but do not get a chance. Tariffs may be third-best to the second-best of a wage subsidy, if the latter is infeasible. And tariffs do bring in budget revenue.

3.3 Privatization and 'State Desertion'

Privatization takes time. It has been delayed by the economically unnecessary and costly emphasis on restitution of property to former owners; and by the search for the 'best' method of privatization. There has been an unfortunate focus on revolutionary experiments in mass privatization through free distribution of state assets to the population, which is not a short-cut and does not instantly create functioning markets for assets or appropriate mechanisms of corporate governance.

Meanwhile, the authorities should immediately take steps to reverse the 'state desertion' that has left state-owned enterprises floundering: commercialize them, pay attention to their management and the environment in which it operates, redirect managerial incentives, improve corporate governance in so far as is possible without privatization, and rehabilitate industrial policy. The experience of Central Europe shows that we cannot trust the market to select and eliminate negative value-added activities and to develop those that do have good long-run prospects. The market cannot and will not restructure the large state-owned enterprises – and they are too big to fail, until they are broken up and there is some expansion elsewhere in the economy. Simply citing Erhard, the Wirtschaftswunder, and Ordnungspolitik will not solve these problems (and is a misuse of history). The *modus operandi* and experience of the Treuhandanstalt confirm that even Germany recognizes that. But we cannot trust the old *nomenklatura* to guide the restructuring any more than the market. This is therefore a major challenge for foreign advice and advisers.

3.4   Financial Restructuring

A financial cleanout is long overdue. The market cannot and will not work if credit markets do not function. They will not, as long as banks do not enforce debt contracts. Enactment of bankruptcy laws is not sufficient for initiation of bankruptcy proceedings; there must also be appropriate incentives for creditors to foreclose. Until incentives are changed, the government cannot successfully delegate credit allocation in general and associated control rights over closure in particular. Moreover, when there are major credit market failures, privatization alone is unlikely to promote substantially greater efficiency. These problems are widespread throughout CEE and the former Soviet Union.

'Creditor passivity' may arise when the expected value of the debtor's assets is less than the costs of enforcing bankruptcy, or when there is an 'option value' in waiting to see whether the debtor's fortunes may improve. Moreover, if banks are severely undercapitalized, have extensive non-performing loans, and face political pressures to finance struggling state firms, they may plausibly conclude – on the basis of experience – that their debtors are 'too big to fail' and will eventually be rescued by the budget.

The greater the creditor passivity of banks, the more probable is creditor passivity in inter-enterprise relations. This may make matters worse: it increases uncertainty about the liquidation value of individual firms; it increases systemic risk by creating an interlocking network that may in aggregate be too big to fail; and it redistributes liquidity from sound to potentially unsound enterprises. But the solution lies in bank–enterprise relations: when banks press vigorously for bankruptcy of those unable to service bank loans, enterprises will take a tougher line with their customers in order to secure their own cash flow.

In these circumstances, it is urgently necessary and quite feasible to recapitalize the banks; to institute strictly cash-limited fiscal subsidies to those loss-making state-owned enterprises that are to be kept going on industrial policy grounds (see above); and in a second stage, to mark to market the debt and physical assets of state firms that are to be privatized.

Not to have done this immediately and comprehensively was the single most important error in sequencing, with the greatest cost to restructuring and to output.

3.5   Regional Trading Arrangements

Some of the lost intra-CMEA trade could and should be re-created. Within the former Soviet Union, and between it and its former CMEA partners, a substantial part of the problem is that the switch to the market has been incomplete. After the initial shock of liberalization, there is a serious coordination failure – markets are not yet functioning. The enforced move to barter has created great inefficiency and has brought a dramatic fall in the volume of transactions and consequently of output. The most urgent measure is to create the simplest institutional framework for monetary exchange – a payments or settlements mechanism with a mutually acceptable means of exchange and facilities for organizing transactions. Grand schemes for payments unions are a distraction; they are not feasible (and perhaps not desirable). But if we believe in the market, the least we can do is to create the institutional framework for it to function. This is the quickest way to raise output in the short run, or at least to stop it from falling yet further.

4   New Policies for the Central European Countries

Some of the lessons of the experience we discuss in section 3 are now relevant not so much to the Visegrad four, but rather to the rest of Central and Eastern Europe and the countries of the former Soviet Union. Here we set out specific policy guidelines for the countries covered in this project.

4.1   Dealing with the Fiscal Crisis

Developing a modern tax system and administering it effectively are key areas where massive Western technical assistance is required. Much of this is under way, but efforts should be redoubled. A value added tax and personal income tax should be the key instruments. Corporate profits taxes should become much less important; but firms should be given strong incentives to plough back profits into investment. It may not be too early to contemplate a modest rate of capital gains tax, especially in view of large-scale redistribution and concentration of wealth. Free disposal of state assets increases the fiscal pressure, since it will require higher taxes or lower expenditures to compensate for the former direct yield on state assets paid to the state budget.

The major effort for budgetary equilibrium must come from increasing tax revenues and cutting subsidies to loss-making firms. Some social welfare benefits are overly generous. On the other hand, there is no justification in incentive effects for cutting off unemployment benefits after a limited duration if there will be no jobs to find. Spending on infrastructure, education and health has been grievously squeezed, and the negative social and political effects of the deterioration in public consumption are just as important as the positive effects of improvements in private consumption.

4.2   Financial Restructuring

The CSFR and Hungary have taken limited measures to recapitalize the banks and deal with the overhang of enterprise debt. Hungary seems set for a wave of bankruptcy declarations and enforced liquidations. The Polish government has obtained World Bank assistance and is mobilizing the former 'stabilization fund' to support a plan for partial recapitalization of the banks and reduction of enterprise debts. Hidden, quasi-fiscal subsidies going to state firms through the banks must give way to open, cash-limited subsidies directly from the budget; the commercial banks' balance sheets must be made strong enough for them to emerge from 'creditor passivity'; and the debts and assets of firms must be valued realistically. Only then will financial discipline be possible; only then can the capital market function. There are still major tasks, too, in developing financial institutions, still few and thin. Here the banks and government bond markets should take priority over stock markets for some time to come.

4.3   Privatization and Reversing 'State Desertion'

Delays in privatization and the aversion to anything like industrial policies must be overcome. The politics of privatization become more, not less difficult as time passes. This argues for avoiding complex schemes and using the full range of alternative privatization techniques now available. Every remaining opportunity to break up large firms should also be taken. There is no time for ambitious experiments; all modes of privatization should be employed simultaneously. With the commercialization of state enterprises, their taxation regime should be the same as that of the private sector, without discriminatory taxes or dubious tax bases.

Even when bankruptcy does become possible, restructuring will need guidance, and the international agencies should be offering as much help as possible. In the circumstances of economies in radical transformation, short-run profitability may be a bad indicator of the capacity of a firm to restructure and adapt under good management responding to appropriate incentives and with some access to capital. Non-viable (or value-destroying) state firms, or parts of them, should close as soon as possible. The remainder will need access to investment finance, as will new small and medium enterprises. Post-privatization failures will be frequent, and unemployment will continue to rise until the growth of new and viable old firms can take up the slack.

4.4   Incomes Policies

If foreign demand is elastic and domestic suppliers can respond, lower real wages can provide an important competitive edge in the production of tradables. In a tranquil, growing economy, lower wages may stimulate investment demand by more than the depressive effect on consumption demand. In the turmoil and uncertainties of economic transformation, however, and in an already declining economy, an abrupt fall in real wages is simply a negative demand shock. The very sharp reductions of real wages in Poland in 1990 and the CSFR in 1991 were excessive, and their reversal was inflationary. It is important to try to maintain the stability of real wages at a realistic level through formal or informal incomes policies. That will not be possible unless growing unemployment is cushioned by an effective social safety net and labour market institutions.

4.5   Trade and Investment

Both foreign and domestic investment require a properly constructed, secure legal framework; and the latter will in many cases need appropriate financial intermediation. This institution-building should now take the highest priority.

The Europe Agreements constrain the possibilities for these countries to impose non-discriminatory tariffs. If broad-based import surcharges are still allowable, however, they should be considered seriously.

These countries must now pursue normal, stability-oriented macroeconomic and monetary policies. Their fiscal problems and the relative underdevelopment of their financial markets make this difficult, but not impossible. The exchange rate will continue to play a key role, the more so as trade participation rises still further. There are strong arguments here too for stability – not in the sense of trying to impose monetary discipline with a fixed nominal exchange rate, but rather by keeping the real exchange rate stable and competitive.

Reintegrating these countries into the world economy is not inconsistent with re-establishing and developing regional links. For example, harmonizing on the same standards implies harmonizing with each other, as in approximation of laws under the Europe Agreements. Moving towards free trade with the Community impels them to seek free trade with each other, because otherwise their producers will export to other countries in the region under conditions inferior to those available to Community producers (this has indeed required the Visegrad free trade area). There is a wide range of opportunities for regional cooperation in tourism, financial services, and physical infrastructure. But the main effort should be directed towards developing intra-industry trade among the countries of the region, as well as corresponding cross-border investment. The simple introduction of automatic multilateral clearing, i.e. the transferability of bilateral trade balances among trade partners, could help preserve or restore the trade flows that still correspond at least temporarily to comparative advantages. And that will provide the base for developing trade in new areas.

5   A Historical Footnote

What have the new governments done that could not have been attempted by the old governments if they had wanted to? In view of the slow pace and limited scope of privatization so far, perhaps not very much. But the old regimes did not want to open trade, as they were seeking to maintain integration in the CMEA bloc under Soviet dominance; they did not want to liberalize prices and discard administrative allocation (except Hungary). Most important, when they did want to undertake such measures (Poland 1988), they did not have the domestic political legitimacy necessary to undertake the stabilization measures of the 1990-1 programmes, or the support from abroad that has been enjoyed by their democratic successors. Hence the old governments could not have done what the new governments have done. Now the new governments must do much more.

Note

This chapter builds on the previous studies published by the Commission in *European Economy* no. 43 (1990) and *European Economy* Special edition no. 2 (1991). It draws on material in the country study chapters as well as a wide range of the literature, including our own previous writings. In view of its synthetic and policy-oriented character, however, we have omitted the scholarly apparatus of detailed bibliographical references. We are grateful to all those who collaborated in the project. The views expressed are entirely our own, not those of our respective institutions.

2   Czech and Slovak Federal Republic: a solid foundation

Jan Svejnar

1   Introduction

In this paper I provide a broad, up-to-date assessment of the economic transformation of Czechoslovakia. I start in section 2 by offering a historical perspective on the problem. In section 3, I then identify the external shocks and the principal stabilization and transformation measures undertaken since the revolution of November 1989. In section 4, I review the main economic, social and political developments in the 1989-92 period, and in section 5 I outline the main policy challenges faced by the Czech and Slovak governments in 1993 and thereafter. In section 6, I provide a brief evaluation of the economic, social and political aspects of the transformation.

In preparing this paper, I have drawn on raw data as well as on a number of studies, including those that I have written or co-authored earlier.[1] My conclusion is that Czechoslovakia embarked on the transformation path with a memory of its historical tradition of economic success in the 1920s and 1930s, with a terrible economic, political and social legacy from 40 years of the communist system, and with a determination to join the European Community in the shortest possible time frame. Enjoying popular support for a major systemic change, the Czechoslovak government adopted a bold transformation programme and, despite numerous problems, succeeded remarkably in stabilizing the economy within a short period of time. The population bore the brunt of stabilization as production and real earnings in state-owned enterprises fell dramatically. This impact, which was more pronounced in Slovakia, generated different political and social reactions in the Czech Republic from those in Slovakia and was one of the reasons for the split of Czechoslovakia into the Czech and Slovak republics on 1 January 1993. Since experience from developing countries indicates that macro stabilizations tend to unravel if microeconomic transformations are inadequate, the main challenge for the Czech and Slovak republics now lies in successfully transforming their enterprises and farms so as to resume economic growth before a potential onset of popular unrest.

2   Background

Czechoslovakia provides an interesting example of a country that became underdeveloped as a result of an externally imposed system. It is also a country that maintained relative macro stability and thus entered the transition in a better position than the other transforming socialist economies. Finally, within the Soviet bloc countries it displayed one of the most equal distributions of income as measured by the Gini coefficient (Yotopoulos and Nugent, 1976).

Before World War II, Czechoslovakia was a democracy, with an average GNP per capita similar to that of Austria, industries that were at the forefront of technological developments and products that were known worldwide for their superb workmanship.[2] The level of economic development was very unequal in the two parts, however: the Czech GNP per capita exceeded that of Austria, while that of Slovakia was significantly lower. The Czech lands were historically heavily industrialized; Slovakia was historically an agricultural economy. A remarkable fact is that, as a result of six decades of government policies stressing economic integration and regional development, Czechoslovakia entered the 1990s with negligible differences in per capita GNP between the Czech and Slovak parts.

An unfortunate result of the four decades of Soviet-imposed communist rule is the relative economic backwardness. While comparable to Austria's GNP on the brink of World War II, by 1990 Czechoslovak GNP per capita was estimated by the World Bank at US$3,300, which was comparable to that of Venezuela, Gabon and Yugoslavia, but only slightly above one-fifth of that of Austria.[3] Many Czechoslovak products were of mediocre quality, selling at a discount and with some difficulty, in the West. The discrepancy between the Czechoslovak and Western GNPs increased further in 1991 and 1992 as the officially recorded Czechoslovak GNP declined by an estimated 16% in 1991 and continued to decline in 1992 (see Table 2.1).

This remarkable transformation of a relatively advanced economy into an underdeveloped one occurred over four decades. During the post World War II reconstruction of 1945-7, the country was still run as a market economy, although major parts of industry, banking and insurance were already nationalized. After the February 1948 communist takeover, Soviet-type planning was imposed on the economy, the remaining private enterprises were nationalized[4] and priority was given to heavy industry. Czechoslovak foreign trade was forcibly reoriented from world markets towards the relatively less developed Soviet bloc countries.

The Czechoslovak government adhered to the Soviet-type planning system faithfully throughout the 1950s and early 1960s. The economic slowdown in the early 1960s led to a series of reform attempts, which culminated during the Prague Spring of 1968. In this remarkable period, the reformed communist government instituted a short-lived programme of partial price liberalization, strove to separate economic policy from political decision-making and tolerated increased enterprise autonomy and workers' participation in enterprise management. Central planning was re-imposed after the 1968 invasion of Czechoslovakia by Warsaw Pact armies, and it remained virtually intact until the late 1980s. From a historical perspective, it is also important to note that 1968 was the turning point when Czechoslovakia became a federation with significant autonomy accorded to the Czech and Slovak republics.

Interestingly, Czechoslovakia's faithful adoption and maintenance of the Soviet economic system was coupled with adherence to its historical monetary and fiscal conservatism. In 1919, one year after the creation of the country, Czechoslovakia's finance minister, Alois Rasin, had already taken effective measures to halt within Czechoslovakia the hyperinflation that raged throughout the former Austro-Hungarian empire. By temporarily closing the Czechoslovak border, stamping the Austro-Hungarian currency that was in circulation in the Czechoslovak territory at the time and recognizing only the stamped currency as legal tender, he turned Czechoslovakia into an island of stability while hyperinflation continued in all the neighbouring economies. This initial conservatism was followed throughout the two decades of democracy and also until the final phase of the communist rule. Unlike most other socialist economies, Czechoslovakia hence entered the post-1989 economic transformation in a state of relative economic stability and only limited external indebtedness.

2.1 An Historical Overview of Economic Performance

Even if one were to treat the World Bank estimates of the Czechoslovak GNP per capita as downward biased, the profound decline of Czechoslovakia's position relative to advanced market economies is indisputable. As a result, one has to accept the official as well as Western data on Czechoslovakia's long-term economic growth with caution. The data indicate that the most impressive rate of growth occurred during the First Five-Year Plan (1949–53), when the officially measured net material product (NMP) increased at nearly 10% a year. This pace proved unsustainable, however, and in the second half of the 1950s NMP reportedly grew at a much lower but still highly respectable 7% annually. The 1961–5 period witnessed virtual stagnation and led to the subsequent reform. Growth resumed at about 7% during the 1965–70 reform period and the economy still registered almost 6% annual growth during the next five years. A major slowdown to 3.6% set in between 1975 and 1980 as the first oil shock turned the terms of trade against Czechoslovakia within the Council for Mutual Economic Assistance (CMEA) and agriculture recorded poor performances.

The 1980s witnessed a further slowdown in economic growth. The world recession, rising input prices and restrictive government policies resulted in a 1.8% growth rate in the first half of the 1980s. As can be seen from Table 2.1,

Table 2.1 Production, Employment and Unemployment, 1985–92

	1985–9	1989	1990				1990	1991				1991	1992[1]	
			Q1	Q2	Q3	Q4		Q1	Q2	Q3	Q4		Q1	Q2
Real NMP														
Index, CSFR		100.0	91.8	99.4	96.0	108.6	99.0	87.5	81.8	71.8	77.3	76.9	70.0	69.7
% change[2]														
CSFR	2.0	0.7	–	–	–	–	-1.1	-4.6	-11.4	-16.0	-19.5	-19.5	-20.0	-17.5
CR	1.6	0.9	–	–	–	–	-1.1	-4.9	-11.7	-16.0	-19.0	-19.0	-18.0	-15.0
SR	2.6	0.2	–	–	–	–	-5.8	-5.2	-11.1	-16.0	-18.0	-18.0	–	–
Real GNP														
Index, CSFR	–	100.0	94.5	100.2	97.6	106.1	99.6	91.7	87.4	76.6	79.3	83.8	78.2	77.6
% change[2]														
CSFR	–	–	–	–	–	–	-0.5	-3.0	-8.0	-12.5	-15.9	-15.9	-14.7	-13.0
CR	–	–	–	–	–	–	-1.1	-1.9	-10.0	-12.3	-14.1	-14.1	-17.4	-14.0
SR	–	–	–	–	–	–	–	–	-8.0	-13.0	-14.0	-14.0	-18.0	-15.0
Real ind. production (% change)[2,3]														
CSFR	2.4	0.7	-2.9	-3.0	-3.7	-3.7	-3.7	–	-15.1	-19.8	-23.1	-23.1	-25.9	-18.9
CR	2.3	1.3	-2.9	-2.8	-3.7	-3.5	-3.5	-8.7	-14.4	-18.8	-22.5	-22.5	-22.7	-18.5
SR	2.6	-0.8	-3.1	-3.6	-3.9	-4.1	-4.1	–	-16.7	-20.5	-24.9	-24.9	-25.5	-18.8
Real agric. production (% change)[4]														
CSFR	1.4	1.7	–	–	–	–	-3.9	–	–	–	–	-8.4	–	–
CR	1.0	2.3	–	–	–	–	-2.3	–	–	–	–	-8.9	–	–
SR	2.3	0.6	–	–	–	–	-7.2	–	–	–	–	-7.4	–	–

Table 2.1 Production, Employment and Unemployment, 1985–92 (continued)

	1985-9	1989	1990 Q1	1990 Q2	1990 Q3	1990 Q4	1990	1991 Q1	1991 Q2	1991 Q3	1991 Q4	1991	1992[1] Q1	1992[1] Q2
Employment (% change)[2,5]														
CSFR	0.7	0.3	-0.7	-1.3	-1.7	-2.5	-2.5	-8.4	-9.7	-11.1	-12.5	-12.5	-13.4	-12.2
CR	0.6	0.6	-0.8	-1.3	-1.6	-2.5	-2.5	-8.4	-10.0	-11.2	-12.9	-12.9	-15.0	-13.8
SR	0.9	-0.2	-0.7	-1.3	-1.9	-2.7	-2.7	-8.2	-9.1	-10.7	-11.7	-11.7	-12.3	-11.0
Unemployment rate (%)[6]														
CSFR	–	–	–	–	–	0.8	0.8	2.3	3.8	5.6	6.6	6.6	6.5	5.5
CR	–	–	–	–	–	0.1	0.1	1.7	2.6	3.8	4.1	4.1	3.7	2.7
SR	–	–	–	–	–	1.0	1.0	3.7	6.3	9.6	11.8	11.8	12.3	11.3

Notes:
1 1992 data for CSFR, CR and SR are preliminary, data for 1990–2 have not yet been made consistent across CR, SR and CSFR.
2 Cumulative percentage change relative to the period up to the same quarter in the preceding year.
3 1991 and 1992 data include small and private enterprises.
4 Percentage change relative to preceding year. Data are not collected on quarterly basis.
5 Average number of employees in the state and private enterprises.
6 End of quarter (year) data. Employment = average number of employees in the state and cooperative sectors.

Sources: Federal Statistical Office and Czech Statistical Office; Dyba and Svejnar (1992).

the situation did not improve markedly in the second half of the 1980s, as the growth rate of NMP was only 1.95% a year in the 1985-9 period. With many observers noting that inflation was being increasingly underestimated, the 1980s can arguably be seen as a decade of economic stagnation (see e.g. Dyba, 1989).

Other indicators also signalled deterioration in economic performance and increasingly desperate attempts by the communist government to maintain a degree of public support. The share of net fixed investment in NMP fell from 20% in 1975 to a mere 13% in the late 1980s, and the share of consumption rose. Export growth slowed down in the 1980s, and exports to economically troubled developing countries were increasingly accompanied by trade credits. Within CMEA, Czechoslovakia became a net creditor, especially vis-à-vis the USSR and Poland. This was increasingly, albeit reluctantly, financed by borrowing in the West.

The secular deterioration of economic performance was brought about by a number of factors. The centralization of all economic activity after 1948 initially created phenomenal growth as the command system could rapidly mobilize existing resources. The other engine of growth was the rapid increase in inputs, which temporarily sustained a respectable growth rate. The shortcomings of the centralized system, which gradually became overwhelming, were the perverse incentives, limited innovation, inefficient allocation of resources, and rigidities. These latter factors became especially important as demand patterns started to change, input growth could no longer be sustained at high rates and the quality of marginal inputs declined. The situation was further aggravated by the isolation of Czechoslovakia from world markets and its extreme reorientation towards trade within the CMEA. This reorientation contributed to the increasing technological backwardness of Czechoslovak industry and its vulnerability to disruptions in the protected CMEA markets.

3   The Principal Measures During Stabilization and Transition

3.1   The Start of Economic Transformation, 1989–90

A number of initial reform steps, undertaken in 1989-90, paved the way for more substantial changes in January 1991 and thereafter. Even before the November 1989 'Velvet Revolution', the communist government had reduced somewhat the role of central planning. The November 1989 revolution ushered in a liberally oriented transitional government and created strong expectations of a radical economic transformation from a centrally planned to a market economy. The new government immediately devalued the koruna (Kcs) vis-à-vis the convertible currencies, revalued it vis-à-vis the rouble and tightened budgetary policies for 1990, setting itself the target of a 1.0-1.5% budget surplus. The government also declared that the introduction of a market economy and integration with the Western economies were to be the key to re-establishing economic prosperity. Specific proposals for the strategy of economic transformation were quickly put forward (see e.g. Svejnar, 1989), but disagreement also emerged within the government about both the overall direction of the economic transition and the nature and timing of specific measures. As a result, it was not until 24 May 1990 that a government economic strategy, reflecting the above principles, was officially adopted as a formal resolution.

The parliamentary elections of 8–9 June brought in a coalition that broadly favoured the market-oriented transformation. The elections brought about major personnel changes in the federal parliament, with the broadly based Civic Forum and Public Against Violence together winning 170 of the 300 seats, the Communist Party retaining only 47 seats and the Christian Democratic Alliance capturing 40 seats. Less extensive personnel turnover took place in the executive branch since many of the ministers of the transitional government belonged to the newly formed coalition of Civic Forum, Public Against Violence, and the Christian Democrats. The new government in principle adopted the 24 May economic resolution, but few significant economic measures were adopted in the immediate post-election period. The two important measures were the elimination of a negative turnover tax, which was accompanied by a Kcs 140 per month compensation for each citizen on 9 July 1990, and the gradual start of negotiations of new commercial policies with various market economies and organizations such as the European Community.

The main reason for delaying the economic transformation was the fact that other factors made rapid progress on designing and implementing an economic transition problematic. The most important of these factors were the inability to achieve consensus on a specific economic programme within the executive branch of the federal government, the desire of the newly elected parliament to play a major role in shaping economic laws and policies, the need to create a completely new legal framework for economic activity,[5] and the onset of difficult negotiations over the relative powers and jurisdictions of the federal and the two national (Czech and Slovak) governments.

On 1 September 1990, the government formally submitted to parliament a 'Scenario of Economic Reform'. The document contained the first detailed set of economic and social principles, specific measures and time parameters. It was also a political document reflecting the major compromises that had been speedily concluded within a relatively short period.

On the macroeconomic front, the scenario placed top priority on a strict anti-inflationary policy, with all other macroeconomic goals (growth, employment and balance of payments) being subordinate 'within reasonable limits'. Specific measures that were to ensure the success of this strategy in 1990 were a zero growth of the money supply and a budget surplus of at least 1.0–1.5%.[6]

Measures proposed for 1991 were a continuation of the previously established policies, but they were more far reaching in that they included a restrictive monetary policy, a 2.0–2.5% budget surplus, a convertible koruna (Kcs) for current account transactions, and a positive real interest rate.

The proposed micro policies stressed the need to induce an efficient allocation of resources, to introduce new institutions and to minimize the social costs of transition. The main measures identified in this context were: (a) a major tax reform emphasizing value added tax, a personal income tax and an 'enterprise' tax, (b) a budgetary reform stressing independence of units and transparency of budgetary allocations, (c) a process of de-etatization and privatization of property, (d) price liberalization, (e) internal convertibility of the koruna, (f) reduction and retraining of redundant labour, (g) legalization of collective bargaining and a stiff tax on wage increases, (h) restructuring of social security and health care systems and their gradual separation from the state budget, and (i) limited elements of structural (industrial) policy based on Czechoslovakia's comparative advantage.

The proposed measures varied in terms of specificity, consistency and timing. The tax reform proposal, for instance, listed a detailed set of taxes but, despite the fact that the government was elected for only two years, the implementation of the tax reform was scheduled over a period of three years. The backbone of the tax proposal, the value added tax, was to be phased in only in 1993. The proposed privatization package consisted of a rapid auctioning of small properties such as restaurants and workshops, speedy restitution of certain types of properties confiscated by the previous government, a somewhat slower commercialization and privatization of medium-sized and large firms, and transformation of agricultural cooperatives into cooperatives of owners and joint stock companies. The privatization of medium-sized and large firms would rely on a variety of methods, including investment vouchers (to be used by citizens to buy shares of enterprises), preferential sale of shares to employees, sales of shares or entire firms to foreign investors, and leasing of firms. The backbone of the proposed microeconomic programme was the liberalization of prices, which was to take place for a significant proportion of commodities on 1 January 1991. In this realm the proposal was both emphatic and cautious, noting the need for various forms of price regulation and the need to link price liberalization with the opening of the economy to imports. The principle of internal convertibility obliged enterprises to sell their foreign exchange to the banks but promised unrestricted opportunities to buy foreign exchange for international transactions.

The variety of views among the architects of the scenario could perhaps best be gauged by comparing the economic and social sections of the document. In contrast to the subordinate position given to income growth, employment and social security in the restrictive package of economic measures, the social programme stressed the social and environmental orientation of the forthcoming market economy and placed priority on social justice, employment, workers' incomes and social security. It declared that a significant decline in real incomes was unacceptable and called for an *ex ante* social agreement on the acceptable limit. The proponents of this social programme lost in the subsequent debates and the social aspect was by and large subordinated to the more austere economic part of the reform package by the end of 1990.

The parliament approved the scenario but, from the standpoint of implementation, the striking feature was the large number of laws and decrees that were to be drafted and passed before the major parts of the reform would be launched on 1 January 1991. This indeed proved to be a major burden and the resulting fatigue was increasingly visible. The introduction of some widely expected measures (e.g. the privatization of small enterprises) was consequently delayed.

3.2 Transformation Measures Undertaken in the 1991–2 Period

On 1 January 1991, the government launched a major set of reforms, consisting of liberalizing 85% of producer and consumer prices, devaluing the koruna and pegging it to a basket of five Western currencies (primarily the Deutschmark and the US$), introducing internal convertibility of the koruna together with a 20% import surcharge, controlling the growth of wages, and activating a social safety net.[7]

These radical measures were introduced in the context of a proclaimed determination to pursue restrictive macro policies, and they were supplemented by a strong push to speed up the privatization process, attract foreign capital, promote the growth of private firms, decrease government subsidies to firms as well as some other government expenditures (e.g. on arms), and generally reduce the role of the state in the economy. In many respects, the measures introduced by the Czechoslovak authorities in January 1991 resembled those launched by the Poles a year earlier.

The broad quantitative targets declared by the government for 1991 were to limit inflation in terms of the GDP deflator to 30%, GDP decline to 5–10%, unemployment to a 4.5% annual average rate, and real wage decline to 10%. The target for the current account was a deficit of Kcs 2.5 billion. The goal for 1992 was to remove most of the remaining price controls, keep the increase in money supply within the 10–15% band, maintain the existing exchange rate policy, continue the wage controls for firms with 150 or more employees, continue the privatization of small firms and launch the privatization scheme for large enterprises. The government also aimed at reducing interest rates, providing strong indirect support for small enterprises, increasing the efficiency of the banking sector, and further liberalizing foreign trade.

The government generally persevered in pursuing the policies but it did not reach all its targets. As one can see from Table 2.2, bank credit to state

Table 2.2 Credit to Enterprises and Households, 1985–92 (Kcs bn)

	1985-9	1989	1990 Q1	1990 Q2	1990 Q3	1990 Q4	1990	1991 Q1	1991 Q2	1991 Q3	1991 Q4	1991	1992 Q1	1992 Q2
Bank credit to state enterprises[1]														
CSFR	524.3	530.9	524.4	532.9	540.3	529.8	529.8	558.4	586.6	599.9	575.3	575.3	574.0	564.9
CR	355.1	360.5	314.3	387.6	395.4	383.0	383.0	397.1	414.2	420.0	403.7	403.7	398.1	390.5
SR	169.2	170.4	210.1	145.3	144.9	146.8	146.8	161.3	172.4	179.9	171.6	171.6	175.9	174.4
Bank credit to private enterprises[1]														
CSFR	–	–	–	0.5	1.4	3.4	3.4	9.3	24.7	40.5	71.4	71.4	85.4	125.7
CR	–	–	–	0.4	1.1	2.8	2.8	7.7	20.5	33.1	55.5	55.5	64.3	94.4
SR	–	–	–	0.1	0.3	0.6	0.6	1.6	4.2	7.4	15.9	15.9	21.1	31.3
Inter-enterprise debt (credit)[1,2]														
CSFR	25.0	7.2	10.6	13.8	27.8	53.6	53.6	76.4	56.8	–	–	–	–	–
CR	18.7	4.8	6.4	8.3	18.0	37.8	37.8	56.5	32.1	–	–	–	–	–
SR	6.3	2.4	4.2	5.5	9.8	15.8	15.8	19.9	24.7	–	–	–	–	–
Inter-enterprise debt (credit)[1,3]														
CSFR	–	–	–	–	–	–	44.9	78.6	123.4	147.1	145.4	145.4	143.3	123.7
CR	–	–	–	–	–	–	31.8	55.6	88.8	100.2	101.7	101.7	98.8	79.3
SR	–	–	–	–	–	–	13.1	23.0	34.6	46.9	43.7	43.7	44.5	44.4

Table 2.2 Credit to Enterprises and Households, 1985–92 (Kcs bn) (continued)

	1985–9	1989	1990 Q1	1990 Q2	1990 Q3	1990 Q4	1990 Q1	1991 Q2	1991 Q3	1991 Q4	1991	1992 Q1	1992 Q2
Bank credit to households[1]													
CSFR	42.1	46.9	44.5	47.1	47.2	50.0	50.0	51.2	51.6	52.7	55.4	55.4	56.3	55.7
CR	26.5	29.5	27.2	29.8	29.9	31.8	31.8	32.4	33.2	33.9	36.2	36.2	37.4	37.2
SR	15.6	17.4	17.3	17.3	17.3	18.2	18.2	18.8	18.4	18.8	19.2	19.2	18.9	18.5

Notes:
1 End of quarter (year) data.
2 Frozen payments due to insufficient balances in the bank accounts of debtor enterprises (bank data).
3 Unpaid obligations past maturity date (enterprise accounts).

Sources: Federal Statistical Office, Czech Statistical Office and the Czechoslovak State Bank; Dyba and Svejnar (1992).

Table 2.3 Money Supply, Interest Rate, Exchange Rate, and External Debt, 1985-92

	1985-9	1989	1990				1990	1991				1991	1992	
			Q1	Q2	Q3	Q4		Q1	Q2	Q3	Q4		Q1	Q2
Money supply (% change)[1]														
M0	5.5	8.8	2.9	6.5	7.7	8.4	8.4	-1.1	3.4	9.5	20.0	20.0	-2.5	7.5
M1	4.0	0.5	-7.4	-2.5	-5.3	-6.4	-6.4	-3.4	-1.1	9.8	28.8	28.8	-4.1	0.8
M2	5.8	3.5	-2.3	-0.2	-1.5	0.5	0.5	-0.3	5.6	12.4	27.3	27.3	2.0	7.1
Nominal interest rate (%)[2]														
Loans	5.1	5.0	5.4	5.4	5.6	7.6	5.9	14.7	15.1	14.2	13.9	14.5	13.5	13.7
Deposits	3.1	3.2	2.6	2.7	2.8	3.3	2.8	7.6	8.2	8.6	8.0	8.1	8.7	6.9
Exchange rate (Kcs/US$)[2]														
Commercial	15.1	15.1	16.5	16.6	16.0	22.7	18.0	-	-	-	-	-	-	-
Tourist	-	-	37.6	30.2	27.0	31.0	30.9	-	-	-	-	-	-	-
Auction	-	121.2	78.8	48.0	34.3	41.1	50.4	-	-	-	-	-	-	-
Parallel market	33.7	42.4	41.5	36.3	33.3	41.0	38.0	34.1	31.7	32.5	30.8	32.3	30.2	30.0
Official (unified)	-	-	-	-	-	-	-	27.9	30.3	30.5	29.2	29.5	28.8	28.8
External debt[3] (US$ bn)	6.2	7.9	7.4	7.1	7.6	8.1	8.1	8.3	8.8	9.3	9.4	9.4	8.9	9.8

Notes:
1 End of quarter (year) data reflecting changes relative to the end of the previous year.
  M0 = Currency; M1 = M0 plus demand deposits; M2 = M1 plus time deposits and foreign currency deposits.
2 Average rate in respective quarter (year).
3 End of quarter (year) data.

Sources: The Czechoslovak State Bank; Dyba and Svejnar (1992).

enterprises and households was managed conservatively. It rose in nominal terms but fell in real terms in 1991; it fell in both nominal and real terms in 1992. In contrast, bank credit to private enterprises rose from almost zero in mid-1990 to Kcs 71.4 billion at the end of 1991 and Kcs 125.7 billion in mid-1992. Credit to private firms thus amounted to 12% of credit extended by banks to state enterprises in 1991 and 22.3% in the middle of 1992. This shift in lending towards the private sector was clearly in the spirit of the transformation. Yet the general sentiment among the new entrepreneurs was that credit was too restricted and expensive.

All three measures of money supply (M0, M1 and M2) increased at less than half the rate of inflation in both 1990 and 1991 and continued to be tightly managed in 1992 (Table 2.3). This restrictive money supply policy was accompanied by rising (and still not freely set) interest rates. The protected banking sector was also allowed to establish a sizeable spread between the interest rate on loans and deposits, thus enabling it to build up reserves and raise the salary levels of employees. The unified exchange rate was set near the parallel market rate and the differential between the two became minimal. The foreign debt increased from modest US$8.1 billion at the end of 1990 to US$9.4 billion by the end of 1991 as the country borrowed US$2.135 billion in 1991.[8] The increased debt was, however, fully reflected in increased foreign currency reserves, which rose from US$1.2 billion in December 1990 to US$3.3 billion in December 1991. There was no significant evolution in the size of the debt in the first half of 1992.

Fiscal policy was somewhat less under control (see Table 2.4). After finishing 1990 with a minor surplus, registering significant budget surpluses in the first six months of 1991 and still achieving small surpluses until October, the government estimates that it ended 1991 with a Kcs 22.1 billion deficit. While this estimated deficit constituted only about 3% of budget expenditures, it reflected a potentially problematic trend. In particular, the early surpluses were brought about primarily by (a) high enterprise income and profit taxes, which reflected the initial profitability after price liberalization,[9] and (b) the still relatively low level of unemployment compensation and other expenditures. As enterprise profits declined and additional state expenditures on health and education were approved by republican parliaments in October, government expenditures began to exceed revenues. It is interesting to note that, while unemployment rose dramatically during the year, the level of unemployment compensation expenditures did not reach the level of reserves allocated for this purpose. Rather, the achievement of zero inflation led to pressure to increase government expenditures, which were automatically processed by the banks. The initial success with inflation thus reduced fiscal coordination and resulted in reduced policy control.

For 1992 the government intended to decrease agricultural subsidies as well as to reduce the benefits and improve the targeting of the social safety net. The

Table 2.4   Fiscal Budgets of CSFR, 1989–92 (Current Kcs bn)

	1989	1990	1991	1992[1]
Revenue	306.7	339.9	460.9	307.5
Turnover tax	74.7	108.5	123.1	79.0
Income & profit tax	74.1	79.0	129.2	77.7
Payroll taxes	78.2	79.6	150.4	107.8
Other revenue	79.7	72.8	58.2	43.0
Expenditures	312.2	339.1	483.0	304.8
Subsidies to enterprises	51.4	48.7	59.4	24.7
Social security	91.6	95.8	123.8	90.7
Subsidies to local budgets	52.5	58.1	72.0	23.2
Other expenditures	116.7	136.5	227.8	166.2
Surplus (deficit)	–5.5	0.8	–22.1	2.7

Note:
1   January–August data.

Sources: Federal Ministry of Finance; Dyba and Svejnar (1992).

goal was to reduce current expenditures and increase investment expenditures in real terms. At the federal, Czech and Slovak levels, the governments generally succeeded in keeping the budget in balance until the last quarter of 1992, when a mild deficit developed. Yet, the first signs since the division of Czechoslovakia on 1 January 1993 indicate that both the Czech and Slovak governments are adhering to conservative budgetary policies.

3.3   External Shocks

In assessing the effect of the Czechoslovak stabilization and transition policies, one must bear in mind that these policies were carried out in the context of disintegration of the CMEA and decline in economic activity of its traditional trading partners. The absorption of East Germany by West Germany in 1990 represented the first shock, as East Germany was a major trading partner, accounting for approximately 10% of Czechoslovakia's foreign trade. A further shock came from the disintegration of the Soviet economy (which in 1988 accounted for 33.4% of Czechoslovak exports)[10] and the reduced demand from recession-stricken East European trading partners. Finally, the switch from CMEA trade to free trade based on world prices on 1 January 1991 resulted in a significant shift in the terms of trade against Czechoslovakia. Official calculations point to a 26% worsening of Czechoslovakia's terms of trade in the first quarter, 28% in the second quarter and a cumulative 22% decline in the first three quarters of 1991.

A major attempt by Rodrik (1992) to estimate the impact of the Soviet trade shock on Czechoslovakia suggests that the 1990–1 impact was very sizeable – amounting to an income loss of about US$3.4 billion or about 7–8% of GDP. Rodrik's calculation takes into account the terms of trade shock, the removal of import subsidies and export taxes shock and the loss of markets (loss of rents associated with selling goods to the USSR at higher prices than to Western markets) shock. While Rodrik uses incomplete data and makes a number of assumptions, his approach is on the whole quite conservative (ignoring for instance the multiplier effect), and the actual impact might have been even greater.

4 Economic, Social and Political Developments in 1989–92

4.1 Statistical Trends

As can be seen from Table 2.1, the slowdown in NMP growth to 0.7% in 1989 turned into an estimated 1.1% decline in 1990 and a 19.5% decline in 1991. There was a further decline in the first quarter of 1992 and a levelling-off thereafter. The sizeable decline in 1991 was accounted for primarily by a 23.1% fall in industrial production, as agriculture declined by a more modest 8.4%. Slovakia experienced a somewhat greater decrease in industrial production (24.9%) than the Czech lands (22.5%), but also a shallower decline in agricultural production (7.4% vs. 8.9%, respectively). The Czechoslovak authorities started to calculate GNP in 1991 and their estimates suggest that this indicator of performance registered a 16% decline in 1991. On a quarterly basis, this indicator of performance appears to have fluctuated without a significant trend since mid-1991.

There are several important deficiencies in the official data. First, price increases tend to be overestimated as a result of structural changes in reporting. In particular, data from shops indicate that there was a smaller decline in sales during the 1990–2 period than is generally assumed, thus pointing to an overestimation of price increases for a given value of sales. Second, the data underestimate the growth of the private (informal) sector, which escapes the official statistical and tax coverage. Hence, although the data in Table 2.1 try to cover all enterprises, it is not clear to what extent they are successful. Finally, foreign trade appears to be underestimated as mirror statistics from the OECD (reported in Table 2.11 below) point to higher levels of Czechoslovak exports and imports than the Czechoslovak customs data (see also Rodrik, 1992).

As is evident from Table 2.1, the modest growth in employment over the mid-to-late 1980s turned into a decline in 1990. With a 2.5% decrease in 1990 and 12.5% fall in 1991, enterprises clearly carried out sizeable reductions in employment. This is further accentuated by the fact that average hours worked declined in most enterprises due to the elimination of overtime and other measures. Nevertheless, employment has so far declined less than has production. The pattern that has emerged is that the initial labour force reductions usually took the form of retirements and laying-off of immigrant workers. This was followed by a freeze on hiring and eventually lay-offs. Among the Czechoslovak workers, the group that was the hardest hit at first were hence the labour force entrants (especially young people) as insiders in state enterprises temporarily insulated themselves from the impact of the external shock and the transition. Interestingly, as lay-offs began to take place, they affected individuals in the inverse order of age, with the older (pre-retirement age) workers suffering the lowest unemployment rate.

As the unemployment data in Table 2.1 indicate, Czechoslovakia maintained a virtually zero unemployment rate until the second half of 1990. Unemployment became a serious phenomenon in 1991 as the overall rate rose from less than 1% at the start of the year to 6.6% at year end. The Czechoslovak government estimates that about one-third of the reported unemployment was fictitious, covering individuals who were gainfully employed or not actively looking for work but who succeeded in collecting unemployment benefits. Interestingly, unemployment began to decline in 1992 as the private sector absorbed unemployed workers and the state enterprises still maintained relatively large labour forces.

There has been a remarkable asymmetry across the Czech and Slovak republics in the unemployment dynamics. While employment declined by about 2.5% in 1990 and 12.5% in 1991 in both republics, unemployment rose much more rapidly in Slovakia. By the end of 1991, the unemployment rate was 4.1% in the Czech lands and 11.8% in Slovakia. It is not clear to what extent this enormous discrepancy reflects a faster rise in the private informal sector in the Czech Republic or a more liberal approach to unemployment compensation and severance pay policies in Slovakia. Information obtained by the author from both the Czech and Slovak Ministries of Labour suggests that the latter factor is important in explaining the differential unemployment rate. The formation and effective functioning of the District Labour Offices, which register and screen the unemployed, were slower in Slovakia and even now the Czech offices are much more strict in enforcing the eligibility criteria for unemployment compensation. Another important factor that accounts for the differential unemployment rate in the two republics is the greater opportunity for the citizens in the Czech Republic to work as guest workers abroad, namely in Austria and Germany. It is interesting to note that the unemployment rate started falling in both republics in 1992.

After decades of seeming stability,[11] consumer prices registered an 18.4% increase in 1990 and a major 53.6% rise in 1991 (see Table 2.5). The 1990 increase was brought about primarily by the removal of the negative turnover

Table 2.5 Prices, Wages and Consumption, 1985–92

	1985–9	1989	1990 Q1	Q2	Q3	Q4	1990	1991 Q1	Q2	Q3	Q4	1991	1992[1] Q1	Q2
Consumer price index[2]														
CSFR	1.0	1.4	2.4	3.1	13.6	18.4	18.4	40.9	49.2	49.5	53.6	53.6	1.8	3.0
CR	1.0	1.5	2.2	2.7	13.3	17.5	17.5	39.3	48.0	48.1	52.0	52.0	2.2	3.8
SR	0.9	1.3	2.3	3.8	14.0	19.2	19.2	44.9	51.6	53.4	58.3	58.3	1.4	1.9
Producer price index for industry[2]														
CSFR	0.2	-0.7	0.3	0.4	0.5	16.6	16.6	48.1	53.7	53.0	54.8	54.8	2.9	5.2
CR	0.4	0.1	0.5	0.6	0.7	15.6	15.6	48.7	54.2	54.5	56.6	56.6	3.2	6.0
SR	-0.2	-2.7	-0.2	-0.1	0.0	19.4	19.4	45.3	51.5	48.7	50.6	50.6	2.3	3.6
Nominal earnings (% change)[3]														
CSFR	2.0	2.4	3.6	2.7	2.8	3.6	3.6	6.0	10.5	12.2	16.4	16.4	21.2	22.1
CR	2.0	2.4	3.5	2.6	2.7	3.4	3.4	5.8	13.8	12.3	16.3	16.3	21.3	23.0
SR	2.1	2.6	3.7	2.9	3.0	3.9	3.9	6.1	10.8	12.2	16.6	16.6	20.5	19.7
Real personal consumption (% change)[2]														
CSFR	2.9	1.8	–	–	–	–	1.1	-26.0	-37.1	-34.3	-33.1	-33.1	-4.6	5.0
CR	2.8	1.6	–	–	–	–	1.7	-24.0	-29.0	-33.5	-29.0	-29.0	–	–
SR	3.3	2.1	–	–	–	–	0.5	–	–	–	–	–	–	–

Notes:
1 1992 data are preliminary.
2 Refers to end-of-quarter (year) data which are cumulative, reflecting changes relative to the end of the previous year.
3 Percentage change relative to the same period in the preceding year.

Sources: Federal Statistical Office and Czech Statistical Office; Dyba and Svejnar (1992).

Table 2.6 Consumer and Producer Prices in 1991 (% Change Relative to Preceding Month)

						Month						
	1	2	3	4	5	6	7	8	9	10	11	12
1991:												
Consumer prices												
CSFR	25.8	7.0	4.7	2.0	1.9	1.8	-0.1	0.0	0.3	-0.1	1.6	1.2
CR	25.8	6.1	4.3	2.4	1.9	1.8	-0.3	0.0	0.3	0.2	1.4	1.1
SR	25.9	8.8	5.8	0.8	1.9	1.8	0.5	0.5	0.1	-0.4	1.7	1.9
Producer prices in industry												
CSFR	24.0	19.3	0.1	2.9	1.7	-0.8	-0.5	0.4	-0.4	0.0	0.9	0.6
CR	20.4	22.4	0.9	3.0	1.5	-0.8	-0.1	0.6	-0.3	-0.2	1.2	0.4
SR	33.0	12.3	-2.7	2.6	2.2	-0.6	-1.5	0.2	-0.5	0.4	0.1	0.7
1992:												
Consumer prices												
CSFR	1.0	0.5	0.4	0.5	0.4	0.3	0.8	0.6	1.8	-	-	-
CR	0.9	0.7	0.6	0.6	0.5	0.4	0.6	0.6	1.9	-	-	-
SR	1.2	0.2	0.0	0.1	0.2	0.2	-0.2	0.6	1.7	-	-	-
Producer prices in industry												
CSFR	1.0	1.9	0.1	0.5	1.1	0.6	0.6	0.0	0.3	-	-	-
CR	1.0	2.0	0.2	0.8	1.3	0.6	0.7	0.2	0.5	-	-	-
SR	0.9	1.7	-0.3	-0.1	0.8	0.6	0.5	-0.4	-0.1	-	-	-

Sources: Federal Statistical Office and Czech Statistical Office; Dyba and Svejnar (1992).

tax in July and the devaluation of the koruna in the autumn. The 1991 price increase, whose dynamics are captured in detail in Table 2.6, reflected the large-scale price liberalization on 1 January 1991, followed by the liberalization of some remaining commodities later in the year. As can be seen from Table 2.6, the 1991 price liberalization resulted in a 26% jump in consumer prices in January and a gradual tapering off of inflation in the following five months. Indeed, consumer prices still increased by 7% in February and 5% in March, but the monthly rate of increase remained at or below 2% in the second quarter. The economy registered complete price stability from July to October, but then consumer prices rose again by 1.6% in November and 1.2% in December. Figures for 1992 indicate that the authorities succeeded in keeping the annual rate of inflation under 12%. With the introduction of the value added tax in January 1993 there has been a sizeable and as yet not fully documented price jump for many commodities. It remains to be seen whether this is a temporary or a permanent phenomenon.

While the price rise associated with the July 1990 elimination of the negative turnover tax was accompanied by a compensating adjustment in incomes, other price increases and the price liberalization of 1991 were carried out in the presence of relatively tight controls on wages, at least through the first half of 1991. As can be seen from Table 2.5, nominal earnings increased by a mere 3.6% in 1990 and 16% in 1991. Real earnings, measured as nominal earnings relative to the consumer price index, hence declined by 12.5% in 1990 and 26% in 1991. Personal consumption, which still registered a modest 1.1% increase in 1990, declined precipitously by 33% in 1991. Social consumption declined by 10% in 1991. The fall in the conventionally measured living standard has thus been considerable for an average consumer. At the same time, the success of the stabilization programme was undoubtedly aided by the ability of the authorities to keep the labour cost per worker down. As can be seen from Table 2.5, nominal earnings rose at the end of 1991 and in 1992, thus mitigating somewhat the dramatic fall in living standards in the early part of the transition.

There also appears to have been a considerable widening of income differentials and stratification in social status. For many individuals, especially those losing in relative terms, this has been hard to accept. The ability of the government to keep the social peace has thus been a remarkable achievement and it remains to be seen if the situation will remain as peaceful in the future.

The restrictive economic policy, external shocks and the nature of the transformation process also resulted in a major decline in investment activity. As can be seen from Table 2.7, real net fixed investment rose by a mere 2.9% in 1990 and declined by a full 20% in 1991. It is clear that, with low product demand, restrictive macro policies and uncertainty over the transfer of property rights, enterprises opted to cut down on investment. Unfortunately, no reliable data on investment could be obtained for 1992.

The savings data, reported in Tables 2.7 and 2.8 in nominal terms, imply a

Table 2.7 Investment and Savings, 1985–92 (% Change)

	1985–9	1989	1990 Q1	1990 Q2	1990 Q3	1990 Q4	1990	1991 Q1	1991 Q2	1991 Q3	1991 Q4	1991	1992[1] Q1	1992[1] Q2
Real net fixed investment[2]														
CSFR	2.8	3.1	–	–	–	–	2.9	-10.0	-28.3	-22.0	-20.0	-20.0	–	–
CR	2.3	1.7	–	–	–	–	2.7	-12.0	-20.0	-15.0	-13.0	-13.0	–	–
SR	3.5	4.1	–	–	–	–	3.2	–	–	–	–	–	–	–
Savings of population in korunas[2]														
CSFR	2.3	4.6	0.8	1.2	0.9	-2.6	-2.6	-1.2	0.1	2.6	12.7	12.7	3.0	4.7
CR	5.8	4.0	0.9	1.4	1.1	-2.0	-2.0	-0.8	1.9	4.6	14.7	14.7	3.0	5.5
SR	4.4	5.8	0.7	0.9	0.4	-3.9	-3.9	-2.3	-3.7	-1.8	8.5	8.5	3.1	3.0
Savings of enterprises in korunas[2]														
CSFR	6.0	2.8	-18.7	-14.1	-15.4	-15.8	-15.8	0.0	7.4	11.3	34.9	34.9	2.8	4.7
CR	–	–	–	–	–	–	–	3.3	10.4	15.0	31.3	39.3	6.5	8.0
SR	–	–	–	–	–	–	–	-7.5	0.6	2.9	25.3	25.3	-6.3	-3.6

Notes:
1 1992 data are preliminary.
2 End of quarter (year) data reflecting changes relative to the end of the previous year.

Sources: Federal Statistical Office, Czech Statistical Office and the Czechoslovak State Bank; Dyba and Svejnar (1992).

Table 2.8 Savings in Foreign Currencies, 1990–2 (Kcs bn)

						Month						
	1	2	3	4	5	6	7	8	9	10	11	12
1990:												
Enterprises	–	–	3.9	4.3	4.8	6.0	6.1	7.6	8.7	11.2	12.7	18.0
Households	2.1	2.3	2.8	1.8	2.0	3.7	3.9	4.2	3.2	7.1	6.5	10.2
1991:												
Enterprises	15.0	15.5	14.1	21.7	21.2	21.1	21.5	21.6	22.8	21.8	19.5	19.8
Households	11.3	12.6	14.0	15.4	16.7	18.2	19.2	21.1	22.3	23.2	24.4	26.6
1992:												
Enterprises	20.0	19.4	21.9	21.9	26.6	26.0	26.1					
Households	29.8	31.2	35.1	36.3	37.6	39.8	42.3					

Note: End of month data.

Sources: The Czechoslovak State Bank; Dyba and Svejnar (1992).

decline in the propensity to save in korunas and a rising propensity to save in foreign currencies. This trend was somewhat reversed in the second half of 1991 as price stability and the fixed nominal interest rate policy resulted in high real interest rates on koruna deposits.

As can be seen in Table 2.2, a major response of enterprises to the restrictive monetary and fiscal policies has been an increasing reliance on inter-enterprise debt (credit). There are two data series that permit one to assess the extent of this phenomenon in Czechoslovakia. The first one – frozen bank payments due to insufficient balances in the bank accounts of debtor enterprises – captures the extent of insolvency of firms as reflected in their inability to meet deadline payments through banks due to insufficient funds. The series shows a major and continuous rise through the first quarter of 1991 in both republics, exceeding 10% of total bank credit to all enterprises from the third quarter of 1990 on. The series registered a significant decline in the Czech Republic in the second quarter of 1991, just prior to the banks' decision to discontinue the collection of these data.[12]

The second data series refers to unpaid obligations of enterprises as shown in enterprise accounts. This series has been collected continuously since 1990 and it has the advantage that it also contains direct inter-enterprise debt that is not channelled through banks. The series depicts a major rise in inter-enterprise debt from Kcs 45 billion at the end of 1990 to 145 billion at the end of 1991. Hence, while the inter-enterprise debt was equal to 8.4% of the total bank credit to enterprises at the end of 1990, by the end of 1991 it had jumped to 22.8%. This is a significant rise that potentially represents an enormous problem for the government and the banks. It also in large part explains why virtually no state enterprises have gone bankrupt in the presence of the seemingly very restrictive macroeconomic policies and great external shocks. The government has been aware of the problem and in the autumn of 1991 it allocated Kcs 50 billion from its (future) privatization income to the banks for the purpose of increasing their capitalization and partially (selectively) reducing the bank debt of promising enterprises. In 1992, the series has shown a tendency towards decline, but many analysts also increasingly question its accuracy. The problem hence most likely remains but its analysis becomes increasingly difficult.

Finally, turning to foreign trade, one can see from Table 2.9 that, after registering a trade deficit in 1990, Czechoslovakia appears to have achieved a surplus in 1991. Moreover, while trade with the (former) socialist economies accounted for more than 60% of total trade in 1989, this share dropped to about 50% in 1990 and 40% in 1991. Trade in non-convertible currency basically disappeared in 1991 and Germany replaced the Soviet Union as Czechoslovakia's main trading partner, accounting for almost a quarter of Czechoslovakia's foreign trade. As the official data reported in Table 2.9 suggest, the geographic restructuring has not avoided a major real decline in the physical volume of Czechoslovakia's foreign trade. For the first six months of

Table 2.9   Czechoslovak Foreign Trade, 1989–92 (Current Kcs bn, fob)

	1989	1990	1991	1992[1]
Exports	217.5	216.5	321.2	176.7
1. 'Socialist' countries	132.3	106.7	126.3	43.5
2. Market economies	85.2	109.8	194.9	133.2
Imports	214.7	246.3	293.7	171.7
1. 'Socialist' countries	133.8	125.7	125.9	62.7
2. Market economies	80.9	120.6	167.8	109.0
Surplus (deficit)	2.8	–29.8	27.5	5.0

Note:
1   January–July data.

Sources: Federal Statistical Office; Dyba and Svejnar (1992).

1991, the official estimates put the decline in the physical volume of exports at 30% and imports at 31%. Estimates for the January–November period indicate a much smaller 15.5% decline in the physical volume of exports but still a sizeable 28.9% decline in imports. The official data hence suggest that the volume of Czechoslovakia's foreign trade has shrunk considerably but that in terms of exports a turnaround has been achieved since mid-1991. In relative terms, exports represented 29% of GDP in 1989, 26% in 1990 and an estimated 30% in 1991.

In this context it must be stressed that the official Czechoslovak data, based on customs statistics, are at great variance with OECD data. As Rodrik (1992) shows, OECD statistics show much greater trade activity between Czechoslovakia and major OECD members. For instance, in the first quarter of 1991, Czechoslovak statistics showed that Czechoslovak exports to OECD countries fell by 19% while OECD statistics showed an increase of 12%. Similarly, as data in Tables 2.10 and 2.11 indicate, there was a major (about 35%) increase in the dollar value of Czechoslovak exports to and imports from OECD countries in 1991. While part of this surge was accounted for by the falling value of the US dollar, there was a significant volume increase as well. Since the Czechoslovak Statistical Office itself questioned the validity of the official data, it seems that the OECD statistics provide a more accurate picture.

4.1.1 Privatization
A salient feature of the Czechoslovak transformation process is the rapid privatization of state property. Indeed, since 1990 Czechoslovakia has moved from being one of the most state dominated economies to a situation in which it

Table 2.10   Czechoslovak Imports from OECD Countries, 1989-92 (monthly averages, US$ mn)

Country	1989	1990	1991 Q1	1991 Q2	1991 Q3	1991 Q4	1991	1992 Q1	1992 Q2
OECD	306.0	406.0	518.0	461.0	458.0	658.0	565.0	–	–
EC	219.0	277.0	406.0	347.0	340.0	487.0	394.0	517.0	–
EFTA	68.2	106.3	86.3	92.1	98.3	138.7	103.4	129.2	145.9
USA	4.5	7.4	10.2	9.7	8.0	13.5	10.3	14.2	28.0
Japan	4.6	4.2	7.3	4.2	5.4	6.0	5.7	9.0	9.2
Austria	31.6	64.1	52.2	55.0	63.0	91.6	65.5	84.4	93.4
France	19.4	23.9	80.2	27.7	22.6	33.9	40.1	35.3	62.7
Germany	121.9	160.7	231.4	216.6	232.3	320.5	250.2	337.4	368.3
Italy	23.8	32.4	30.9	40.6	29.2	49.1	37.9	52.6	66.1
Netherlands	14.1	16.3	18.7	17.7	16.1	26.2	19.6	27.4	30.0
Spain	4.3	4.7	5.6	4.5	2.4	5.0	4.3	5.9	7.5
Sweden	9.0	12.2	11.0	9.8	10.0	15.6	11.6	19.2	11.7
Switzerland	18.1	20.8	19.0	19.4	18.9	23.7	19.8	19.8	25.9
UK	17.9	19.7	18.9	16.3	14.8	26.5	19.0	26.0	28.4
Yugoslavia	35.2	38.6	24.7	27.0	n.a.	n.a.	n.a.	n.a.	n.a.

Sources: OECD, *Monthly Statistics of Foreign Trade*; Dyba and Svejnar (1992).

Table 2.11   Czechoslovak Exports to OECD Countries, 1989-92 (monthly averages, US$ mn)

Country	1989	1990	1991 Q1	1991 Q2	1991 Q3	1991 Q4	1991	1992 Q1	1992 Q2
OECD	347.0	408.0	476.0	500.0	546.0	678.0	551.0	–	–
EC	238.0	285.0	359.0	381.0	416.0	532.0	423.0	531.0	–
EFTA	76.2	84.3	80.7	77.5	83.0	100.9	85.5	97.2	118.2
USA	7.2	7.3	9.2	10.1	13.0	15.8	12.0	17.8	17.9
Japan	10.8	10.7	10.3	11.4	7.7	12.9	10.5	10.5	13.9
Austria	42.4	47.1	44.2	46.7	53.1	68.1	53.0	61.8	85.5
France	22.4	29.0	28.9	30.4	31.3	35.4	31.5	39.8	41.1
Germany	110.7	140.2	215.1	220.5	259.8	328.2	255.9	334.9	371.3
Italy	33.8	39.9	38.5	49.0	43.5	72.5	51.5	68.1	77.0
Netherlands	16.0	18.6	22.2	21.7	21.2	25.3	22.6	16.0	22.9
Spain	7.3	7.3	7.3	9.2	8.3	11.2	9.0	12.7	14.2
Sweden	9.6	10.4	10.9	9.8	9.8	10.7	10.3	12.9	11.6
Switzerland	10.4	9.9	9.9	10.3	8.9	10.8	10.0	10.4	11.4
UK	21.4	20.1	16.5	19.1	19.8	21.5	19.3	22.3	26.8
Yugoslavia	40.8	43.1	52.6	68.2	n.a.	n.a.	n.a.	n.a.	n.a.

Sources: OECD, *Monthly Statistics of Foreign Trade*; Dyba and Svejnar (1992).

has rapidly privatized the great proportion of state assets.

As in most transitional economies, the privatization process has proceeded at two levels, focusing on small and large units, respectively. The privatization of small and medium-sized enterprises and other economic units started in the autumn of 1990 and has been relatively successful. While proceeding slower than originally forecast, by June 1992 the government had auctioned off about 27,000 units and returned a similar number to previous owners through property restitution. The restitution process also involves housing, thus creating a precondition for the future establishment of a real estate market. By June 1992 the proceeds from the small-scale privatization amounted to about Kcs 35 billion (about US$1.2 billion). In comparison, the amount of foreign investment in 1991 was about US$650 million. In December 1992, the Czechoslovak government estimated that by mid-1992 it had auctioned off about two-thirds of all the units that were scheduled to be privatized within the small-scale privatization process.

The process of privatizing approximately 6,000 large Czechoslovak enterprises (about 4,400 of which were in the Czech Republic and 1,600 in Slovakia) was divided into two waves, with each wave consisting of several rounds of bidding. The first wave, which took place in 1992, involved over 3,000 units (2,210 in the Czech lands), thus covering about one-half of all units planned for privatization. The second wave, presumed to cover the rest of the firms, is scheduled to take place in 1993. However, in view of the partition of Czechoslovakia into two independent republics on 1 January 1993, the second wave may proceed at different speeds in the Czech and Slovak republics. The Slovak officials in fact report that the voucher method may be used only as a subsidiary method in the second wave.

Within the first wave of large-scale privatization, enterprises were privatized on the basis of privatization projects, which were selected from a number of competing projects by the Czech and Slovak Ministries of Privatization and by the Federal Ministry of Finance. Projects could be submitted by any domestic or foreign individual or group. In the first wave, the number of submitted privatization projects per firm averaged 3.8; for some firms the number of submitted projects was in excess of 20.

Of the total number of 3,100 firms that entered the first wave, 1,491 were privatized either entirely or at least in part through the voucher method by which individual citizens could use vouchers, distributed almost free, to bid for shares in firms.[13] The book value of shares allocated for the voucher privatization scheme in the first wave was Kcs 300 billion (about US$11 billion).

Within each wave, the process of converting points into shares took place in rounds of bidding. Between May and December 1992, the voucher privatization process went through five rounds. After the fourth round, with almost 80% of all shares allocated for the voucher scheme placed, the government decided to make the fifth round the last one. Since the system's iterations failed to converge, the government used brute force to terminate the process.

The general assessment is that the process of distributing vouchers and converting them into shares was an awkward and cumbersome one. Nevertheless, it succeeded in transferring 93% of shares allocated for voucher privatization from the state to individual citizens and to the investment privatization funds (IPFs) that formed spontaneously and into which citizens placed their voucher points. Hence, however inelegant, the Czechoslovak example indicates that transferring a large fraction of state ownership to a large number of citizens is feasible. The issue that remains unresolved is whether the individual citizen-shareholders and investment funds will generate a structure of corporate governance that will alter enterprise behaviour towards greater efficiency.

4.2   Social Issues – Unemployment and Migration

While the overall unemployment picture has already been discussed along with other economic indicators in section 4.1, in view of the orientation of this paper it is worth examining some of its social aspects in more detail.

4.2.1 The Unemployment Compensation Scheme

The Czechoslovak government put into place an unemployment compensation scheme in January 1990 – almost immediately after the November 1989 revolution. The scheme entitled anyone who was laid off, or who graduated from school, to one year of benefits according to the following schedule:

(a) the first six months of unemployment: 65% of the individual's net average income over the previous year if the individual was laid off for organizational reasons, 60% of net average income if laid off for other reason, Kcs 1,580 monthly if seeking work for the first time;
(b) the second six months of unemployment: 50% of net average income;
(c) if in retraining, 70% of net average income.

The scheme was quite favourable to the worker. Although there was a minimum benefit of Kcs 1,580 there was no ceiling (unlike Western unemployment insurance programmes). In addition, again unlike Western systems, there was no requirement on the minimum number of months the person had to have been employed prior to receiving benefit. Moreover, many people who were out of the labour force could be eligible for benefit after a certain period. For example, mothers caring for children under 3 years of age were eligible for unemployment benefit after one year of child care. Similarly, people were also eligible after one year of: (i) caring for handicapped children; (ii) being registered as a job applicant; (iii) receiving a disability or widow's pension; (iv) suffering from an illness; or (v) being detained or imprisoned or serving in the army.

A new, more restrictive scheme was introduced on 1 January 1992. In the new scheme, only an individual who either worked, studied, or took care of a child up to 3 years of age for 12 months during the previous three years qualifies for unemployment benefit. No one else is eligible. Moreover, since January 1992, the maximum period during which an individual may receive unemployment benefit has been shortened from one year to six months (those undergoing retraining are covered for one year). Third, the amount of unemployment benefits for 1992 was set at 60% of net average income in the last quarter of employment for the first three months and 50% for the next three months. (Those being retrained receive 70% during the retraining period.) The minimum amount of benefit was set at Kcs 1,200 (approximately US$40), which is the subsistence level set by law. The maximum was set at Kcs 3,000 (approximately US$100), or Kcs 3,600 (approximately US$120) for those in retraining.

Before January 1992, it appears that many districts in the Slovak Republic allowed individuals to collect severance pay and unemployment benefit concurrently. Since this date, concurrent receipt of severance/leave pay is not permitted. A person who is granted severance pay or leave pay in their last employment can be granted unemployment benefit only after the expiration of the severance pay (usually zero to five months, since severance pay may represent up to five months' salary).

Job applicants become eligible for unemployment benefit seven days after submitting a request to the employment office. Benefit is terminated at the end of six months of benefit or sooner if the applicant: (a) did not turn up at the employment office on a preset date; (b) refused a suitable job; or (c) refused retraining.

As mentioned earlier, the labour offices were given the right to create new employment either through subsidies to employers or through lump-sum payments for the creation of a small business. If applicants decide to start a private enterprise, they are obliged to inform the employment office about their registration request. During the period prior to running their business, or if their gross income is lower than Kcs 800, they remain on a list of job applicants and are eligible for unemployment benefit. If applicants intend to run a business in a given sector for at least two years, they may obtain a government contribution for the creation of their job up to 12 times the amount of the average benefit paid by the employment office during the last calendar quarter. New business potential and efficiency must be supported by expertise.

If there is no demand for additional workers in an applicant's profession, the labour office offers the individual a one-shot possibility of retraining. The applicant and labour office sign an agreement on retraining; if the terms of the agreement are broken by the participant, he/she may have to bear the costs of the retraining programme.

If applicants are unsuccessful in finding a job during the six-month period, they remain on the employment office database. They may apply to the Department of Social Affairs and Health Services of the local district municipal office for social benefits (welfare).

The evolution of Czechoslovak unemployment compensation hence demonstrates clearly the initial desire of the government to provide a generous safety net and its subsequent realization of the need to limit the extent of benefits in view of abuse as well as mounting budgetary pressures. The social impact of the emergence of unemployment and of the reduction in unemployment benefit had significant political repercussions in Slovakia, which suffered high unemployment, and it contributed to the eventual partition of Czechoslovakia.

4.2.2   The Czech vs. Slovak Unemployment Phenomenon

What explains the differences in the Slovak and Czech unemployment rates? Since the political partition of Czechoslovakia was primarily driven by economic factors, and the same factors may seriously influence future developments, this question deserves attention.

From Table 2.1, it appears that differences in domestic demand are not driving the disparity between the two republics' rates, since declines in employment were comparable in the two republics, if not slightly greater in the Czech Republic. However, employment in small firms may not be properly represented in these data. It is generally thought that in the Czech Republic there is much faster growth of employment in small enterprises (with fewer than 100 employees). Vavro (1992, p. 3) claims that the number of Czech employees in small firms grew by 250,000 in 1991 while the figure for Slovakia was only 30,000. He claims that this is the most important factor explaining the disparities between the two republics' rates.

Assuming that the employment statistics underrepresent employment in the Czech lands, Vavro argues that another major demand-side reason for disparity in the unemployment rates is the differing impact of the fall in the CMEA market on each of the two republics.[14] Since the industrialization of Slovakia occurred mainly during the communist period, much of its industrial production was aimed at the CMEA market. In 1991, when Slovak exports to the former CMEA had already fallen to 72% of 1989 levels (Vavro, 1992, p. 10), the Slovak Republic still depended on this market for 42.0% of its exports, while the former CMEA market constituted only 29.4% of the Czech Republic's exports. Clearly, the financial strain that has characterized this region since 1990 has had a significantly negative effect on demand for Slovak exports, particularly in such branches as machines and electro-technical industry, 85% of whose exports were previously aimed at states with non-market economies. Although the full effects of the resulting drop in production on employment have yet to be revealed, workers in Slovak industries have been negatively affected.

Another factor of less importance on the demand side is the relative ease with which Czechs can work in Germany and Austria owing to their advantageous location. The data reported in Table 2.12, which cover the entire federation, indicate that foreign employment nearly doubled in 1990-1. Foreign employment, however, accounts for only a small fraction of total employment (0.9% in 1991) and clearly mainly helps people in border regions.

Table 2.12 Czechoslovak Citizens Employed Abroad, at 31 December 1990 and 1991 (Number of Persons)

	31 December 1990	31 December 1991
Germany	14,300	31,600
Austria	6,800	8,830
Italy, Greece (mostly seasonal)	2,000	4,000
Trade contracts (CIS, etc.)	2,000	1,290
Without permission (estimate)	10,000	20,000
Total	35,100	65,720

Sources: Federal Ministry of Labour and Social Affairs; Ham, Terrell and Svejnar (1992).

On the supply side, several factors seem to be at play. The most important factor on the supply side is the difference in the ethnic composition of the Slovak and Czech republics. There are more gypsies in Slovakia, and the incidence of unemployment is higher among the gypsies. Vavro (1992) notes that 55,400 gypsies were unemployed in March 1992. Of these, 44,700 were in Slovakia, meaning that gypsies accounted for 47% of total unemployed in Slovakia at that time. On the other hand, they accounted for only 14% of the unemployed in the Czech Republic in that month. Data from the Slovak Ministry of Labour indicate that the unemployment rate for gypsies in Slovakia in December 1991 was 42.9%, while the rate for the entire Slovak Republic was only 11.8%. Similarly, the unemployment rate in April 1991 was 16.6% for gypsies and 4.6% for the entire Slovak Republic.

A second reason why the number of unemployed might be higher in Slovakia relates to the more benevolent administration of unemployment insurance benefits. Slovaks were allowed to receive severance pay at the same time as they were receiving unemployment benefit.

Lastly, Vavro notes that the ranks of the unemployed in Slovakia might be inflated by the fact that older pensioners in Slovakia continued to work and receive pensions. In 1990-1, 186,000 pensioners working in the Czech Republic left work as opposed to 50,000 working pensioners in Slovakia.

Tables 2.13 and 2.14 provide alternative comparisons of the Czech and Slovak labour markets. From Table 2.13 one can see that the percentage growth in the number of workers unemployed in the Czech lands is usually lower than the growth in Slovak unemployment, although the growth rates appear to follow the same general trend. It is interesting to note also that, in both the Czech and Slovak lands, the growth in female unemployment is greater than the growth in male unemployment until the end of 1991, at which point the trend is reversed. Another way to view the difference in the two labour markets is the ratio of the number of unemployed to the number of vacancies. This is shown in Table 2.14 for the period October 1990 to April 1992. We see that there were many more workers than vacancies in the Slovak lands in this period, with both labour markets bottoming out in December 1991, when there were approximately 37 unemployed workers for each vacancy in the Slovak lands compared with only 9 unemployed workers per vacancy in the Czech lands. As with the unemployment rate and the growth in unemployment, conditions improved in 1992.

Table 2.13   Monthly Rate of Change of Unemployment by Gender, February 1991 – April 1992 (%)

Date	Czech Republic Total	Male	Female	Slovak Republic Total	Male	Female	Czechoslovakia Total	Male	Female
Feb 1991	26.93	–	–	28.04	24.72	31.74	27.49	–	–
Mar 1991	0.00	–	–	22.27	23.71	20.75	11.34	–	–
Apr 1991	42.77	–	–	22.82	23.27	22.33	31.61	–	–
May 1991	10.83	7.89	13.85	17.92	16.27	19.71	14.53	12.32	16.87
Jun 1991	17.81	8.69	26.72	17.52	14.29	20.93	17.65	11.75	23.66
Jul 1991	18.84	14.92	22.11	22.09	22.66	21.53	20.58	19.25	21.81
Aug 1991	10.39	5.69	14.09	13.05	10.58	15.54	11.84	8.51	14.84
Sep 1991	10.62	10.19	10.94	9.52	7.13	11.83	10.02	8.40	11.40
Oct 1991	4.50	3.00	5.58	7.81	7.04	8.53	6.31	5.34	7.11
Nov 1991	2.94	4.07	2.14	7.46	7.46	7.46	5.45	6.07	4.94
Dec 1991	1.94	3.78	0.62	6.81	7.49	6.19	4.69	5.99	3.62
Jan 1992	4.26	7.38	1.94	5.77	7.51	4.17	5.13	7.46	3.17
Feb 1992	-5.90	-4.57	-6.95	-0.03	1.70	-1.67	-2.49	-0.77	-4.01
Mar 1992	-10.29	-10.93	-9.78	-3.72	-1.76	-5.65	-6.38	-5.24	-7.42
Apr 1992	-13.45	-14.26	-12.80	-3.64	-3.69	-3.59	-7.45	-7.46	-7.44

Sources: Federal Ministry of Labour and Social Affairs; Ham, Terrell and Svejnar (1992).

4.2.3 The Demographic Characteristics of the Unemployed

Since the unemployment effects of transition may have a differential effect across gender and age groups, I briefly report on the gender and age characteristics of the unemployed. The data on the proportion of females among the unemployed (Table 2.15) tend to indicate that their share in unemployment

Table 2.14   Unemployed/Vacancy Ratio, October 1990 – April 1992

Date	Czech Republic	Slovak Republic	Czechoslovakia
Oct 1990	0.45	1.32	0.66
Dec 1990	0.70	2.58	1.10
Jan 1991	1.21	6.22	2.05
Feb 1991	1.97	10.26	3.34
Mar 1991	1.97	13.02	3.75
Apr 1991	2.94	19.01	5.26
May 1991	3.19	21.95	5.89
Jun 1991	3.96	24.69	7.21
Jul 1991	4.36	28.90	8.10
Aug 1991	4.34	29.85	8.17
Sep 1991	4.61	29.88	8.57
Oct 1991	4.72	33.05	9.00
Nov 1991	4.78	35.82	9.37
Dec 1991	4.58	36.82	9.25
Jan 1992	4.40	32.38	8.82
Feb 1992	3.64	33.01	7.72
Mar 1992	2.97	29.69	6.61
Apr 1992	2.35	25.18	5.55

Note: Unemployment figures for the Czech Republic in Feb and Mar 1991 are exactly the same.

Sources: Federal Ministry of Labour and Social Affairs; Ham, Terrell and Svejnar (1992).

is larger than their share in employment in both republics and even higher in the Czech Republic than in Slovakia. Unemployment rates for December 1991 confirm that the incidence of unemployment is higher among women: 4.8% for women vs. 3.5% for men in the Czech Republic and 12.7% for women vs. 11.0% for men in the Slovak republic (see Table 2.16). For more detail on the relative position of men and women in the labour market, see also Paukert (1991).

In Table 2.17 one can see the proportion of unemployed in each age group from the first quarter 1991 to the first quarter 1992 in the Czech lands, with a shorter time series available in the Slovak lands. From the longer Czech time series, we see a dramatic rise in the proportion of unemployed who are teenagers between the first quarter and the third quarter of 1991, with the proportion falling back in January 1992 with the tightening of the unemployment insurance regime.[15] From a policy point of view, one may be more concerned with the workers aged 20-29 and 30-39, since together they comprise 55-60% of the total unemployed and are at a more important stage in their labour market careers. Those in the 20-29 group seem especially hard hit; their unemployment rate at the end of 1991 was approximately 10%, substantially higher than that of any other non-teenage group.

Table 2.15   Female Proportion of Unemployment, April 1991 - April 1992 (%)

Date	Czech Republic	Slovak Republic	Total
Apr 1991	49	48	49
Jul 1991	56	50	53
Oct 1991	59	52	55
Dec 1991	57	52	54
Jan 1992	56	51	53
Apr 1992	56	49	52

Sources: Federal Ministry of Labour and Social Affairs; Ham, Terrell and Svejnar (1992).

Table 2.16   Male-Female Unemployment Rates, at 31 December 1990 and 1991 (%)

| | 31 December 1990 | | 31 December 1991 | |
	Female	Male	Female	Male
Czechoslovakia	1.07	0.88	7.32	5.93
Czech Republic	0.82	0.66	4.81	3.47
Slovak Republic	1.62	1.35	12.65	11.03

Sources: Federal Ministry of Labour and Social Affairs; Ham, Terrell and Svejnar (1992).

4.3   Political Developments

As I have indicated above, in many respects the economic outcomes (e.g. output and employment) were similar in the Czech and Slovak republics during the 1990-2 period. In some visible areas (such as unemployment), the outcomes were strikingly different.

The differences in unemployment were widely interpreted as reflecting a more negative impact of the economic transformation on Slovakia than the Czech lands. A significant part of the Slovak population in turn attributed this impact to the particular economic policies pursued by the federal government in the 1990-1 period. Together with nationalist factors, these perceptions contributed to the election of governments with different economic, social and political orientation in the Czech and Slovak republics in June 1992. In the Czech Republic the winning parties were essentially those that had pushed through the economic reforms since 1990, while in Slovakia the winning coalition espoused a more gradual and socially oriented transformation of the

Table 2.17 Age Structure of Unemployed, 1991–2 (%)

Quarter	Age 0–19	Age 20–29	Age 30–39	Age 40–49	Age 50+
Czech Republic:					
1Q91	11	33	27	21	8
2Q91	13	31	27	21	8
3Q91	22	29	24	19	7
4Q91	19	29	25	20	7
1Q92	14	30	27	21	8
Slovak Republic:					
3Q91	17	31	29	16	6
4Q91	17	31	29	16	6
1Q92	13	30	31	19	6
Czechoslovakia:					
3Q91	19	30	27	17	6
4Q91	18	30	27	18	7
1Q92	14	30	29	20	7

Note: Unemployment data concerning age structure are unavailable in the Slovak Republic before 3Q91.

Sources: Federal Ministry of Labour and Social Affairs; Ham, Terrell and Svejnar (1992).

economy. There are also indications that while the Czech leaders wish to reorient their economy primarily towards the West, the Slovak leadership wishes to re-establish some of the interrupted links to the East.

The inability of the Czech and Slovak members of the federal parliament to agree on numerous bills during the 1990–1 period and the post-1992 election demand of the Slovak leadership for a major transfer of powers from the federal level to national governments resulted in the summer of 1992 in negotiations between the main Czech and Slovak political parties about political separation of the two republics. In the summer months of 1992 these negotiations led to an agreement to split Czechoslovakia into two republics on 1 January 1993. This party-to-party agreement was approved by the governments and parliaments of each of the republics. After longstanding opposition, the agreement was eventually also approved by the federal parliament in November 1992. It was never submitted to a popular referendum as demanded by the Czechoslovak Constitution. Paradoxically, while the majority of citizens in each republic were indicating in opinion polls their desire to keep Czechoslovakia a single state, the country separated peacefully.

5   Policy Challenges for the Czech and Slovak Governments

In the very short run, the principal issue facing the Czech and Slovak governments is how to minimize the transition costs associated with the division of Czechoslovakia. The imposition of inefficient border controls in January 1993 has undermined the free flow of goods and endangered the traditional trade and cooperation. Both governments have realized the danger of interrupting trade flows in the two highly interdependent economies and are in the process of negotiating simpler customs practices.

The second problem whose gravity was underestimated was the pressure that would develop on the Czechoslovak koruna after the split. Indeed, while the Czech and Slovak governments claimed until the end of 1992 that the single currency would be maintained at least until June 1993, the popular expectation of a significant devaluation of the Slovak koruna vis-à-vis the Czech koruna has resulted in rising deposits by Slovak enterprises and citizens in Czech banks and in a run on foreign exchange. The central bank (which still operates for both republics) has had to suspend convertibility and it appears that the separation of currencies will take place much sooner, despite the fact that neither republic is quite ready. The lack of preparation ranges from the unavailability of new banknotes in both republics (stamped Czechoslovak banknotes will be used instead) to the virtual non-existence of a central bank in Slovakia.

In the medium term, the two countries will strive to re-impose macroeconomic stability while speeding up the microeconomic transformation. The macro stability has been disturbed by the budgetary deficits recorded at the end of 1992 and by the inflationary jump connected with the introduction of the value added tax in January 1993. The budgetary deficits were relatively mild, and in principle they could be contained. With all the easy budgetary cuts carried out, however, future reductions in government expenditure will be politically harder to implement. The January 1993 inflationary bout appears to be significant and its dynamics are hard to judge. Some of it is apparently connected with inadequate explanation of the nature of the value added tax and the fact that it is to be substituted for the traditional turnover tax. Many small businesses are reported to have simply added VAT on top of the turnover tax. More fundamentally, the question arises whether the inflationary jump was due principally to other reasons (expectations of a change in policy, delayed cost push, etc.) and what its repercussions might be.

On the microeconomic side, the main problem facing the two governments is how to improve the performance of the remaining state and newly privatized firms. In many respects, the transformation has been postponed by the rapid fall in real wages, the rise in inter-enterprise indebtedness and the willingness of banks to lend to old client enterprises. No major bankruptcies have taken place, because the government delayed the implementation of the bankruptcy law. Since foreign capital has been flowing into Czechoslovakia (and especially

Slovakia) in only moderate amounts, one can expect that the real adjustment will result in plant closures and higher unemployment. In this context, women and young people are likely to be the hardest-hit groups.

6 Evaluation

By applying restrictive macroeconomic policies, the Czechoslovak government succeeded in rapidly extinguishing inflationary pressures brought about by the sudden liberalization of about 85% of all prices on 1 January 1991. The ability to eliminate inflation in three to six months and maintain significant price stability for almost two years was impressive. The economy has also adjusted remarkably in that the private sector developed rapidly in response to the removal of administrative restrictions, price liberalization and provision of bank credit, and exports picked up after an initial period of major decline.

On the negative side, the Czechoslovak economy has plunged into a much more severe recession than was officially expected. The recession has to a significant extent been caused by external shocks associated with the disintegration of the CMEA, and it is also exaggerated by systematic errors in data collection. Nevertheless, the restrictive government policies have clearly also played a part.

In undertaking the tough measures, the Czechoslovak government greatly benefited from the willingness of the population to undergo a painful transition. In Slovakia, however, a significant part of the population deemed these measures to be excessive and in June 1992 they voted in a government that is expected to undertake a more moderate set of transition policies. The Czech–Slovak differences in economic policies also added to the nationalistic factors in bringing about the split of the country on 1 January 1993.

A major problem is the fact that state enterprises have by and large avoided the impact of the restrictive policies by relying to an increasing extent on inter-enterprise debt (credit). This debt has risen fast and, despite the macroeconomic restriction, few enterprises have been forced to restructure or close down so far. The impressive stabilization exercise has thus been accompanied by only limited enterprise restructuring. The expected remedy for this problem is the large-scale privatization, the first wave of which was carried out in 1992. There is no doubt that the success and further acceptability of the transition depend very much on the impact that this first privatization wave will have on enterprise performance.

In trying to assess the Czechoslovak transformation so far, it is apparent that the key ingredients on the positive side have been the relative political unanimity about the desirability of a fundamental economic transformation in 1989, 1990 and 1991; the traditionally conservative macroeconomic policy, which resulted in relative economic stability at the outset of the transition; the willingness of the government to undertake strong measures (including restrictive macroeconomic policies and privatization of small firms); popular support for the painful transition; and the proximity to the German and Austrian markets (including the labour markets).

The major factors that might endanger the transformation process would be difficulties in implementing the Czech–Slovak split, the costs of adjustment associated with this split, slow and inadequate transformation of the large enterprise sector, protectionism on the part of Western partners, and general political and social instability. One should also note that factors related to historical resource transfers, different economic structure and perceived uncertainty are likely to make the transition more difficult in Slovakia than in the Czech lands.

Notes

The paper benefited from comments by David Begg and other participants at the project workshop in Brussels. I would also like to thank Josef Kotrba for valuable research assistance.

1   See e.g. Svejnar (1989, 1992), Dyba and Svejnar (1991, 1992), Ham, Terrell and Svejnar (1992) and Begg (1991).

2   As Gelb and Gray (1991) indicate, in 1938 the GDP per capita in Austria and Czechoslovakia was US$400 and US$380, respectively.

3   The estimated GNP of Czechoslovakia naturally depends on the methodology used. Some other studies generate higher estimates of Czechoslovak GNP.

4   Private agriculture was collectivized or converted into state farms.

5   An alternative would have been temporarily to adopt a modified set of Western (e.g. German or EC) laws. In view, however, of the voluminous nature of Western legal statutes and the paucity of skilled translators, it turned out to be simpler to create a new set of Czechoslovak laws.

6   These goals were in fact pursued from the start of 1990.

7   Unlike some other transforming economies, Czechoslovakia had a relatively well-developed social safety net.

8   The loans were provided as follows: IMF US$1,313 million, World Bank US$205 million, the European Community US$248 million, G24 US$89 million, and the financial sector US$280 million.

9   The high profitability reflected both the fact that enterprises accumulated raw material inventories before price liberalization and the custom of paying income and profit taxes on the value of delivered rather than paid-for goods.

10 See Rodrik (1992).

11 As mentioned earlier, the long-term price stability under the communist regime was in part generated at the expense of shortages. In addition, it also reflected data manipulation in the construction of the baskets of commodities for price indices.

12 The decision to discontinue the collection of the data was related to the disintegration of the traditional monobank system and the reported difficulty in tracking frozen payments across the growing number of commercial banks.

13 For details see, for instance, Svejnar and Singer (1993).
14 Our future work with micro data will examine whether differing demand factors are leading to longer unemployment durations in the Slovak lands.
15 The higher unemployment of the young seems to be a characteristic of transitional economies – see the other studies in the *International Labour Review* 130.

References

Begg, D. (1991) 'Economic Reform in Czechoslovakia: Should We Believe in Santa Klaus?', *Economic Policy* 13, 243–86.
Dyba, K. (1989) 'Czechoslovakia 1970–1990: Growth, Structural Adjustment, and Openness of the Economy', *Europäische Rundschau* 3.
Dyba, K. and J. Svejnar (1991) 'Czechoslovakia: Recent Economic Developments and Prospects', *American Economic Review*, 81 (2), May.
(1992) 'Stabilization and Transition in Czechoslovakia', paper presented at the Conference on Transition in Eastern Europe, National Bureau of Economic Research, Cambridge, MA, 26–29 February.
Gelb, A. and Gray, C. (1991) 'The Transformation of Economies in Central and Eastern Europe: Issues, Progress, and Prospects', World Bank, mimeo, April.
Ham, J., K. Terrell and J. Svejnar (1992) 'Recent Developments in the Czech and Slovak Labour Markets', Report to the National Council for Soviet and East European Research.
Paukert, L. (1991) 'The Economic Status of Women in the Transition to a Market System: The Case of Czechoslovakia'. *International Labour Review*, 130(5-6), 613-33.
Rodrik, D. (1992) 'Foreign Trade in Eastern Europe's Transition: Early Results', CEPR Discussion Paper No. 676, June.
Svejnar, J. (1989) 'A Framework for the Economic Transformation of Czechoslovakia', *PlanEcon Report* 52, 29 December, 1–18.
(1992) 'Labor Market Adjustment in Transitional Economies', Part III, *Recent Developments in the Czechoslovakian Economy with Special Reference to Labor Markets in Transition*, Report to the National Council for Soviet and East European Research, November.
Svejnar, J. and M. Singer (1993) 'The Czechoslovak Voucher Privatization: An Assessment of Results', paper presented at the 1993 American Economic Association Meetings, Anaheim, CA, 5 January.
Vavro, A. (1992) 'príčin rozdielneho vývoja nezamestnanosti v SR a ČR' ['Analysis of the Reasons for the Evolution of Different Unemployment Rates in the Slovak Republic and the Czech Republic'], transl. Sharon Fisher. Bratislava: Slovak Commission for Economic Strategy, May.
Yotopoulos, P. and J. Nugent (1976) *Economic Development*, New York: McGraw-Hill.

3 Czech and Slovak Federal Republic: a new approach

Valtr Komárek

1 General Background

The economic reform that is being undertaken in CSFR today is associated with a complex of serious macroeconomic problems. These problems are felt in unexpectedly high inflation, which reached 60% in 1991, and in strong suppression of household purchasing power as well as that of companies, and of all aggregate demand in the national economy. Warning signs of the sales crisis were the decrease in industrial production in 1991 by about 23%, and much more in the construction industry. In spite of severe devaluation, falling exports are unavoidably reflected in the accelerated growth of unemployment. These inflation trends, recession and mass unemployment affected broader macroeconomic, macrosocial, structural and foreign economic relationships and threatened to tighten the downward spiral of overall economic efficiency and lower the standard of living, including the environment. These warning signs cannot be belittled by ideological and theoretical textbook commentaries and must be subjected to serious analysis, including the definition of ways and means for overcoming them.

Detailed macroeconomic analyses, microeconomic analyses of industrial, construction and agricultural companies, and investigations in both republics and in selected regions prove that the present economic difficulties and their heavy social impact on the population have two basic causes:

(1) the social, economic and environmental heritage of the past totalitarian system,
(2) mistakes in the conception of economic reform.

The burdensome heritage of the totalitarian system cannot be underestimated. It fundamentally distorted the industrial structure and the whole economy, created internal debt, and mortgaged the future. This is manifest in the technical and technological backwardness of production levels, in the infrastructure, in the environment, in the dampening of economic motivation and of the creative capabilities of the population, in long-term isolation from advanced world markets, in an absolute shortage of convertible currency, and in low levels of competitiveness, labour productivity and overall economic efficiency. This is connected with the huge economic difficulties of the CSFR's East European neighbours and their negative influence on its foreign trade. At the same time, it is necessary to recognize the extraordinary breadth and scale of Czechoslovak industry: its per capita production in many important products and in aggregate ranked it among the relatively most industrialized producers in the world. It is also necessary to acknowledge the long-renowned traditions of crafts and industrial production, and the generally broad education and relatively good qualifications of the population.

The second cause of the present economic difficulties and problems lies in strategic mistakes in economic reform. Many years of research, theoretical discussions and practical reform efforts in many Central and East European countries, as well as their theoretical comparison with the development of market economies and economic theories in the West, have all resulted in certain ideas about the strategic profile of an economic reform that would be suitable for our historical situation.

These ideas, as summarized by, for example, the Institute for Forecasting of the Czechoslovak Academy of Sciences, were concurrently coming to the conclusion that the real functioning of the market mechanism, including the full application of world market influences, is possible only through close relations among the existing economies to overcome the initial economic imbalances connected with wide structural and price distortions. For this reason I suggest that the market system, hastily applied to deeply unbalanced economies (internally and externally) that are historically rooted and long conditioned, cannot function rationally.

A barrier to the rational functioning of the market was the complete nationalization (or collectivization) of all production and service companies, with the accompanying absence of not only business experience, business cadres, and a business environment, but also of the primary accumulation of resources for speedily overcoming monopolistic influences, for immediately coping with the new competitive environment, and for immediate and mass privatization.

The introduction of uniform mechanisms of free play of supply and demand (with liberated prices and exchange rates) into these initial imbalanced states and distortions necessarily means that purchasing power concentrates in formerly preferred foci of heavy industry and productive consumption, to which will be directed new supply flows to the detriment of the population and of long-term advantageous exports. The unconditional liberalization solution unavoidably mixed the more moderate imbalance in the consumer market with the huge imbalance in inter-enterprise supplies and investments in one big unbalanced pot, and there is only one way to avoid overheating – the steep reduction in overall aggregate national economic demand. The exclusively market solution of this operation leads to the reproduction of initial deficits in generally worse deficit levels, with an unavoidable decline into a general recession and foreign indebtedness. The final bill for the whole operation must be paid by the people to the detriment of consumption.

The transformation of the economy given these initial conditions was therefore formulated as a relatively complex and mutually intertwined long-term process, in which the rational functioning of the market system geared to economic prosperity can be achieved only by the combined application of a whole series of simultaneous measures to overcome the initial imbalance and the broad macroeconomic, price and structural (internal and external) distortions caused by this imbalance.

This concept of the reform strategy could have become a more concrete programme of the government. Its first stage linked the swift and mass privatization in the business sphere, restaurants, other services and small industry with de-monopolization and de-bureaucratization of medium and big industry management. This programme relied on macroeconomic and structural regulation to dampen excess demand in the least effective foci and to support new supply, primarily by means of selective financial and other economic tools. Prosperity was to follow the resulting rise in effective demand. This programme anticipated a clear definition of real structural policy as well as a programme for the introduction of new technologies, the modernization of industry and agriculture, the realization of an ambitious programme to enhance competitiveness and the development of an export offensive, the expansion of active tourism, infrastructure and the whole sphere of services. It strove to create bases for market development for goods by consistent improvement of price relations with a view to the gradual liberalization of prices. Simultaneously it anticipated the building of a financial market without delay – but with respect for all its needs for banking and a stock exchange network – and gradually extending the foreign currency and capital markets together with the development of large privatization, including the linking of capital and production with reliable foreign capital centres, the formation of a labour market, etc. It set in motion policies on housing, research and development, the school system, the health service, the environment, etc. The realization of the programme was planned in conditional and binding sequences and stages.

The lack of patience and nationwide consensus has led to opportunistic policy and politicians gaining favour with the radicalized masses through much more radical political ideas, which in turn were further radicalized ideologically, including the reform concept. In this context, the economic reform became highly ideologized and politicized and, instead of being based on scientifically expert documents, it was propounded on the basis of hastily assembled eclectic prescriptions from current standard macroeconomics in combination with stereotyped proposals for anti-inflation and pro-export monetarist programmes aimed at developing countries, elaborated in recent years by American theorists. These developing countries, primarily Latin American, got into difficulties and still suffer from foreign indebtedness, high inflation and state bureaucratic interventions, supported by the corrupt management of state industries and some services.

For this reason, the proposed remedies were reduced to the following relatively simple scheme:

(1) Restrict the enormous state bureaucracy, corruption and irrational state interventions in the economy; therefore apply deregulatory, liberalizing and privatizing measures.
(2) Devalue to support exports because you can proceed only by way of price competition, to the detriment of domestic wages and consumption.
(3) Severely suppress private demand by an extremely restrictive currency and fiscal policy to dampen the existing inflationary trends as well as the new inflationary consequences of devaluation.
(4) Hold back the growth of consumer prices and freeze wages, pensions and savings because a decrease in consumption is necessary to deal with the pro-export and anti-import consequences of devaluation and also to break the inflationary spiral.

Essentially, these simple reform schemes were exported to Central and Eastern Europe by such theorists as Professor Jeffrey Sachs, who, after a short stay as adviser in Bolivia, became an adviser to the Balcerowicz group, which in 1989 was preparing the reform in Poland. A simple and ambitious prescription for the recovery of developing countries by shock therapy started to be applied to the complicated, but at the same time hopeful, economic situation of countries like the CSFR and Poland just when this treatment had largely failed in those developing countries.

Perhaps the most concentrated expression of the lack of realism in such an application is Sachs's thesis that: 'Convertibility has long seemed to be a distant dream for many economists in Eastern Europe, however, it can be achieved by severe devaluation, combined with restrictive macroeconomic policy' (*The Economist*, 13–19 January 1990, p. 24). The fact that CSFR exports per capita are only US$1,000 against US$7,000–10,000 per capita in the Netherlands, Sweden, etc., presents no problem: according to Sachs, the convertibility of the currency need not be based upon the necessary volume of convertible goods.

The elegance and simplicity of the prescription, accompanied by lucid textbook commentaries, have become attractive to all who were not aware of the specific complexity but hopeful economic situation of countries like the CSFR. The radical atmosphere required radical conceptions of the simplest transparency and categorical emphasis. Only strong politicians could, in a serious field like the economy, stand up to opportunist radicalism. The political sobering up after the triumphalistic mood of the years 1989 and 1990 is seen at least in international political circles. The economic sobering up will follow. It will concern not just a sobering up but overcoming certain well-organized interest groups.

The ideologically violated conception of economic reform in the CSFR *a priori* distorts the government's economic policy. The so-called 'Scenario of Economic Reform' not only represents this framework of economic policy but directly dictates some basic measures of government economic policy, for example, the devaluation to Kcs 20–24 per dollar (as explicitly mentioned in the scenario), the liberalization of prices, the liberalization of foreign trade, the introduction of internal currency convertibility, the elimination of negative turnover tax, the restrictive currency and budgetary policy, the control and restriction of wages, immediate and general privatization, etc.

On this basis, the reform policies of the CSFR since the second half of 1990 changed – from the original gradual conception to the 'Big Bang' of shock therapy. Shock therapy, as defined by dozens of Western armchair economists, calls for a complete change-over from a command economy to a market economy in a relatively short time, generally two to three years. This speeded-up process typically involves making the currency convertible, eliminating subsidies, decontrolling prices, privatizing industry and eliminating restrictions on imports. These steps, it is believed, will set the stage for future growth and renewal based on sound market principles after a brief adjustment period.

Unfortunately, shock therapy is out of touch with reality. It ignores the impact of such an approach on the vast educated, skilled classes of Eastern Europe. In Czechoslovakia, where radical reforms had been in place for a year, the outcome in 1991 was a 23% fall in industrial output, an increase in the unemployment rate from zero to 6.5%, an inflation rate of 58%, a one-third decline in domestic demand and a 15–16% shrinkage in the gross domestic product. Although these are the consequence of 40 years of communist mismanagement, their sudden intensity results from the shock therapy.

Furthermore, there is no available evidence, statistical or anecdotal, that these negative phenomena are reversing. In fact, a strong case can be made that they are accelerating and are more the result of shock therapy than of structural deficiencies in the economy as a whole. Poland, which began shock therapy about six months earlier than Czechoslovakia, has suffered an even greater deterioration.

The issue is one of time, not intent. East European economists agree on the need to establish market economies. The question is whether it should be done over two years or ten. To put matters in perspective, consider that it took the UK more than 12 years to make the transition from its brand of socialism to capitalism, even under the spirited leadership of Margaret Thatcher. The privatization started in 1978 has yet to come to full fruition; major UK public companies, including British Telecom, are not yet fully privatized. Can the democracies of Eastern Europe be expected to proceed any faster? Can public enterprises be expected to withstand the rigours of international competition without the same degree of preparation West European institutions have enjoyed?

Moreover, shock therapy ignores the basic concept of a division of labour in an advanced industrialized society. Most of the people of Czechoslovakia, Poland and Russia have committed their lives to developing highly specialized skills for heavy industries. Vast numbers of these people are being asked to abandon their training and experience, and, without an adequate adjustment phase, to participate in an ill-organized 'market' building itself up from scratch.

In Hungary, this plunge was not as painful as elsewhere in the former Soviet bloc because its economy was more geared towards agriculture and commerce. But in Czechoslovakia, whose economy is oriented towards heavy industries, this means beginning anew, without the mainstays like capital goods and steel that stabilize all modern economies. The results tear at the country's social fabric.

Instead, East Europeans need to draw on their strengths in key manufacturing sectors, like precision instruments in Czechoslovakia, in order to join the world economy. Major industries – electronics, for example – need to be protected until they have been prepared, with the help of Western technical aid, to compete. Governments need to make sure their citizens are not cast adrift.

This approach would allow the industries time to stabilize. It would provide breathing space for the creation of a banking system able to channel domestic savings to support corporate growth based on market principles. Tax revenues could be funnelled into infrastructure projects to build a hospitable environment for foreign and domestic investment, while creating jobs and stimulating domestic demand in much the same way that public works like building a highway system or putting a man on the moon do in the West.

In spite of the gross inefficiencies of communism, domestic demand in Czechoslovakia was sufficient to sustain a modicum of economic well-being in 1989. Why was it insufficient to do so in 1991? The excessive and needless damage of shock therapy is largely to blame.

Because of the fall in purchasing power, newly freed prices rose and the value of the currency fell, and domestic demand dropped nearly 50% in real terms in 1990-1. In addition, Czechoslovak trade, which had been directed towards its former Soviet bloc partners, was given no time to reorient itself westward. Lastly, existing mechanisms for capital investment (mainly the various state ministries) were eliminated, resulting in a decline in investment of more than one-third.

Not all elements of shock therapy are misguided. For example, allowing the currency to 'float' against Western currencies, as prescribed by the International Monetary Fund, is certainly a crucial early step. But, taken as a whole, the radical approach largely eliminates the role of government in the economy virtually overnight. I know of no country that could withstand such a shock.

To quote Samuel Johnson, 'The chief differences among men are over means, not ends'. Shock therapy is untested outside the economic laboratories of Cambridge, Massachusetts. Its vision of the market has never been completely realized in any industrialized nation in this century, including the United States. It is a means that could bring about an awful end, particularly when one considers its current application in Russia and the ex-Soviet republics, where conditions are more complicated and serious than in Eastern Europe. There, the social implications could have geopolitical and even military overtones.

It is time to rethink shock therapy. We should enlarge the discussions now under way with the West to address critical long-term social implications.

2   Specific Initial Conditions

The paths taken by the Central and East European countries for their transition from totalitarianism to democracy and from a centrally planned economy to that of a market-oriented economy are the subject of much theoretical discussion. Professor J. K. Galbraith, for instance, calls the reform strategy proposed by Professor Sachs madness, and we could enumerate many completely contradictory views. More and more frequently we hear objections stating that the reform proposals of radical American professors and the IMF are based on conditions normally existing in developing countries and do not respect the historical specifics in countries such as Czechoslovakia. There are even forecasts predicting that such reforms will not result in raising these countries to the level of the developed ones but will probably lead to their falling into the developing world. This will then contribute to the creation of a new burden of competitive pressure in the cheap export of mass products as well as the requirements of financial assistance from the developed countries.

In all these connections the determination of the efficiency and competitiveness of the countries with a previously centrally planned economy, as well as of the comparable volume of their GDP, consumption, wages, labour productivity and other macroeconomic relations, was and still remains the crucial question in the formation of theoretical concepts as well as of practical economic policy. These economies show many structural as well as value distortions. The price levels as well as the levels of wages, taxes, profits, depreciation, credit, etc., differ significantly from those in market economies, and the non-existence of a convertible currency complicates the determination of realistic exchange rates and the evaluation of comparative advantages and performance as well as reliable inter-branch comparisons. The point was, and still is, the adequate expression of the national aggregate in real international value.

Until 1990 the official exchange rate of the dollar amounted in the CSFR to

Kcs 5.60, which was approximately the internal purchasing power parity of the koruna. There was also a so-called tourist exchange rate – the official rate of about Kcs 11 to US$1 granted to foreign tourists. Then there was the trade exchange rate expressing the relationship of the koruna to the dollar calculated on the basis of an average achieved in total exports (or so-called 'reproduction costs' per dollar), which amounted to about Kcs 14.50, and finally, the black market exchange rate of Kcs 35 per dollar. The extreme values, i.e. the purchasing power parity and the increasingly officialized exchange rate on the black market, have had a range of approximately 1:6, and depending on that change, the macroeconomic characteristics of the CSFR were also altered.

Nevertheless it is evident that the CSFR is a developed country, although ranked near the bottom of the scale of developed European countries. With a GDP of US$9,500 per capita in purchasing power parity, or about US$6,000 in a simulated exchange rate of the convertible currency, it lies between Greece, Spain and Italy and not on the level of the developing countries of Latin America where the per capita GDP amounts to US$1,500–2,000.

The realistic assessment of the development level of the CSFR is not only a methodological problem, but a principal question of political economy and practical economic strategy. On this assessment depends whether the CSFR should choose an economic reform and political strategy that will be similar to the strategy of the developed countries of Western Europe practised since the middle of the 1960s, or one that is nearer the economic policy of the developing countries of Latin America and Asia. This decision will also shape the development of economic relations between the CSFR and, on the one hand, developed countries and, on the other, those countries still in the process of development. This last question also has broader implications concerning the entire Central and East European region.

A deeper analysis of the problem leads to the conclusion that the economy of the CSFR (and similarly of some other former countries with a centrally planned economy) has a dual character. On certain macroeconomic parameters it is close to the developed countries, and on some others it resembles the developing ones. This is not by chance. It is a special hybrid caused by concrete historical events during which the developed economies of Central Europe (and some neighbouring regions of Eastern Europe) came under the supremacy of the semi-feudal Soviet empire, which was more Byzantine than European. They became a sort of metropolis of this Eastern empire, suppliers of know-how, technology and machinery and importers of fuel and raw materials. This situation was very favourable for them from the point of view of direct exchange, but in this bloc they became isolated from the developed world and had to depend on the autarky evolved within the framework of the CMEA.

Crucial to this development was, as has already been mentioned, the historical fact that Czechoslovakia entered the CMEA as an already developed country. In 1938, the economic level of the Czech part of the republic (i.e. two-thirds of its total population), characterized by a GDP of about US$220 per capita,[1] was in 10th-15th place in the world, oscillating between the levels of France, Belgium and the Netherlands. The programme of 'socialist industrialization' adopted after 1945 led to a further growth, especially of heavy industrial branches and engineering. In the first three decades of its post-war development, the physical volume of Czechoslovak industrial production grew according to official statistics about 2.5-3 times and according to the corrected index about 1.5-2 times faster than production in most industrially developed countries. If we compare the per capita production of a representative sample of 15 key industrial products[2] with that in other industrially developed countries, Czechoslovakia was seven times in first place, twice in second place and once in third place.[3]

To summarize, we might conclude that calculations based on a per capita ratio would show that the CSFR has probably the largest traditional industrial potential in the world. But one cannot derive any conclusions from this concerning the overall economic level of the country and its international position. This depends mainly on the modern concept and structure of the industry, its efficiency and final economic results. The hypertrophy of heavy industry created an excessively large domestic market for the means of production. Central planning, and the fact that most of the products were sold to a not very demanding foreign and domestic market, led to a tendency to 'produce for production's sake' (i.e. for stock and to create reserves, which did not have a positive effect on the economy), to export at disadvantageous prices partly on credits that had little hope of ever being repaid, to import to fulfil production targets, and to invest in equipment an increasing proportion of which remained unutilized. All this strongly modified the relationship between the industrial and economic potential of the country and its actual economic level. Between these two poles of the Czechoslovak economy's basic characteristics lies its real efficiency. To assess this real efficiency and real economic level we can use the outcome of international comparison projects initiated by UN bodies, which, in order to compare economic levels, convert the product volume according to the purchasing power parity of the currency, which was ascertained by comparing the relative prices of hundreds of products and services taking into account the average 'weight' of each of them in the structure of the utilized GDP in the compared countries as well as their qualitative differences.[4]

Czechoslovakia did not participate in these international projects, but we performed an indirect estimation. It is based on data concerning some member countries of the former CMEA (i.e. Hungary, Poland and Romania) that were involved in an international comparative project (ICP), and their comparison with the data on mutual trade within the CMEA community. A similar method was used in the above-quoted *Review of Income and Wealth*, in which the GDP per capita for Czechoslovakia in 1985 was 7,424 ID (International Dollars) in 1980 prices, representing more than 9,000 ID in current prices. The data of the

Institute for Forecasting of the Czechoslovak Academy of Sciences were constructed in the same way; they are based on comparisons of the CMEA countries instituted by the Statistical Commission of the CMEA, according to which the utilized national income of Hungary oscillates around 80% of the Czechoslovak level. These calculations indicate that the GDP per capita of the CSFR reached about US$9,000 in 1990.

Czechoslovakia's economic potential and the volume of its production place the country in the group of economically developed states. Therefore the economic policy of the CSFR cannot be the same as the Portuguese and even less the Mexican, Argentine or Turkish policy. Nevertheless, there exist opinions stressing the similarity of the development level of these countries and of the CSFR and evaluating the latter's lag behind the developed market economies at a quarter to half a century. From these alarming 'findings' is derived the call for a renewal of a high quantitative growth of the social product and of industrial production in the CSFR, which is presented as the only way it could reach the present level of the Western countries of the lowest rating, at least by 2010.

In view of the relatively high economic level of the CSFR, the frequently recommended imitation of the overall economic and technological policies applied by the highly dynamic, newly emerging industrial countries (mainly those of Southeast Asia) is not sufficiently justified. Though it can hardly be denied that – thanks to cooperation with and capital from developed market economies – these countries are able to produce some goods more competitively than can Czechoslovakia, the overall measure of their industrialization, their production equipment and infrastructure, the employment and consumption of their populations, their educational level and lifestyle, are entirely different.

Contrary to the strategies applied by developing countries, the CSFR could advance on a path similar to that of the small developed European countries that, at the advent of the new technologies, immediately started to introduce radical structural changes. They reduced the traditional branches of heavy industry, as well as the standard branches of light industry, as they were able to take advantage of the high qualifications and adaptability of their labour force. The CSFR too could master these structural and technological changes – although with a certain delay – if the necessary preconditions of economic strategy and mechanism were created for it.

At the same time, as already mentioned, the Czechoslovak economy also reveals certain characteristics and parameters that are more typically found in developing countries than in fully developed economies. These reflect mainly its low integration into the international division of labour, especially into inter-branch and enterprise cooperation, joint production and trade. In contrast with US$6,000–9,000 exports per capita, which is typical of the small developed economies of Western Europe, the Czechoslovak statistics for 1988 mention about US$1,500 and now, after the disintegration of the CMEA, this amount is even lower. Thus imports not only of high technology but also of consumer goods are reduced to an entirely insufficient level.

If we emphasize the relatively high level of the total social product of the CSFR, we also have to take into account the high material and energy intensity of its production, which requires significantly more raw material inputs and a greater circulation of all other materials for achieving the GDP mentioned above than does production in other developed countries (see Table 3.1).

Table 3.1   Energy and Material Intensity per US$1,000 GDP in 1985

	CSFR	Average of comparable developed countries
Consumption of primary energy (gigajoules)	20.0	13.3
Consumption of crude steel (kg)	77.1	27.0
Consumption of concrete (kg)	72.0	36.3
Railway transport (gross tonne kilometres)	998.0	160.2

Source: *Synthetic Forecast of the CSFR to the year 2010*, Prague: Institute for Forecasting of the Czechoslovak Academy of Sciences, 1988, pp. 40, 42.

The inefficient use of productive resources is also proved by the level of labour productivity measured by Net Material Product (the equivalent of GDP), which reaches about 50% of the average in the developed countries.

Typical, too, is the backwardness of the service sector, which accounted for about 40% of total Czechoslovak employment in 1988, compared with approximately 60% in the developed countries of Western Europe. On the other hand, the shares of heavy industry in GDP and employment are 20% and 17.5% respectively in the CSFR, against 12% and 3% on average in the developed countries of Europe (plus Japan).[5]

These facts show that the Czechoslovak economy has large growth reserves, so that economic transformation could be combined with economic growth and it would not be necessary to sacrifice the real standard of living.

3   Real Course of the Economic Transformation in 1991

A great many influences are active during the transformation process. To make this network of events more transparent, we have to expose the most relevant interconnections and the basic mechanism of the entire process of the actual development of the economy. This means that we have to move from purely theoretical speculations to the world of reality, in the sense that the real beginning of this process can be considered to be the large devaluation. Leaving aside the first small devaluation in January 1990 (from about Kcs 15 to Kcs 17 per US$), the devaluation in October to Kcs 24 and in December to Kcs 28 per

US$ (with the later bank modification to about Kcs 30) had an inflationary impact as domestic cost and price levels tended to rise by more than half. In addition, the price liberalization of 1 January 1991 gave monopolistic producers complete freedom to raise prices. A price shock was the result in the first month, and in January and February price increases (compared with December 1990) already surpassed 34.6%. In fear of spiralling inflation, the government restricted wages (gradually a slow increase in average wages was permitted, and later a partial revaluation of the salaries of public employees and of pensions was introduced).

Overall, these two poles developed in the following way during 1991 (compared with 1990): consumer prices increased by 157.9%. and average nominal wages grew by 15.8%. That meant a drop in real wages of 27%. This development resulted in a strong reduction in consumer demand, and domestic demand dropped by 39.9% in 1991. Peasants and consumer and food-related enterprises entered a sales crisis on the domestic market.

Other relevant factors and circumstances include the following:

- Exports to the traditional Eastern markets started to collapse, entailing a sales crisis for more enterprises. In 1991, exports to the former group of countries with planned economies dropped by about 28% (compared with 1990). This reduction was naturally partially compensated for by growing exports to Western countries, meaning that the total reduction amounted to only 12% and entire industrial production fell by about 5%.
- The government introduced a strongly restrictive budget and currency policy, which had two basic results:
  (a) First of all there was a severe reduction in budget expenditure on the health service, on education, science, research and culture, on public investments in general and, logically, less expenditure on defence; for example, expenditure on defence fell in 1991 compared with 1990 by 12% (from Kcs 30,992.8 million to Kcs 27,264.9 million), on culture by 5.5%, etc.
  (b) Harsh credit measures were taken regarding industrial, construction and agricultural enterprises. The traditionally high materials and semi-finished product reserves grew in the enterprises. Originally they were a reflection of the defects in the centrally planned economy. Their growth was a reflection on the one hand of rising prices, on the other hand of the crisis in demand – so the need for credit rose explosively. Simultaneously, right from the first inflation round, credit rapidly became more expensive as the lending rate rose to about 24%. The number of enterprises with no possibility of getting new credit increased quickly, and these enterprises stopped paying their debts to other enterprises, causing a chain reaction of inability to pay. By the middle of the year, enterprise indebtedness was already approaching

the alarming figure of Kcs 100 billion, and the government released Kcs 50 million to the banks for a one-off writing-off of debts for promising enterprises. Nevertheless, there was repeated growth of debts, and at the end of the year enterprise debts not only approached the Kcs 100 billion mark again, but surpassed it quite substantially.

Consequently enterprises stopped investing. At the same time they stopped producing and started to dismiss many of their workers and employees. These are the facts:

- Compared with 1990, industrial production in 1991 dropped by an average of 23.1%. After smaller decreases in the first two months, it accelerated and the decrease in the second half of the year amounted to about 30%.
- The drop in construction was even more obvious: 31%.
- As certain household expenditure on food is necessary, the reduction in agricultural production was slower but still quite sharp – the number of slaughter cattle sold decreased by 17.1%, milk sales fell by 16%, etc.

This falling production (especially in industry and construction) led, under the new conditions of a developing labour market, to a rapid reduction in employment. By 31 December 1991, the number of employment-seeking jobless people in the CSFR reached 523,700,[6] having grown compared with the end of 1990 (50,000 persons) by about 470,000 persons. The unemployment rate reached 6.6% of the entire available labour force. In the Czech Republic there were 221,700 unemployed at the end of 1991 (4.1% of available labour), and in the Slovak Republic 302,000 (11.8%).

Among the total number seeking work in the CSFR were 325,000 workers and 63,800 graduates of all types of schools. There were 56,600 job vacancies at the end of 1991 in the CSFR. Much worse than in the Czech Republic was the situation at the end of 1991 in the Slovak Republic, with 8,200 job vacancies. At the end of 1991, 411,700 people received benefit before being placed in a job, of which 247,700 were in the Slovak Republic.

We have to realize, however, that the total number of people out of work is significantly larger than the number of unemployed, as a considerable proportion of the older generation is forced to retire (on old-age pension) and many working women stay at home without seeking employment. Employment in industry and in enterprises with more than 100 employees in December 1991 was 77.7% of the level in December 1990, and in the construction industry the figure was 67.9%. This means a fall in employment in just these two branches of about half a million. Of course, the growth in employment in private enterprises and in firms with up to 100 employees, mainly in construction, was a certain counter-tendency, even if the drop in labour opportunities in big enterprises could not be balanced for the time being. Naturally, the total income level of these groups of the population and their families dropped considerably. This entire development started a recessionary spiral, schematically expressed in the following sequence of events:

(1) The rapid drop in household incomes resulted in a sudden steep drop in consumer demand: domestic purchases (turnover of domestic trade) halved in the first months of the year, causing selling problems for businesses in the consumer goods and food industries, etc.

(2) These enterprises tried to redirect their production to exports, utilizing the large devaluation, but the losses of exports to the Eastern markets partially outweighed the gains in exports to the West (especially in the production of cars); there was an overall reduction in sales and a resulting indebtedness and inability to pay.

(3) This reduction started a chain reaction in investments and all subcontractor firms producing semi-finished products, materials, and raw materials for final production; these enterprises also struggled unsuccessfully with the possibility of using exports to compensate for losses in the domestic market and started to reduce production, investments and employment.

(4) The rapid drop in investment activity – averaging nearly one-third annually – quickly reduced domestic sales of machines, electrotechnical equipment, building activity and building materials.

(5) Another big reduction in employment, combined with exploding unemployment, continued to reduce domestic consumer demand.

(6) The drop in investment activity and employment led to a further round of reduced domestic demand and, therefore, also to reduced sales and production in industrial, construction and agricultural enterprises as well as in transport enterprises, to further growth in their debts, further dismissals, further drop in investments, and so on.

This mechanism of the recessionary spiral, which started with the devaluation and the preference for foreign markets at the cost of domestic demand, is the key problem of the present path of economic transformation in the CSFR, all the more as it was supposed – even according to government forecasts – to continue during most of 1992.

3.1 Conclusion

In order to be able to evaluate the development of the reform in the CSFR and to formulate recommendations for the next stage, we have to be aware of the depth to which the economy really fell. GDP fell by 16% in the course of 1990-1. This was, however, the average decrease over the entire year; in the first quarter it fell by 3%, while in the fourth it was down by 25.2%, as shown in Table 3.2.

Table 3.2   GDP Production of the CSFR, 1990–1, Quarterly Averages (in January 1984 prices)

	Q1	Q2	Q3	Q4	Year[1]
Total GDP (Kcs bn.):					
1990	172.4	182.8	178.2	193.6	727.0
1991	167.3	159.5	139.8	144.8	611.4
Annual fall:					
Kcs bn.	–5.1	–23.3	–38.4	–48.8	–115.6
%	–3.0	–12.7	–21.5	–25.2	–15.9

Note:
1   Estimated

Source: Statistical Information FSU

Even steeper is the drop revealed by the figures on decreasing *industrial production*. The curve for 1991 was at first fairly flat – falling by about 4.5% in January and by about 6.0% in February – but then fell rapidly. In March production fell by 20%, and in the second half of the year it stabilized at 30–35%. In January and February 1992 it dropped further to a level about 35% below the previous year, which is a decrease of 40% over January and February 1990. For an industrially developed country like Czechoslovakia this represents a near catastrophe. Either this deep recession must soon be surmounted or it could threaten devastation of the basic industrial capacity of the country.

To analyse and recommend further steps we naturally have to distinguish to what extent this huge drop is the result of the reduction in domestic demand and to what extent of the external shock, i.e. the disintegration of the Eastern market and the reduction of exports.

In differentiating between internal and external factors in the economic recession, the official analyses usually exaggerate the influence of external factors. Some claim that up to half of the drop has been caused by the disintegration of the CMEA market.[7] An analysis of the development of the individual factors of aggregate demand in industry, however, shows that the rapid narrowing of the domestic market was – in terms of both its rate of decrease as well as its weight in aggregate demand – the main factor in the collapse of industrial production.

Supplies for export (measured in producers' prices) fell by only 5% and as a total did not essentially influence the drop in industrial production. It is a sign of a certain elasticity of the Czechoslovak economy that it was able to replace a large part of the lost exports to the CMEA markets by growth in the rest of its markets. Supplies to the consumer market, whose reduction was extraordinarily large (30%), accounted for most of the drop (nearly three-fifths) in final aggregate demand. The restriction on investment deliveries – reduced by 43% – contributed significantly (by nearly one-fifth) to the total decrease. These facts lead to the clear conclusion that a revival of industrial production will not be possible without the stimulation of domestic demand for consumer goods, as well as and mainly for investments. Among the primary reasons for the reduction in aggregate demand, the disintegration of the CMEA market certainly played a part, but we cannot mask all the others with it. Authors who add all the multiplying effects to this account commit a methodological mistake, mainly by regarding the entire reduction in demand in the CMEA market as a clear GDP loss even if the commodities originally meant for these markets could be exported somewhere else or if the production factors could be released for the production of other goods or else saved.

It is also questionable whether the deterioration in the selling conditions during the transition to clearing in convertible currencies and world prices can be added to the same account, as this was actually mainly a disadvantageous price change for manufactured goods compared with the prices of raw materials, or a more reliable exchange rate of the dollar compared with the rouble, which could also have taken place without the disintegration of those markets. Today it is obvious that the hasty introduction of changes in payment conditions eventually harmed both sides and in itself significantly contributed to the disintegration of the Eastern market. That is true not only of the countries of the former CMEA but also of Finland, which also introduced convertible currencies in its trade with the former USSR; the USSR accounted for one-fifth of Finnish exports, so the drop in the mutual trade played a part in the unusually steep fall of the Finnish GDP, which reached more than 6% in 1991.

Exact calculations of the influence of the losses of the Eastern markets are so complicated as to be disorienting. We shall therefore attempt a simpler explanatory model with parameters equal to or near the reality and taking account of the main macroeconomic circumstances.

In 1990, according to the national accounts, Czechoslovak exports represented 26% of GDP; of these, about half (i.e. 13%) went to the former socialist states. According to various estimates, the physical volume of the exports to these countries decreased in 1991 by between one-third and one-half, depending on whether we calculate on the basis of 'net' price indices, resulting in about a 30% reduction, or whether we also take into consideration the transition to other payment terms; in the latter case, if we calculated on the basis of the basket of physical indices, the drop is more than half. If all the drop in exports to the former CMEA countries represented a net loss, it would amount to 4.0–6.5% of GDP.

The next considerations are more complicated. On the one hand, part of the production meant for export to the CMEA countries, or of available factors of production, was utilized in a different way and the entire export reduction cannot, therefore, represent a net loss of GDP. On the other hand, the loss of final sales, in our case of the exports, caused further losses directly in gross production (with a coefficient of about 2 according to inter-industry balances) and indirectly also in value added to GDP. In a broad generalization we can only state that both influences compensate each other. Evidence of higher exports to other regions does not prove this presumption.

The analysis shows that the fall in exports to the CMEA countries certainly never amounted to as much as half the volume, and more likely was less than one-third of the reduction of real GDP. (Remember that the loss resulting from worse terms of trade is not calculated into the index of production in comparable prices; it only reduces its utilization. It is, therefore, not logical to take it into consideration in the quantification of the influences on this index.)

The issue that cannot be proved by such 'static' quantifications is the influence of the primary impulse on the recessionary spiral. This effect could really have been significant in exports, although a similar situation existed for the primary impulse for the rapid and strong reduction of domestic demand, which was even more significant.

4   Deeper Connections, Influences and Consequences

The key issue of the whole mechanism of transformation by shock therapy is the mutually interconnected circle of devaluation, convertibility and complete liberalization of foreign trade.

Devaluation was supposed to help exports. That is understandable. But less understandable is the enormous rate of devaluation. In view of the fact that for half a century the CSFR did not have an open market or a convertible currency, the determination of the unified exchange rate as the starting point of transformation in 1990 represented quite a problem. According to the basket of commodities and international comparisons, the purchasing power parity (PPP) of the Czechoslovak currency in 1988-9 hovered around Kcs 5-6 per US$ and Kcs 3.5-4 per DM. The market exchange rate for exports into regions with convertible currency in fact got US$1 for goods costing about Kcs 15. This average 'shadow' exchange rate differed so much from PPP because of the different quality and technological level of domestic and foreign commodities, because of the significantly lower prices paid to Czechoslovak exporters, who did not have their trade network, and finally because of the demotivating influence of foreign trade monopolies (i.e. sugar with an 'exchange rate' of Kcs 60 per US$). As 80% of exports to regions with convertible currency had an exchange rate lower than Kcs 15 and as there were extensive reserves, it was possible to consider a realistic exchange rate at PPP (e.g. Kcs 11-12 per US$ and Kcs 7 per DM), or in an extreme case at the level of the existing market exchange rate of Kcs 15 per US$ (Kcs 9-10 per DM). It is true that there was still a black market exchange rate of Kcs 30-33 per US$ and Kcs 15-20 per DM, but that could not be considered to be decisive for a number of crucial reasons. On the one hand, because the state did not offer the population any free currency and demand and supply were managed by interest groups of black-marketeers with high earnings, the distortion of the domestic supply of commodities and domestic prices was such that for food, clothing, shoes, glass and china, etc. the purchasing power relation was Kcs 5–10 per US$ (including rent), while it amounted to Kcs 2 per US$ for non-traded goods and various services and to Kcs 50–70 per US$ for electronic equipment that was in very short supply. Demand by the Czechoslovak population on the black market was dictated by just this price relation for deficit commodities in high demand, and the politically but also financially very limited foreign travel, etc. According to various estimates, the volume of free currency exchanged on the black market represented only a small percentage of the volume that was state regulated. It could be expected that if this stupid policy were to be abolished by increasing the demanded imports of consumer electronics and reducing their prices to a level corresponding to the market exchange rate, if at least a certain supply of free currency were to be officially introduced for the population, if a broad network of exchange offices for tourists were opened, and if more serious steps were taken against the black market in free currencies, it would be realistic to presume that the black market exchange rate would drop quickly in the direction of the market one.

In these circumstances it is not at all clear why the government of the CSFR and its state bank did not try to hold the new official exchange rate at the level of the existing market rate, i.e. about Kcs 15 per US$ and Kcs 9–10 per DM. Instead, they seem to have acted in accordance with the traditional 'textbook' concept that the exchange rate is a special case of a price, the price of foreign currency, and that this price – like any other price – is determined by supply and demand, and these could be ascertained only on the black market.

By taking this step, the way was opened for an enormous devaluation of national capital on the threshold of privatization. (If in 1990 the book value of the basic assets of production and services amounted to about Kcs 4,600 billion in 1984 prices, this means, at a simulated exchange rate compromising between PPP and the market exchange rate, an international value of US$400–450 billion, whereas in the new exchange rate these assets could be bought for one-third of that value.)

This heroic scholarly abstraction – transferred into practice with the courage of astronauts – opens up a completely new area of a sort of 'economic weightlessness' in which all the initial steps of introducing foreign commodities, privatization, as well as domestic and foreign speculation and corruption, 'lose their gravity' by the magic power of foreign exchange, small particles of which had already set in motion large masses of domestic resources. These, of course, move to a great extent into the pockets of those alert mediators.

In its main intention – supporting exports – the devaluation misses its objective. Total exports shrank in 1991. It would certainly be unjust if we connected this reduction with devaluation. The reduction was a result of the disintegration of the Eastern market. The exports of goods to countries with a planned economy (converted into US$ million), developed in the following manner in 1989–91:

1989	1990	1991	Index 1989/90	Index 1990/1
8,782	5,825	4,201	66.3	72.1

The enterprises suffering simultaneously from a drop in domestic demand made enormous efforts to redirect their exports to Western Europe or to the developed countries. The exports of goods to the developed countries developed in the following manner (in US$ million):

1985	1990	1991	Index 1989/90	Index 1990/1
4,501	5,038	5,639	111.9	111.9

Such increases in exports to countries with free currencies also took place, however, in some years of the old regime, for instance in 1988 and 1989, when there was no devaluation. We can presume that this export growth in 1990 and especially in 1991 also resulted from the instinct for self-preservation of enterprises that had lost their market in the East and at home and had to try to keep their sales up by maximum exports. The difference is that under these conditions and in a deep economic recession, the CSFR turned towards large foreign loans.

This entire analysis indicates that the key reform operation – a deep devaluation aimed at introducing so-called 'internal' currency convertibility and the immediate complete liberalization of foreign trade – was obviously a tragic error.

We would like at least briefly to indicate the long-term distortions and difficult problems ensuing for the Czechoslovak economy from this step for the future:

(1) A broad devaluation of domestic capital and completely unprecedented sell-off of Czechoslovak enterprises to foreign firms, far below their value. We have already mentioned that all the Czechoslovak capital earmarked for privatization could in these circumstances be bought for about one-third of its international value, representing a profit for the buyer of about US$300 billion. We only remark that the actual devaluation is even deeper, as the entire privatization is being developed like the discredited 'Blitzkrieg' in an unbelievably short time-span of two to three years. The conditions of a sales crisis, indebtedness and an acute threat of most enterprises declaring

themselves bankrupt, with constantly changing self-appointed managerial teams, corruption, etc., substantially reduce the offer prices. Typical is the fact that quite a large part of the enterprises is being privatized by means of investment vouchers sold at a symbolic price to the entire population. The inhabitants can invest these vouchers in shares in enterprises, naturally without an existing serious capital market and necessary information. That means that they easily become the prey to multifarious private funds, which are growing like mushrooms after rain and even have the right to buy the vouchers for various attractive bonuses from the population and in this way acquire large amounts of capital for a fraction of its value. If foreign resources are utilized in this way at the exchange rates described above, these fractions are really minute.

(2) An enormous domestic wage distortion. The old communist system compensated high accumulation by a relatively low wage. The average Czechoslovak hourly net wage in 1988–9 was about US$3.50 while the gross wage (including social benefits) was US$8–10, compared with about US$10 and US$20 respectively in the best-paying West European countries. Under the pressure of the present exchange rate on those wages, they dropped below US$1. This means that the rapid growth of domestic consumer prices is so far reflected in a deteriorating parity of the purchasing power of the Czechoslovak koruna from Kcs 5–6 per US$ to about Kcs 10–12, reducing the former wage of US$3.5 to about US$2, and this 'free fall' continues. The CSFR is moving with its wage level into the central zone of developing countries. This means that if Volkswagen was paying its workers in Wolfsburg about DM 3,600 average monthly wages and its workers in East Germany about DM 1,500, the wage level at the Volkswagen–Skoda plant in the CSFR will average about DM 250 a month. That, of course, evokes further ominous questions, such as: if wages remain as low as that, will it make any sense for foreign capital to modernize the former Czechoslovak enterprises at all? Or will there, under such conditions, be a mass exodus of highly qualified people from the CSFR?

(3) The introduction, as a result of the deep devaluation, of a very strong inflationary trend. As the Czechoslovak economy opened itself completely, lots of people from neighbouring Germany, Austria, etc. went there to shop. Germany alone has 80 million inhabitants. While the average monthly wage of a Czechoslovak citizen amounts to about Kcs 3,750, the purchasing power of a German citizen in the CSFR amounts to about Kcs 60,000 (about DM 3,200 average income multiplied by Kcs 18 per DM at the official exchange rate). This means that these shoppers are getting an enormous subsidy on their purchases to the detriment of the living standard of the Czechoslovak population. Even more important, in such an open Czechoslovak market, its prices continually converge towards German ones. If a landlady in Prague can get about DM 200 rent for a two-room flat

from a German tenant, she will demand the same from a Czech student. And if a German visitor pays ten times more for a meal and drink in a restaurant than it used to cost in 1989 and still considers it to be advantageous for him, these prices will naturally also be valid for all other foreign visitors and the local inhabitants. A similar situation exists for other services. For the majority of industrial products, Czechoslovak prices are already at the level of German ones, the prices of services are approaching that level, and slowly even food prices are moving up.

That naturally means that:

(a) In 1989, purchasing power parity in the CSFR was Kcs 3.50–4 per DM. For an average monthly wage of Kcs 3,100 that represented an income level of about DM 850 compared with DM 2,700–3,000 average monthly income in the former West Germany.

(b) At the beginning of 1992, prices were nearly double their level in 1989 and the purchasing power parity rose to Kcs 7–8 per DM for an average monthly wage of Kcs 3,800. Living standards in relation to the western parts of Germany markedly deteriorated – DM 500 average monthly wage in the CSFR against DM 3,000–3,200 in Germany.

(c) With the further rise of Czechoslovak prices towards the German level and therefore a parity near the official exchange rate of Kcs 18 per DM, the average Czechoslovak wage, which was slowly approaching the order of Kcs 5,000 monthly, would fall to a real level of DM 200–300 and could hardly be considered to be tolerable. On the other hand, if the present DM 500 is to be preserved or if the former DM 850 is to be restored in the course of the next few years, the Czechoslovak average wage would have to rise from the present Kcs 3,800 to about Kcs 10,000–12,000. That clearly shows the trend of the inflation to come, if average wages are to treble by 1995–7.

(d) The devaluation shock still relatively favours the production and exports of heavy industry, especially of raw materials and materials, with its uneconomically low domestic prices. If the communist hypertrophy of heavy industry was justly criticized, a further deterioration took place in 1991. Table 3.3 shows this fact without commentary.

The depth of the problems springing from the triple shock therapy – 'convertibility–devaluation–liberalization of foreign trade' – is revealed in Tables 3.3 and 3.4. The negative influence on the entire future economic development is evident.

The entire movement of the macroeconomic aggregates and proportions is reflected in the recessionary spiral. If we convert the indices of Table 3.4 into constant 1988 prices, we arrive at the figures in Table 3.5.

Table 3.3 Decline in Industrial Production, 1989–91, Constant Prices
(1989 = 100)

Branch[1]	In comparison with the same period the previous year (%)				
	1990	1991			
		Q1	Q2	Q3	Q4
Industry total	96.3	89.5	83.5	78.7	75.3
Fuels	91.3	99.3	102.4	98.0	94.5
Energy	98.8	100.8	98.3	97.0	96.4
Ferrous metals	97.1	99.6	93.8	84.3	78.2
Non-ferrous metals	–	81.6	70.5	63.0	58.4
Chemicals, rubber, asbestos	90.9	89.7	81.3	77.4	77.3
Mechanical engineering	98.2	90.3	82.3	75.6	69.7
Electrical engineering	93.0	80.8	70.1	65.1	60.8
Building materials	94.0	81.3	75.8	71.3	66.9
Wood working	100.8	97.5	88.0	81.4	73.9
Metal working	94.5	88.2	82.0	71.6	66.6
Paper and pulp	–	106.4	96.2	87.0	81.6
Glass, ceramics, china	98.7	87.2	82.6	77.4	73.4
Textiles	100.4	84.0	75.9	68.8	64.4
Ready-made clothing	95.3	71.1	66.8	65.2	59.6
Leather	98.3	81.5	73.7	68.6	63.5
Printing	108.2	90.2	81.7	77.5	73.2
Foodstuffs	98.2	82.8	81.8	83.1	83.0
Beverages, tobacco	–	68.0	82.2	80.3	82.8
Others	–	95.2	86.0	78.7	–

Note:
1 Enterprises with more than 100 employees.

The most important and largest drop, of the order of one-quarter, appears in personal consumption. That corresponds to the average monthly wage decrease from Kcs 2,901 to Kcs 2,117, i.e. by 27% (in constant 1988 prices). Remember that between 1989 and 1990 there had already been a drop in real wages from Kcs 3,080 to Kcs 2,901 (i.e. 5.8%), so the total drop for the two years was 31.3%. Note, too, government expenditure, where there were significant reductions in expenditure on health care, education, science and research. Total investment shows a smaller reduction than fixed investment, resulting from high additional investment in stock. In the attempt to maintain production and employment, despite losses in sales, enterprises produced for stock. The preservation of employment found its expression in a sharp reduction in labour productivity – by 13.8% in industry and 19.8% in construction between 1990 and 1991 (over the two years 1990 and 1991, 16.3% and 23.0% respectively).

On the whole we can, therefore, observe a rapid drop in the efficiency of the Czechoslovak economy. Apart from the already mentioned phenomena of

Table 3.4   Key Economic Indicators, 1989–91

Indicator	Unit	Year			% change	
		1989	1990	1991 Estimated	1989/90	1990/1
GDP, current prices	Kcs bn.	759.4	819.0	952.5	7.8	16.3
Personal consumption	Kcs bn.	367.9	412.0	421.7	12.0	2.4
Government spending	Kcs bn.	164.3	171.7	210.0	4.5	22.3
Investment	Kcs bn.	210.2	251.2	300.8	19.5	19.7
Net exports	Kcs bn.	17.0	−15.9	20.0	–	–
GDP, 1988 prices	Kcs bn.	748.9	734.3	624.0	−2.0	−15.0
GDP, 1984 prices	Kcs bn.	–	727.0	607.0	–	−16.5

Average monthly nominal wages (excluding farming cooperatives)

	Kcs	3,123	3,238	3,750	3.7	15.8

Average monthly real wages (excluding farming cooperatives)

	Kcs	3,080	2,901	2,117	−5.8	−27.0

Fixed investment, current prices

	Kcs bn.	184.0	204.5	220.0	11.1	7.6
Construction works	Kcs bn.	97.3	103.4	112.7	6.3	9.0
Machinery and equipment						
	Kcs bn.	86.9	101.1	107.3	16.3	6.1
Investment, constant 1988 prices						
	Kcs bn.	177.1	189.4	130.9	6.9	−30.9

Total industrial output (including small enterprises and private sector), constant prices

	Kcs bn.	989.9	950.0	730.5	−4.0	−23.1
of which enterprises with 100+ workers						
	Kcs bn.	926.8	892.7	672.0	−3.7	−24.7

Total construction, current prices

	Kcs bn.	93.7	91.1	86.1	−2.8	−5.5

Gross agricultural production, constant prices

	Kcs bn.	160.7	154.4	141.0	−3.9	−8.7

Growth in labour productivity, constant prices (%)

Industry		1.7	−2.0	−13.8		
Construction		3.8	−4.0	−19.8		

Table 3.5 Key Economic Indicators, 1990–1, Constant 1988 Prices (Kcs bn)

Indicator	1990	1991 Estimated	% change 1990/1
GDP	819.0	683.9	-16.5
Personal consumption	369.5	276.3	-25.3
Government spending	154.0	137.6	-12.5
Investment	225.3	197.1	-12.5
Fixed investment	189.4	130.9	-30.9

producing for stock and of falling labour productivity, we also have to note the extensive losses in depreciation if industrial enterprises have a diminishing daily output and, therefore, also a smaller utilization of their fixed assets – by 30% in the second half of 1991.

The energy intensity of production also grew significantly, as shown in Table 3.6. The total consumption of primary energy resources remained virtually the same in 1991 (a 2.2% decrease) for a 23.1% lower industrial production and 16.5% smaller GDP.

Table 3.6 The Energy Intensity of Production, 1989–90

Primary energy sources	Unit	1989	1990	% change
Production of primary energy	PJ	2,132.4	1,977.7	-7.3
Imports	PJ	1,287.2	1,188.3	-7.7
Exports	PJ	-259.6	-183.7	-29.2
Decrease/increase in stocks	PJ	-22.6	87.2	–
Gross consumption	PJ	3,137.5	3,069.5	-2.2
Coal production	million tonnes	125.4	119.3	-4.9
Electricity generation	million kWh	86.6	–	–
of which nuclear	million kWh	24.58	24.62	0.2

This reduction in energy efficiency is all the more dangerous because it started from a low base. The centrally planned economy was rightly criticized for its low efficiency. Compared with developed countries, its labour productivity was about half, the energy intensity for a comparable unit of net production about double, etc. Economic reform was supposed to exert firm pressure and to motivate enterprises to improve their efficiency.

In reality an enormous squandering of economic resources is taking place. This wastage is connected with three further issues:

(1) The strong inflation shock of the beginning of 1991. Total inflation, expressed in the consumer price index for 1991, amounted to 57.9%, reaching 40% in the first three months of the year. That growth was precipitated by the introduction of completely liberalized prices, at a time when there was no competition and monopolistic state producers tried to see how high prices could be pushed. Prices changed every day, while many commodities were still produced for the low costs of the previous year. At the same time, wages were frozen or nearly frozen. In this way, enterprises were able to increase their incomes without spending more on wages, and many dishonest people in trade and production acquired high speculative incomes for their own pockets. According to information published in the press by the Ministry of Labour of the Czech Republic, an additional Kcs 100,000 million appeared in the Czech Republic in 1991, of which only a few hundred were honestly earned. The real income taken from the population by this one-sided inflation (instead of the classical inflation spiral of prices–wages–prices, this was mostly only price inflation) improved the income situation of enterprises without their earning it, thus again supporting wastage and finally disappearing in the abyss of enterprise efficiency or rather inefficiency.

(2) Devaluation, with a systematic wastage of national resources resulting from the widespread redistribution in favour of foreign investors.

(3) The actual method of carrying out privatization. Parts of the property of collapsing state industry are being generously carved off for speculation of all sorts. Unjustified high expenditure and high income are current phenomena.

In fact nobody now cares about this large property. On the contrary, the government is giving a green light to destructive activities of this kind. The remaining assets of state enterprises are being appropriated by various private firms founded by employees of these firms who are working as employees and as private entrepreneurs in parallel, as well as by various advisory firms that are developing all sorts of rationalization studies and privatization projects. Contracts are concluded with foreign customers that are unfavourable in volume, product mix and prices. Even direct looting of property is unexceptional.

The problem consists in the fact that the ministries are not interested in this property, that cost calculations are no longer carried out and nobody requires them. The management of a state enterprise has usually changed several times during the last few years and, therefore, even their interest in the enterprise's prosperity is low.

The process of privatization deserves special attention – and not just for the above reasons. After all, it is one of the pillars of the transformation.

So far about one-third of former state-owned shops, restaurants and service enterprises have passed into private hands. Instead of the original proposal, supported by the President of the Republic, that this network of services should at first be sold to the employees at book prices, the method of public auctions, guaranteed by local privatization commissions, was chosen. As a result, speculative practices were quite extensively applied. Today it is alleged that shops were bought in great numbers by various interest groups, that 'dirty money' was laundered in this way, that the privatized services were given an orientation differing from the original purpose, thus infringing the traditional, balanced distribution of services, that domestic participants in the auctions were actually used as fronts for purchasers who were exploiting the advantageous exchange rate.

The process of large-scale privatization, i.e. of industrial enterprises, is more complicated and obviously accompanied by enormous problems. It is performed in two ways. On the one hand, there is the process of normal evaluation and public sale of shares, with a preference for foreign tenders, which is managed by the Ministry of Privatization in cooperation with other ministries. The second method consists of the so-called voucher privatization process, with about one-third of the total number of privatized enterprises being offered in equal shares to the whole population for a symbolic, very low price. Every citizen has the right to buy a book of vouchers containing 1,000 investment points, which he can invest in various enterprises nominated by the ministry for the voucher privatization process. The investors should find some information on the efficiency of these enterprises in the published privatization projects, but these do not overflow with relevant information on capital efficiency. That means that citizens invest their investment points in various enterprises of their choosing or because one enterprise is oversubscribed while another is undersubscribed. To make this situation easier for the public, special financial advisory institutions were set up for this purpose – investment privatization funds were to place the shares and take a certain share of the profit. But an unexpected speculation started in this field. Several hundred such funds were established and introduced aggressive acquisition. Using a large number of agents they started to buy vouchers from the public for a certain remuneration. For instance, the Harvard Investment Fund bought 200,000 books of vouchers which people were ready to sell to them on the promise of being paid a bonus amounting to ten times their price (the price of one voucher book with the investment stamp is Kcs 1,035 so the return is about Kcs 10,350). In this way the entire voucher privatization process turned into an entertaining national lottery. The numbers interested in this small but certain profit grew in number and about 7 million people bought voucher books. This means that the value of fixed investments privatized in this way (Kcs 210 billion) shrank to only Kcs 30,000 per head; in the existing inflation that is a minor item of about five to eight times the average monthly wage. It is to be expected that most of the books of vouchers will be bought by investment privatization funds for a much lower sum. For this purpose they are partly using means that are very much favoured by the exchange rate or cash that they would otherwise have difficulty investing – including laundering dirty money. As I said, all this has changed into a quite undignified lottery for the inhabitants who succumb and quite openly hand enormous public wealth to speculators.

Concluding this part, I would like to indicate some – in my opinion – very questionable general aspects of privatization in the CSFR. First of all is the speed with which the state enterprises have to be privatized. About half of the industrial enterprises enlisted in the first wave of privatization in practice have one year for this process. My objection is that even Mrs Thatcher privatized for 12 years, but our government representatives answer by comparing the total value of our state capital with the lower value of enterprises privatized in the UK and, by dividing this value by the UK period of 12 years, they prove mathematically that the CSFR's privatization would take centuries that way. That certainly does not call for any comment. But to turn such a serious matter as the economic, financial, technical, organizational, legislative and labour preparation of the privatization into a mathematical sport is very surprising. And there should not be any doubt that the situation in the UK, where only some dozens of large firms were privatized in an ocean of private property and in a functioning capital market with plenty of experienced managers, etc., was far more favourable than the CSFR's. That means that the calculations should be performed the other way round, if anything: if it took the UK 12 years, then the CSFR needs double the time. Naturally we do not intend to reduce privatization to a time function. But the privatization 'Blitzkrieg' announced in the CSFR necessarily makes the process chaotic. Another problem is the macroeconomic consequences of devaluation, which on average devalued domestic capital to one-third of its international value. Apart from that, enterprises are forced into immediate privatization under the conditions of a sales crisis and mass indebtedness, which sharply reduces the market prices of these enterprises, especially for foreign buyers. Finally, restitution, the courageous return of a large amount of property to the original owners, raises a large number of proprietary–legislative, but also socioeconomic, problems.

In all these connections we can state that the real monetary funds taken from the population, enterprises and public institutions are partially returning to the economy through other channels. Among these belongs a relatively broad stream of income from speculations, the largest sources of which are the mass pilfering of state property connected with the privatization process, and the speculative operations of the much-used foreign economic experimenters rather than businessmen.

Only against this background can we understand the rather surprising facts regarding the development of monetary turnover, finances and the state budget. Officially, a policy of tightening budget expenditure and strict currency policy, presuming restrictions on the diffusion of money in circulation, was introduced. In reality, however, the growing mass of money in circulation is fairly obvious. The available statistics allow comparatively detailed data to be published only for the first 11 months of 1991 (see Table 3.7).

Table 3.7 Key Monetary Indicators, 1989-91

Indicator	1989	1990	1991
Change in money in circulation (Kcs m.)			
November	2,079	3,978	3,512
January–November	6,834	7,679	11,422
January–15 December	11,886	14,202	21,013
Money in circulation (Kcs m.)			
at end November	69,307	75,738	85,075
Planned growth of cash turnover (%)			
Expenditure January–November	4.5	18.6	20.3
Income January–November	4.6	18.7	26.3
Turnover of money in circulation (days)			
1 Kcs in circulation, January–November,			
on an average for	33.4	29.5	27.9

The amount of money in circulation at the end of November 1991 was 12.3% higher than in the previous year (the figures for 1989 and 1990 were 6.3% and 9.3% higher, respectively), that is an acceleration of the dynamics by 3 points. The total addition to money in circulation since the beginning of the year amounted to Kcs 11.4 billion, that is Kcs 3.7 billion more than in the same period in 1990. The turnover of the money in circulation accelerated (since the beginning of the year) compared with the previous year by 1.6 days (against data for 10 months of 1991, it decelerated by 0.1 days). In 1990, the cash turnover balances amounted to four times those of 1989; in 1991 (compared with the same period of 1990), expenditure rose by only 1.7 points and income by 7.6 points.

There are, however, some annual data at our disposal, which signal a serious growth in monetary and financial sources (see Tables 3.8 and 3.9). On the one hand, with inflation of 58% in 1991, a certain growth would be understandable. On the other hand, as we have already shown, this was not real inflation, but more of a currency reform in which real wages fell by 27%, consumer demand dropped by about 30% and production went into a deep recession characterized

Table 3.8   Composition of Czechoslovak Assets, 1989-91, (Kcs bn)

Assets	1989	1990	1991
Net foreign assets	17.8	-4.3	2.3
Foreign assets, convertible currency	37.8	27.7	92.0
Foreign liabilities, convertible	20.0	32.0	90.0
Net domestic assets	530.0	555.0	670.0
Domestic credit	583.6	640.2	771.0
Net credit to government	5.9	54.2	52.0
Net credit to Property Fund	0.0	0.0	25.0
Credit to enterprises and households	577.7	586.0	694.0
Credit to enterprises	530.8	536.0	640.0
Credit to households	46.9	50.0	54.0

Table 3.9   Czechoslovak Liabilities and Deposits, 1989-91, (Kcs bn)

| Indicator | Year | | | % change | |
	1989	1990	1991 Estimated	1989-90	1990-91
Liquid liabilities	547.8	550.7	673.0	0.5	22.2
Money	311.1	291.2	368.0	-6.4	26.4
Currency outside banks	68.0	73.7	88.0	8.4	19.4
Households	62.8	69.0	-	-	-
Enterprises	5.2	4.7	-	-	-
Demand deposits	243.1	217.5	280.0	-10.5	28.7
Households	107.5	103.3	-	-	-
Enterprises	135.6	111.4	-	-	-
Insurance companies	0.0	2.8	-	-	-
Quasi-money	236.7	259.5	305.0	9.6	17.5
Time and savings deposits	232.5	231.7	260.0	-0.3	12.2
Households	170.2	167.4	-	-	-
Enterprises	6.6	10.5	-	-	-
Insurance companies	55.7	53.8	-	-	-
Foreign currency deposits	4.2	27.8	45.0	-	-
Households	1.7	9.8	-	-	-
Enterprises	2.5	18.0	-	-	-
Other items net	53.6	85.2	100.0	-	-
Inter-enterprise credit	7.2	53.6	140.0	644.4	161.2

by a 23.1% annual decrease in industrial production (30% from the second half of 1991).

The policy of severe restriction has failed. The proclaimed policy of national sacrifice remained more of a slogan. While certain strata of the population are making sacrifices, others are rapidly enriching themselves. It would be more accurate to say that this is a sacrifice by some people for the benefit of others. From the social, humanitarian and political point of view it is more regrettable that the sacrifices are made by the socially weakest strata of the population, mainly pensioners, of whom there are 4 million in the CSFR (3.5 million old-age pensioners and 0.5 million disabled people), workers and young workers' families with several children.

At the same time, this development allows us to explain the fact that this rapid drop in real wages and the explosion of unemployment have so far not led to social tensions manifested in mass strikes and other forms of protest. In fact, the newly established, although speculative, entrepreneurs need craftsmen and other workers, and approximately 500,000 workers have registered, apart from their employment, as private entrepreneurs. This enables them to have a second income that in the present chaos is often not taxed. As a result, domestic and foreign entrepreneur organizations are introducing wide variations of income into our economy. One section of the population becomes rich in this way, but another section also receives orders for small-scale building, reconstruction, adaptation and repair work, resulting in small-scale production for the domestic and foreign markets. According to our estimates, the basic source of these incomes is the chaotic disappearance of state-owned industry accompanied by widespread speculative activity, corruption and undeserved enrichment. Only with mass privatization will this source dry up, and social tension will then become visible in a sharper way.

The above failures and deviations of the restrictive policy are also visible in the development of the state budget (see Table 3.10). During the compilation of the 1991 budget at the end of 1990, its savings and anti-inflationary character was declared, but at the end of the first three months enormous increases (of the order of Kcs 15 billion) were observed in income. The unexpected source was the price increase and, therefore, also the transfer to the budget. These surpluses were used up by higher expenditure, and at the end of 1991 money was being spent on such a large scale for all sorts of surprising fees and expenditure that the state budget ended up showing a deficit. Current developments indicate that the relation between budget inputs and outputs is becoming more strained.

A great problem, in my opinion, is the fact that the state budget is not strategically linked with an overall view of credits and bank operations. Credit is out of control and the banking system is not in a good state. The application of restrictions on volumes limited government support for restructuring investments and the import of foreign capital and reduced the availability of credit by means of the high interest rate as well as limitations on government

Table 3.10   Government Budget, 1989–91 (Kcs bn)

Indicator	Year			% change	
	1989	1990	1991 Estimated[1]	1989–90	1990–91
Liquid liabilities	547.8	550.7	673.0	0.5	22.2
State budget and local					
authority expenditures	462.2	464.4	494.7	0.5	6.5
Current expenditure	417.7	–	442.2	–	–
Capital expenditure	44.5	–	52.5	–	–
State budget and local					
authority revenues	455.8	469.8	502.7	3.1	7.0
Income and profits tax	162.3	166.7	198.8	–	–
Payroll tax	113.8	116.0	123.3	–	–
Domestic tax on					
goods and services	133.6	138.9	144.7	–	–
Other	46.1	48.2	35.9	–	–
Balance (deficit)	–6.4	5.4	8.0[2]	–	–

Notes:
1   The 1991 budget included a mid-course correction in July.
2   Actual expected deficit is Kcs 5–10 billion.

guarantees of credits – thereby strongly reducing the elasticity of the banks' behaviour.

During the first three months of 1991 state income developed positively only thanks to a sudden wave of inflation combined with a low level of production costs that still corresponded to the conditions of 1990. Conscious of the short-term and transitory character of state income, the Federal Ministry of Finance relaxed state expenditure. But the ministry reacted to the following negative development of income with extensive restrictions. These restrictions did not correspond to the adaptive abilities of the economy and therefore caused an unnecessary drop in production, which multiplied the state income losses. This is how the cumulative process came into being that ended in the huge state deficit of 1991, which would unfavourably influence the year 1992, and probably even 1993. These negative consequences flowed from the prolongation of the recession. They harm privatization, the inflow of foreign capital and the development of the middle class.

The drop in production and in enterprise profits and the resulting loss of state income led to a situation in which the state deficit resulted not from exceeding the expenditure budget but from insufficient income. The result is a paradox and can be characterized with the words: from restriction to deficit.

The inflexible attitude of the central bank, and in that connection of the commercial banks, had already been signalled by the fact that, for the originally presumed 30% price growth in 1991, the central bank planned a 16% credit growth and in addition determined a uniform credit release of 4% in each quarter of the year. The main price shock, however, took place in January (26% compared with December 1990) and at the end of April prices were already 39% higher. That is how the shortage of money in the economy came into being and grew. In addition, the banks increased interest rates to 24% and the government changed its method of crediting reserves (which amounted to Kcs 150 billion and represented 20% of the national product). The existing interest arrears with the crediting of reserves amounting to 6% rose to 20–22%.

The central bank reacted too late to these developments and did not reduce the discount rate until June (from 14% to 12%) and then by August to 9.5%. The reserve credits were also dealt with later, by restructuring banking resources, by reducing the interest rate and by prolonging the repayment periods. Up to the time when these extreme rates were abandoned, the default risk rose and weakened the banks further.

Businesses reacted to these conditions in two ways, usually in parallel: they limited production without simultaneously restructuring (for which they did not have sufficient financial resources) and they did not pay their suppliers, i.e. they increased total insolvency. These reactions essentially prove the ineffectiveness of a restrictive policy at the micro level. This result probably occurred because this policy included no adequate adaptation programme by means of which the restrictions could have been coordinated. Instead of putting pressure on adaptation, the restrictions only provoked an unintended decline in production. They had no recuperative powers and made limited use of the monetary function. These are exactly the opposite changes to those needed for the development of the market economy.

The basic credit policy of the banks should consist of a consistent application of the criteria for re-funding. It is important that the central bank should attempt to preserve the optimal difference between interest from deposits and interest from credits. This optimum should reflect the actual default risk as well as the need to support the development of the sector outside banking, i.e. the banks' profits should not be created at the expense of the enterprises that are their debtors. This action is especially important as competition in the banking sector is only just starting and so far does not significantly influence the interest rate.

A serious problem that has to be resolved even before the industrial or structural policy is enacted is the old debt burden on enterprises (inherited from the past) and the payments insolvency connected with the new conditions.

The old debt burden is the banks' claims on enterprises. The payment of principal due and interest on these debts would usually ruin the enterprises, which is why bank claims remain unpaid, with the exception of Kcs 50 billion received by the banks in the form of obligations of the National Property Fund.

This represents only a partial solution of the entire problem. (For instance, the industrial enterprises of the Czech Republic were permitted to write off only Kcs 14 billion within this framework, while a more significant solution would require Kcs 50 billion in this sector alone.)

It seems that this problem will have to be treated more seriously by transferring this old debt burden to a long-term state debt so as to liberate enterprises from this yoke. At the enterprise level, this problem cannot even be solved by bankruptcy, in particular because the restructuring of enterprises would in this manner become a reflection of the faulty decisions of central planners in the past and not the result of the influence of market conditions.

In connection with these trends we can expect an intense exacerbation of social tensions. The report of the Czechoslovak government submitted with the draft state budget for 1992 forecast that the economic recession would continue – by another 6-8 points. The reduction in real wages would also continue, as would inflation, though probably moderated at 10-15%. Especially alarming is the government forecast of unemployment – about 1 million unemployed, i.e. 13-14% by the end of the year.

The forecast of the Institute for Forecasting for 1991 and that of the government differed a great deal,[8] but for 1992 they more or less agreed on the above figures – apart from inflation. We expected inflation to be at least twice as high, i.e. 20-30%, rather more than the government.

A really key difference, however, is the government's presumption that the end of the year would see the end of the recession and an economic upturn. We think that, just as the government's presumption turned out to be groundless for 1991, it will also remain doubtful for 1992. There is likely to be a mass wave of bankruptcies of industrial enterprises, because the combination of the sales crisis with the high indebtedness had already brought perhaps one-third of enterprises to the brink of insolvency at the end of 1991. They were able to defer bankruptcy only with credits from the state banks. With privatization of banks and enterprises in the course of 1992, the financial collapse of the most indebted ones becomes unavoidable. That is why we presume that any revival of enterprise investment is just as unlikely as higher income for the state budget and a revival of public investment. And with the forecast of a doubling of unemployment from about 0.5 to 1 million persons and a continued drop in real wages, no revival of consumer demand can be expected. Lastly, we have to count on a further and very sharp decrease of exports to the Commonwealth of Independent States. For these reasons we presume that the economic recession in the CSFR will be long term, involving growing social tension and simultaneous political problems.

One positive feature for 1992 and 1993 will probably be a higher influx of foreign, especially German, capital, although we cannot expect an adequate wage increase and higher investment in modernization. This is very clearly spelled out in the leading German economic journal *Wirtschaftswoche*: experts from various industrial branches in the FRG think that 'The large wave of German investment influx into Czechoslovakia can still be expected.' In comparison with other countries into which German capital is flowing, the CSFR is only half way up the ladder (see Table 3.11). In the first half of 1990 West German investments in the CSFR amounted to DM 1 million, while in the same period of 1991 they were DM 700 million. Out of about 3,000 Czechoslovak joint ventures, one-third are connected with capital from the FRG.

Table 3.11   Direct Investment by West German Enterprises
(1st half of 1991)

Country	DM bn.
Ireland	3.1
Belgium/Luxembourg	2.2
UK	1.4
Switzerland	1.1
Spain	0.8
Czechoslovakia	0.7
France	0.6
Canada	0.4
Austria	0.3
Italy	0.2

Source: German Institute of Economics.

The German investors are mainly attracted by the low wage costs. *Wirtschaftswoche* states that the hourly wage of the CSFR converted into DM amounts to 1.30, while in the FRG it is about DM 36. As regards the new Länder in the east, it is expected that in three years wages there will reach the levels of the western Länder. The West German textile producers calculated that one working minute in the CSFR costs only 21 pfennigs, which is 4 pfennigs less than in Yugoslavia and 9 less than in Portugal and only one-third of what they have to pay to domestic textile workers.

It is not only a question of low wages, however. *Wirtschaftswoche* enumerates more of the advantages: 'Czechoslovak workers have experience, they are well educated and diligent, the trade unions are tame. In addition, the protection of the environment is not yet taken too seriously by the inhabitants of Prague.' It is also possible, however, that under the pressure of such low wages the Czechoslovak workers and their trade unions will stop being so tame and that a further influx of German capital will come up against these barriers.

At present it is difficult to anticipate all the consequences. For the 1992 elections we are already aware of confrontation between the government's shock therapy and the concept of a gradualist solution offered by social democrats. In the latter case, it is a question of diminishing the previously harsh social consequences of the reform. In either case we have to expect serious long-term economic difficulties.

5   Recommendations of 'Policy Options for the Future'

The recessionary spiral has to be broken. We have to change from one-sided restrictions to a policy of revival and long-term growth.

In the first place we have to revive consumer demand. It is not just the social aspects that lead us to this conclusion. It is the key to removing obstacles to enterprise sales, to innovation and growth of production, to the revival of investment activity. Until now the CSFR's economy has been extremely self-sufficient. The Netherlands, with 14 million inhabitants, exports about US$ 110 billion, while Czechoslovakia exports about one-tenth of that, and its imports are determined by that figure. We produce most things ourselves and that has to be overcome in the future, but at the moment it offers us the opportunity to base our future boom on the domestic market, i.e. its expansion on the basis of a systematic and perceivable growth in the real incomes of the population. Naturally, we also have to create the space for export growth, as a higher living standard will mean higher imports and this process could be halted by the barrier of the balance of payments. A gradual, cautious solution involving resolute government support for exports is, however, possible.

A considerable rise in real wages – i.e. 3–5% or more annually – has favourable preconditions: strong industrial, agricultural and construction capacities, although weakened, are still at our disposal and have only to be utilized. Private enterprise and new sources of supplies have been added. The volume of imported commodities is much higher than in 1989. Foreign tourism shows great potential. It is possible to invest in private enterprise, securities and shares, and to buy houses, flats, etc. And the growth of supply has to be supported purposefully. That means we have to change from reducing demand to increasing supply and reviving industrial, agricultural and construction production.

At the same time we need to revive public investment. The old system was biased towards large heavy industrial plants rather than in investing in the maintenance of the housing stock, public buildings, the maintenance and development of communications, the telephone network and especially environmentally sound construction. It has disappeared, but it created a special debt for the future. It is now time to eliminate it, to liberate the resources previously diverted to super-heavy industry, which has low productivity but high investment demands, and to direct them to the benefit of public works, to investment by towns and villages in infrastructure and the environment. That means preparing for a 'boom' in building activity and the broad spectrum of associated production units and craftspeople. The CSFR's domestic building capacity is large, and there is an unusual range of domestic building materials, which means that imports will not play a decisive part.

There is no reason to reduce public expenditure on health care, education, science and culture. Reducing expenditure on education and science means weakening the future of the country. If the real income of the state is continuously lower, it is the result of the general fall in consumption and production, i.e. of losses of profits tax. That means that the policy of revival should enable us to raise public expenditure, whose growth will stabilize prosperity. There are other new possibilities thanks to reductions in state expenditure on armaments, on assistance to some developing countries, etc.

Enormous resources for further economic growth are concealed in the structural changes of our national economy. The inherited hypertrophy of heavy industry ties up large quantities of investments, energy resources, metals and imports. Heavy industry also makes big demands on equipment, energy, materials, etc. and creates a vicious circle of production demand, i.e. 'production for production'. Heavy industry is to a large extent self-sufficient, and the final effect on the population's consumption and exports is small. Czechoslovak production per head of the population is in fact double that in Austria, but consumption is about half. The surplus capacity of our heavy industry must be dramatically reduced, rapidly but purposefully and with the courage to assist the transfer of unused resources into manufacturing branches with a high proportion of skilled labour and into services. This will require a shift from ferrous metals (from the present production of 15 million tons of steel to 7-8 million tons in future), from coal mining (from 100 million tons brown coal to 30-40 million tons), from large-scale petrochemicals and heavy engineering, etc. to medium and light engineering, to more skilled types of chemicals and other branches, to developing services for tourism, etc. New jobs have to be created and big retraining programmes have to be started. The structural changes of the 1970s and 1980s were the main source of the boom in all West European countries. Now it is our turn. But the government has to help – beginning with a long-term programme of structural change and its systematic support, for instance with tax reductions, foreign exchange, but also directed subsidies, etc.

The achievement of the structural changes in the CSFR, however, requires the development of broader *regional cooperation*. Within the framework of the EC it would be useful to create an advisory and financial system for these structural changes. For instance, a 50% reduction of Czechoslovak steel production is a problem for 10-15 years. It is not clear how to achieve this structural manoeuvre. It is probably not possible without actual regional cooperation, mainly with the FRG and Austria but perhaps also with Italy, France, the UK, etc. It is not, however, just a matter of cooperation with the West European countries. Very positive developments are taking place in the CSFR's economic relations with Poland, Hungary and Bulgaria. A matter of some urgency is the establishment of a viable payments union with the new states appearing since the disintegration of the USSR; and the possible renewal of economic cooperation with the East European region, taking into account certain existing integrating bonds in this field. It would also be possible to develop natural micro-regional interconnections between Bohemia and Bavaria, Slovakia and Austria, etc. It would be expedient to organize and coordinate a programme for all these regional cooperations, which could form a promising basis for future development.

At the same time we need a long-term agricultural programme to support effective renewal and an ecological programme to improve the present unsatisfactory situation not only for the future but also in the short term.

It is important to support private enterprise. If we wish to stimulate supply, private producers must be given a 'green light'- state assistance for wholesale trade and stores, means of transport, telephones, cheap credit, exemption from taxes in the early years of their existence, etc. We have to keep to the well-known principle: rich craftspeople and tradespeople equal a rich state (or, even better, 'rich citizens' - rich craftspeople and rich enterprises - equal a rich state).

We should also emphasize special programmes such as the development of foreign tourism (Austria has an income of about US$10 billion per year from it, the CSFR at present not quite US$0.5 billion), the development of automobilism (the entire complex of major roads, garages, motels, petrol stations, etc. up to the actual production and sale of cars, spare parts, servicing, etc.), housing, etc.

That brings us to the social sphere. In accordance with the findings of modern sociology and management theory, we reject a return to the harsh capitalism of the nineteenth century with its principles of forced labour under the threat of unemployment, up to the conservative glorification of Taylorism and its degrading rationalization, changing man into the famous screw. We are in favour of a positive motivation of employees, assisting their creativity, their voluntary responsibility, and their participation in the ownership of property.

In this sense we also have to make a lot of improvements in public education and in health care. Good medical care and education must be accessible to the entire population, regardless of whether they can pay. We have to improve the care of our old population, and develop a programme of active old age, enabling the older generation to participate in university, language or other studies. We have to improve housing opportunities, and medical, hygiene, shopping and other services for old people, and their opportunities to participate in culture, tourism, etc. Improvement in the care of the disabled is essential.

The forecast of 1 million unemployed must not be permitted to come true. The loss of employment causes serious spiritual and social damage, often leading to humiliation for the individual, and shock for the family and children. With a controlled programme of reviving the economy, of structural change, of creating new jobs and training, unemployment can be kept near 4-5%, i.e.

350,000–400,000 people.

Concerning housing, we have to try in the present circumstances, with our income and prices, to keep flats socially accessible. We cannot permit the development of groups of homeless people, of emergency settlements, of shacks without sanitary facilities, etc. Adequate housing must be socially available for each citizen.

We have to care for mothers and children, and for families, especially young families with several children. We have to link children's benefits and maternity benefits to the rate of inflation, and we have to respect the principle of a minimum benefit (for 1992 we considered a level of Kcs 1,300 per person, which naturally also depends on the number of people in a household and the children's ages).

A new danger is developing with the unfortunate spread of pornography and prostitution, the sale and use of drugs, acute alcoholism, growing chronic criminality and other deviations. The present social care system has to be widened by an effective system of prevention and protection reaching into all parts of the country.

5.1 Market Development

In 1991 a large number of hasty pro-market liberalization measures were taken, and it seems impossible for the whole socioeconomic organism to digest them. An undesirable secondary phenomenon is considerable chaos, even extending to widespread and unpunished economic criminality. The state enterprises are devastated, plundered and privatized for a fraction of their real value. The price liberalization, which offers only slight protection to the customer, and minimum competition enable anybody in the network of trade, storage, transport and production to 'fill their pockets' at will. Tens of thousands of speculators, middlemen, black-marketeers, economic swindlers and criminals are springing up.

The contemporary modern market is a very complicated and sensitive organism, which cannot be simply decreed. Our present task consists in transforming the present anarchy and speculation (which is quite similar to an oriental bazaar) into a real market. That means:

(1) Renewing the population's confidence in the currency and creating positive economic expectations, thus strengthening the natural desire to start a family, to build a house, to invest. To that end we have to end the recession and mass unemployment, liberalize and differentiate wages and salaries, support situations in which honest work earns an adequate corresponding remuneration that can be spent in a market that offers a wide assortment of high-quality commodities at moderate prices.

(2) Starting immediately with the formation of an administrative–legislative

and institutional state infrastructure, without which the market cannot function. In the first place this means revenue and tax offices, because at the moment speculators are not paying taxes. Secondly, it means improving the almost non-existent protection of the customer, the registration of craftspeople and artisans, punishing economic criminality, improving price analyses and statistics, demonopolizing economic activity. It also means consciously supporting decentralization, healthy competition and protecting the domestic economy against the pressure of foreign competition.

(3) Developing and introducing a reliable programme for the creation of a domestic capital market. The presumed general and immediate privatization of banks and all monetary institutions, as well as the rapid opening of a domestic stock exchange, cannot be staffed or technically equipped. It would be possible to utilize much more foreign help. The further development and perfection of the foreign exchange market are not based on firm projects and the ambition of achieving the full convertibility of the currency soon is not realistic. It is not yet clear how to achieve the real functioning of the market in the investment sphere. The present submission of investment tenders through the local administration bodies etc. has very few reliable rules. Prices in this sphere reflect complete chaos and arbitrariness. Credit is out of control and the banking system does not work. An analysis of the entire financial and capital situation in the country is necessary.

(4) Improving the market and trade with the Eastern states, which to a great extent are in the hands of speculators and middlemen. There is no payments union and no stable general rules for exchange and evaluation.

These problems are very intense and must be solved systematically and with a target. A programme of systematic support has to be developed for small private enterprise, for the foundation of small and medium firms, for the creation of a keen but healthy competitive environment and for the gradual formation of all segments of the market, of personal, institutional, technical and other prerequisites for their rational function.

5.2 Privatization

Privatization is a necessary process, and optimal conditions have to be created for free enterprise. The problem, however, lies in the present hasty, uncontrolled privatization process, with speculators and various unreliable domestic and foreign firms influencing it to an increasing extent. In Austria, Italy, France but also in the UK, privatization took 10–20 years, in spite of the fact that there was a predominant sector of private owners. Very concrete, valuable experience was gathered there, but we are ignoring it. Some decisive measures have to be taken to put this essential process on a serious, prosperous footing.

First of all the course to be taken by the small-scale privatization has to be precisely defined. Many of the shops, restaurants and service enterprises are still waiting to be privatized. Continuing with the current practice will increase the risk that privatization will be abused by foreign speculators, by interest groups and for the dangerous practice of laundering dirty money. There is sufficient evidence that it is becoming increasingly difficult to meet the population's basic shopping needs, while 'boutiques' are spreading irrationally, and many will end in bankruptcy. For the remainder of the small-scale privatization we should return to the original proposal, which was supported by the President of the CSFR, of giving employees the priority to buy them.

For the path of the large-scale privatization, we mainly have to define the strategy of the process precisely, bearing in mind that it is not an independent campaign but that there is instead an organic interconnection between privatization, the workers and employees as well as the management of each enterprise in order to revive and stabilize the enterprises and thereby the economy. It should also be decided that 51% of the shares of leading enterprises are to remain in the hands of national capital. The bonds between the government programme of structural changes and improvement of the environment should also be defined. The concept of the privatization project should be directed more towards the strategy of the given enterprise, i.e. the optimal changes in the production programme, raising the technical level and quality on the basis of a marketing analysis in conformity with it. The stages of denationalization, installing a professional management with long-term interests and the gradual selling of shares (with a fixed maximum share of foreign capital, domestic capital and employees' capital) should also be connected with it.

The process of establishing joint stock corporations, and of announcing and selling shares should be fully entrusted to reliable financial capital, i.e. with the temporary, guaranteed and controlled participation of selected foreign banks, agreed between governments (e.g. the Vienna or another stock exchange, etc.). No amateur actions by employees of the Ministry for Privatization should be permitted.

The entire privatization process should be under public control, from supervision by parliamentary commission to regular conferences of representatives of all political parties and the press. Each large privatization should be evaluated by a commission of experts with the participation of representatives of the public and, a month before the signing of an agreement, the entire draft should be published.

5.3   Budget and Currency Policy

The state budget has to be transformed from an instrument of economic restriction back to its original purpose of ensuring public expenditure by the state at a civilized level. This concerns mainly health care and education, the development of towns and villages, infrastructure and the environment, apart from the necessary costs of administration, the judicial system, the police and defence (pensions are paid from the accumulated means of enterprises and employees are financed autonomously from the pension fund).

In addition, the state budget should finance the government's economic policy, its concept of structural changes, the agricultural programme, etc. To that end it would grant certain subsidies and tax and foreign exchange reductions in order selectively to support particular programmes and activities. Most important in this respect are subsidies for research and development, tax reductions for investments in high-technology branches with good prospects, subsidies for the production and export of agricultural products, support for training programmes, support for plans to expand exports, etc.

A special task of the state budget is the elimination of the damage caused to the environment and the infrastructure in the past. Compared with 1989, there should be new opportunities resulting from a reduction in the costs of defence, from granting less aid and subsidized exports to some developing countries as well as from new resources. For the years 1991–2 we can presume that there will be 150,000–200,000 new millionaires in the country. That represents property growth of about Kcs 300–400 billion. Here we have to introduce firm financial control. Imposing a 30% tax on this property, not all of which was respectably acquired, permits the state greatly to increase its budgetary income and to invest publicly about four times as much as at present. That is the strategic path along which lie the possibilities of introducing essential changes in favour of reviving investment and the economy as a whole and in the direction of significantly greater care for the environment, the infrastructure, housing and public funds.

5.4   Monetary Policy

There is a need to change to a policy of long-term currency stabilization after the anti-inflation restrictions (more theoretical than practical). The currency is being debased through:

(a) transferring the former investment money of state enterprises into normal circulation by means of the new millionaires stealing state funds and with them financing their personal employees, their purchasing of extravagant cars, etc.;

(b) mobilizing previously frozen currency reserves in foreign financial centres and with the speculators, black market money exchangers and smugglers,

and putting them into circulation for privatization but also for corruption;
(c) laundering dirty money from abroad;
(d) the rapid increase in the volume of money in circulation at the same time as the rapid decrease in production and sales in domestic trade. This stabilization policy will mean not increasing the volume of money in circulation for the next few years. To finance future economic growth, external capital inputs and overcoming the present immobility of enterprise resources should be sufficient. We should start with a precise currency analysis, which the state bank will have to submit to parliament and the public.

5.5 Inflation

The present inflation is – in spite of its high annual rate of 60% – not real inflation. It is cost inflation caused by devaluation combined with a simultaneous wage freeze. It is more of a currency reform or exorbitant price growth than a classical inflation connected with rising wages followed by rising prices, etc. This classical inflation will probably be unavoidable in the next few years, but we must avoid reducing the living standard of the population (pensions, wages and salaries must be systematically and equitably raised). Theoretically the given problems can be solved with deflation, i.e. with a combination of revaluation and an overall adjustment of the price level downwards by 20–30 points. This has some advantages but would be difficult to carry out because of the measures already embarked upon. A more suitable method (for the next few years) is controlled inflation at 30%, then 15% and finally 10% a year.

5.6 Correcting Relative Prices

At the beginning of the reform we faced the problem of overcoming extreme price distortions. Now the disintegration of the price system is threatening us. Simultaneously we have the old relative prices, resulting from a purchasing power parity of Kcs 3.5-4 per DM in 1988 and the new price level and relative prices with an exchange rate of Kcs 18 per DM, together with a reciprocal opening of our market and the German or European markets. If we leave this process to develop unhindered, it will pose great problems for the CSFR's price development and will be an obstacle to the transition to normal world relations. Cars, for instance, and other industrial products are becoming very expensive in relation to wages, purchases of cars are falling rapidly, and the population is losing its motivation. In contradiction to the theory of comparative advantage, imports of machinery and complementary technology are losing their attractiveness, thus affecting the opportunity to produce and export more sophisticated products requiring skilled labour. On the other hand, there is a marked increase in the profitability of exploiting exports of raw materials and semi-finished products. It is necessary speedily to submit proposals for improving relative prices by means of indirect financial instruments, i.e. taxes and social subsidies, as well as changes in the exchange rate and interest rates in order to achieve within five to six years a rationality approaching the present state of relative prices in the developed market economies.

5.7   Foreign Exchange and Exchange Rate Policy

The triple devaluation in 1990 from Kcs 15 to 28 and then 30 per US$ was a great shock to the stability of the Czechoslovak economy. In 1989, the purchasing power parity amounted – according to comparative consumer baskets and international comparisons – to about Kcs 5.50-6 per US$. From the point of view of real foreign purchasing power, a market exchange rate based on the cost of earning one unit of convertible currency with exports amounted in the last few years to Kcs 14.50 per US$. Finally there was the black market on which people bought foreign exchange, not to purchase normal products, which in comparison with abroad were cheap in the CSFR and where purchasing power parity held, but to purchase those products in shortest supply, i.e. consumers' electronic goods and similar products for which the domestic price was kept extremely high for subjective, largely political reasons, at a level of about Kcs 70 per US$. That is how an exchange rate of Kcs 30-35 for the US$ came into being between the estimates of Western sellers and of domestic buyers (as expressed by the blackmarketeers and their organization). In the past, about 20% of free currencies were bought according to that exchange rate, which now officially applies to all free currencies. This has given an immediate advantage to the foreign partner. It also means favouring foreigners in the sale of the national domestic wealth. With 80 million Germans as our neighbours, this cheap price of the Czechoslovak koruna in relation to the DM is of particular significance, and there is even a danger of a certain economic colonization.

For all these reasons we should start with revaluation. But the problem is that the inflation wave has already strongly lifted the level of the purchasing power parity and the domestic costs of earning dollars. PPP can be estimated according to the price index at about Kcs 10-12 per US$ and the cost of earning dollars at Kcs 28 per US$. In this situation we would really have to combine revaluation with deflation. According to comparative macroeconomic models, that would mean reducing the exchange rate to a point mid-way between the two estimates above, i.e. to about Kcs 20 per US$ and about Kcs 12 per DM, at the same time as intervening to adjust the domestic price level by reducing the level of basic products by about 20 points with further pressure by the state, mainly as a customer, on the price level.

Another method would be to utilize controlled inflation together with the continuing domestic growth of prices and wages, with an annual inflation rate of

30%, slowing to 20% and then 10%, and maintaining the present exchange rates with a view to compensating for their negative influence gradually with the rise of domestic prices. Compensation in relation to the FRG would be reached only over the course of a number of years. In the meantime, the solution could be the introduction of several different exchange rates – for tourism, trade, convertible operations, etc.

Both of these methods have still to be studied, but, in terms of organizational integration into the overall context of the economic policy, we would prefer the inflation variant. According to our short-term estimates, gradual transition to real convertibility would need a ten-year period. It is also conditional on a rise in competitiveness and in exports to developed country markets. For that period our domestic industry has to be protected against the harshest effects of foreign competition, to allow a rapid modernization of technology and of the entire economy and the elaboration and introduction of an ambitious programme to raise the competitiveness of Czech industry.

Naturally, this is only an outline of the further development of the economic transformation in the CSFR and suitable changes in the actual economic policy. Essentially these are limited suggestions that need further elaboration.

6   The Problems in 1992

The economic situation in the CSFR in 1992 was better than in 1991, but it was also more complicated: the annual rate of inflation was only 12% and unemployment stopped growing, but the fall in industrial and agricultural production continued and the general economic decline in 1992 was estimated at about 8–10% GDP.

At the end of 1992 we cannot say that these negative tendencies have definitely been overcome. But views differ. One group believes that the economy is picking up and is approaching prosperity, while others fear that the solution of the actual problems of production efficiency is being postponed with the threat of a consequential wave of bankruptcies. We shall now attempt an objective synthesis.

First, there was an improvement in the development of industrial production as compared with 1991. Although industrial production fell by 20.2% for the period January–June 1992 as against the same period in 1991, the rate fell to 15% in May and to 11% in June.

This improvement should not be overemphasized. If industrial production in January 1992 within the framework of the CSFR fell to only about 55% of the 1989 levels, we would not expect the fall to continue at the same intensity – otherwise we would come close to zero during 1993. On the basis of available information, including state budget documentation and published government statements, a rise in industrial production as against 1991 is estimated at only about 6–8%. It is important to remember the overall monthly industrial production curve showing a fall in production for 1991: production in January–February fell by only about 5%, in March–April by 15%, in May–June by about 20%, and in the following period by 30–35%. It is therefore understandable that, in the face of the expected overall moderate fall in the annual average, we should expect a large fall during the first few months and then a rise in the course of the later months of the year. For this reason 'the rise from the bottom' is not straightforward; we may even talk about 'a wave near the bottom'. The dramatic fall in industrial production during 1991 had complex consequences and their elimination will necessarily be a long-term process. We should realize that the average fall in production by 24% in 1991 and by about 45% if we compare the period October 1991–January 1992 as against 1989 was quite extraordinary from an international and historical point of view. This was the result not only of reform restrictions, but also of the collapse of the Eastern markets (by about one-third). Thus climbing out of this recession is a long-term problem. A return to the production levels of 1989 will take until about 1995–7.

We should not, however, consider just simple quantitative production curves. The decline had a complex character. The restrictions removed subsidies from businesses, agricultural cooperatives and the population. Thus they complicated the already precarious financial position of businesses and further reduced overall buying power and consequently effective demand by creating an excess of domestic supply. This had a double-edged character: there was positive pressure on the economy and the competitive efforts of companies losing markets, but there was also a quite rapid global fall in opportunities in the domestic market in general.

The large-scale devaluation during the second half of 1990 and the liberalization of prices at the beginning of 1991, which gave industry access to enormous profits, deeply affected the financial restrictions on companies. Thus a kind of unique economic miracle occurred, in which companies experiencing falling production and sales achieved huge profits in the first half of 1991. Despite all the problems, this made it possible for the companies to have a bearable financial situation by creating the resources to maintain excess employment and to transfer huge profit shares to the state budget. Two levels of company efficiency were created. One was at the level of economic phenomena with the positive development of company efficiency and positive profit transfers to the state budget, with resultant wide-ranging interrelationships and consequences on the surplus state budget, a reduced rate of unemployment and a rising margin of exports over imports. The second visible level of efficiency was deep within the real economic processes and was marked by:

(1) A steep fall in labour productivity, which in the course of 1991 fell in industry by about 15%. This is the more disturbing because under the conditions of the former centrally planned system the CSFR's labour productivity fell behind that of the developed Western countries by about

40% on average.

(2) A rapid rise in the energy and financial demands of production: during the rapid fall in domestic production in 1991, the domestic consumption of electrical energy hardly fell at all. Industrial production fell by 24% and total GDP by 16%, but the total domestic consumption of energy (in the face of a fall in the real incomes and demands of the population) fell by only about 5%.

Under the conditions of central administration, Czechoslovak energy consumption was about double that of the developed Western countries. If heavy industry production was previously subject to great over-capacity, then, with the steep fall in sales and production in 1991, energy intensity of production rose by about one-third.

The surge in company receipts after the first impact of devaluation and the price rises on the basis of their liberalization led to the eventual transfer of the price increases in company outputs (domestic and foreign sales of products) to company inputs and thus into overall domestic cost levels. The profitability of domestic production began to fall sharply and at the end of 1991 was almost exhausted – which is evident in Table 3.12.

Table 3.12   The Development of Cost Efficiency in 1991 (%)

Q1	Q2	Q3	Q4	Year
15.41	9.11	6.94	1.99	8.31

Note: For all economic organizations except so-called small organizations and financial and insurance institutions.

'Clever' company practice has opened up a further insurance outlet: the mutual finance of companies through the rise in company debt. Without further comment this is expressed in Table 3.13. The current volume of company debt is about Kcs 200 billion. What is important is the fact that even this chain of mutual company loans punctuated by bank loans is slowly being weakened. Its weaknesses are particularly evident in companies where liabilities far surpass claims, companies that nobody wishes to finance. The links are on the verge of collapse with the consequent destabilization of the whole chain.

It is necessary to state that the CSFR's industrial sector is threatened by a wave of bankruptcy, which at present is probably held at bay by the following factors:

(1) extensive inter-enterprise credit;
(2) the continuing and strengthening 'basic survival' in which old fixed assets,

Table 3.13   Delayed Settlements in 1991, by Quarter (Kcs bn)

	1.1.91[1]	31.3.91	30.6.91	30.9.91	31.12.91	Yearly rise
CSFR totals	49.9	76.4	123.5	147.0	170.6	120.7

Note:
1   Position as at 1.1.91 based on estimates presented at 31.12.90.

which have scarcely half their value and most probably one-third as against current purchase prices increased by inflation, are being depreciated, while the previous meagre imports of machinery from the developed countries have fallen further, as have investments, so that the modernization of industry is at a standstill, investments in scientific research are falling, etc.;

(3)   structural changes that the previous centrally planned system delayed for 20 years and that are being postponed further, and the relatively increasing bias of the economy to heavy industry;

(4)   the further postponement of investments in the environment;

(5)   hidden and postponed inflation, whereby companies are paying reduced energy, water and transport charges, lower wages, and lower ecological charges, while the raised depreciation rates are not included in the costs;

(6)   the creation of a clear short-term cushion through large-scale devaluation in 1990, which will be followed by inflation for several years (in that the new exchange rates have increased the real purchasing power of the domestic currency fivefold); the currency parity may last up to the time when the so-called reproduction costs equivalent to US$1 will rise from about Kcs 14.5 in 1989 to Kcs 35, which on present trends would occur during the second half of 1993, with further knock-on effects also in 1994.

It remains only to evaluate briefly the probable impact of the division of the Czechoslovak Federation into two states. The main prognoses are very different.

(1)   The rather pessimistic script of the economic team of Federal Centrale foresaw a steep fall in production and employment, strong inflation, devaluation, etc.

(2)   The Vienna Institute for Comparative Economic Studies also forecast difficulties. The prognosis of FSI and its leader was fairly optimistic, but even this maintained that the dissolution of the Federation as at 1 January 1993 would mean for the Slovak Republic a 6% GDP reduction, a 17.3% rise in unemployment, 19.2% inflation and at the same time devaluation of the koruna to Kcs 35 per US$. In the Czech Republic these consequences would be more moderate, for example an overall fall in GDP of 2.1%. At the

same time differences in economic policy (tax, fiscal and monetary) are expected, and it will not be possible to maintain a common currency.

Even the Governor of the Czechoslovak State Bank, known for his conservative stands, admits the future existence of two currencies with varying convertibility by the exchange rates of convertible currencies. Some of the preliminary calculations based on structural pricing models show that such measures could lead to an increase in current company prices of about 50%. Similarly it would be possible to discuss market losses for quite a number of Czech companies that are monopoly suppliers to the Slovak market. There are further problems of cooperative relationships, usually with multiple dimensions. These are the simplest relationships. The financial relations of the companies are more complicated. Value analyses signal large differences in the debt burden, in profitability and in the wages share.

A complicated chain of mutual debt exists between Czech and Slovak companies, while quite a number of them are close to complete insolvency. Thus they may settle their debts only after complete dissolution, when neither would have the means for such settlement. This applies to some more than others. It is the same with the large network of organizationally differentiated Slovak and Czech banks that administer this company credit. Overall, credit relationships are ill-defined and confused and there is the risk of the complete collapse of company finance. An important role should be played by further steps in the economic reform.

Notes

1 According to calculations based on the *Statistical Year Book of the League of Nations, 1938–9*, the publications of the State Planning Commission for Czechoslovakia and the work of Colin Clark in *The Economist* of 1960.
2 Steel, coal, electric power, concrete, plastics, wool and cotton textile fabrics, gas, sulphuric acid, newsprint, shoes, meat, wheat flour, beer. For an assessment of the volume of engineering we used the share of employed persons in the national economy.
3 The rating for purely modern products of electronics, biotechnology, specialized chemistry, etc. would be entirely different.
4 In the 1970s see the work of an expert group headed by I. B. Kravis, A. Heston and R. Summers, *World Product and Income: International Comparisons of Real Gross Product* (Baltimore/London: The Johns Hopkins University Press, 1982). More recently, see the updating by A. Heston and R. Summers, 'A new set of international comparisons of real product and price level estimates for 130 countries 1950–1985', *Review of Income and Wealth*, No. 1 (1988).
5 Comparable developed countries are: Austria, Switzerland, Belgium, the Netherlands, Finland and Denmark; some other small ones (Norway and Sweden) are not included in our comparison because of their different conditions, caused by their larger raw material resources, etc.

6   Data from the Federal Ministry of Labour and Social Security.
7   See the article by the President of the Federal Statistical Office, J. Šujan, in the weekly *Ekonom*, No. 4, or the discussion with the Minister of the CSFR, V. Dlouhý in *Ekonom*, No. 8, 1992.
8   The government assumed a 5% drop in GDP and a 15% inflation rate, while the Institute for Forecasting of the Czechoslovak Academy of Sciences forecast a 15–20% decrease in GDP and 55–60% inflation, and the reality is – as already mentioned – 16.5% for GDP and 58% inflation.

4   Hungary: sound money, fiscal problems

Werner Riecke and László Antal

1   Introduction

This study will put most emphasis on the economic problems of transition. It will primarily attempt to investigate the role and scope of financial (fiscal and monetary) policy in ensuring a smooth, safe transition to the path of a market economy. One of the main questions is whether stabilization can be achieved without serious shocks and social conflicts and within a reasonable time horizon.

This starting point contains a preconception, namely, that if extreme conflicts such as hyperinflation, loss of confidence in the domestic currency and dollarization, economic anarchy or increasing corruption can be avoided, then the so-called 'shock therapy' – which is usually accompanied by a two-digit decrease in economic performance and a serious once-and-for-all price increase, and a large fall in domestic demand – could also be avoided.

This approach is supported by the fact that Hungary started its route to a market economy under relatively favourable conditions. One starting point was the introduction of the New Economic Mechanism in 1968, which aimed to mix elements of the market economy with the framework of economic planning. This process suffered setbacks in the 1970s and was speeded up somewhat in the 1980s. In this way the basic monetary terminology of a market economy became familiar to state administration and enterprise management; at the same time the dependence of managers of state enterprises on the administration became looser. The market for consumer goods ceased to be a typical shortage market from the middle-to-end 1960s. This is shown no better than by the fact that the black market price of convertible currencies never exceeded the official exchange rate by more than 50–60%, and the difference has now practically disappeared.

Within the agricultural sector in particular, private entrepreneurship had long been possible on the small private plots attached to the cooperatives. This private activity created 30–40% of household income in agriculture.

The reform of 1968 created further scope for private entrepreneurial activities, but outside agriculture the growth of the secondary economy lacked an appropriate legal framework. Only at the beginning of the 1980s did private entrepreneurship and partnerships for small-scale economic activities get a legal framework. This opened the way for entrepreneurs, whose activities were at first closely related to the public sector and later on directly to the market for consumer demand. This course enabled two-thirds of all employees to remain in the public sector, while at the same time augmenting their income through private activities. This was a typical strategy in the 1980s. An investigation in the middle of the 1980s showed that the average employee spent 20% of his spare time in private activities.

These events are extremely important, because all participants in the economy – central government institutions and enterprises, private entrepreneurs, households and even agencies financed directly by the state budget – were able at least partially to acquire the capabilities and the knowledge that are needed to run a market economy. This learning process came into its own between 1987 and 1991, when the most important parts of the legal framework for a market economy were created.

Hungary was thus able to avoid the paradoxical situation – which indeed occurred in all other transforming economies – that all the newly created institutions formally fulfil the legal requirements of a market economy, but the behaviour of the economic actors and the attitude of the whole system are driven by the past.

Looking at Hungary's economic development over the last two and a half decades also shows that the process of establishing a market economy has become irreversible. Of course temporary steps backwards and partial centralization attempts cannot be excluded. But there is no chance for the re-establishment of bureaucratic coordination procedures, where the expectations of government institutions decide the path of economic activity. This irreversibility depends on past developments as well as on the social and political changes throughout Eastern Europe and on Hungary's new binding links with and dependence on the Western world.

2   Characteristics of Economic Policy

The establishment of the institutions of a market economy started in Hungary years before the change in the system. The first step was the creation of the two-tier banking system in 1987 (at the end of 1991, 36 commercial banks were operating in Hungary). This was followed by a tax reform in 1988, which included the introduction of a personal income tax with full globalization and the value added tax. (The Law on the Taxation of Enterprise Profits was passed a year later.) The core of the tax reform was the abandonment of the possibility to change tax rules by government decree. In 1989 the Law on Associations came into force, which provided free choice for the legal form of entrepreneurship. Until this law, private activity was restricted to forms with unlimited liability, and this law made public and private limited companies a possible choice for private entrepreneurs. As a result of the Law on Associations, the unfavourable treatment of private businesses and cooperatives compared with the state enterprise sector disappeared. Somewhat later, in 1990, the limit on the number of employees in purely private associations (maximum of 500) was also abolished and – which is even more important – restrictions on the sale or leasing of fixed assets by state enterprises to private businesses or even on taking a share in private associations also disappeared. The introduction of the principle of limited liability into the private sector eliminated one of the most serious restraints on the development of this sector.

In 1990, after a break of more than 40 years, the Budapest Stock Exchange was re-established. In the second half of 1991, laws on the central bank, on banking, on bankruptcy and on accounting were passed by parliament. These new laws came into being already marked by Hungary's move towards the unifying Europe, and took EC recommendations into account even in the regulatory details.

At the same time, it is true that these laws will lead to an increase in bankruptcy proceedings, that reserve requirements will reduce the profits of the banking sector and that all this will cause a downturn in the expected tax revenue of the budget. The same effect can be expected for the accounting law, which allows the application of the lowest value principle in asset valuation. The new regulation will thus eliminate fictitious incomes.

Taking all this into account, we may state that since 1987 an unbroken sequential line is observable in Hungary's economic policy. This policy has some characteristics worth mentioning.

The core of this economic policy is the comprehensive liberalization process, which covers foreign trade, prices, interest rates, wages (after some delay) and, last but not least, the free choice of forms of entrepreneurship, including rights of establishment for foreign investors. The liberalization programme started in 1989 and envisaged the abolition of all restrictions on entrepreneurship within three years. This process has now more or less successfully ended.

The process of import liberalization is shown in Table 4.1. There are no final data for 1991, but the share of liberalized imports is approaching the theoretical maximum of 85% (in the last phase only agricultural products remained on the list of products whose import is controlled by administrative measures).

The first step in this import liberalization included investment goods, consumer durables and spare parts. This was followed by a radical liberalization of raw materials and a cautious liberalization of other consumer products. For example, the share of manufactured goods from convertible currency areas compared with domestic investment was 15% in 1988 and 21% in 1990. There was only a slight increase in convertible currency imports overall, which had a

Table 4.1   Share of Liberalized Import Products, 1989 and 1990
(% according to turnover)

Sector	1989	1990
Mining	0	7
Steel	0	68
Machinery	86	90
Construction materials	31	30
Chemical products	2	75
Light industry	6	44
Other industry	0	41
Food processing	60	61
Industry	43	74
Agriculture	24	39
Forestry	0	100
Total imports	42	72

crowding-out effect on imports from rouble areas and a much less serious effect on domestic production.

Some safeguards were included in the policy of import liberalization. For example, in the case of consumer good imports there was a so-called global quota set by the Ministry of Foreign Economic Relations, and convertible currency was distributed in the framework of public tenders. But, although at first traders' import demands exceeded the quota, there was an over-allocation of licences by the ministry. In 1991, only 75% of the global quota was used – demand for final consumer goods proved to be limited and was different in structure from the expectations of traders.

As will be shown later, the import liberalization did not lead to a worsening of the current account and did not – as some people feared – lead to serious bankruptcies among domestic producers. It is of course also true that with the exception of electronics there was no pressure from imports on the domestic price level.

As Table 4.2 shows, there was also a significant and continuous liberalization in the area of prices. In 1991, the degree of price liberalization reached the practical maximum of 90%.

The third stage of liberalization was freedom for entrepreneurship. The number of companies and of small enterprises shows a significant upward trend since 1988 (see Table 4.3). The enormous increase in the number of companies is due mainly to the establishment of small partnerships. These companies are not able to compensate for the losses arising from the inadequate structure of manufacturing enterprises, but nevertheless the process of structural change has

Table 4.2 Degree of Price Regulation, as a Percentage of Total Turnover, on Final Consumption Products, 1987–90

Regulation	1987	1988	1989	1990
Administrative pricing	38	22	19	16
Price changes subject to official registration	21	21	12	6
Price consultation[1]	-	5	7	1
Free pricing	41	52	62	77
Total	100	100	100	100

Note:
1 Consultation on prices included agreements between the main producers and users of the product without intervention by the authority.

Table 4.3 Number of Companies, 1 January 1988 – 1 February 1992

	Total	State enterprise	Limited company Private	Public	Cooperatives
1 Jan 1988	9,597				
1 Jan 1989	10,811				
1 Jan 1990	15,235	2,399	6,242	365	7,546
1 Jan 1991	26,700	2,363	18,317	646	7,641
1 Apr 1991	29,470	2,357	26,837	777	7,666
1 Jul 1991	38,122	2,362	30,949	868	7,738
1 Oct 1991	42,401	2,278	35,581	968	7,740
1 Feb 1992	57,000				

begun. Unfortunately, state enterprises with more than 2,000 employees still account for 85% of industrial production, while, at the end of 1991, 70% of all companies had fewer than 20 employees, 13% had 20–50 employees and 12% had 50–300 employees.

The path of liberalization of interest rates on loans as well as on deposits does not show a clear statistical pattern, but in 1990 the last restriction, on private household deposits, was abolished. Thus liberalization in this area is also finished.

Lagging a year behind liberalization, a range of deregulation measures came into force. Because regulation is meaningful only within the context of a planned state sector, deregulation is successful if there is a real, demand-controlled private sector.

Another element of the economic policy towards the market economy was the continuing abolition of centrally planned special treatment, including financial support for selected enterprises, consumer price subsidies and preferential tax treatment of certain branches. This liberalization attempt has also reached a successful conclusion. Budget subsidies, including those on housing, developed as shown in Table 4.4.

Table 4.4   Budget Subsidies, 1985-91

Year	Ft bn.	% of GDP
1985	160.2	
1986	172.6	16
1987	191.3	
1988	186.5	
1989	207.0	
1990	198.9	
1991	188.0	7

Taking into account accelerating inflation (the CPI rose 35% in 1991), subsidies decreased in real terms by 60%. This process was less intentional than one would expect. IMF pressure and mid-year budget corrections in several years led to the decrease – proportionally and in real terms – in subsidies. The 1991 budget survived without the usual package of interim adjustments, but ended up with a Ft 114 billion deficit instead of the approved Ft 79 billion.

Much more interesting is the fact that, despite the decline in subsidies (including consumer price as well as production subsidies), the ratio of general government revenue (central and local budgets, the Social Security Fund and extra-budgetary funds) to GDP was 62% in 1990-1, which is only 2-3 points less than in the years 1986-7.

Hungary's economic policy is characterized by gradualism, by the avoidance of abrupt changes. Gradualism was present not only in the avoidance of extreme currency devaluations and a serious drop in real incomes, but also in the liberalization of foreign trade, prices, etc. This was possible – and politically desirable – because Hungary's economy did not suffer from serious market distortions, shortages or corruption, and there was no loss of confidence in its currency as the ruling means of exchange and payments. From this point of view, the fall in real GDP (12% during July 1990– July 1992) and the level of unemployment (8.5% at the end of 1991) seem to be better than expected, especially when compared with other East European economies in transition.

A significant change occurred in the treatment of monetary aggregates.

While the monetary programme has been an important part of any IMF stand-by credit condition since 1982 and while monetary policy became meaningful only after the creation of the two-tier banking system in 1987, it was not until 1988–9 that the quantity of money and the amount of domestic credit started to become closely monitored targets. Prior to this period, monetary aggregates were simply a consequence of planning and related budgetary decisions. This increase in the role and scope of monetary policy had not only an institutional but also a sociological background: the weakness of the political system prior to the democratic elections in the spring of 1990 diverted attention from the central bank. The National Bank of Hungary (NBH) took advantage of this situation and was able to concentrate on the control of inflation and on the external balance. This *de facto* independence was recognized *de jure* only at the end of 1991, when the Law on the Central Bank was approved by parliament.

The management of the external debt was always the task of NBH. Hungary's gross foreign debt in convertible currencies was US$2.1 billion at the end of 1973. The rise in raw material world market prices at that time and the lack of any adjustment effort in Hungary's economic policy led to a steady increase in this debt to US$10.5 billion at the end of 1979. From 1979 to 1984 the nominal level of the amount of gross debt was relatively stable, hovering between US$10.2 and 11.5 billion. The period from 1985 to 1987 saw a virtual doubling of this debt to US$19.6 billion at the end of 1987. After that the debt level was around US$20 billion. It was US$21.3 billion at the end of 1990, but this was mainly an accounting issue, related to the weakness of the dollar at that time. Hungary's gross debt was US$22.3 billion at the end of 1991, accompanied by a comfortably high level of foreign exchange reserves (US$4 billion).

Per capita debt can be easily calculated, because of Hungary's 10 million population: a US$20 billion debt means a US$2,000 per capita debt. This figure is often used in international comparisons, but in our view it is a little bit misleading. This approach would expose the United States and Hungary as highly indebted countries, whereas China and the former USSR would always get a good rating. South Korea is risky, but Romania is a reliable candidate for loans, etc.

Export performance and future growth prospects seem to us a better starting point for the evaluation of the debt situation, but before analysing debt service ratios let us have a closer look at developments in the past, raising and at least partly answering the usual questions regarding resource outflows, the debt trap, etc.

A resource outflow is defined as a trade surplus and other items on the current account that have to be maintained at a certain level only to cover interest payments on the existing amount of debt. This trade surplus can of course be inflationary in the absence of sufficient voluntary saving, but it is primarily an ideological rather than an economic term. If we think about resource outflows as created by the interest burden of outstanding debt, we overlook two important facts:

(1) resource outflows are preceded by significant resource inflows, which created the foreign debt; and
(2) interest rates are simply minimum requirements on the expected return of investment.

Regarding the first aspect, we may calculate a cumulative time series from 1973 to 1990. It shows that the cumulative outflow first exceeded the resource inflow only after 15 years, in 1990. The question of causality may also be raised. On the one hand economies like the Hungarian one are considered to need forced savings (or inflation, shortages, high domestic interest rates, etc.) in order to cover interest payments on foreign debt by trade surpluses. On the other hand, nobody says that Germany or Japan 'suffers' from its trade surplus, which is probably created by the fact that in these countries there are more incentives to save than to invest. Especially in Hungary – and in contrast to its neighbours – often during the last two decades economic policy had to choose between austerity (selecting it only very seldom), higher inflation or an increase in foreign indebtedness. There was no serious increase in shortages in the goods and services market.

Regarding the return on investment, the analysis would also have a political dimension. From the purely economic point of view it is true that there is no direct relation between the increase in foreign debt, domestic investment and export performance. Export performance was much more dependent on the restrictiveness of monetary and fiscal policy than on the first two variables. In other words: investments, based on government decisions during the last few decades, frequently proved to be inefficient and not justified by the demand of international markets. A large part of trade deficits in several years served only to avoid serious declines in the standard of living of the Hungarian population. In fact, in Hungarian economic statistics nothing is smoother than the time series of real private household consumption. This fact leads us to the political return on investment: US$20 billion is the price for the most peaceful transition in Eastern Europe. It is the price for Hungary still being an island of stability in this region, and, because of this, more than half of foreign direct investment in Eastern Europe is attracted by Hungary. All told, this is a price worth paying.

The question remains of course – coming back to the purely economic approach – whether or not Hungary will be able to pay the price in the years to come.

The debt trap approach says that once a certain debt level is reached – as compared with the possible economic performance of a country – the interest payments themselves will be the driving force behind the further and unavoidable increase in the country's debt. This may be true for some countries, but time series for Hungary show that the largest increases in foreign debt were never connected with the interest payments of those years. The periods with the largest increase in Hungary's foreign debt are closely connected with government-initiated big investment decisions, large budget deficits and loose monetary policy.

The years from 1989 in many aspects reveal a new picture of the Hungarian economy. The import liberalization mentioned above did not lead to an uncontrollable increase in imports, but rather helped to double exports in the following three to four years. The inflow of foreign direct investment, which exceeded US$1.5 billion (in cash) in 1991, has become a new counterpart for the financing of current account deficits, and has reduced the pressure on economic policy to improve the external balance at any price.

The increase in exports was caused not by special incentives but rather by domestic demand management. It was also a precondition for a smooth change that Hungary's export structure had already changed prior to the breakdown in CMEA trade (see Table 4.5).

Table 4.5   The Share of Rouble Exports in Hungary's Total Export
Turnover, Current Ft Basis (%)

1980	49.4
1984	46.7
1985	49.0
1986	52.6
1987	48.7
1988	41.7
1989	37.8
1990	27.1
1991 (estimated)	16.0

3   Monetary Policy behind the External Balance

Before examining the prospects for Hungary's monetary policy we can consider past experience. The foreign debt increase in the past reflected domestic monetary and fiscal policy. The monetary approach to the balance of payments seems to be an appropriate framework for this analysis.

In terms of pure economic theory, the amount of money in the economy is the sum of domestic credit and net foreign assets:

$$M = DC + NFA$$

In a small open economy with a fixed exchange rate the amount of money is determined purely by the demand for money. This is a function of real GDP and the price level. The latter equals the world price level times the exchange rate:

$$M = f(real\ GDP, P)$$
$$P = PW * ER$$

This means on the one hand that the instrument of monetary policy is domestic credit creation. On the other hand, the equation above in terms of change (*d*) implies that the increase or decrease in foreign debt depends on whether or not domestic credit creation exceeds the increase in demand for money:

$$dNFA = dM - dDC$$

Hungary of course was different from the usual case of a small open economy because of its trade regime. If there is administrative control on imports, there cannot be a direct link between the world market and the domestic price level.

What happened in all those years prior to import liberalization? The increase in domestic credit exceeded the increase in the demand for money, so that it was possible to direct the excess demand in the domestic market into two channels: a further increase in foreign debt or an increase in the domestic price level. We may call this the 'inflation–current account trade-off' of Hungary's economic policy.

The exchange rate policy had its own rule in this trade-off. Since the exchange rate was fixed but the domestic price level could increase independently from the rise in world market prices (because of the limited access to imports), from time to time exchange rate adjustment was unavoidable. In our approach these devaluations do not add to the inflation rate, since the devaluations were rather caused by the difference between world market and domestic inflation. Of course, by an almost 90% liberalization of imports, the role of the exchange rate in stabilizing the price level has been increased.

It is worth mentioning that in this trade-off relation a third possible way to respond to excess demand would have been an increase in shortages in the domestic market. This never happened during the last two decades in the Hungarian economy, because excess demand was in fact covered by excess imports and because, even under administrative price control, prices did follow the signals of the markets at least with some delay. As a result there was no 'monetary overhang' in Hungary, which is a big advantage in the transformation process.

Of course questions are often raised about Hungary's foreign debt. Is the debt manageable now and in the near future? Is rescheduling a possible option?

Looking at different debt service ratios, time series show an improvement from July 1990 onward, and an even more significant improvement is expected in the future. This is caused mainly by three factors:

(1) the increase in the foreign debt stopped in 1990-1 (in terms of net debt);
(2) the NBH succeeded in improving the maturity profile of its long-term debt, and it was able to reduce the share of short-term debt;
(3) there was a large increase in convertible export revenues after July 1990. Exports now exceed the US$10 billion level.

As the debt service ratio reaches the 30% benchmark, there should be no serious problem about financing Hungary's foreign debt in the coming years. Financing the outstanding debt is the key word: if there is no doubt about the country's willingness and ability to service its debt, then no problem will arise in replacing maturing loans with new ones. In the case of a non-increasing debt, the only burden of the debt is the interest payment, which will represent less than 15% of exports in Hungary over the next few years.

Undoubtedly, debt service is crucial to this approach: if there were any attempt to change this attitude – no matter whether it is called rescheduling, debt relief, maturity extension or whatever – there would be an enormous increase in adjustment costs. Let us list the main factors:

(1) Amortization and new credits range between US$2.5 billion and US$4 billion a year. A change in Hungary's debt policy would bring only a small reduction in principal payments, but would cause loss of access to private capital markets, which are the main sources of debt refinancing. Thus attempts to ease the situation would result in a much larger outflow of resources.
(2) The inflow of foreign direct investment would slow down.
(3) There would be capital flight from the US$1.5 billion foreign exchange deposits of Hungarian households.
(4) Import financing would become more expensive.

Taking all this into account, to pay on time seems to be the cheapest solution in the medium term. In the longer term it does not seem reasonable to attempt to build a civil society, a pluralistic democracy based on a free market with massive foreign aid.

If we look only at the issue of debt, the question regarding Hungary's future prospects has a simple answer: with increasing exports and with a real growth in GDP, Hungary will 'outgrow' this debt. Increasing the denominator is the simplest solution. Hungary had a US$20 billion debt with US$5 billion of exports – which did look very dangerous; it now has a US$20 billion debt with US$10 billion of exports, which seems to be manageable. And, if Hungary succeeds in achieving US$20 billion of exports a year, its foreign debt will no longer be the main issue of economic policy.

Since the debt was created by, or at least with the assistance of, monetary and fiscal policy, however, the problem will not disappear without appropriate adjustments to the monetary and budget policy. This is indeed the real challenge of the future.

From the monetary point of view, we can call on the monetary approach to the balance of payments. Let us look at the structure of the monetary survey:

Assets	*Liabilities*
(Ft bn.)	(Ft bn.)
$NFA-1,000$	$M1,500$
$DC2,500$	

(This balance sheet is highly stylized, but it indicates the appropriate magnitudes.)

The problem of indebted countries is that the amount of domestic credit is much greater than the amount of money. And, of course, a large share of domestic credit is the liability of the budget. In such a situation monetary policy aiming at external equilibrium has to ensure that the nominal increase in domestic credit equals the nominal increase in the demand for money. A simple calculation: 5% real growth plus 5% inflation with stable velocity would mean a 10% increase in the demand for money; according to our monetary survey, this would mean an Ft 150 billion increase.

Targeting an Ft 150 billion increase in domestic credit, which is a 6% increase in outstanding domestic credit, in fact means a very restrictive credit policy, because of the 10% growth in nominal GDP. For example: monetary policy was considered successful in 1991, but external and internal equilibrium was achieved with a 27% increase in broad money and a 10% increase in domestic credit.

In the longer run, such a policy can be maintained only if the share of the budget in the increase in domestic credit is reduced year by year; or, in other words, if the budget deficit is decreasing or even switching over to a surplus. This was not the case in 1991: the approved budget for that year had a deficit of Ft 79 billion, and the out-turn was even higher: a Ft 114 billion deficit. In 1991 it was possible to finance this by relatively high – and unexpected – household savings. The price is paid in the form of a relatively high level of interest rates.

The 1992 budget also included a Ft 70 billion deficit, but even rough calculations show that at least an additional Ft 50 billion should be expected. The higher budget deficit may have various implications:

(1) inflation may not decrease from 35% in 1991 to 20–25% in 1992, or

(2) the level of domestic interest rates may remain high, even while the inflation rate decreases, or

(3) a new period of increasing foreign indebtedness may begin (together with a decrease in the currently comfortable level of foreign exchange reserves).

Taking all this into account, the future of Hungary's foreign debt problem depends on the public sector (budget) reform, which seems to have been a little bit slowed down by the Hungarian government. The necessary measures are becoming even less likely as we approach the next election date (1994). Monetary policy on its own – even with an independent central bank – will hardly be able to ensure the internal equilibrium needed to achieve external equilibrium.

4   Privatization

The really new element in economic policy in the transition process is privatization. The creation of the legal and institutional framework began in 1987, but the process achieved a level worth mentioning only in 1991. The Hungarian approach, which is very different from that of other East European countries, relies on selling state property to foreign and domestic investors, giving tax incentives and – in the case of domestic investors – offering preferential loans too. Leaving aside the issue of compensation for former owners – which has a magnitude much less than expected – there is no redistribution and no other artificial, populist procedure of creating small shareholders. Large-scale privatization, however, is a contradictory process anyway and there is probably no first-best solution.

The legal framework for privatization was created between 1987 and 1992. From 1987, domestic legal entities could create private and public companies, at that time based on a law of 1875. In 1989, the so-called Transformation Law was passed, giving a chance to state enterprises to become limited liability companies. The same year, the Law on Protection of Foreign Investment in Hungary was passed, and foreigners could take shares in Hungarian companies up to 50% without any official authorization. (The 50% limit was later lifted.) Also in 1989, the new Law on Associations passed parliament. This was the basic law of privatization (of state property), and it induced the growth of the existing private sector. The State Property Agency (SPA) was established in 1990, but the same year a Law on the Defence of State Property also came into force. This was to prevent the sale of state property 'below value'. Unfortunately, the status of the State Property Agency was changed too. While it used to report to parliament, it is now directly under government control. In 1991 the Law on Concessions came into force and now, with the exception of real estate and land regulation, the legal infrastructure of privatization is complete.

Results are rather difficult to interpret. The book value of state enterprises is around Ft 1,900 billion, of which Ft 500 billion is accounted for by enterprises that will remain in state ownership. In 1990, there was no remarkable privatization (while Ft 5 billion privatization revenue was expected); in 1991, the privatization revenue of the State Property Agency was Ft 40 billion, not much below the expected Ft 50 billion. Ft 10 billion are reported for January 1992. The privatization of 500 enterprises is in process, and the State Property Agency has invited in consulting companies and given more room for privatization initiated by enterprise management to speed up the process.

Privatization is much more costly than previously expected: the operational costs of SPA, compensation and foreign consulting companies take part of the revenue. Local governments and employees also take a share. But even considering this burden, the Hungarian privatization creates net revenues, while for example the German Treuhand makes serious losses.

4.1   Some Fiscal Issues of Privatization

Revenue from privatization creates unexpected windfall profits. While this revenue was negligible in 1990, the Ft 40 billion cash flow to the SPA in 1991 is a considerable amount. The reduction of domestic budget debt from privatization revenues would make room for a greater involvement of the banking system in financing the enterprise sector without violating overall limits on domestic credit creation. This was the strategy of 1991. However, the Law on the Central Bank requires privatization revenues created only by loans provided to buyers of state assets to be cleared against old outstanding budget debt. This is a kind of interest rate swap, improving the profit and loss account of NBH. Ft 20 billion of the privatization revenues of SPA in 1992 were directed to general budget revenues. For the rest – if there is any – there was constant competition between different goals: creating new jobs, infrastructure investment, bailing out the Social Security Fund, etc. The problem is not the wide range of competing goals but the creation of new extra-budgetary funds, making it even more difficult to start the reform of the public sector. Clearing net revenues of privatization fully against outstanding old budget debt would give the monetary sphere the most scope for lending to the enterprise sector, but including this revenue in the regular budget would also have an advantage: the government is forced to keep the privatization process going, even if some political forces are trying to slow it down.

5   Present Situation and Prospects for the Near Future

It seems to be a historical fact that, with gradual liberalization and the increasing role of cautious monetary policy, Hungary's economic policy based on continuity was able to manoeuvre successfully between different dangers. For the time being, the transition process could be managed at an acceptable social cost. The first stage of the transition period has come to a successful end. The market economy has become irreversible.

This process was less successful in structural reforms, having positive effects only in the long run. The reforms of the pension and health care systems are extremely sensitive issues and have been postponed. As the time of the next elections approaches, the likelihood of long-term reforms decreases. The public sector is still too big, but to operate on it simply by linear expenditure cuts is no longer a possible solution.

Concerning the social basis of the systemic transition, the optimism of the first phase is past. This is due to the fact that, after years of stagnation, the political changes were followed by the accelerating breakdown of the Eastern markets. Prior to 1989, Hungary was the most reform-oriented country of the region, and now it is only one among many. Public opinion polls show that Hungary's people are the most pessimistic in Eastern Europe.

Table 4.6 GDP and Components, Development in Real Terms, 1989–91, 1980=100

Indicator	1989	1990	1991
GDP	114.9	110.3	101.5
Domestic demand	104.1	98.9	91.5
Private consumption	109.1	104.7	98.5
Public consumption	115.2	114.0	111.8
Real income per capita	114.4	112.6	109.2
Real wage per employee	93.5	88.7	80.7
Unemployment ratio (%)	0.1	0.5	7.3
Investment	90.2	84.8	75.1
Industrial production[1]	99.0	91.5	73.2
Construction industry	98.7	83.3	75.8
Convertible exports[2,3]	163.6	186.9	178.0
Convertible imports[2,3]	178.1	207.0	206.0

Notes:
1 Statistics are gathered only on firms with more than 50 employees.
2 Volume data, based on Ft values of foreign trade.
3 Data for 1991 include the effect of the change to dollar accounting in Eastern trade and the breakdown of the CMEA.

The Hungarian economy has been stagnating for over a decade. The data in Table 4.6 show that the performance level of the Hungarian economy was almost the same in 1991 as it was at the beginning of the 1980s.

Within this general framework of stagnation, there was significant growth in two areas:

(1) the development of convertible currency foreign trade turnover, which includes the effect of the profound reorganization of the trade structure, and
(2) the number and the increasing role of small entrepreneurs.

According to expert estimates (official statistics are not available or not reliable), enterprises with fewer than 50 employees contributed 26-28% to GDP in 1991. Thus, their share has doubled compared with the mid-1980s.

On the other side, the production of medium and big state enterprises is still decreasing, and at an even faster rate. This can be illustrated by the month to month data for 1991 (see Table 4.7).

Table 4.7   Production Indicators for Industrial Enterprises with more than 50 Employees in 1991 (same month of previous year = 100)

March	June	September	October	November
83.4	76.8	73.7	72.9	70.3

It is very likely that the fall in production in large state enterprises (with more than 1,000 employees) is even greater. Given their liquidity problems and likely bankruptcy proceedings, it is unlikely that the growth dynamics of the private sector will be able to compensate for this.

The government seems to be too optimistic. While the decrease in real GDP was 7-9% in 1991 (the decrease in economic performance was probably less than shown by the Central Statistical Office figures), the government expected a 0-2% increase for 1992. In fact, the downturn in a major part of the state enterprise sector has not yet come to an end. The unemployment rate was above 8% at the end of 1991, and may exceed 12-13% by the end of 1992. The expanding private sector is not yet able to compensate for the expected bankruptcies of the big state enterprises, so the budget is extremely vulnerable.

This implies that, having reached the bottom in 1991, there will probably be a smaller decrease in real GDP in 1992; inflation will be lower, but not as much as expected in official projections. The transition will go on. Public sector financing reform has become unavoidable.

A peculiar feature of Hungarian development is the expansion of market-like segments of the economy and market-like behaviour in a large part of society, combined with the continuing predominance of the state in income redistribution and business unit ownership. These tendencies created the unparalleled situation in Eastern Europe that, in establishing the legal and institutional framework of the economic transition process, the second phase should now be introduced. By withdrawing the state from the economy, market operations and market judgements should come to dominate in the significant areas of the economy and society, but at the same time the political authorities still consider the economy to be an important area or means of carrying out political will.

This peculiar feature, whose final outcome is hard to foresee, forces analysts to consider two possible alternatives. The key question of the first option, not taking political arguments into account, is what would be the most favourable fiscal policy in terms of Hungary's future economic development. The key question of the other option is what consequences might emerge from the unchanged tendencies experienced in 1991-2 and from an unaltered government policy?

Obviously, actual processes will fall between these two extremes, but exactly where depends largely on the extent of political accommodation and the pace at which the underlying contradictions surface.

6   Budget – Public Finance

The lack of a stable government budget led to a peculiar development process in the past few years. The 1988 introduction of the taxation reform was complemented by a budget position close to equilibrium. In contrast, the sudden miscalculation in the current balance of payments in 1989 (in deficit by US$1.4 billion) cannot solely be attributed to the uncoordinated customs, tax and foreign exchange supply measures applied when liberalizing travel, for in 1989 there was a significant budget deficit as well. In 1990, the budget surprisingly closed without a deficit, and there was a surplus on the current balance of payments. Since most of the underlying measures responsible for this were taken in late 1989, this surplus can be taken as a farewell present from the last pre-transition government. Since then, financial trends have taken a turn that reflects both the division of control over economic policy (which is partly a favourable phenomenon) and also the effects of forever postponing the Treasury reforms.

On the basis of the balanced budgetary position in 1990, and taking into account the known collapse of the CMEA, the Ministry of Finance forecast a deficit of Ft 79 billion for 1991. The actual deficit finally amounted to Ft 114 billion, and only a third of this derived from lost revenue related to rouble trade. The 1992 budget projected a Ft 70 billion deficit, but the actual deficit was Ft 78 billion after only the first five months. These trends indicate that current revenues and expenditures and the institutional structure of the Treasury are resulting in a deficit that is growing year by year and that will become impossible to finance as early as 1993 or 1994. The widening gap between revenues and expenditures is the result of factors that will continue to apply for some time:

(1) The first is economic recession, which became deeper than expected in 1991 and is going to last. A natural consequence of this is shrinking tax bases. Recession, however, is also parallelled by a wave of bankruptcies that is shaking corporate liquidity, so talking about budget revenues that need only to be collected does not seem very logical. Rather, using (or maybe abusing) the priority of tax obligation will contribute to a deepening recession.

(2) Privatization also reduces tax revenues, not just because companies with foreign partnership can make use of tax allowances designed especially for this reason, and not just because the local entrepreneur is 'a cheat by nature', but mostly because the emergence of a real ownership interest is accompanied by a constant struggle to cut costs within the bounds of legality. Presumably, public sector institutions given the same number of tasks to perform, but with less central funding, will need to turn against the patron state.

(3) A special role is played by the value added tax. Not only does the wide gap between products taxed at the normal 25% rate and those with 0% tax distort consumer price ratios, but owing to the classification system, when the economy is in recession people tend to purchase products taxed at 0%, thus reducing VAT income. That is why a significant drop is expected in budget revenues.

(4) On the expenditure side, individual entries increase at the same speed as nominal GDP growth. The so-called 'large distribution' mechanisms which, in the case of money transfers, are supposed to equalize incomes, actually support all social classes uniformly. These mechanisms allocate less than necessary to those in need and over-support the well-to-do. Without a change in the redistribution principles, and under pressure from the bottom-up inflationary push, either these mechanisms will become impossible to finance before long, or the already middle range tax burden – in conjunction with the 54% social insurance contribution – will become a major obstacle to the further development of private enterprises.

(5) Almost the same situation prevails where public sector institutions provide the population with free services (kindergarten, school, medical care). Inefficient redistribution also arises in these areas, and the government institutions in their current form are facing competition from the private sector. Moreover, the question arises whether a normal relationship between profit and non-profit organizations should have been established before a part of central government tasks were transferred to local governments.

(6) In contrast to the much-criticized modifications of the old preferential housing loans, central government's subsidies of interest and repayments are still surprisingly high. A need for a reform of housing project financing emerges, when most people believe this has already taken place.

In relation to the 1992 budget deficit – which was well in excess of the approved figures – the government argument was that the extent of overspending contributed to lessening the recession because it created, or at least sustained, domestic demand. That is to say, all budgetary packages aimed at reducing the expected level of deficit would only exacerbate the economic recession. Meanwhile, it was argued that it was possible to finance even the 1991 deficit from the capital markets and that this liquidity would also be available in 1992, mainly from private savings.

This argument was as wrong as it was dangerous or contradictory. It was contradictory because it perceived the private propensity to save as satisfactorily high, while it assumed a further drop in domestic demand. It was wrong because it was the National Bank of Hungary that granted a loan of Ft 40 billion to the Treasury in order to top up its current assets (this happened back in late 1990), and another loan of Ft 60 billion to finance the deficit. The truth is that, in late 1991, the Treasury current account balance was Ft 62 billion, which was not used up until the first quarter of 1992. Private investors played only a small and indirect role in financing the rest of the deficit, since commercial banks purchased high-interest government securities in large quantities. This was possible because banking sector liquidity had significantly increased from the second half of 1991 – not just because of rising savings and the influx of foreign capital, but also because the number of commercial banks' short-term loans had dropped dramatically. This trend was mainly due to the high business risks involved and the high nominal interest rate, which in late 1991 and early 1992 meant a considerable real interest rate. This contributed to the high capital inflow, as speculators made use of the large gap between expected devaluations and interest rate levels.

By 1992, the Treasury and the government had apparently lost control over fiscal processes. The fact that the 1991 deficit, which was expected to reach Ft 78 billion at most, turned out to be Ft 114 billion was not the result of a derailment or a wrong forecast. This is backed by the fact that the 1992 budget's Ft 70 billion deficit was 'fulfilled' as early as the end of March. The Ministry of Finance then forecast the deficit to be expected at year-end to be Ft 120 billion, then Ft 140 billion, and finally more than Ft 200 billion. Guidelines for the 1993 budget now include a deficit of Ft 240 billion. The need for a comprehensive reform of the expenditure side has been taken off the agenda. The inability to control on the revenue side in budget entries can be explained by the uncertain position of the finance minister.

A classic vicious circle has thus emerged, and the way out will be found only if a better economic climate evolves in parallel with a lower budget deficit and a significant drop in the state's redistributive role. Current economic policy shows no sign of such a change.

7   Balance of Trade

In 1991, a particular feature of the Hungarian economy disappeared. For more than two decades the current balance of trade deficit had always been a mirror-image of the budget deficit. In 1991, the budget position worsened compared either with the previous year or with the scheduled figures. This – in addition – happened in a year when the agreement with the IMF allowed a deficit of US$1.2 billion owing to price advantages in rouble trade. By the end of 1991, foreign exchange reserves amounted to some US$4 billion. If we analyse the internal structure of these figures, it becomes clear how weak was the basis of this balanced position (see Tables 4.8 and 4.9).

Table 4.8   Some Items of the Balance of Trade Dollar Accounts, 1989–91 (US$m.)

	1989	1990	1991
Exports	6,446	6,346	9,258
Imports	5,909	5,998	9,069
Balance of trade	537	348	189
Balance of tourist industry	(349)	345	560
Balance of interests	(1,387)	(1,414)	(1,331)
Balance of unilateral current remittances	126	727	860
Current balance of payments	(1,437)	127	267

Table 4.9   Short- and Long-term Operations of the Capital Balance, 1989–91 (US$m.)

	1989	1990	1991
Collection	3,343	2,827	4,077
Repayment	1,946	2,547	2,409

Even NBH figures indicate that the balance of trade, although remaining positive, has gradually worsened. (Figures given by the Ministry of Foreign Economic Relations differ significantly from those of NBH.) The slight surplus on the current balance of payments in 1991 and 1992 was due to the tourist industry surplus and the balance of the so-called unilateral transfers, which in practice means an increase in the volume of private foreign exchange accounts. The increasing foreign exchange accounts can be attributed to taking out loans well in excess of repayment obligations, and, of course, to the influx of foreign capital (not shown in the table), which should be combined with extra imports of investment goods in an expanding economy.

There is no guarantee that these tendencies will continue. The fragility of the tourist industry balance is shown by the 1989 figures. If some measures to protect domestic manufacturers emerged, then private imports would again gain momentum. The amount of private foreign exchange accounts should be secured by appropriate foreign exchange reserves, especially if we have only vague ideas about the reasons for the increase in this instrument.

8 A Possible Financial Policy in the Medium Run

In 1992 the state budget and the related redistribution mechanisms – especially social insurance and the Solidarity Fund – experienced tensions to such an extent that even a supplementary budget, aimed at increasing revenues and reducing expenditures, would not be certain to prevent major deficits. We have to admit a considerably larger need for Treasury financing. Should there be an even partial capital market financing, it will keep interest rates high. Another scenario is also imaginable: NBH could be asked to grant loans directly to finance part of a major deficit. In this case, we might have to reckon with the inflation rate not decreasing at the desired speed. For the time being, it is not predictable when this will be reflected in a decrease in foreign exchange reserves and, related to this, a rise in consumer goods imports.

There is no doubt about the inevitability of institutional reforms, but even if this is clearly demonstrated to the population by hardship under existing institutions, a tough preparation phase, time-consuming professional preparation and the necessity for political marketing must be taken into account. A Treasury reform package should go hand in hand with an expansion of capital market (and not deficit financing) instruments and ownership rights.

The programme of expenditure cuts should focus on the following areas:

(1) In the case of social transfers paid in money, the principle of automatic entitlement should be abandoned. At the same time, consistent application of a means test is challenged by the limited administrative capacity of local governments; moreover, subjective decisions made by the 'bureau' are still regarded with suspicion in Hungary. A compromise therefore might be to gross up these transfers and include them in the tax base.

(2) A more difficult and even more unavoidable step would be a total or partial application of market principles to the wide range of social payments in kind. This will be difficult, because there is virtually no possibility of making recompense in money, an opportunity that could have been taken five years ago, and in an economy becoming somewhat liberated from tax and contribution burdens, rising individual costs can be compensated for only by performance-based extra income. The decreasing demand by

women for employment might ease the burden of the changes.

(3) Removing state predominance in these areas would give a greater room for manoeuvre, and not just for private initiatives. The expansion of voluntary insurance will create a demand on capital markets, which is indispensable to sustain the privatization process. And, last but not least, stabilization of expectations of a falling inflation rate and a steady decrease in inflation itself are further inescapable preconditions of the process. There is no truth to the view, more and more becoming a government standpoint, that abandoning the anti-inflationary policy would permanently ease the structural problems of an over-centralized economy. Currently we are witnessing a stabilization that is getting more and more unstable.

9   Recent Economic Figures

The 1992 state budget deficit, originally scheduled to be Ft 70 billion, will possibly amount to Ft 180 billion, as outlined in the supplementary budget submitted by the government to the parliament. The supplementary budget did not even make any effort to include fire-fighting measures to increase revenues or decrease expenditures; it simply asked parliament to approve capital market financing of the vast deficit.

Meanwhile, the Minister of Finance admitted that the 1992 deficit might exceed even Ft 200 billion, which is equivalent to 7.5% of GDP. It might also be worth mentioning that the Economic Research Institute, which forecast a deficit of Ft 150 billion when the Ministry of Finance (MOF) foresaw only Ft 120 billion, was subsequently merged with the Central Bureau of Statistics.

What is most important and interesting for the moment is to uncover the direct causes of the deficit and what implications can be derived with regard to the position and perspectives of the whole economy. In conclusion, we discuss the planned extra issue of government securities worth Ft 100 billion, which cannot be without consequences for the banking sector.

The expenditure side is less responsible for the huge increase in the deficit, since only the items 'private housing projects' and 'financing special funds' exceed scheduled figures by a few billion forints. Taking into account savings on other expenditure items, total budget expenditures did not exceed scheduled figures. This, however, might well happen in the second half of the year, since the item 'financing special funds' mainly consists of the Solidarity Fund, which funds unemployment benefit, and whose deficit tends to increase over time. Miscellaneous savings entail cuts in, or delayed remittance of, budgetary financing of public sector institutions. The financing had been agreed by parliament, but was cut by a secret government clause.

The real breakdown took place on the revenue side, where there were significant shortfalls. Less than 40% of corporate taxes scheduled for the first half of 1992 came in. It is striking that monetary institutions (the National Bank of Hungary included) were able to pay only 10% of the amount expected in corporate taxes and dividends. Only import duties came in steadily, and they exceeded the schedule. Contrary to this, the Minister of Finance dismissed the head of the customs department in the first half the year, as being the main source of budget deficits.

By and large, the business sector was able to produce slightly more than 50% of the revenue expected by the Treasury.

A somewhat different picture is seen in the case of turnover taxes and personal income tax. The latter brought in slightly over 60% of the expected payments, but the value added tax and consumption taxes brought in more than 80% of the expected revenues.

What does all this mean? First, that in Hungary the lowest slump is in private consumption. Contrary to this, the Ministry of Finance, governed by some kind of pre-Keynesian consumption shortage theory, blames a low private propensity to consume for the economic recession. Second, recession trends are already signalled in private incomes, as revealed in the tax returns. Third, the recession is at its worst in the corporate sector, not excluding the commercial banks.

The government has already modified its conceptions about 1992's economic trends. For example, real GDP will not grow, but only stagnate, and private consumption will stagnate, or even decrease by 3% (in our opinion the two should be reversed: a decrease in GDP and a stagnation in private consumption), the international balance of trade will break even, and the current balance of payments may close with a surplus of Ft 300–600 billion. It is true that the trade balance surplus in the first four months of 1992 was Ft 600 billion, and that there was almost Ft 500 billion surplus on the current balance of payments. Foreign exchange reserves increased by another US$1 billion, coming close to US$5 billion.

According to data provided by the Ministry of Foreign Economic Relations, exports grew by 20% in current dollars and imports decreased by 14% in the first four months of 1992. Unemployment is now increasing at a slower pace. This development is overshadowed by the MOF assumption that, if the economic upswing begins in 1993, unemployment will increase further until the end of that year, reaching some 1 million. That would be an unemployment rate of more than 20%.

The import downturn was the sign of a continuing crisis, and the export performance was partly due to companies that are able to export only at the cost of generating losses, or using up equity, until they inevitably go bankrupt.

Meanwhile, the Treasury hoped to finance the 1992 deficit, which had almost tripled since being approved, on the basis of the high savings propensity of households. The behaviour of the banking system is not always rational either. So far, interest rates have not declined in line with the drop in inflation and tremendously high real interest rates emerged, including on the deposit side. The amount of corporate loans decreased, however, and the interest rate on the short-term inter-bank market dropped to 23%, the same rate as for short-term Treasury bills (these are used as a current account by the Treasury). This market has attracted the banks' free capital assets, exceeding Ft 100 billion, and the Treasury therefore perceives that, owing to this increased liquidity, it is urgent to finance the deficit with securities of longer expiration dates. At the same time, banks' losses are on the increase, and after closing down the Realty Bank and two deposit banks, the State Bank Supervision is now restricting the operations of two other banks at risk of bankruptcy.

Several commercial banks have simply stopped trading their high-interest securities instead of lowering interest rates. Sooner or later private investors' propensity to invest will drop, or savings will be transferred to tax-free foreign exchange deposits, since the opportunity is given by the foreign exchange allowances, which increased from the annual US$50 to US$350 from 1 July 1992. If the Treasury enters the market – in the hopes that new securities will be purchased to a lesser extent by private investors and to a larger extent by banks – it will become strikingly evident that it is not budgetary overspending that is holding back the economy from recession, but, on the contrary, that it is contributing to the downturn. It is also not encouraging that, by a modification of the Banking Act, banks are restricted in making provisions before paying taxes.

5   Hungary: gradualism needs a strategy

Kálmán Mizsei

1   Introduction

The authors of a recent analysis of Hungary have wisely noted that 'it is not particularly instructive ... to take the years 1990 and 1991 and compare, with normative objectives, Hungarian performance with say, Czechoslovak or Polish performance. The recent phase of the Hungarian experience is, however, extremely interesting in itself' (Dervis and Condon, 1991). In other words, it is not enough for us Hungarians to be satisfied, if we look around and see that Hungary has outperformed most of the other post-communist countries in the last three years.

First, as the quotation indicates, Hungary, after 20 years' experience with market socialism, was at a different stage in the creation of a market economy than were the others. Second, the poor performance of, let us say, the Bulgarian political structures is no consolation when judging Hungary's achievements. Economic policies in the other transforming economies have sometimes been poorer than those in Hungary; political situations have also been less promising in many places. But I want this analysis to be guided by the above quotation and, in particular, I want to judge Hungarian performance in the light of its potential to catch up with the developed market economies after four decades of devastating experience with socialism.

This paper was originally prepared in April 1992 and was revised in January 1993. Its main focus, however, is still the period before mid-1992.

2   Political and Social Constraints on Economic Reforms

Probably the most important difference between the systemic transformation of Hungary and the whole of the rest of the region was that 1989 was much less of a threshold in Hungary than elsewhere. I am referring here to the *gradualist* nature of the Hungarian development. Analysts usually draw attention to the significance of the economic reforms (New Economic Mechanism, NEM) in

1968. Here let me point out that the deeper reason was political, and 1968 was already a repercussion. The core event was 1956, after which the Hungarian Socialist Workers' Party (HSWP), out of fear of the people, pursued a much more consumer-oriented policy throughout the next three and a half decades than any other communist country. At the same time, the HSWP was able to avoid any major collision with Soviet geopolitical interests. Therefore the continuity of diverging from the Soviet-type economy was not interrupted, unlike in Czechoslovakia in 1969 and in Poland in 1981.

The main features of the Hungarian economic system in the Kadar period, in comparison with the rest of the region, were:

(1) an agricultural policy combining collectivization with more liberal regulation of the cooperatives than elsewhere (neither the Polish nor the Soviet model) (see Juhász and Magyar, 1984);
(2) reform of the regulatory system of the state sector in 1968;
(3) liberal treatment of the grey economy in fields where the state was not able to provide a politically tolerable supply of goods;
(4) a second wave of liberalization and opening from 1981 (quasi-privatization steps, joining the IMF, liberalization of tourism);
(5) a third set of liberalization measures after the failure of acceleration of growth from 1987 (gradual import and price liberalization under pressure from the IMF, spontaneous privatization starting in 1988).

Some of these elements are to be found in the development of other communist economies. Poland in particular can be mentioned here: a second economy, partial reform in 1982 and privatization in the late 1980s are the key points. No communist country, however, produced the organic, gradualist reform path that was so characteristic of Hungary, although very significant retreats (like that in the early 1970s or the growth-oriented adjustments of 1985) are also part of this development. The sense of pragmatic gradualism has become a deeply rooted feature of Hungary's macroeconomic management more than in any other socialist state.

This is a fact not only of the economy in Hungary but also of social developments. By the time of the collapse of the Soviet empire, Hungary was a more westward-looking, pluralistically minded country than any other in the region, with a significant history of private wealth accumulation and semi-Western consumerism.

The other important social feature of the Hungarian transformation is that it has been much less of a political revolution than that in any of the East European countries. It is generally true that the political upheavals were made possible because the imperium became deeply dysfunctional for Russia. In Hungary, the additional factor was a different role of the Communist Party in the society than elsewhere. While in the rest of the region the party could be regarded entirely as a foreign agent alien from the society and as one that only destroyed, the HSWP could be seen at least partly as a pragmatic semi-reformist elite. Its split (led by the reform communists, Németh and Pozsgai) into a 'socialist' (read: reformist) and a 'fundamentalist' wing made it possible for new political organizations to develop as early as 1989.

As a result of the organic political transformation as well as of the above-mentioned deeply rooted pragmatism, Hungary was the only country in the region that was able to produce a unique combination of a *relatively* well-structured political party system with a workable set of political (constitutional, electoral and parliamentary) rules. At the beginning of 1993 Poland still does not have constitutional clarity in terms of whether it wants presidential or parliamentary rule; the parliament, as a consequence of disastrous election rules, is deeply fragmented. The relatively good performance of the Polish economy has occurred *in spite* and certainly not because of the political setting so far. Czechoslovakia has just split into two entities and the end of disintegration is still not in sight; monetary disintegration will probably come sooner than was envisaged by the politicians, and there is a legitimate fear that even the customs union might not survive. The Czech Republic seems to be stable politically and has great economic prospects; this is by no means the case with Slovakia. The political system is (understandably) still fluid in Slovenia and Croatia as well. The disintegration of some countries of the post-World War I settlements poses new challenges, but the good news is that now not only are Hungary and Poland ethnically relatively homogeneous countries, but so are the Czech Republic and Slovenia. Their economic transformation should not be disturbed by ethnic conflicts. These happen to be the countries with the best chances of rapid economic reform anyway.

Hungary compares very favourably with Poland and Czechoslovakia. It has a clearly parliamentary system, with a 4% minimum threshold for parties, which boosts the concentration of political alliances (and works against fragmentation). The first free elections had a good combination of proportional and German-type election rules, although they were procedurally too complicated. The first three years of operation of the parliament have revealed a remarkable stability of the party structure and, in particular, of the governing coalition, in spite of the continuous public struggle of the Smallholders' Party for a bigger share in power and then the split in its parliamentary group.

The largest governing party and the largest opposition party were able to agree on mutual self-restraint after the election. As a result of the deal, the Alliance of Free Democrats (the Hungarian acronym is SZDSZ) made it possible to eliminate a constitutional requirement of a two-thirds vote for some less significant legal acts. In exchange, the state president was chosen from the ranks of SZDSZ. Although tactically the SZDSZ got less from this bargain than it could have, the country benefited because the deal made the legislation workable (previous rules had been shaped in the communist past and could not be applied now as the role of the legislative body became serious), while the president has counterbalanced the efforts of the ruling parties to amass more political power than that to which they are legally entitled. The overwhelming popularity of the 'opposition' president also helps to balance political power in the country.

The generally positive balance of the political transformation (especially in comparative perspective) cannot hide the unresolved shortcomings and persisting challenges of Hungarian democracy. The most serious problem is that, because of general despair and disappointment among significant parts of the population and declining living standards of a large segment of society, the governing elite is unpopular. Moreover, it contains clear and strong tendencies to try to limit democratic procedures in the country. Two partly interrelated sources of danger to democracy should be mentioned here.

First, the Hungarian Democratic Forum (MDF) has emerged as a movement built on national grievances. The nation has still not come to terms with the historical traumas of the twentieth century (world wars and the ensuing peace settlements as well as the horror of Soviet dominance). Some other political groups, especially the Smallholders' Party, also play the national card in a sometimes irresponsible way. Therefore the potential danger is always that collectivist (national) goals might overshadow the basically individualist targets of market economy reform as well as of democratic rules of the game. The MDF campaigned against 'spontaneous' privatization in 1990, and such groups in its parliamentary faction are still very active and loud (especially the so-called Monopoly Group). The influence of collectivist tendencies can be seen in almost every recent legislative act of parliament.

Even the danger of outright nationalism cannot be ignored. In late 1992, following an infamous pamphlet by István Csurka, one of the vice-presidents of MDF (Csurka, 1992), the ruling party made radical moves in that direction. MDF has changed so much primarily because of its unpopularity. Many people left the movement after realizing the discrepancy between its pre-election promises and its performance in government. The activists who remained in it are now afraid of losing power and influence after the next elections (due in spring 1994). In order to prevent that happening, they are trying to limit the scope of democracy. Even mass demonstrations against the president of the republic are not rare. The governing elites have a dubious attitude towards the emergence of paramilitary groups (mostly based on young skinheads) in society. The MDF is also fighting hard in order to gain strict control over the mass media. The party feels it cannot rely on objective media, because if it did, it would not have any chance of winning the next elections. The Csurka phenomenon, primarily because of its anti-Semitic obsession, has shaken the reputation of Hungary as leader of the transformation in the region.

The second threat to democracy and reform arises because the governing parties and the government have started to create strongly clientelist structures in the state and the business community since around mid-1991. A prelude to this was the confidential analysis by Mr Kónya, leader of the MDF parliamentary group, of the political situation in September 1991, which was publicized by the opposition. Since then, every nomination by the government has reflected its conscious efforts to build up a clientelist state. The replacement of Mr Surányi by Mr Bod as president of the Hungarian National Bank (NBH) in late 1991 caused a huge domestic and international outcry. In this case a highly qualified and internationally appreciated professional was dismissed in spite of his strong loyalty and devoted work to the government goals. Another example of the clientelist tendencies of the government is the filling of institutions of privatization with close confidantes of the government and paying very little attention to professional competence.

It would go beyond the scope of this paper to analyse the roots of the lack of legitimacy in Hungarian politics.[1] In any case, the legitimacy of the recent parliamentary structure is not yet satisfactory. Large parts of society think that the members of the legislature act in the same way as did those in the communist era. The most visible example of the not fully legitimate status of parliament and its government was the taxi drivers' blockade in November 1990. While in that case the government stood up for the rule of law, since then it has itself respected the spirit of legality less and less.

Some new political movements try to play on popular disappointment with politics in general and thereby to secure their future role in the political life of the country. This does not seem to be a very serious danger, because none of the political forces outside the parliamentary game have yet been able to gain mass support. More worrying is that, if the general public do not protect democracy energetically enough as a crucial public good, the political system might become less resistant to the power-centralizing efforts of the new governing elite. The experience of new democracies shows that the crucial psychological breakthrough is usually the second, and not the first, election. It is vital for Hungary that it experiences truly democratic elections in 1994. If it does, the prospects of success in building a market economy will be quite good. The role of the West in securing democracy in Hungary is crucial: since integration with the West is a common goal in the country, clearly expressed conditionality of this support makes an enormous difference.

3 Monetary Policy and the Independence of the Monetary Authority

3.1 Anti-inflationary Measures

Monetary policy has been the success story of Hungarian macro policy not only in the post-communist period but starting as early as 1988. In fact one can quite convincingly argue that the components of Hungary's relative success in the region (besides the poor performance of most of the rest) are the legacy of earlier reforms, the sustained monetary discipline over the last four years, discipline and a sufficient level of social consensus in wage setting and the practice of 'spontaneous' privatization. From the second half of 1991 even a visible deceleration of inflation and inflationary pressures has emerged in Hungary. This success has to be attributed to the tough monetary policy and the ability of the government to maintain a minimum of discipline on the expenditure side of the budget (at least until 1991). No toughness by the monetary authority could have compensated for a runaway budget deficit. Also important is the fact that the elimination of price subsidies increased inflationary pressures up to 1991; by 1992 the level of subsidies was very minor.

On the other hand, it is also true that the major failure of government policies since 1989 has been that they have delayed the promised, and very much needed, reform (restructuring) of the public sector. Since this should inevitably contain very sensitive measures in various fields of welfare policy, it is generally expected that in the term of the present parliament there will be no real public sector reform. Without it, however, one cannot hope to lower the level of the public sector deficit, which reached 4% of GDP in 1991 and climbed to a very dangerous 8% in 1992 ('Összeomlott...', 1992).

This, of course, limits the central bank's possibilities. A further problem is that the large and sustained deficit makes it impossible (together with the bad portfolios of the largest banks) to decrease the spread of interest rates, thus making investments very costly. Hungarian economic policy is in a vicious circle: after many years of restrictions they want to generate growth but high nominal (and lately also real) interest rates keep investment activity rather low. The deficit and high yields on government securities make investment in the public sector increasingly lucrative, while the private sector suffers from the high price of credit. It should also be noted that the irresponsible policy of the Ministry of Finance (MOF) is also dangerous because the recently issued state bonds will mature after the term of office of the present government and legislature. In this way they put a heavy burden on the next generation to make life less conflictual for themselves.

In any event, 1992 was a peculiar year for the Hungarian financial markets. The simultaneous introduction of the banking law (with its reserve requirements against bad loans), the bankruptcy code and the new accounting rules caused the liquidity gap of the enterprise sector to surface with a dramatic explosion. The portfolio of the banks has deteriorated enormously; they have had practically no profits and their situation even forced the government hastily to introduce a rescue operation at the end of 1992. In this situation, and also because the National Bank of Hungary (NBH) had deliberately expanded the money supply more rapidly than was justified by inflation, the banks have been left with (a probably temporary) excess liquidity. It was quite easy for the central bank to do this because the inflow of foreign capital and the large current account surplus would otherwise have imposed a need to act strongly to counter their impact on

Table 5.1   Interest Rates in Hungary, January–November 1992

Month	Differences between credit and deposit interest rate levels		Average rate of interest (%)
	Maturity within a year	Maturity over a year	
January	6.6	-1.3	31.5
February	8.6	2.3	31.5
March	8.4	-3.0	28.7
April	9.0	3.3	24.6
May	9.5	3.0	26.6
June	10.0	3.6	23.9
July	12.6	6.1	17.0
August	13.1	8.0	16.5
September	12.2	10.6	17.6
October	12.2	8.3	16.3
November	–	–	15.5

Source: NBH (1992) pp. 31 and 33.

the monetary figures.

On top of these developments, the savings propensity of households did not deteriorate compared with 1991. This situation enabled the banks on the one hand to finance the budget deficit, and on the other hand to reduce the deposit rates radically. The seriously worsening portfolio of the financial institutions, however, did not allow the banks to reduce the lending rates simultaneously. They followed the trend at a much slower pace (see Table 5.1). The banks have become very cautious, while the range of possibly liquid clients has narrowed enormously at a stage in the transformation when the banks have not yet developed sufficient technical skill to evaluate the creditworthiness of companies. This situation is temporarily convenient for the Treasury because there has been ready demand for its safe short-term and long-term securities, and even the interest rates were able to decline quite dramatically in this market. The very large spread between the rate of inflation and the price of credit has, however, made it almost impossible to invest from bank credit and in this way to generate economic growth in 1992. *In this situation the single most important cause of delay in economic recovery is the huge budget deficit.*

One also should note that the very considerable achievement of the National Bank of Hungary in maintaining monetary equilibrium and relatively low inflation (see Table 5.2) in the turbulent years of 1990 and 1991 was accomplished through extremely drastic measures, and the monetary authority does not yet have the tools to 'fine-tune' the realization of monetary targets. One clearly has to differentiate between instruments and performance here. While the performance has been good, one should not forget that the introduction of

Table 5.2   Consumer Price Indices as a Percentage of the Previous Month,
January 1990 – November 1992

Month	1990	1991	1992
January	107.7	107.5	103.2
February	105.3	104.9	102.7
March	102.7	103.7	101.9
April	102.5	102.4	101.3
May	100.8	102.2	101.5
June	100.4	102.1	100.6
July	102.6	100.9	100.3
August	102.9	100.2	100.8
September	101.5	101.5	102.4
October	101.5	101.3	102.5
November	102.1	101.4	101.6
December	101.7	101.6	–

Source: NBH (1992) p. 14.

sophisticated instruments for maintaining the targets is partly still to come. In 1992, partly because of the deliberate actions of the monetary authority to maintain excess liquidity in the banking sector and partly because of the overwhelming impact of the deficit on the financial markets, it was the Treasury instruments that shaped the interest rates on the inter-bank markets as well.

In the stormy period of the last three years of transformation, the lack of sophisticated tools for monetary policy did not cause practical problems because sophisticated monetary planning was almost impossible anyway. The extremely rapid structural changes in factors determining monetary targets put the NBH in a rather peculiar situation. Quick and decisive reaction to changes in the course of the year was a much more important asset than anything else. NBH coped with this challenge very well. For instance, for 1991 the expectations of the government and the IMF were that the loss of Soviet markets would cause a large balance of payments gap, with the current account deficit reaching about US$1.2 billion. This assumption was based on the expected terms of trade losses as well as on the supposed inability to reorientate trade flows at a sufficiently high rate to Western markets. A further expectation was that it would also cause large budget deficits and a sharp drop in economic activity. While the latter expectations have been fulfilled, external balances have been much better than expected. Trade reorientation was extremely rapid, with the growth of exports to the OECD countries reaching 30% (CSO, 1992a). The other source of favourable external balances was a qualitative jump in the level of foreign investment. Investments in the form of cash payments amounted to US$1.2 billion in 1991. Lastly, nobody expected the incredible jump in household savings from 5% to 11% of incomes, which to a large extent financed budget deficits. This had never occurred in the past; deficits were always financed from external sources.

The main thrust of monetary policy, as it turned out, had to be to sterilize the massive inflow of hard currencies throughout 1991. One of the necessary distorting features of the Hungarian monetary system has been that it has encouraged savings in hard currencies, even in comparison with savings in forints. This distortion was coupled in the past with the one-sided concentration of monetary planning on domestic money, while quite neglecting the impact on inflation of changes in the stock of foreign assets, in spite of the fact that exchange of hard currency assets into forints was automatic. It was understandable in the period when Hungary was on the brink of financial insolvency and foreign exchange regulation was quite restrictive. The good results of 1990 and 1991, however, as well as gradual liberalization of foreign exchange regulation imposed new tasks upon the authorities; foreign exchange holdings became increasingly important in establishing monetary targets.

Because of the discrepancy between the interest rates on the Hungarian and major foreign credit markets and because since 1990 there has been a tendency for a real appreciation of the Hungarian currency, both demand for and supply of foreign exchange have been rapidly increasing. This is in spite of the fact that foreign exchange loans have been very expensive by international standards. In 1991, for instance, it was not unusual for firms to pay a 16–18% total interest rate cost on short-term (less than one year) dollar credits, which was greatly in excess of the cost of such credits on the international money markets. This was manageable for firms in 1991–2 because they rightly expected a real appreciation in the forint, but the question emerges, when will the real appreciation of the forint end? The banks do not bear a foreign exchange risk, but the enterprises (which usually have a quite low level of financial prudency) will have to. It might cause a further deterioration in their liquidity. In addition, termination of the policy of real appreciation of the forint could be very detrimental for savings in Hungarian currency, as the withholding tax still applies only to savings in domestic currency.

Demand of households for foreign exchange was also very high in the first two years of the 1990s, partly because confidence in the Hungarian currency was still not re-established after years of relatively high inflation, and partly also because of the already mentioned distortions. The budget still receives a 20% withholding tax on forint interest rates which does not apply to convertible currency deposits. Until 1991, the banks themselves were encouraged to collect hard currency savings by the population because they could get automatic and unlimited refinancing in domestic currency at relatively low interest rates. This changed in 1992. In addition, since August 1992, households have gained more access to 'tourist currency'. Lastly, the supply of foreign exchange has also been very large because of the appreciation of the forint in real terms and because of the role direct foreign investment has to play in the privatization process.

As a result of these sometimes contradictory developments, the Hungarian currency markets have become mature. The process was strengthened by the opening of a limited inter-bank foreign exchange market in 1992. Although Hungary has resisted declaring the convertibility of its currency, the actual strength of the forint has been impressive. While current account convertibility has been available for companies, the rush of households on hard currencies has disappeared to the extent that the black market in currencies virtually does not exist any more, in spite of the still prevailing limitations on foreign exchange.

Because of the scale of the need to sterilize the inflow of foreign exchange (the difference between the projected and the actual balance of payments position was almost Ft 150 billion!), monetary policy had to face an unresolved dilemma in 1991: the harsher the restrictions on forint assets, the higher the incentive to convert foreign currencies into forints in the Hungarian banking system. This resulted in an excessively strong improvement in the external position of the country. Foreign reserves increased to almost US$4 billion by the end of 1991, i.e. the level of almost five months' import financing. In 1992, the liquidity problems of the enterprise sector were primarily responsible for the continuation of the domestic recession, and consequently the strong improvement in the trade balance. Nevertheless, this and other developments mentioned above pushed up the reserves to about US$6 billion, which covers imports for about seven months. Now the costs of increasing the reserves are much more expensive than the rate of return on the foreign exchange assets. Since the country has fully restored its international creditworthiness, and because of the government's perception that it has to generate visible economic growth if it is to succeed in the 1994 general elections, the authorities are planning a slightly worsening current account balance, compared with 1992. Since Hungary's external position has room for improvement, and the debt overhang is still considerable, any easing of balance of payments considerations should be watched very carefully.

Continuation of large surpluses on the current account cannot be a goal either, because it would further restrain domestic economic activity (other than direct foreign investment in privatized firms). One should, however, note that all previous efforts to relax monetary stringency led to inefficient growth, causing an intolerable deterioration in the external position of the country. Have the structural reforms gone sufficiently far to secure a healthier credit allocation, leading to an export-led growth push? This question can be answered after an analysis of the banking sector and the structural reforms themselves.

The sustained effort of the monetary authority to squeeze domestic demand, accompanied by a manageable wage mechanism and the sustained attempt by the government to decrease consumer price subsidies, finally produced what can now be seen as a turning point in inflationary trends in 1991. Consumer price inflation in the first month of that year was still 7.5% (on a monthly basis) owing to the elimination of subsidies, but then inflation sharply decreased to 4.9% in February, to 3.7% in March, 2.4% in April and below 2% from June on. Although the yearly inflation rate was 35% in 1991, in the second half of the year the increase in prices was much lower than that, computed on a yearly basis. (The official statistics compute inflation as an average, comparing months with the same months in the previous year. Because of the price increase in the first two months of 1991, this method of computation was not sensitive to the deceleration in inflation in the second half of the year.)

Since much of the elimination of price subsidies is behind us, consumer price inflation in fact decelerated to 25% in 1992, which is the upper limit of government estimates. The producer price index has been even more impressive, reaching only about 12% in 1992. However, without much greater budgetary stringency as well as more dynamic structural reform (the creation of domestic competition through privatization but also through anti-monopoly practice, sustained import liberalization, execution of bankruptcy rules, etc.), the ultimate goal of keeping inflation to single figures cannot be achieved. It would, of course, have serious consequences for the exchange rate policy and, accordingly, for the goal of convertibility of the forint.

The government expects a consumer price index increase in the range of 15–17% in 1993. This would mean a further deceleration of inflation. Since some basic parameters of the macroeconomic equation will still be quite uncertain (in particular the balance of payments position of the country, but also domestic demand for credit), one can only say that this target is within the range of possible developments. I would not be surprised either, however, if inflation were closer to the performance in 1992. Certainly there is no immediate danger of a price explosion as a result of the huge budget deficit. It poses, however, a serious long-term problem.

3.2 External Debt Management

In the period of the political transformation, many foreign experts advised Hungary to stop paying its external debt or at least to initiate renegotiation of it. Indeed, in the EC quite a few analysts thought that servicing the debt fully is a bad concept. One of the political parties (the Alliance of Free Democrats) also urged changes in the debt management strategy in the 1990 election campaign. Criticism from domestic political forces and experts intensified again when the news about the Polish debt reduction deal was revealed. The NBH firmly stood its ground on maintaining a full commitment to the international obligations. It might have seemed a rather dubious strategy at the time, but retrospectively the advantages of it appear to be overwhelming.

Hungary's position on the financial markets has markedly improved, and its debt burden has been sharply decreasing.[2] Another important aspect of this worth mentioning is that the adopted strategy kept the morale of the Hungarian government rather high, whereas the Polish situation is the opposite: instead of regarding Balcerowicz as a national hero for achieving as much as 50% debt forgiveness, he was criticized throughout 1991 and partly even in 1992 for not achieving more. Moreover, the procedure has taught people to think that if Poland became insolvent it would be natural for the world to rescue it. Imparting this attitude instead of responsibility for one's own business should not be the aim or the unintentional consequence of international cooperation. It is not that debt forgiveness is bad in any circumstances or was so in Poland (in fact, in the Polish case international assistance was justified), but that even in seemingly clear cases like that of Poland there might be a long-term political price to pay for the deal. Hungary, on the other hand, should be able to capitalize on fully servicing its international debt.

In 1992, the trend of the previous years continued: the balance on both the current and the capital accounts was favourable. Hungary's gross and net debt decreased if measured in ECU (in dollar terms both have increased because of the devaluation of the US currency). None the less, Hungary's external situation is still far from being safe. The debt service/exports ratio was still 34.6% in 1991 and somewhat less in 1992, while a 25% ratio could be regarded as more or less safe. Massive inflows of foreign direct investment have made the situation less painful than expected, but there is of course no guarantee that the wonderful balance on the capital account will be reproduced in subsequent years. Another potentially vulnerable element in the situation is the high propensity to save in foreign currencies. This is heavily dependent on confidence; if this is damaged, the whole situation could be destroyed quickly. The issue also ties up with the problem of exchange rate management.

In 1990–2, the National Bank of Hungary pursued a policy of real appreciation, i.e. the size of devaluations has lagged behind the inflation rate. This policy was in the cross-fire of criticism in the government in the whole period. In particular, the minister responsible for international economic relations criticized, sometimes openly, the exchange rate policy, claiming that it would lead to a low level of export growth. However, in exactly this period the export expansion in the convertible currency area exceeded the rate of any earlier period as well as all expectations.

The exchange rate policy of the NBH focused in this period on anti-inflationary efforts, while the underlying assumption prevailed that strict monetary policy and the collapse of the CMEA markets would force economic actors to turn westwards anyway, so that the deterioration in the current account position would at least be tolerable. Furthermore, some argued that too strong a devaluation would make the state enterprises lazier, since, in contrast to 'normal' private businesses, they strive not for profit maximization but for a 'tolerable' level of revenues. This means that real devaluations would decrease their incentive to export to the West. We do not have any reliable model of enterprise behaviour, but the fact is that hard currency exports have grown astonishingly. One can also assume that the state firms' combination of a poor liquidity position and short-term vision has made them cut export prices to profitable levels. It is also a fact that the liquidity position of the large industrial firms deteriorated quite rapidly in 1991 and 1992.

The other factor, usually overlooked, is that real appreciation has been possible partly because of the efficiency gains through import and price liberalization as well as structural reforms. Since both were almost completed in 1991, the 'liberalization bonus' is unlikely to continue for long. As we shall see in section 4, the opposite might happen: there is a strong tendency to soften the effects of the liberalization measures. Incidentally, this is another important reason for being disappointed about the scale of the budget deficit: if the deficit were sufficiently lower, inflation could be pushed down close to that of the OECD countries (German inflation in particular is relevant here) and the foreign exchange policy would be much easier.

So in 1992 the crucial question was whether the practices of the previous year, i.e. periodic devaluations of less than the inflation rate could be sustained? The general understanding in the NBH at the end of 1991 was that the 5.8% devaluation in November 1991 was the last such substantial change in the exchange rate and from then on devaluations would occur more regularly but on a much smaller scale, i.e. less than 1% a month ('Leértékelés...', 1992). Dates of devaluations would not be announced beforehand.

Nomination of the new head of the central bank altered this process; devaluations have been much less frequent than originally planned and altogether the forint has appreciated by about 6% in real terms according to the producer price index in 1992. (According to the consumer price index, the appreciation has been much larger.)

Hungary has also chosen to reach currency convertibility gradually. This contrasts sharply with the current tendency in the region that early announcement of 'internal convertibility' is aimed at anchoring the economic policy to responsible monetary policy as well as to rapid structural reforms. The paradoxical result is that convertibility has become non-sustainable (as in Yugoslavia in 1990) or completely illusory (as in Romania), while the cautious Hungarian approach has produced an extremely gradual approach of solid convertibility. In spite of lagging behind in rhetoric, it is clear that the strongest currency in the post-communist world is the Hungarian forint. While the early announcement of current account convertibility has proved sustainable in Poland and the Czech Republic, a hasty declaration of capital account convertibility might lead to a failure because these economies are still too weak to resist larger-scale speculative transactions against their currencies.

Ahead in Hungary lie liberalization of current account transactions for the population (the first step being the increase in the yearly tourist money supply), completion of foreign trade liberalization and capital account transactions for domestic firms and households. Still, the above-mentioned distortions of the

Hungarian financial system make the process somewhat vulnerable. Liberalization of foreign exchange transactions for the population, for instance, might convert parts of savings into foreign currencies, causing some strain on debt management. Unexpected adverse tendencies in inflows of foreign direct investment or in exports might also challenge some administrative measures. Of course, in a world of ideally functioning macroeconomic management, the recent Hungarian situation would allow the earlier announcement of convertibility and acceleration of its expansion. The recent Hungarian economic management, however, is far from being that perfect; in this case cautiousness is highly justified.

4   Public Revenues and Spending

The worst aspect of government performance in 1991-2 was most probably the central government budget. The problem is at least threefold. First, the government has not been able to lower the deficit to economically tolerable levels. Second, the government redistribution of incomes is very high: general government expenditures are still 66% of GDP (1991 data), an almost unbearable burden on an economy like Hungary's. (One should note, however, that these data are not consolidated; in a net sense the redistribution of GDP would amount to somewhere between 54% and 60%.) The third problem is that the government has not even started to reform the major mechanisms of government spending. Since most of these mechanisms are politically very sensitive, the prospects of serious reform of a basically communist-type welfare structure in a basically market environment have been postponed for at least another three years.

The 1992 budget plan envisaged a deficit of about 2.5% of GDP (Ft 70 billion); this would not have been unbearably high, but it was already clear during its debate in parliament that the deficit in reality would go up at the very least to Ft 120 billion (4% of GDP). In fact, the deficit exceeded the most pessimistic expectations and reached Ft 190 billion, about 7.5% of GDP. The plan seriously overestimated the revenues from corporate income tax, especially from the banks. The new, very much needed, accountancy regulation has forced firms and banks to show their real financial position in their books. In the case of the banks, an explicit government requirement is to reach the capital adequacy ratio, corresponding to EC regulation and BIS standards, in three years. To achieve this, the banks must increase the level of their reserves quite dramatically. That means, however, seriously shrinking budget revenues. This crisis has led the Ministry of Finance to 'ask' the large state-owned commercial banks to 'submit' those funds to the ministry that were previously refunded on the basis of excess corporate income tax bill. Eventually, most of the banks gave short-term credit to the fiscal authorities. The danger of this kind of procedure is a possible escalation of *ex post* measures of the state budget.

The government, despite earlier statements, has made extensive use of its privatization revenues for financing the current deficit rather than paying back public debt. In addition, the deficit of the Social Security Fund was to be partly (to the extent of Ft 14.7 billion in 1992) reduced by 'capitalization' of the organization (see also section 7). The total revenue of the State Property Agency (SPA) was Ft 40 billion in 1991, and there is strong pressure for part of the SPA revenues to be used for restructuring ailing state enterprises and to provide subsidized loans to small private businesses. All these goals could be achieved only through a miraculous acceleration of the privatization process (see section 10). Although revenues from privatization have grown considerably (to about Ft 70 billion), they were only able to ease the pain of the financial troubles of the state. By financing current deficits through privatization revenues, the government cheats itself (and the population) since later governments will have to carry the burden of recent, very expensive, public indebtedness. The government can crowd out alternative investments only by offering much higher interest yields than banks and securities.

The 1993 budget is already a pre-election one, meaning that the expenditure side is not significantly curtailed but rather further broadened. This will be even more so the case with the budget in 1994; the first reform steps can be expected from the new government in 1995 and by then the strains of delays in the previous period will have built up quite seriously.

One might wonder if my worry is not exaggerated. After all, many governments (for instance those of Belgium and Italy) run deficits that are usually higher than that of Hungary until 1991. In addition, in that year the net savings position of households improved dramatically. For the first time for decades, the government was able to issue longer-term (three years) State Bonds, and more have followed. Lastly, the deficit of the consolidated public sector was smaller, only 1.3% of GDP.

The situation is, however, more complicated than this. There are many arguments for trying to reduce the budget deficit more than in some smoothly functioning market economies. The economy is in the final phase of a long stabilization period that started in 1988. The recession is deep not only because of this but also because of the collapse of Soviet and East European markets. The stock of poorly performing loans in the banking sector is huge. A very high share of household and enterprise savings are located and still go into hard currencies. Because of all these factors the spread between the interest rates of deposits and credits is large; high interest rates on credit limit the ability of the enterprise sector to invest. The budget is not only crowding out businesses but also pulling up the market lending rates and thus further depressing investment demand (Jaksity, 1992).

Finally, the huge (in relation to GDP) budget revenues are being 'consumed' by the public; the level of public investment is in fact extremely low, while that of welfare items is high. For all these reasons, the government might have to pay a heavy price for postponing structural reforms of the budget (Riecke, 1992), in terms of high future inflation, and postponing the start and moderating the intensity of the expected recovery.

A World Bank team prepared a two-volume document at the end of 1991 on how the deficit and high budgetary engagement in the Hungarian economy could be moderated. The political arithmetic, however, makes it virtually impossible that the government will initiate that before the 1994 elections, meaning that implementation cannot start until 1995. The major findings of the confidential World Bank paper have been discussed in Dervis and Condon (1992). The authors' suggestions are rational from an economic point of view and thus even more clearly underline the significance of political doubts about the required adjustments on the expenditure side. They suggest reducing subsidies from 7% to 1% of GDP, which would face a quite enormous reaction from the peasants, who have representatives in the government.

The welfare systems are another huge source of government spending. The largest single item is of course the pension system, taking 10% of 1991 GDP (see section 8). It is clear that the low retirement age is very odd for a country like Hungary (55 years for women and 60 years for men with a general entitlement). The government pretends, however, that it does not want to touch it and will continue to do so until the elections due in 1994.

The tax-raising capacity of the government was especially poor (relative to expenditure) in 1991, despite the fact that Hungary has the most reasonable tax system among the post-communist economies. Figures suggest that the concern of some Western analysts about the erosion of the tax base might be justified. The government planned a 20% increase in tax revenues of the central budget for 1991 over 1990 (the inflation rate being 35%). It was, however, able to collect only 12% more (in nominal terms), which was way below the price index (see Table 5.A1). The biggest surprise was the nominal fall in enterprise profit tax. The fall in registered economic activity also affected indirect taxes, however, once believed to be an easy item to forecast. VAT revenues were short of the plan by Ft 20 billion, 6.25% of the total. Customs revenues similarly underperformed.

Part of the problem is that, because of the heavy tax burden, a large part of the economy still operates underground in spite of the otherwise favourable climate for private enterprise. Privatization has not caused a shrinkage of the shadow economy, expected by many. Although VAT is more collectable than profit tax and personal income tax, to a certain extent it is also hit by the general tendency to under-register activities and of course by the recession in general. This is a very complex problem, inherited from the communist past. What is needed is a long-term, sustained effort simultaneously to decrease the tax burden on individuals and businesses and to build up a strong tax administration. Neither activity can be successful without the other. The understanding of the enormous importance of this was missing in the original Kupa programme,[3] which has now been practically abandoned by the Antall government.

The domestic debt of the state was Ft 1,740 billion at the end of 1991. This is about the same magnitude as the foreign debt, since the cause of foreign indebtedness was, unlike in other East European countries, mostly deficit financing in the last two decades. The domestic debt is about 75% of the roughly Ft 2,400 billion GDP, representing only a slightly larger proportion than the EC average (*Magyar Hirlap*, 21 February 1992). Recent growth of the debt, however, threatens a self-perpetuating process that might disrupt the financial system were it to be maintained in the long run.

5   Price and Foreign Trade Liberalization

Hungary's experience with price and import liberalization is very interesting. When speaking about 'Hungarian gradualism', analysts often confuse the gradual, but still very rapid, liberalization measures in these fields with the 'gradualism' of economic reforms in the last two decades. Indeed, in contrast to the textbook cases Hungary has implemented its shift from a socialist semi-market, semi-shortage system towards an essentially market economy basically by these two measures. In some other post-communist countries this shift was compressed into a once-and-for-all set of measures because it was assumed that step-by-step liberalization would not be feasible politically. Hungary has been able to manage it, and now almost all prices and 90% of imports are liberalized.

6   Incomes Policies

One of the most important questions of macroeconomic policies in the transformation period (whatever their length) of the East European countries is whether they are able to keep wages under control on a long-term basis in the still huge state sector. Hence the need for incomes policies. So one of the distinctive features of the Hungarian 'gradualist success story' is that liberalization in this field has been very cautious and incomes policies have been able to achieve a steady decline in real wages in the state sector (see Table 5.3).

The data reveal two interesting phenomena if compared with Polish figures. First, the bad news is that the growth of nominal wages accelerated systematically from 1983 but it has been a slow, steady and thus relatively controlled process. There was a quite strong jump in 1989 and again in 1991, but nothing in comparison with the frenetic move of wages in Poland. The second interesting phenomenon is the steady decrease in employees' real wages. The only exception is the 1985–6 acceleration episode when the trade balance also deteriorated. Even in 1989, the year of political transformation, the outgoing Németh government showed remarkable self-restraint in its incomes policies. We wonder if the same level of responsibility will characterize the present government in 1993 and especially in the 1994 election year?

Table 5.3   Nominal Wages, the Price Index and Real Wages of Employees, 1982-91 (Previous Year = 100)

Year	Net nominal wages per employee, average	Consumer prices	Real wages per employee
1982	106.1	106.8	99.3
1983	104.0	107.4	96.8
1984	105.6	108.2	97.6
1985	108.3	106.9	101.3
1986	107.4	105.4	101.9
1987	108.1	108.5	99.6
1988	110.1	115.8	95.1
1989	118.2	117.2	100.9
1990	122.3	128.9	94.9
1991	127.2	135.0	94.2
1992	121.5	123.0	98.8

Note: 1991 data are preliminary while data for 1992 are rough estimates and contain only firms with more than 50 employees.

Sources: *Magyar Statisztikai Évkönyv*, 1990 and 1987; and Central Statistical Office (1992).

Especially important is that the present government was able to decrease real wages in the two critical years of transformation, 1990 and 1991, when the fall in the East European markets made this obligatory. An important further positive effect of real wage decreases has been that they have exerted steady pressure on employees to quit the state sector and to try to open a small private business or to be employed in one.

In the last few years, the rate of wage growth has been determined by the inflationary impact of price liberalization and of the elimination of subsidies. In these years the engine of inflation was not (as often in Poland or Yugoslavia and recently in some other transforming countries) wage growth but liberalization. Of course, if wage increases could be reduced, this would have a positive impact on inflation as the demand barrier would more seriously affect sellers. On many occasions, especially at the beginnings of years, the trade unions strongly protested, sometimes going on strike, against wage regulations that caused real wage losses, but the level of political consensus as well as the relative weakness of the trade unions secured manageable compromises (Körössényi, 1992).

The task was different during the 1992 negotiations. Previously, the inflation rate had grown almost year by year. Therefore the money illusion helped to achieve a moderate real wage fall. As other inflationary factors have been moderated (not much has been left for price liberalization and for cuts in subsidies), the main immediate enemy to anti-inflationary policy is inflationary expectations. Their significance was greater in 1992 than that of the budget deficits. Therefore a very brutal agreement on nominal wages in 1992 could have lowered price inflation much more than has in fact happened. But its immediate cost in terms of real wage losses would also have been proportionately larger; the long-term benefits of lower inflation were not appropriately represented in the negotiations.

Until 1988, wage regulation was quite centralized in Hungary. The usual notions about the cautiousness and gradualism of the Hungarian transformation hold perhaps most for this aspect of regulation. It also demonstrates, together with price and import liberalization, the idea that the Hungarian economic transformation cannot, except in some segments, be related to the year(s) of political turnaround, since serious liberalization steps started really in 1989. In 1988 the government found itself under increasing political pressure from the National Council of Trade Unions and the Chamber of Commerce (later Economic Chamber) to relax wage regulation. The government, knowing that the complete elimination of wage regulation would cause a Polish-like wage–price spiral, took refuge in a more relaxed system of regulation. The separate wage (incomes) regulation was abolished but enterprises had to add the increase in their wage fund to their profits before taxation if the increase was more than half the increase in value added in the enterprise. That meant that, in the case of excessive wage growth, the whole increase was taxed with the enterprise profit tax (a flat 54% at that time). If the increase was below this limit, the enterprise could avoid the extra tax.

The other positive side of the new system was that it eliminated most of the earlier exemptions (12 government decrees were annulled). Only smaller firms with a wage bill of less than Ft 20 million could be exempted (Tóth, 1990). The regulation encouraged a reduction in the number of wage-earners because the basis for the regulation was total, and not average, wage costs. The wage increase in 1989 was partly due to the new regulation, partly to the initial burst of new small firm starts. The other important event was that the National Council for Interest Reconciliation (the Hungarian abbreviation is OET) was formed. The OET advised enterprises to restrict themselves to a 3–10% wage increase, without much success.

In 1990, a large cut in real wages was necessary, given the very serious problems in East European trade and the near-insolvency in the external balances of the country. The political balance was even more fragile than a year earlier. To the credit of the economic record of the Németh government, even in this situation it did not relax the wage policy any further. The external adjustment was eased by a 5% plus real wage cut. Similarly, the Antall government stood firm in the negotiations at the end of 1990 (in spite of the political handicap caused by the taxi-drivers' blockade in November 1990). Since the government could not get broad agreement from the trade unions, it maintained the semi-regulation (or shadow regulation as it was called by one analyst) in the field of wages.

For the first time regulation was not based on the performance (value added or profit) of the firm. Those enterprises not exceeding 18% growth in the wage bill had no problems; those between 18% and 28% had to add the sum above 18% to their pre-tax profit, i.e. were liable to the flat-rate profit tax, while firms increasing their wage bill beyond 28% had to add the whole increment to the profit. The government applied the regulation to virtually all economic units except joint ventures and small firms (less than Ft 20 million yearly wage bill) (Góczánné, 1991; Popper, 1991). There was no discussion of differentiating between the different ownership forms, although economic rationality would have called for it. It is not just that in private firms there is a natural limit to wage growth, but, by liberalizing the wage policy for private firms and fixing it in firms with majority state ownership, the economic policy could have built into the system an aggressive incentive for enterprises to transform into predominantly private firms. The other option could have been what the Poles applied – differentiating between the incorporated sector (whether private or not) and the state sector.

Progressive personal income tax was introduced in Hungary in 1988 and this undoubtedly helped to keep wage growth under control; higher than 'planned' increments would have incurred progressive, i.e. increasingly high, taxation.

The regulation of wages in 1992 was more complicated than the previous rules as it was not clearly established at the outset but depended on the behaviour of the firms. If the average level of wage growth in the economy did not exceed 23%, no wage regulation would apply. If it did, however, the firms exceeding 28% would have to add the *whole* increment to their profits, i.e. it would be liable to the flat-rate profit tax. Moreover, if the inflation rate was above 21%, the OET was to decide in December about the appropriate adjustment of the key numbers. The good news is that this formula was agreed in OET, i.e. this time social consensus was achieved between the government and the representatives of the employees and employers. The agreed formula nevertheless carries some risks as well. First of all, the system would tolerate an almost 2% real wage increase. If the liquidity position of the firms allowed, they might increase their average wages (since there had been a shift from regulation of the wage bill towards average wages) by an additional 5 percentage points without risking the penalty tax. The government was counting on the cautiousness of firms and on the fact that the liquidity positions differed so greatly that even the 28% ceiling was enough to achieve an average below 23%. The regulation now applied to any firm with more than 10 employees, i.e. even joint ventures were not exempted.

The system worked reasonably well in 1992 partly because the liquidity pressure was particularly strong as a result of the new bankruptcy regulation. This combined with the changing labour market in consequence of unemployment considerably to decrease the upward pressure on wages. One can, however, read a slightly different message from the data as well: in spite of the extraordinary liquidity situation of enterprises, there was still an approximately 21.5% wage increase, i.e. real wages decreased only marginally. It means that one cannot yet assume that the socialist phenomenon of strong upward pressure on wages is already behind us. In a different macroeconomic situation it might come back, although certainly not in its clear 'socialist' form.

The whole system also cries out for lower-level (local, branch, etc.) agreements because of the general shortage of information. The regulators, trying to decentralize responsibilities, themselves attempt to establish such practices. This might make the wage negotiations overpoliticized at times when the enormous organizational changes would otherwise require much more (especially downward) wage flexibility. Under the banner of liberalization of wage policy, other rigidities can be implanted. Furthermore, the present system might exacerbate wage competition among state enterprises if their liquidity position allows that. Thus even some relaxation of monetary policy would shift liquidity from the enterprise sector to households, causing an adverse impact on the trade balance. The government might have been able to bring inflation under control more rapidly than it did in 1992, since wages could have pushed up the incomes of households as well as the costs of the firms. I do not, however, expect a dramatic impact on inflation from the side of wages. Economic barriers already work more strongly here than in the case of the central budget. It would nevertheless be a mistake to think that the potential for wage–price inflation has already totally disappeared from the Hungarian economic system. For that we have to wait until the share of the private sector becomes overwhelming.

7   The Labour Market and Unemployment

Open unemployment appeared in Hungary relatively late, basically in 1990. Its level has increased steadily, however, month by month, during the transformation and reached about 12% of the active population at the end of 1992 (see Table 5.4). Actually the rate of growth of the number of unemployed has shown some significant deceleration recently, but one should wait for some time before drawing any conclusion from this. The situation is much worse in the eastern and north-eastern part of the country, while in the west it is only about 8–10%. The situation is best in Budapest where the rate of unemployment is only 5.9%, although recently the growth in unemployment has been sharpest in the capital.

Unemployment hits the unskilled workforce hardest, but educated young people are now increasingly experiencing it. Unemployment has grown very rapidly: its level was still only 80,000 (1.7%) at the end of 1990, while it will be around 900,000 by the end of 1993 (17–18%) according to official forecasts. As a new phenomenon, rural unemployment grew rapidly in 1992, reaching 120,000 (according to earlier forecasts) at the year-end.

In regional comparison Hungary's position is not that bad though; only in

Table 5.4 Main Data on Unemployment at the End of Periods,
December 1991 – October 1992

Period	No. of registered unemployed ('000)	Unemployment rate (%)
Dec 1991	406	7.5
Jan 1992	443	8.2
Feb	455	8.4
Mar	478	8.9
Apr	503	9.3
May	523	9.7
Jun	547	10.1
Jul	587	10.9
Aug	601	11.1
Sep	617	11.4
Oct	627	11.6

Source: NBH (1992) p. 12.

Romania and the former Czechoslovakia are the unemployment rates lower. In Romania, this is due to the slowness of the transformation process and a very low level of social protection, while in Czechoslovakia the level of unemployment is lower only in the Czech Republic; in Slovakia it is similar to that in Hungary.

Since unemployment is a relatively new phenomenon, the Hungarian government's reaction has been very slow and very passive until now, although it might cause the government parties a lot of pain at the next parliamentary elections. Spending has gone overwhelmingly on paying unemployment benefit from the budget of the so-called Solidarity Fund (SF). SF is financed from the wages of the employed and by the employers: employees pay 1% of their gross wages into the fund, while employers paid 5% from 1992. This, together with high social security contributions, strongly discourages legal employment, hence the danger of establishing a vicious circle: entrepreneurs hide employment from the authorities for tax reasons and are encouraged to reduce employment, while the bill of the SF grows. The central budget has guaranteed full support for the SF should it become exhausted; it was clear even when the system began that the growth in unemployment has systematically exceeded government predictions. The budget is also unable to spend more on public works, especially infrastructure projects, because of the high 'idle' deficit caused by overspending on welfare.

The main source of active policy against unemployment is the Employment Policy Fund (EPF), which had a budget of Ft 16.5 billion for 1992 (the Solidarity Fund was planned to have Ft 42 billion). More than half of this was spent in a decentralized way by the regional bureaus of the Fund. Experience with active employment support has not been too good. Only 26,000 people were involved in professional re-education programmes up to early 1992. Most of them (5,000) were from Budapest, where the unemployment rate is the lowest anyway. About one-third of the decentralized resources of the EPF were spent on direct employment creation in 1991, but even this established only 9,000 working places.

A very negative experience has occurred with the programmes aiming to turn the unemployed into entrepreneurs. Credits with low repayment costs turn out to be very risky not only for the state but also for the inexperienced would-be entrepreneurs. Only very few have really lost their employment and are potentially good individual entrepreneurs. Only 1,000 new entrepreneurs have been created by this method, and nobody knows how many of those have simply profited from the availability of cheap credit.

In Hungary, as in Poland and Czechoslovakia, unemployment benefits were too generous at first. As unemployment growth exceeded expectations, the government was forced to decrease the benefits. From the beginning of 1992, benefit was payable for 540 days (previously 720 days). During the first 360 days the benefit is equal of 70% of the previous year's average monthly income; in the remaining 180 days it drops to 50%. Because of the serious budgetary situation and large-scale abuse of the system, in 1993 the span of unemployment benefit was further reduced to one year. The primary reasons for abuse are that, on the one hand, control is lax and opportunities of jobs in the 'black economy' are plentiful and, on the other hand, the minimum wage is too high. Therefore, many enterprises can offer only unskilled jobs at less than the minimum wage, so that such workers' wages are only marginally more than unemployment benefit.[4] The lesson from this is that fighting unemployment is a complex task. It should incorporate flexibility of the wage system, an unemployment scheme that does not encourage the refusal of legal jobs, an efficient retraining scheme and some mechanisms of public infrastructure construction works for the unemployed.

Unemployment will be a major issue in Hungarian politics in the years to come. The challenge is to find free-market solutions to the problem in the face of two dangers: the not-too-pro-market government either might continue to pay too little attention to the phenomenon, or, realizing the political threat in rising unemployment, might react administratively by imposing various kinds of limitations on the freedom of employers.

8   Allocation of Labour – The Role of Public Sector Projects

A potentially sensible way of increasing employment is public works, which have been rather underutilized until now. I see significant potential here for several reasons. The first is rising unemployment. Since unemployment was almost non-existent before the recent economic transformation, its rapid growth is a real worry throughout the country. Of special concern is the fact that a growing proportion (already 20% at the beginning of 1992) of the unemployed are young, educated people who have not found employment after school. Another reason for intensifying plans for public works is the very poor state of public infrastructure in the country. Moreover, it might be relatively easy to find some foreign assistance for infrastructure projects like highway building with broader European implications.

The government is increasingly aware of the underutilized potential of public works. In 1991, on average only 11,400 people were employed on such schemes countrywide, while by October 1992 their number had increased to a mere 18,000 (*Pénzügyminisztérium, 1992*). The government hopes to create some additional employment by taking advantage of the opportunities in concessional highway construction, channelling them into the needs of the 1996 World Expo. Another government initiative is the continuation of the M3 freeway to the Hungarian–Ukrainian border. The north-eastern region of the country is the most severely hit by economic restructuring, and this project could benefit it in many ways. While these are sensible moves, they come quite late given that the free fall in economic activity had started two years before the government launched the policy.

Another important project with international significance, the Trieste–Budapest freeway, although much discussed in the Pentagonale group, has not made progress in the last three years. The project would be interesting because it could link Hungary to the part of the EC south of the Alps. This is an important consideration for a country in which Germany looms so large in its trade relations. The project would deserve strong EC backing since it has major significance not only for Hungary but also for Slovakia. Finally, another project with European significance would be the continuation of the M5 freeway to the Serbian border. With the break-up of Yugoslavia, Hungary has become a major transit country towards Greece and Turkey from the northern part of the EC. In fact, Hungary's geographical potential for that role has always been better than that of Yugoslavia but the earlier geopolitical situation did not allow it to be exploited. Now Hungary should look at this freeway with much more care and should demand EC backing for its construction. Since road infrastructure is so underdeveloped in Hungary, the rate of return on well-designed projects is unusually high, as they eliminate serious bottlenecks. The problem to be overcome in these projects is the constraint on direct financing from the state budget.

9   Explicit and Implicit Social Contracts – The Welfare Systems

In section 4, I dealt with the budget expenditure dimension of the welfare systems. However, the operation of the welfare systems is a burning issue in itself too. The government has done almost nothing since 1990 to reform the obviously disintegrating systems, and the liberal opposition, for somewhat ill-conceived ideological reasons, has not produced strong alternatives either. The record of the Hungarian Socialist Party (supposedly having social democratic values) and the trade unions has also been poor because their social concern has also been limited to criticizing something for which they, as the ex-government party, bear at least as much responsibility as the present regime.

The present government undoubtedly inherited a mess in this field, but not one major structural reform has occurred during its term.[5] The past system was characterized by universal entitlement to social security and by a total integration of the system into the central budget. Therefore it is impossible and meaningless to compare contributions with social security payments. In the last decade, as the inefficient socialist economy was no longer able to maintain an inefficient socialist welfare system, the quality of services fell dramatically.

Its burden is especially quantifiable in the catastrophic fall in the real value of pensions in the last decade, as revaluation has failed to catch up with inflation. The situation is similar, though not that easily quantifiable, in other fields as well. Paradoxically, because of the poor design of the system, especially its over-generous entitlement rules, its social costs have grown steadily over the last four decades (see Table 5.A2).

As Augusztinovics (1993) emphasizes, the cornerstone of the problem is that, although separation of the social security system has gradually occurred in recent years, it has not been correspondingly capitalized (funded). Her argument is quite convincing: ex-employees have not received (in the form of some kind of an asset portfolio) any part of the net capital formation that has occurred over the last four decades or so. She believes that the most modest estimate of this would be 40–50% of the 'tangible national wealth'. Of course there are problems with handing over such a huge package of state-owned assets to the present very inefficient and incompetent social security system, owned by the state. International evidence also tells us that public pension funds have not been the best portfolio managers in the capital markets. It is quite clear, however, that, without some degree of recapitalization of the system, the present pensioners and middle-aged and older employees will remain in a hopeless situation; their future cannot be solved through otherwise very desirable alternative private pension schemes.

The system in itself is also very inefficient. It is unable to collect firms' arrears of social security contributions, and its current operations are very poorly managed. The recent liquidity crisis of enterprises has obviously had an adverse effect on payment arrears in the economy, including the Social Security Fund (SSF). The backlog of unpaid contributions more than doubled in 1991 to Ft 52 billion (Tóth, 1992).

Worst of all, the fundamental reform of the retirement age has as a result been postponed. It is an unbearable burden on a relatively poor and also substantially ageing country's productive population that men retire and get a guaranteed pension at the age of 60 and particularly that women do at the age of 55.

Denied the net capital formation of past social security contributions and obviously also large budgetary injections, and being very inefficient anyway, the system needs to charge very high contributions to employers. Firms have to pay 44% of the gross wages of their employees into the Social Security Fund, while wage-earners pay 10%. Here I disagree with Augusztinovics, who argues that, since this is a contribution to both the health service and retirement, it is not excessive. In fact it makes Hungarian labour much less competitive than it would be just on the basis of wage differentials compared with the EC (Hungary's major trading partner). Also, it is a practical question: high contributions are a deterrent to labour-intensive investment and clearly encourage employers to conceal labour illegally. The system creates higher than necessary unemployment and encourages a rather large shadow economy. A mixture of lower contributions and capitalization of the SSF could ease the situation. Furthermore, quite strong incentives should be given to building up private pension schemes.

On the institutional level so far, the SSF was separated from the general budget in the late 1980s and the health system was shifted from the central budget to become the responsibility of the SSF. In both cases, because of the poor financial and strong institutional position of the Ministry of Finance, the operation was not equitable, i.e. the SSF was left with a worse long-term financial position. In 1991, this resulted in a deficit for the SSF, which was equivalent to the payment arrears of the economy to the social security system.

The financial situation of the Social Security Fund is not completely hopeless, but concerted action to combine privatization of some social security functions with capitalization of the SSF and a simultaneous modest unburdening of the business sector could slow down the pauperization of great masses of the population, especially the elderly. The government cannot ignore the rapid growth in the numbers living below the official minimum subsistence level. Just in the group of pensioners, Augusztinovics's sober estimate shows well above 1 million of the 10.5 million total population of the country are getting pensions below the social minimum!

What makes the situation particularly troublesome is that any major and meaningful reform of any part of the welfare system would further worsen the budget deficit before it yielded savings. For example, partial privatization of the pension system would mean that a large part of the better-paid strata would quit the state system, and consequently their contributions would disappear. In the present budget situation, this would be very painful, and any major move forward will need very significant foreign assistance.

10   Demonopolization and Competition Policy

In the communist recent past, a straightforward pro-privatization ideology was impossible until the very end of the Németh government. Therefore, and also because the state enterprises had been strongly centralized, mainstream reformist thinking went in the direction of *demonopolization*, more particularly breaking up large state enterprises. This ideology was born when import regimes were highly centralized, i.e. foreign competition could not be assumed. The demand by reformers to 'create' competition by increasing the number of (still state-owned) actors led to a decentralization campaign in the early 1980s. That campaign finally foundered on the resistance of the branch ministries, however, and only the food industry was reshaped through the elimination of most of the branch-based trusts. Nevertheless, modest decentralization of the highly concentrated state companies continued throughout the whole of the 1980s. The Ministry of Finance usually supported (sometimes with financial incentives) the division of large enterprises. Later, from 1988 one of the favourite methods of 'spontaneous' privatization also incorporated decentralization of the enterprise structures (see section 11 and Mizsei, 1990).

The number of firms has increased extremely rapidly in the last few years. The prelude to this process was undoubtedly the passing of the Company Act at the end of 1988. Since then a real explosion has occurred (see Table 5.5).

Table 5.5   The Number of Economic Organizations with Legal Entity, Year-end 1988–92

	Total	of which	
		Limited companies	Joint stock companies
1988	10,811	450	116
1989	15,235	4485	307
1990	29,470	18,317	646
1991	52,756	41,206	1,072
1992	66,121	54,222	1,584

Source: CSO (1992b).

The data are somewhat misleading because most of the new entrepreneurial units were products of the somewhat odd transitional legal regulations of the early 1980s and had to change into corporate structures or private enterprises in the late 1980s and in 1990. Therefore they do not represent new establishments. The impressive organizational innovation in the economy is without question, however, especially if we take into account that the limited or joint stock company form is much clearer in the legal sense than the previous inter- or intra-enterprise working associations (for the term and description see Marer, 1986).

Furthermore, the number of unincorporated private units is also huge, exceeding 500,000 at the end of 1991. It is encouraging that one cannot see any relaxation of the boom of new establishments even in 1991.

According to the estimates of the Central Statistical Office (CSO), industrial production decreased by 23.2% in companies employing more than 300 people, while it increased by 50% in firms employing fewer than 50 workers in 1991 – although it is also true that the former were still responsible for 84.1% of total industrial production, and the latter for only 6.1% (see Table 5.6). In industrial exports the concentration is even higher.

Table 5.6   The Structure of Industrial Production, Employment and Export
Production, 1991

| Size of firm according to employment | Production | | Employment distribution (%) | Export production distribution, current prices (%) |
	Distribution, current prices (%)	% change over 1990		
> 300	84.1	-23.2	76.4	88.1
50–300	9.8	- 4.3	16.6	8.8
< 50	6.1	+50.1	7.0	3.1
Total	100.0	-19.1	100.0	100.0

Source: CSO (1992a), p. 11.

In terms of employment in the whole economy (i.e. not just in industry), concentration is much lower. Firms with more than 300 employees employed only 8.8% of the active population in 1990 compared with 23.3% in 1988 (see Table 5.7). Concentration in industry is obviously much higher, since most of the small firms are in the trade and service sectors.

The anti-monopoly regulation of the present period started with the Company Act in 1988, which limits the cross-ownership of joint stock companies and protects the rights of the smaller shareholders. The act did not try to prevent cross-ownership in other corporate forms, however, although limited companies became much more typical than the joint stock form. The Transformation Act of mid-1989 has a broader scope: it affects every corporate form (Voszka, 1991).

The Competition Act was introduced at the beginning of 1991. As Voszka shows, this law follows primarily German legal practice by penalizing not the existence of a monopolistic situation but the concrete abuse of that situation. The regulation gives the Competition Agency broad scope for discretion in forbidding or permitting a monopolistic situation. Permission can be given, for example, if it would improve international competitiveness.

Table 5.7 Changes in the Size Structure of the Hungarian Economy, 1988-90 (%)

| Year | Number of employees | | | | | |
	<20	21-50	51-300	> 300	No data available	Total
1988	18.7	14.5	28.2	23.3	15.3	100.0
1989	33.5	15.7	22.7	17.2	10.9	100.0
1990	55.9	14.0	15.2	8.8	6.1	100.0

Source: Voszka (1991), Table 4.

The main problem with the Competition Act is that it does not provide any competence to review the existing large state monopolies inherited from the socialist past. The preliminary drafts in 1989 envisaged the formulation of some transitional rules, which would have given some competence to the Competition Agency. It was precisely the leading architects of competition policy and law, however, who resisted the broadening of their competence. Their actions were influenced by the bad example of the administrative decentralization campaign in the early 1980s. One should ask, however, if the democratic political power structure could not have produced a different outcome had a modest decentralization campaign been launched. At least an overview of the organizational structure of state enterprises should have been accomplished after the political changes. The new government elite has missed this chance in spite of the suggestions of experts, including those in the Blue Ribbon Commission (Hungary, 1990). One thing is certain: any effort to review the organizational structures will meet with much more resistance and will require more political effort than it would have done in the second half of 1990. As Voszka rightly stresses, now no legal act prescribes state action against *existing* monopolies.

Apart from the legal structures, i.e. automatic mechanisms against monopolies, the government established a Demonopolization Committee by means of a decree in early 1990. Not only the way this committee was established, but also the efficiency of its work, reminds one of the Coordinating Committee of the early 1980s. The committee worked under the chairmanship of the secretary of state in the Ministry of Finance and involved people from the Competition Agency, the SPA, and representatives of branch ministries. Because of the negative attitude of the latter, the committee was not able to establish any list of firms that would be divided. Because of the forthcoming election in 1994 it is decidedly unlikely that any administrative action aimed at decentralization will occur in the foreseeable future. The government has lost a unique political opportunity to break up at least some of the obviously harmful state monopolies in order to prevent the creation of private monopolies out of them. One should note that the usual argument, that import liberalization makes this kind of 'administrative' interference in the organization of the state enterprises unnecessary, is somewhat shortsighted since privatization of the state monopolies would create very strong incentives to abuse monopoly powers to maintain import restrictions like quotas, temporary tariffs, anti-dumping protection, etc. This kind of pressure has already grown visibly in the last two years.

One should also note that the formation of the State Holding Corporation (SHC) has created a new, even more powerful state holding structure with a lot of opportunities to soften the budget constraint. The branch ministries also bargained for extending the list of state firms that could enter the umbrella organization. And it is also obvious that, contrary to the goals of privatization, the political forces behind the establishment of SHC were very much interested in pulling in as many profitable enterprises as possible. After the formation of the holding it will be much more difficult to privatize them than it would have been without it, despite statements to the contrary by the politicians responsible for the privatization and management of state property.

11   Privatization

Very few data are available with which to draw a realistic and detailed picture of the scope of the privatization process and the share of private and privatized firms in the production of GDP in Hungary. According to Mr Csepi, director of the State Property Agency (SPA), the privatization revenues of his organization amounted to Ft 40 billion in 1991. That might be about 2% of the enterprises' assets potentially subject to privatization. In another comparison it is less than 5% of the budget revenues in the same year; 85% of this money was paid in hard currencies, suggesting that effective domestic demand for privatizing firms was still extremely low. This US$770 million is more than 50% of total foreign investment in 1991. By the end of 1991, 20% of state enterprises were incorporated but, according to Mr Csepi, only 10% of ex-state firms were controlled by private investors (*Tözsde Kurir*, 30 January 1992). In 1992, the transformation of state enterprises accelerated but the share of private ownership decreased, compared with the earlier transformations. The dynamism of the so-called 'spontaneous' privatization decreased very significantly in 1992.

One should not, however, disregard the fact that, because of the very nature of the Hungarian privatization process, the most significant means of privatizing the economy is increasing the capital of existing firms as well as grassroots emergence of new private establishments. It is particularly difficult to measure the share of the private sector in GDP. According to the rather conservative estimate of KOPINT (1992a), the private sector is probably generating 30–40% of GDP, not counting the 'grey', unregistered sector.

11.1 Restitution

Because of the composition of the coalition government (which gives a significant role to the Smallholders' Party), reprivatization (restitution) was an issue for almost one and a half years after the elections and before restitution could be enacted. It was clear to the MDF politicians, as to almost everyone in Hungarian society, that reprivatization is not rational economically (most of the previous structures cannot be re-established), nor is it particularly justified from a social point of view (not only ex-owners but society at large were the victims of socialism). Therefore the government tried to minimize the costs of the politically inevitable; the way to do it was the Restitution Act.

The act envisages not reprivatization of assets but rather compensation for them. Compensation is regressive and the maximum amount is Ft 5 million (US$64,000), a relatively modest sum. It is paid not in cash, to prevent the burden from shifting to the state budget, but rather in the form of vouchers to be used to acquire shares or other forms of privatized state assets. The exception is agriculture, where vouchers can be used to acquire land through auctions. The threshold is 1947: it is promised that unlawful nationalization before that date and political grievances will be compensated at a later date.

As many of us expected, the problems have only become more complicated with the issuing of the compensation vouchers, as it turns out that there is a shortage of attractive assets to privatize in exchange for the vouchers. The situation is somewhat similar to that in the former Czechoslovakia and in Poland (if mass privatization eventually takes place), in that many owners of vouchers or the like would probably want to get rid of their securities (or even the certificates) and this will decrease the real value of the paper. The early expectation was that the market value of that paper (or the shares bought by the vouchers) would reach only 30% of the face value.[6] Although the actual market value is higher since the government issued a limited amount of bank shares (those of the Budapest Bank and Inter-Europa Bank), the vouchers cause continuous problems for the government. Organization of the issuing and distribution of the vouchers has been poor, and alternative investments with the vouchers (i.e. life insurance) have been unpopular because they would yield very insignificant regular payments. There is a strong and very obvious discrepancy between the irresponsible slogans of the government about restitution and the real possibilities for the Hungarian state to compensate the population for past grievances. At the same time, the government is sinking deeper and deeper into the morass of escalating demands from different groups for compensation for political grievances, etc. The damage has not yet been great from the macroeconomic point of view. It is just that the policy is not clear and explicit.

11.2   Decentralized Privatization

The legal basis for decentralized privatization, one of the foundations of Hungary's (relative) success story, was established by the late communist elite (for a detailed analysis of this, see Mizsei, 1990). In order to meet the enterprise managers' demands to allow foreign investment in state firms, as well as to help to solve their increasingly acute liquidity problems, parliament passed the Corporate Act at the end of 1988. The simultaneous validity of this law and the Act on Foreign Investment (itself very liberal) as well as of the 1984 legislation on the rights of the enterprise councils, resulted in the possibility of decentralized decision-making on incorporation, not only of whole firms (separately legislated in 1989) but also of parts of state enterprises. Top managers of state enterprises thus got the opportunity to become 'privatization agents' (Urbán, 1992). Because of public concern, a corrective legislative act imposed some (limited) state control over the process in early 1990. In this paper, I shall not give a detailed picture of the story of spontaneous privatization, in particular because the statistical evidence is still highly incomplete, owing partly to poor statistics (discussed earlier). The process is still going on and for a while it will have some dynamism, although many claim that it is slowing. Spontaneous privatization is one of the most important reasons Hungary has attracted such an overwhelming share, compared with the country's size, of foreign direct investment in the region. Foreign investment reached at least US$1.5 billion in 1991, out of which US$1.2 billion was invested in cash, contributing to the strong balance of payments performance and to building up a fairly safe reserve position. Preliminary data indicate that this scale of investment was repeated in 1992.

One should, however, also pay attention to signals that the spontaneous privatization component of foreign investment declined in 1992. Generally, managerial initiatives were far less dynamic than in earlier years. There is a certain dilemma about how to proceed with spontaneous privatization since the risk of corruption is obviously present. The government's reaction is at least threefold. In the course of building up its clientelist structures, the government is more and more concerned about the status quo in general. To meet the needs of the branch apparatuses (and also to satisfy World Bank demands for a more stable regulatory environment for state firms) as well as to establish positions for its clientele, the government has organized the State Holding Corporation (SHC) along the lines of the Italian ENI. The list of state enterprises incorporated in SHC has grown, and more and more profitable ones have been pulled in (see Table 5.8). For them, privatization is most probably being postponed. This is obviously bad news, especially as poor firms might be bailed out at the expense of the good ones because they belong to the same corporate structure. Furthermore, it is very dangerous to create such a huge holding organization, to which as much as 40% of the state assets (in terms of book value) might belong (Urbán, 1992).

Table 5.8 Transformation of State Enterprises into Corporate Entities, 1991–92

Date	Number	Value of property (Ft bn.)	
		Book value	Value accepted on transformation
31 December 1990	27	26.19	41.47
31 December 1991	218	345.07	465.20
31 January 1992	242	350.90	473.15
28 February 1992	260	359.40	484.78
31 March 1992	277	362.82	492.82
30 April 1992	292	366.09	494.53
31 May 1992	343	560.40	1,274.40
30 June 1992	373	572.46	1,295.49
31 July 1992	430	576.34	1,302.14
31 August 1992	445	577.31	1,303.43
30 September 1992	468	579.32	1,310.71
31 October 1992	514	609.09	1,338.84

The government has been right to think that the enterprise councils are a relic of the past system and that it should incorporate each state firm rapidly. This is a legitimate concern, but one should also care about establishing strong incentives towards privatization. This is, however, tailing off now, and, with the prospect of elections in 1994, the pace of privatization will almost certainly slow down in 1993.

In despair at the poor record of the State Property Agency in centralized privatization, the government introduced a new scheme in autumn 1991 in order to accelerate spontaneous privatization. *'Self-privatization'* is targeted at the relatively smaller firms (at first those with less than 300 employees and Ft 300 million assets, but then extended; now involving potentially Ft 95 billion of state assets). The declared goal has been that these firms *must* be privatized quickly. The state enterprises themselves choose a consultant from the list of about 50 private consultants picked by SPA. Afterwards the consultant acts in the name of SPA, and the state enterprise has no right to veto its privatization scheme. The SPA exercises only random control over the process. A quick sale of most of these firms was expected, but lack of demand as well as uncertainty following the wave of bankruptcies in the first half of 1992 slowed the conclusion of deals. By the middle of 1992, only 20 firms had been sold and 150 incorporated out of the more than 400 enterprises included in the programme.

Although it is too early to evaluate the self-privatization process, its assumed success has encouraged the government to expand the model. After a stormy intra-government struggle, the SPA announced the 'second wave' of self-privatization in autumn 1992. Here the upper limit is 1,000 employees or

Ft 1 billion asset value, but the limits are to be treated flexibly.

Another important method of privatization in Hungary is the 'investor-initiated path'. Investors, mostly Western, pick firms and negotiate with the SPA. Some significant cases (a refrigerator factory, sugar factories, a canning factory, etc.) have already been handled this way.

11.3 Privatization by the SPA

Centralized privatization has a very poor record. In 1990 the First Privatization Programme (FPP) was initiated in order to sell 20 firms. In spite of the fact that even here the job was leased out to consultant firms, the results are meagre: only 3 of the 20 privatization cases have been completed so far. Similarly, the privatization of most of the quality hotels, utilities, Hungarian Telecom, etc., has not yet been concluded. The management of centralized privatization should be improved considerably within the SPA.

The sale of a majority stake in Malev, the Hungarian airline, to Alitalia, the Italian airline, however, has been concluded. This deal, the first in the airline business in the region, has brought in considerable foreign exchange as well as the hope of massive investment in the profitable but underfunded company. In late 1992, two successful privatizations through the capital market aimed to improve the reputation of the rather dormant stock exchange.

11.4 Small Privatization

The small privatization has so far produced much less spectacular figures than in Poland or in Czechoslovakia. A significant part of the large trade networks were able to escape piecemeal sale by incorporating themselves earlier. After the passage of the Pre-privatization (Hungarian jargon for small privatization) Act, the SPA was able to involve 10,000 shops in the scheme. Of these, 20% proved to be inappropriate for small privatization. Only 30% of the remaining 8,000 can be privatized fully, while the rest will have to be rented to private entrepreneurs. The process will probably take some three to four years to complete. Some 4,000 units were sold or leased during 1991-2. In sum, the establishment of small private shops and other retail outlets in their own right without involving privatization is far more significant than small privatization itself (*Jelentés...*, 1992).

One of the serious problems of small-scale privatization (or renting to private entrepreneurs) is that, by auctioning, the SPA sometimes achieves excessively high prices. In order to compensate for this, various cheap credit schemes have been started. While these might be justified in the case of larger bids by *domestic* buyers (still not a totally riskless exercise because there is no guarantee that the management of the acquired assets will be sound), when faced with strong foreign bidders cheap credit only pushes up the price of the small assets, which could lead to unfair competition if not all the applicants have access to the preferential rates. If it is generally available, what preferential credit means in practice is the channelling of budget resources into the SPA and local government hands through the intermediation of privatization. Preferential credit should be abandoned in the case of small privatization, and the sellers should assist with appropriately lower prices. Another problem is that too many transactions in fact involve only lease contracts rather than straight sale of ownership. Where possible, sale should be given a clear preference.

12   Bankruptcy and Liquidation

Bankruptcy has been regulated by law only since 1 January 1992 in Hungary. In spite of this, among the post-communist countries of the region, with the exception of Yugoslavia (because of the earlier institutionalization of the market economy there than elsewhere), bankruptcy has the longest history in Hungary. Liquidation was first regulated through a government decree in 1986, and restructuring (composition) in 1988 also by decree.

Most of the cases filed with the courts were filed by businesses not receiving their due payment. Out of 528 cases in 1991, only 8 were initiated by banks and just 5 by the Social Security Fund. For different reasons these players had little motivation to do so (KOPINT, 1991). All available evidence suggests that, quite understandably, the liquidity position of enterprises (especially the larger ones) deteriorated during 1991. Payment arrears to the Social Security Fund and the tax authority grew much more rapidly than inflation, i.e. the financial discipline of firms clearly worsened in this period.

A general problem is the lengthy process of liquidation and composition cases in courts. The main reasons have been the overburdening of inexperienced

Table 5.9   Number of Liquidation Cases in the Hungarian Economy, 1986-91

Year	Number of applications to liquidate a firm	Of these, for reasons of insolvency
1986	5	–
1987	71	10
1988	144	9
1989	384	40
1990	630	62
1991	528[1]	78

Note:
1   Data for the first half of the year.

Source: KOPINT (1991).

court staff, uncertainties over asset evaluation, lack of experience of the players and abuse of the law, especially by smaller companies. In the case of large companies, an additional problem is their political and social significance and sometimes their bargaining power.

One of the novelties of the Bankruptcy Law, passed in the autumn of 1991, is that it obliges enterprises to file for financial restructuring (called 'bankruptcy'[7] in Hungary) within eight days if their payment arrears exceed 90 days. If an enterprise has experienced restructuring proceedings in the previous three years, it has to file for liquidation. One rightly expected a large increase in the number of bankruptcy cases after the new law's introduction.

The law provides for Chapter 7 and Chapter 11 type (liquidation or financial reorganization) cases. In financial reorganization, firms have 90 days (this can be extended by the court by another 30 days) to arrive at a restructuring agreement with their creditors. Unanimous consent is required. Both regulations are rigid; 120 days might not be enough to structure a complicated deal for a large organization, while unanimous consent gives ample room for free-riding on the side of small creditors.[8] The law provides for a 'debtor in possession' solution to corporate governance in insolvency but the creditors may demand the nomination of a trustee at their expense. The rights and duties of the incumbent management and the trustee are, however, not clearly defined.

In spite of some inconsistencies, the new law is an important and, in the post-communist economies, unprecedented step towards the rule of law in the economy. It is fair to say, however, that the Bankruptcy Law assumes a functioning market economy and does not reflect the peculiarities of the Hungarian economy in its transformation.

Most Hungarian analysts expected an avalanche of enterprise bankruptcies as a result of the passing of the new law. The first mass filing of bankruptcies occurred on 8 April 1992. In fact, that month witnessed a major wave of filings. Its scale was less dramatic, however, than many analysts and the whole economic and popular press indicated. In May, the number of new filings had already decreased substantially and in June the figures returned to the pre-April magnitudes (see Table 5.10).

Nevertheless, while the number of new reorganization and liquidation cases can be regarded as normal, the overall situation cannot. Because the bankruptcy process is so slow, the backlog of unfinished cases is huge and growing. They represent 9% of the firms; however, their weight in the economy is obviously much greater. At an international bankruptcy symposium, organized by the author, the Minister of Finance revealed that one-quarter of Hungarian GDP is produced in organizations in the process of reorganization or liquidation.

The single most important barrier to implementing the Bankruptcy Law has been the extremely limited capacity of the courts, compared with the large number of cases. The Budapest Court is responsible for processing 30–40% of bankruptcy cases. Yet the court has only eight judges qualified to conduct

Table 5.10   Number of Reorganizations and Liquidations filed in 1992

1992	Reorganization		Liquidation	
	Initiated	Finalized	Initiated	Finalized
1st quarter	786	285	2617	120
April	2259	205	1281	161
May	201	465	837	202
June	145	482	927	166
July	154	300	699	219
August	113	69	701	210
1992 total	3658	1806	7062	1078

Source: Heti Vilaggazdasag, 28 November 1992, p. 90.

bankruptcy cases. On average, one judge deals simultaneously with 147 restructuring and 337 liquidation cases. Delays are therefore formidable at the courts.

One cause of the seriously inadequate capacity of the courts is that neither the Ministry of Finance nor the Ministry of Justice realized at the time of elaborating the new Bankruptcy Law how many new cases would occur as a result of the new regulation.

The Economic Collegium of the Budapest Court repeatedly urged the government in 1991 to extend the financial resources of the court by Ft 1 billion so that the apparatus could meet the increased needs. This investment is relatively minor compared with the enormous direct economic importance of the bankruptcy regulation. Yet the government did not clearly appreciate the benefits of the Ft 1 billion investment and did not transfer any significant additional financial resources to the commercial courts.

The second bottleneck at the courts is the lack of well-qualified judges. In the hurry to prepare and manage quick-fix programmes, the less spectacular, but vitally important longer-term institution-building sometimes gets less attention. Communism did not need a legal system in the Western sense. It is not easy to rectify this damage. Nevertheless, special programmes should have been launched to improve the professional level of judges. Similarly, fields of the legal profession that were neglected before the political transformation, such as bankruptcy, should be included in the regular legal training at universities.

Because of the tremendous burden on them, the judges usually do not start proceedings on time. If at all possible, they send back an application by referring to technical errors. Even if this does not happen, the courts initiate proceedings not within 15 days after filing but usually after a few months.

By the end of August 1992, roughly half of the reorganizations filed had been initiated. It is important to emphasize that a relatively large proportion of these actually arrived at some conclusion. Roughly two-fifths of the cases were finalized by then and almost two-thirds of these ended in agreement between the debtor and creditors. This is noteworthy even if it is known that, because of lack of experience, in some cases this only means a postponement of liquidation. Also, one might be surprised at the proportion of successfully concluded agreements in the light of the requirement of unanimous consent. Some creditors might have been motivated by the incredible slowness of liquidations; this is a powerful weapon in the hand of debtors, since creditors would enter the liquidation process with the prospect of recovering only a very small share of their assets after a very long period of time.

Experience shows that creditor passivity (Mitchell, 1993) was at least partly overcome in Hungary in 1992. This has been the first such situation in the whole transforming post-communist Europe. One should, however, emphasize the partial nature of stronger creditor activity. So far, mainly suppliers have initiated bankruptcies. Their eagerness is often motivated by the effort to avoid the bankruptcy of their own business. The question in this respect is whether, if the process eases, either by modification of the regulation or because the courts are unable to provide a credible procedure because of long delays in handling particular cases, this activity will be maintained. In other words, so far the new Hungarian regulation has contributed to the clarification of property rights but the process has not yet become totally irreversible, especially now that the banks are being much more lenient towards their clients. Their motivation is also rational and justified: having such a huge increase in doubtful and non-performing assets in their books, they would like to spread out the bankruptcies over time.

Still, even for the banks, 1992 was a tremendously important year of learning. Experience shows that some of the banks adjusted their internal organization considerably in order to secure better credit evaluations as well as to process doubtful cases more efficiently.

In the short run, the draconian measures of the Bankruptcy Act have caused some further contraction of GDP in Hungary. My hypothesis is that the most important single reason for the prolonged decline in GDP in 1992 was the massive wave of bankruptcies. One can reasonably argue, however, that, with this bill implemented, economic reform in Hungary is now ahead of the other transforming economies in this field. But the introduction of the new rules could have been better designed.

In the case of many large state firms or enterprise conglomerates (sometimes with complicated ownership structure), the government has not taken the risk of letting the bankruptcy legislation be applied impartially. It has been announced that 13 industrial giants, which had specialized in the Russian market until the end of the 1980s, will receive special treatment.[9] In some cases, this means state subsidies so that privatization of parts of the firms can move ahead; in other cases subsidies or debt forgiveness are not connected with privatization but are perceived as a necessary investment in the salvation of an important national industry. Almost all the enterprises on the list are from the machine-building and chemical branches. With the creation of the list the Hungarian government kept up the tradition, long a target of strong criticism in the economic profession, that some large firms are treated as 'particularly important' and receive preferential treatment from the central authorities. Now the scale of the privileges is different: in the early 1970s the Central Committee of the Communist Party singled out 50 firms for extra privileges. Similar dangers stem from the creation of the State Holding Corporation at the end of 1992. It is highly doubtful if the rigour of the Bankruptcy Law will reach the companies belonging to the SHC. It might well turn out that the political bargaining power of the SHC will be able to protect and, ultimately, to subsidize them.

13   Trade Restructuring – Shift of Exports to Western Markets

Hungarian trade reorientation was the strongest, together with that of Poland, among the East and Central European countries in 1990 and 1991, although even in the past Hungary was by far the most westward-oriented country of the Soviet bloc. Nobody in Hungary expected such a strong reorientation, which was a result of very restrictive monetary policy and of surprisingly successful adjustment at the firm level to the new market conditions. As mentioned in section 3, the export boom happened in spite of the real appreciation of the domestic currency. Moreover, import liberalization has brought producers access to supplies onto a rational basis, and many enterprises were able to benefit from this.

Trade data were very unreliable during the whole of 1991. One reason for this is that the data collection had to shift from export and import permissions to customs evidence. The other problem is that the structure of trade changed so dramatically that comparison with 1990 raises many methodological problems. Manipulation of the trade data was also an instrument of the political conflict between the Ministry of Foreign Economic Relations (MFER) and NBH. MFER tried to make the picture bleaker than it really was and therefore they counted foreign investments in kind, as well as leasing and the import part of cooperation with foreign firms, as 'normal' imports. After a public dispute over the issue, the MFER produced so-called gross and net import data sets.

According to the broader concept, the foreign trade deficit in 1991 was US$1.5 billion, but according to the more realistic, narrower one it was only US$400 million (*Világgazdaság*, 13 February 1992). One should also take note of the fact that, in spite of the extraordinarily good results in 1991 (given that the Soviet market collapsed, while Hungary had to pay for its vital imports from the Soviet Union in hard cash), the trade balance shows a US$1.35 million deterioration compared with 1990. This is more than 12% of the total export volume in 1991.

Even in the middle of the 1980s the CMEA region accounted for half of Hungarian exports. In 1990, its share was only 27% while in 1991 it was a mere 19%! Exports grew most dynamically to the EC countries. In 1991, 47% of export revenues came from exports to the markets of the European Community. Their share was 36% in 1990. The share of the EFTA countries grew from 12% to 15%. Hungary's biggest export market is the united Germany, with more than a quarter of total exports. The share of the Soviet Union decreased to 13%, while that of Austria was the third largest at 11%.

Interestingly enough, deliveries of industrial consumer goods grew fastest in Hungarian exports to the German market. A significant factor might be that East German consumer goods 'exports' to West Germany became too expensive owing to strong implicit appreciation of its currency after the monetary union. Therefore parts of that market niche might have been filled by cheap, low-quality Hungarian goods. However, the export dynamism of industrial consumer goods to the whole EC region has been very strong – up 96% in current forint prices (KOPINT, 1992a). The other main items of Hungarian exports to Germany (and also to Austria) are foodstuffs and low value-added materials.

While a positive feature of trade reorientation is that Hungary is competing in markets that demand greater quality, the shift of exports from the Soviet Union to the EC also means that the branch structure of exports (and also of industrial production) *in general* has become seemingly less 'developed'. The high share of machinery and manufactured industrial goods in Hungary's Soviet exports in the past represented a 'quasi-developed' branch structure, however, as Jánossy rightly noted as early as the late 1960s; 1991 and 1992 illustrated the truth of this analysis: the reorientation of the more sophisticated industrial products has proved to be the most problematic, although their export expansion towards Western markets was relatively strong. The reason for this is that the dynamic export growth of machines to Western countries has not compensated for the sudden collapse of the once (artificially) large Soviet and other East European markets.

In 1992 the main trend continued: exports grew fastest to the EC (although Germany's share slipped a bit) (see Table 5.11). The share of developed countries increased further, while that of developing countries actually decreased further. As regards the East European region, the worst is over, and both exports and imports increased substantially. In spite of the fact that the forint appreciated further in real terms, the trade balance too improved in 1992: exports grew in dollar terms by 12% (because of the devaluation of the US currency – in volume terms it is significantly less, about 5%) while imports shrank by 3%. As suggested in section 3, however, it is not at all clear if this exchange rate policy is sustainable in 1993.

Hungary, like Poland, signed its Association Agreement with the EC at the end of 1991 (for a summary analysis of the treaties, see CEPR, 1992). The treaty

Table 5.11: Geographical Trends of Hungarian Foreign Trade,
January–June 1992

Country	Imports Value (Ft bn.)	Imports Index (Jan-Jun 1991 = 100)	Exports Value (Ft m.)	Exports Index (Jan-Jun 1991 = 100)
Total turnover	408,494	96.4	402,668	119.0
East European countries	111,019	123.0	83,462	122.4
USSR	86,520	146.2	58,357	126.5
EC	168,031	97.8	198,692	132.1
Germany	88,323	99.3	107,928	126.2
EFTA	77,662	99.3	57,540	109.8
Austria	55,338	100.6	42,119	113.4

Source: NBH (1992)

is the subject of controversy, primarily because many observers believe it is not generous enough. So far, opening of the EC market has secured the dynamism of export expansion of the Visegrad countries. In the coming years, however, improvement will be very modest, and the oft-quoted aphorism seems to be particularly justified in this case: if the West does not let the goods of the East in, it will have to face people coming out.

14 Restructuring of Production

The collapse of the markets for Hungarian firms has left economic policy unprepared as far as industrial policy is concerned. Changes were quite dramatic in 1991–2, but their character is not yet clear. The share of the OECD countries in Hungarian exports has increased enormously, while the market share of the Soviet Union and other ex-CMEA countries has decreased.

Trade reorientation has also meant that the Hungarian industrial structure shifted towards a higher share of less sophisticated, more energy-consuming production. Detailed data are available only for firms employing more than 50 people, which makes the picture of changes in the branch structure of production somewhat distorted. According to these incomplete data, the strongest decline (34.9%), occurred in the machine industry in 1991. Its share in total industrial production fell from 20.8% to 17.2%. Within the industry, the decline was steepest in the more high-tech industries such as electronics as well as the strongly CMEA-dependent car industry. In these sub-branches, production was down over 40% from the previous year. The collapse was also strong in the metallurgical and construction materials industries (see Table 5.12).

The decline in the chemical industry was about average (18.5%), but without the more capital-intensive and less labour-intensive oil refining and gas production the shrinkage was stronger, about 26.7%. In the rubber and pharmaceutical industries, the collapse was 30%, while in the production of fertilizers and pesticides it was more than 40%.

At the same time, mining activity fell by only 10.9%, production of electrical energy by only 8% and the food industry by 9.7%.

Table 5.12   Industrial Production in Firms with More Than 50 Employees, 1989-91

Branch	1989	1990	1991	Distribution among branches (%) 1990	1991
		Previous year = 100			
Mining	94.8	88.2	89.1	5.6	6.4
Electrical energy	102.2	100.2	92.0	7.0	8.2
Metallurgy	104.4	81.0	67.3	9.1	7.8
Machinery	100.2	83.8	65.1	20.8	17.2
Construction materials	98.4	95.0	67.0	3.3	2.8
Chemical industry	96.1	94.6	81.5	20.5	21.3
Chemical industry without energy sub-branches	96.4	91.9	73.3	11.7	10.9
Light industry	95.2	88.3	75.1	12.0	11.5
Food industry	101.0	99.1	90.3	21.1	24.3
Total industry	99.0	90.8	78.5	100.0	100.0

Source: CSO (1992b).

Industrial capacities have been increasingly underutilized in the period of the market reorientation. Data are available only for firms with more than 300 employees. Machines were used for 53.2% of total available time in 1990, but only 41.8% in 1991. The average number of shifts has also decreased from 1.60 to 1.26. While industrial productivity decreased by 19%, employment also fell. Therefore the labour productivity decline was only 10.2%. (In industries with more than 50% utilization of machines this is only 9.4%.)

The decline in industrial production halted in 1992 at the level of December 1991. Since there was a continuous decline in 1991, the yearly data actually show about 12% drop for 1992. In the last months of 1992, however, production was higher than in December 1991, revealing the beginnings of a possible slight economic recovery (NBH, 1992).

The big question is how the industrial culture, established in the era of forced socialist industrialization, can survive the recent shock. This is the core of the debate about industrial policy in each of the East European countries. Different political structures produce different balances of power between supporters of orthodoxy in economic policy and representatives of more interventionist policies. Quite apart from the validity of the two philosophies, however, one should stress that the interventionist camp has not been able to present any appealing alternative to the policies of financial stringency in any of the countries of the region. One reason is that the structural changes have been so sweeping that analytical thinking could not keep up. Another reason is that the information system of the economy has collapsed, and analysts have moved *en masse* into government; they are overburdened with bureaucratic duties and cannot make serious efforts at structural analyses of the changes and comparative advantages of their countries' economies. Third World analogies are totally misplaced: in Hungary the question is not which branches should lead an industrialization process, but which will close down as a result of opening up to international cooperation.

Interventionist ideologies seem to have much less political support in Hungary than in some other transforming countries, except the Czech Republic. This statement needs to be qualified: the Balcerowicz group in Poland was less interventionist than the Antall government, but it lacked the political stability needed to realize its perhaps more radical reform programme. Hungarian slowness and pragmatism seem to work relatively well in regional comparison. On the other hand, the efficiency of the Hungarian government was also seriously weakened by the fact that both philosophies were represented in the government and often caused serious policy debates. In the first Antall government, the Ministry of Industry teamed up with MFER and with Mr Matolcsy, head of the Prime Minister's cabinet, against the financial stringency represented by the Ministry of Finance under the leadership of Mr Rabár. After personnel changes in the government in December 1990, the internal conflicts of the government became less intense, but the economic policy concept of the MFER (for instance) completely differed from the Kupa programme.

The situation can also be characterized with the statement that, whatever the intensity of the attacks on the policies of the Ministry of Finance in different situations, the fragile situation of the budget always prevented the development of strong interventionism. Since Hungary's political mechanisms are stable, the government's internal fights have never caused political crisis, so the interventionist alternative has not yet received any strong mandate to realize its vision, unlike in Poland under the Olszewski government. However, even there the government's room for manoeuvre was so small that it could not destroy the achievements of the Balcerowicz programme. On the other hand, the political parties backing the present Hungarian government are much more inclined to accept various kinds of state interventionism than are the two liberal opposition parties. Therefore, and because the government wants to produce some spectacular results for the 1994 elections, the political consensus over the orthodoxy of economic policy is quite fragile. In 1992, the voices demanding the acceleration of growth became very loud again in government circles.

The government has not elaborated any alternative ways of cushioning industrial firms from the combined effects of the collapse of the Eastern markets and the restrictive economic policy. In 1989, it was already clear that the main export companies, oriented to the Soviet markets, should be privatized by finding strong Western partners able to finance product restructuring. In reality not many such privatizations have been achieved in the period of the Antall government. The general reason for this, beyond the particularities of each case, is the rather poor organization of cooperation between the affected government institutions. In consequence, the value of these firms has drastically declined as their liquidity position has deteriorated. (The Tungsram case, the only privatization success story among large industrial exporters, was decided upon under the Németh government, as were the large foreign investments in the car industry.)

The most important case of poor management of state assets in big industry is that of Videoton. The company had been in bad shape since 1989, but the government had not been able to attract foreign investors or to solve industrial conflicts over the number of workers to be laid off. Eventually a decision was made according to which the leading industrialist of the governing party was able to buy decisive influence in one of the largest Hungarian companies with a very low cash payment for the investment. The public risk of this decision is high: Videoton needs a massive capital injection, which Mr Széles is unlikely to be able to provide. The advantage of a multinational company would have been that it could have helped with market access, which Mr Széles does not have. Moreover, a multinational company would have been much more likely to be able to provide the necessary management expertise than the Hungarian owner, who has successfully managed a rapidly growing but still rather small (compared with Videoton) private firm. In other words, there is a great risk that the politically influential owner will now succeed in attracting more financial support (direct or implicit subsidies) from the state.

One also should note that other troubled industries have also eventually been bailed out by the government when political risk has been involved. This was the case with the whole mining industry, as well as with the Szd metallurgical works. I do not, however, want to blame the government too much for its cautiousness: ultimately it bears the political risk of the social tensions that the liquidation of firms and whole branches would entail. What is worrying is that this cautiousness and conflict avoidance might become a general attitude of the government, although since 1992 it has been able to risk more decisive action than in 1991, when the market reorientation in itself caused sharp conflicts.

The government has done virtually nothing towards restructuring firms in trouble. In early 1991, the two camps in the government had a heated debate about the possible effects of the dollarization of Soviet trade. Industry demanded large subsidies, which the MOF tried to resist. Financial orthodoxy triumphed, but the government could perhaps have designed other, less costly, institutional solutions. The export guarantee institution is still not in place after years of preparation. And, more importantly, a financial institution with the goal of restructuring deeply indebted firms was not set up until mid-1992. The government should probably have encouraged debt–equity swaps of the creditor banks. Swapping of the debt proved to be very successful in the Tungsram case; but no conscious government action followed. On the contrary, the banking law is very strict on the issue of bank equity holding.

In the autumn of 1992 the government singled out 13 state enterprises, mainly large industrial firms, for special financial rescue operations. This action will certainly have some budgetary consequences, but the scope of planned government action in terms of the enterprises involved is still relatively modest.

In regard to active interventionism by the state, in the Hungarian case (and probably elsewhere in Eastern Europe) the real efforts should at this stage be concentrated much more on catching up in productive infrastructure than on promoting the development of particular industrial branches. Even that, however, cannot be achieved without a much deeper involvement of the international private sector than would have been the case a few decades ago; the state budget is simply too overburdened to undertake financing of even the most urgent infrastructural projects.

15   Financial Institutions and Intermediation

Although banking is dealt with last in this paper, that does not at all mean a low ranking on the long list of yet unsolved problems of Hungary's economic transformation. On the contrary, apart from the large budget deficit (and the huge size of the government sector itself), banking should be the highest priority of the government. Hungary, like the other communist economies, started from 'communist-type banking', i.e. a monobank with administrative distribution of cheap credit. On the other hand, Hungary started its banking reform in 1988, a year earlier than Poland and a few years before the other countries of the region. This of course makes a difference; however, the Hungarian banking system is also burdened with a huge stock of inherited bad loans and very second-rate credit evaluation practices. The money market is still somewhat oligopolistic (Várhegyi, 1992): in 1990 the three largest banks were responsible for almost half of the credits to the enterprise sector. The situation is constantly changing, but it will take time to overcome the inherited distortions of the credit market.

The prudential regulation in the new banking law (passed in autumn 1991; *Magyar Közlöny*, 1991b) has imposed tough requirements that are particularly difficult for the major creditor banks to meet. The task is not so difficult in the case of smaller banks. The asset portfolios of the large banks, inherited in rather poor shape from the central bank in 1988, deteriorated further in 1991 because of the situation in the Eastern markets. The other requirement of the new banking law, which is quite hard for the large banks to meet, is that a bank cannot have a single debtor with more than 25% of the bank's equity. Just as the enterprise sector was very concentrated in the past, so too was the credit allocation of the large banks.

Part of the problem, however, is the very low level of expertise in the banking sector after four decades of communism. Obviously, the key question in this respect is how to privatize in order rapidly to improve the professional level of banking operations but at the same to preserve a strategic position for the Hungarian state during the transitional period in the three (four if the National Savings Bank is also counted) major financial institutions. The government's somewhat justified concern has been that regulation is chaotic and the market is still fragile and distorted, so that privatized and potentially foreign-controlled banks could gain huge profits just because of the low cost-sensitivity of the state-enterprise-dominated clientele. With hindsight, though, it is clear that Hungary would have been much better off if in 1989 and 1990, exploiting the favourable momentum, it had tried to privatize at least a couple of the large banks by inviting strong foreign professional investors.

The privatization strategy that has been adopted favours gradual progress through an increase in capital mainly by outside investors. The Law on Financial Institutions requires the state to decrease its stake in banks below 25%, but only after five years (by 1997). On the other hand, no investor, except other banks, can go above 25% either. Informally the SPA thinks that bank privatization will be a long process, the pioneers of which will probably be the Foreign Trade Bank (which is not burdened with a bad portfolio and inherited the profitable foreign trade financing business) as well as the Budapest Bank, which is in a less comfortable situation but has a competent and loyal top management.

The medium-sized banks have been steadily increasing their market share in Hungary, partly because they have not inherited a loan portfolio from the past but also because these are usually joint venture operations; therefore their professionalism is higher, and they also have better access to foreign sources. In 1990-1, it was a highly profitable business to borrow abroad and to lend in Hungary. The Hungarian enterprise sector has been able to pay quite high interest rates even on hard currency loans, because of the generally expected real appreciation of the domestic currency. The foreign-owned banks had better access to the international capital markets, so they could benefit from this situation.

The wave of bankruptcies in 1992 led to a dramatic deterioration in the portfolio and in the balance sheets of the large banks. Since this coincided with the maturing of the government's plans to privatize the banks, the situation became very difficult, since if the government did not do anything about it the large state banks would have shown large negative profits for 1992. Therefore, at the very end of the year, the Ministry of Finance hastily prepared a 'credit consolidation' scheme. This allows banks to sell their bad assets to the Hungarian Investment Corporation, a newly created state institution for the support of restructuring. Loans that were declared bad in 1991 sell at 50%, assets that turned out bad in 1992 are traded at 80%, and some credits, listed by the State Property Agency, sell at face value. The assets will be replaced by 20-year government bonds. By the end of 1992 it was not clear if the government or the banks were supposed to supply the bonds. Since the conditions were not clear but time was pressing because of the end of the year, the contracts give both parties the opportunity to withdraw any part of the assets from the package by 31 March. While it is undoubtedly important to clean up the banks' portfolio, this hastily arranged settlement carries the risk of a large future cost.

16   Conclusions

At the end of 1992, Hungary could be regarded as a mixed economy. According to dispassionate, in fact rather conservative, estimates, 30–40% of GDP was being produced in the legal private sector; free pricing and liberalized trade were dominant and there was no danger of any foreseeable retreat from this. Privatization was proceeding and the country had an Association Agreement with the European Community that entails a deepening of the already quite considerable integration of the country with developed Europe.

Yet one cannot say that the transformation is already over and that there cannot be an accident on the road. The reason for this is a set of unsolved problems, both political and economic, which, if mismanaged, might lead to unfavourable developments. The political system is fairly well designed, but the level of consensus about its rules is not high; within the governing parties rather dangerous far-right ideologies are vociferous; the private sector still does not have a dominant role in the economy, and there are political forces that would like to develop the system more in a clientelist–statist direction than towards a free market; the budget taxes away and redistributes about 60% of GDP and is in chronic imbalance; banks are struggling with their bad portfolios; growing unemployment is not being handled properly, and one cannot rule out a growth in social tensions. The Kupa programme (the official economic programme of the government) has quietly been abandoned.

And yet in general the prospects of the Hungarian economy are fairly promising. Before 1990 Hungary was regarded as the only relatively successful and reforming country of the region; in 1990 the Polish 'Big Bang' diverted attention from Hungary. In 1991–2, with political chaos in Poland and more modest economic results than expected, as well as because of Hungary's good performance in 1991, attention switched back to Hungary; it was once again seen as the most successful transformer. This relatively high respect obtained especially in the international financial and business community.

In the autumn of 1992 the 'who-is-the-best-transformer' international game changed again. The surprisingly good and moderate performance of the Polish political elite under the Suchocka government increased confidence in Poland, while the emergence of 'Csurkaism' discouraged many analysts of Hungary. I expect more turns of the tide in the near future, as the transformation is in its fragile phase.

In contrast with the adequate performance of the Hungarian economy, the government is extremely unpopular in the country, according to every opinion poll conducted since the taxi-drivers' blockade (November 1990). Where does this discrepancy come from?

An easy answer would be that any government in the region introducing transformation measures would be highly unpopular. This is not entirely true, however; in Czechoslovakia, for example, the party of Mr Klaus is *the* most popular one in spite of Klaus's strong connection with the economic reforms. In comparison, the dynamism of reforms in Hungary is not that spectacular. In fact, reform measures have not been significantly more dynamic than under the Németh government. There is a legitimate argument that the success of the present period is due to the combined effect of the factors mentioned in section 3: sustained tough monetary policy, political consensus over the wage mechanism, the entrepreneurial climate in the country quite independently of the government, and the inherited and unchecked privatization by sale to incumbent managers and workers.

Empirical knowledge about the sociological effects of the recent transformation is very limited. A recent empirical study (Kolosi and Róbert, 1992) tries to give a picture of the losers and winners of the transformation. First of all, the study does not support the popular conviction that the transformation has caused a general fall in real incomes. The picture we get from the empirical analysis is rather that the broad lower strata of the population became slightly poorer between 1989 and 1991, except for the poorest, whose income position did not deteriorate. On the other hand, those who used to belong to the higher income groups before 1989 had better opportunities to gain from the transformation in terms of their real income position. Thus the income differentials in Hungarian society have clearly increased.

No occupational category can be demonstrated as 'winning' or 'losing'. It is certainly not true that a white-collar job would have been an advantage or that a blue-collar occupation would have been a disadvantage at the start. The earlier trends continued, however, in that those who could shift from the state to the private sector as entrepreneurs or employees have gained, while the ones who have remained in the state sector have been the likely losers. The empirical evidence also shows that younger men have proved to be more mobile than other sections of the society. Past managers have also been generally more entrepreneurial than others. The biggest losers have been the pensioners, as their real incomes have dropped quite significantly. This can hardly be regarded as the consequence of the last two years' transformation, however, since this tendency had already prevailed in the previous decade.

One quite dramatic development has been the increase in the number of people living below the *social minimum* in the last two years. But again: the real situation is much less disastrous than some sociologists and journalists try to suggest. According to Kolosi and Róbert (1992), the proportion of the population below the minimum level has grown from 9% to 15% - a dramatic increase, but a far cry from the often quoted 30% or 40%. Investigation of the income position of households rather than individuals shows that changes still depend much more on changes in the structure of the family (death, birth of child, divorce, etc.) than on the job mobility of the family members. Generally, the economic transformation has not (at least until now) had intolerable consequences for Hungarian society, nor has it dramatically changed the previous social structure.

Hungary has quite a good chance of producing the 'success story' of the region, as Dervis and Condon (1992) predict. One should, however, underline the odds against this. First of all, the government still does not have a workable economic programme. Good improvisation has been a great asset (of the NBH, especially), but it is high time an economic strategy was developed. The so-called Kupa programme has been quietly abandoned and the government seems to lack the intellectual capacity to elaborate a workable programme. This is a problem because otherwise the country could strive to compete with Vienna (and soon also with Prague) for the role as the leading financial and business centre in the region. Infrastructure development also needs a well-designed and structured strategy.

The other serious problem is that reform of the 'state sector' has been postponed indefinitely; the government lost its one chance right after the 1990 elections. Without reform, not only will a viable budget equilibrium be difficult to achieve, but the huge expenditure is a heavy burden on businesses and makes the recovery slower and less robust then it could otherwise be. Lastly, privatization seems to be losing its momentum, although a majority of firms are still in state hands.

The troubles of the other countries in the region pose a twofold additional threat to Hungary's prospects. First, international capital will be less interested if the country's neighbours have gloomy prospects. Second, the Bretton Woods institutions are so preoccupied with the difficulties of Poland, the Balkan countries and now also the Commonwealth of Independent States that they are satisfied with a performance that is outstanding in the region but falls well below the potential of the country.

The set of necessary policy emphases is clear from the above analysis:

(1) The government should face the painful but inevitable reform measures in the welfare sphere in order to be able to balance the central budget at a lower income redistribution level.
(2) Bank solvency and privatization should be a priority, so that bad credit allocation does not spoil the chances of recovery after stabilization.
(3) Privatization should move ahead quickly and in a decentralized way so that

the private sector dominates the economy before the end of the century.
(4) Public productive infrastructure, including Western assistance to it, should also be in the forefront of the activities of the Hungarian government.
(5) Because of the political situation, one cannot expect any active steps in these areas before the next general election, due in the spring of 1994.

Notes

1   For a good although quite partisan assessment, see Kis (1992).
2   For a superb brief analysis of the issue, see Dervis and Condon (1992).
3   The government's officially recognized four-year economic programme, announced in early 1991.
4   This mechanism has been extensively studied by János Köllö. I owe these observations to him.
5   See an eloquent and brief description of the past and present system in English in Augusztinovics (1993). Another, more extensive, analysis of the same topic is to be found in Tóth (1992).
6   'Kárpótlási jegyek a tözsdére', *Magyar Hirlap*, 17 February 1992.
7   The wording of the Hungarian Bankruptcy Law is very misleading because of this. 'Bankruptcy' in reality means financial restructuring (or composition) while 'liquidation' is the term for the Chapter 7 type procedure.
8   A superb analysis of the Hungarian legal situation was provided by Mark Homan of Price Waterhouse following a meeting organized jointly by myself and the Hungarian Ministry of Finance in October 1992. I learnt a great deal from the meeting as well as from the written comments of the Western participants.
9   'Tizenkét plusz egy valságkezelö program', *Magyar Hirlap*, 16 November 1992.

References

Augusztinovics, M (1993) 'The Social Security Crisis in Hungary', in I. P. Székely, and D. M. G. Newbery (eds.), *Hungary: An Economy in Transition,* Cambridge: Cambridge University Press.
CEPR (1992) 'The Association Process: Making It Work. Central Europe and the European Community', London: CEPR Occasional Paper No. 11.
CSO (1992a) *Tájékoztató 1991. év föbb gazdasági és társadalmi eseményeiröl,* Budapest, Central Statistical Office, February.
(1992b) 'Áttenkintés az 1991, ev föbb gazdasági és tarzadalmi esseményeiröl', mimeo.
Csurka, I. (1992) *Néhány gondolat a rendszerváltás két esztendeje és az MDF uj programja kapcsán.* Budapest: Magyar Fórum.
Dervis, K. and T. Condon (1992) 'Hungary: An Emerging Gradualist Success Story?' Paper for Conference on Transition in Eastern Europe, Cambridge, MA: NBER, February.
Góczánné, T. E. (1991) 'Vállalati szemmel az 1991. évi bérszabályozásról', *Munkaügyi Szemle.*

Hungary (1990) *Hungary in Transformation to Freedom and Prosperity. Economic Program Proposals of the Joint Hungarian–International Blue Ribbon Commission,* Budapest, April.

Jaksity, Gy. (1992) 'A költségvetési hiány tökepiaci hatásai', *Figyelö,* 30 January.

Jelentés a magyar privatizációról, 1991 (1992) Privatizációs Kutatóintézet, Budapest, February.

Juhász, P. and B. Magyar (1984) 'Néhány megjegyzés a lengyel és a magyar mezögazdasági kistermelö helyzetéröl a hetvenes években', *Medvetánc,* Nos 2–3.

Kis, J. (1992) 'Gondolatok a közeljövöröl', *Magyar Hirlap,* 24 December.

Kolosi, T. and P. Róbert (1992) 'A rendszerváltás társadalmi hatásai', *Valosag.*

KOPINT (1991) *Melléklet a konjunkturajelentés 1991/3. számához. A gyors változások területei a magyar gazdaságban* (Adatok, tények, elemzések), Budapest: Kopint-Datorg Institute for Economic Market Research and Informatics, October.

(1992a) *Konjunkturajelentés 1992/1.*

(1992b) *Konjunkturajelentés 1992/3.*

Körössényi, A. (1992) 'Demobilization and Gradualism: The Hungarian Transition, 1987–1992', prepared for Overseas Development Council, manuscript, September.

'Leértékelés tyúklépésben. Hétfôi interjú Surányi Györggyel' (1992) *NAPI,* 24 February

Magyar Közlöny (1991a) '1991:IL.tv. A csödeljárásról, a felszámolási eljárásról és a végelszámolásról', *Magyar Közlöny,* No. 117.

(1991b) '1991:LXIX.tv. A pénzintézetekröl és a pénzintézeti tevékenységröl', *Magyar Közlöny,* No. 132.

Marer, P. (1986) 'Economic Reform in Hungary: From Central Planning to Regulated Market', in *East European Economies: Slow Growth in the 1980s,* Washington DC: Joint Economic Committee, Congress of the United States.

Mitchell, J. (1993), 'Creditor Passivity and Bankruptcy: Implications for Economic Reform', in C. Mayer and X. Vives, *Capital Markets and Financial Intermediation,* Cambridge: Cambridge University Press.

Mizsei, K. (1990) 'Experiences with Privatization in Hungary', Paper presented at World Bank conference, mimeo, June.

(1991) 'Sokkal jobb nem lehetett. Vita a kormány új programjáról', *Magyar Hirlap,* No. 48, p. 9.

NBH (1992) National Bank of Hungary monthly report, August.

'Összeomlott a költségvetés', (1992) *NAPI,* 16 April

Pénzügyminisztérium (1992) *Tájékoztato az 1992. évi gazdasági folyamatokról,* December.

Popper, L. (1991) 'Bérszabályozás! Bérszabályozás?' *Munkaügyi Szemle.*

Riecke, W. (1992) 'Ülünk az inflációs bombán', *Figyelô,* 16 January.

Tóth, G. (1990), 'Elöre? Vissza? Egy helyben?' *Munkaügyi Szemle.*

Tóth, I. Gy. (ed.) (1992) 'The Hungarian Welfare State in Transition: Structure, Developments and Options for Reform', Paper prepared for the Blue Ribbon Commission.

Urbán, L. (1992) 'Privatizáció, újraállamosítás', *Népszabadság,* 23 February.

Várhegyi, É. (1992) 'Az egységes Európa kihívásai és a magyar bankrendszer', *Európa Fórum* 1(2), October.

Voszka, E. (1991) 'A privatizáció és a szervezeti decentralizáció összefüggései', mimeo.

Table 5.A1 Hungary: General Government Tax Revenue, 1986–92 (Ft bn.)

	1986	1987	1988	1989	1990 Plan	1990 Actual	1991 Plan	1991 Estimated	1992 Plan
Central government tax revenue	516.8	589.0	697.1	789.5	915.4	940.5	1126.5	1050.6	1305.5
Income taxes	98.3	120.4	123.6	147.9	181.9	211.1	292.1	284.1	384.4
Individuals	3.4	5.2	5.0	27.7	29.7	55.0	132.1	138.2	188.9
Enterprises	94.9	115.2	118.6	120.2	152.2	156.1	160.1	144.9	162.3
Payroll taxes	167.6	179.6	207.8	271.3	317.9	324.7	400.9	367.6	481.3
Social security contributions									
Employees	31.6	34.7	45.2	53.6	62.0	63.0	77.2	78.5	132.2
Employers[1]	101.6	113.2	139.0	224.9	268.0	272.0	337.2	304.8	362.0
minus government	–	4.2	0.0	21.0	25.6	27.6	36.0	42.7	46.1
Self-employed	8.1	7.9	9.3	13.8	13.5	17.3	22.5	27.0	38.5
Taxes on wages and earnings	26.3	28.0	14.3	0.0	0.0	0.0	–	–	3.8
Property taxes	17.8	19.8	0.8	–	–	–	–	–	3.8
Net wealth, corporate	17.5	19.8	–	–	–	–	–	–	–
Confiscation and other	0.3	–	0.8	–	–	–	–	–	–
Taxes on goods and services	218.2	239.5	360.5	368.1	415.6	404.6	433.4	398.9	469.2
Consumer turnover tax and excises	105.5	127.5	211.8	230.7	252.2	249.0	319.7	299.9	359.0
Producer differential turnover tax	57.3	60.6	93.9	65.9	85.5	83.0	27.0	34.0	26.0
Other domestic taxes	16.8	16.8	11.9	2.6	2.9	2.5	2.6	3.0	14.9
Import duties	32.7	34.7	36.3	48.9	57.5	53.5	81.0	63.0	68.3
Other taxes on foreign trade	5.9	–	6.6	20.0	17.5	16.6	–	–	–
Other taxes	14.9	29.7	4.4	2.2	0.0	0.0	3.1	2.1	1.0
O/w: For local authorities	–	–	–	–	–	–	–	–	–

Table 5.A1 Hungary: General Government Tax Revenue, 1986–92 (Ft bn.) (continued)

	1986	1987	1988	1989	1990 Plan	1990 Actual	1991 Plan	1991 Estimated	1992 Plan
Local government tax revenue	51.9	57.7	68.4	73.9	79.7	88.3	67.9	64.8	92.0
Income taxes	31.3	35.0	61.3	66.5	74.5	74.5	46.9	47.0	63.0
Individuals	5.0	4.3	61.3	66.5	74.5	74.5	46.9	47.0	63.0
Enterprises	26.3	30.7	–	–	–	–	–	–	–
Wage tax	13.3	14.6	–	–	–	–	–	–	–
Property taxes	5.4	5.4	6.2	6.2	4.1	6.9	–	–	–
Taxes on domestic goods and services	1.8	2.3	0.9	1.2	1.1	0.0	21.0	17.8	29.0
Other taxes	0.1	0.4	0.0	0.0	0.0	6.9	–	–	–
Total tax revenues	568.7	642.9	760.9	836.0	956.7	991.3	1144.1	1064.4	1326.3
Memorandum item:									
Social security contribution of local government	–	3.8	4.6	27.4	38.4	37.4	50.3	51.0	71.2

Note:

1   Starting in 1989, includes increased transfers to the Social Security Fund from budgetary institutions and local authorities following the unification of contribution rates.

Sources: Ministry of Finance; IMF, *Government Finance Statistics,* and Fund staff estimates.

Table 5.A2 Hungary: General Government Subsidies and Transfers, 1986–92 (Ft bn.)

	1986	1987	1988	1989	1990 Plan	1990 Actual	1991 Plan	1991 Estimated	1992 Plan
Current subsidies and transfers	390.3	401.6	458.2	537.8	562.8	595.2	633.9	601.2	633.3
Central government subsidies[1]	172.6	191.3	186.5	207.0	189.1	198.9	184.3	186.1	134.5
Consumer subsidies	59.8	66.7	44.4	44.1	39.9	40.8	31.3	42.0	17.5
Producer subsidies	15.8	16.3	14.1	5.7	7.3	7.3	26.0	25.5	18.2
Agricultural support	13.7	15.2	16.2	12.4	9.4	7.5	–	3.3	4.0
Tax rebate to exporters	21.3	24.2	18.9	22.0	17.7	24.0	27.5	26.0	26.0
CMEA price equalization	41.5	51.0	57.7	43.7	43.0	43.6	10.4	2.9	–
Import subsidies	2.9	0.1	2.8	2.1	0.3	0.0	–	–	–
Other grants	9.0	8.0	6.5	7.2	2.7	3.0	4.5	5.4	3.8
Housing loan subsidies[2,3]	8.6	9.8	25.9	69.8	68.8	72.7	84.6	81.0	65.0
Central government transfers[4]	210.0	202.4	261.6	321.4	369.2	391.5	442.6	403.1	483.1
Social security pensions	99.4	110.1	130.0	156.5	186.0	202.5	262.4	260.1	310.5
Other social security benefits	42.7	44.6	85.7	113.0	156.6	156.7	156.5	111.8	105.5
Extra-budgetary funds	33.7	35.4	35.8	29.4	23.6	21.0	18.6	31.2	67.1
Other current transfers[5]	34.2	12.3	10.1	22.5	3.0	11.3	5.1	–	–
Local government subsidies	7.7	7.9	10.2	9.4	4.5	4.8	7.0	12.0	15.7
Capital transfers[4]	17.1	26.0	20.5	11.0	6.7	7.7	8.0	12.6	11.7
Central government transfers	12.3	20.4	12.3	1.4	0.6	7.7	8.0	12.6	11.7
Local government transfers	4.8	5.6	8.2	9.6	6.1	0.0	–	–	–
Total subsidies and transfers	407.4	427.6	478.7	548.8	569.5	602.9	641.9	613.8	645.0

Table 5.A2 Hungary: General Government Subsidies and Transfers, 1986–92 (Ft bn.) (continued)

Notes:
1 State budget classification.
2 Includes Ft 12.2 billion, Ft 18.5 billion and Ft 22 billion reclassified from capital expenditures for 1989, 1990 (Plan) and 1990 (Actual) respectively.
3 Includes Ft 5.1 billion carried forward to 1988 in official presentation of subsidies on interest premiums payable on 1 January 1989; and Ft 6.9 billion of similar expenditure included in the official presentation of the 1989 budget.
4 Net of transfers within the general government.
5 Includes transfers abroad and transfers to non-profit institutions.

Sources: Ministry of Finance; IMF, *Government Finance Statistics*, and Fund staff estimates.

Table 5.A3   Impact of Budget Reform Proposals (% of market price GDP)

	1991	1995	Change
Expenditure adjustment, net			−7–8
Reductions, gross			−12
Subsidies	7	1	−6
Housing purchase	3	0	−3
Consumer price subsidies	1.5	0.4	−1.1
Transport	0.7	0.4	−0.3
Producer subsidies	2.5	0.6	−1.9
Production	1.5	0	−1.5
Export	1.0	0.6	−0.4
Pensions	10.3	8	−2
Family allowances	3.2	2	−1
Sick pay	1.2	0.2	−1
Maternity and child care benefits	0.9	0.8	−0.1
Privatization and profit-oriented CBIs	1.7	0	−1.7
Increases, gross			4–5
Employment and Solidarity Funds	1.4	2.4	1
Other Social Assistance (cash)	1.0	2.1	1
Education	4.5	5–6	1
Health care	5.5	6–7	1
Transport infrastructure	0.6	1.3	0.5–1
Impact of 1992–3 tax reforms			−2
Revenues of profit-oriented CBIs	1.5	0	−1.5
Net budgetary savings			3–4
Adjustment required for macroeconomic consistency			3.5
Memorandum items:			
General government expenditures, 1991			58
Account consolidation[1]			9–11
Adjusted expenditures, 1989			47–49
Net expenditure reduction			7–8
General government expenditures after reform			39–42

Note:
1   Inadequate accounting of CBI expenditures results in large unclassified expenditure and possibly large double counting of expenditure and revenue. Recorded General Public Services expenditure and Other Economic Affairs and Services expenditures are thought to be the most affected accounts. In the EC, the average shares of GDP devoted to expenditures on General Public Services and Other Economic Affairs and Services are 2.5% (ranging from 1.0% in Spain to 4.1% in Ireland) and 1.1% (ranging from 1.0% in Ireland to 1.6% in the Netherlands) respectively. In Hungary they are 7.5% and 7.4% respectively. Proper account consolidation should result in a decline in recorded expenditures (and revenues) in these categories to the levels found in the EC, which would imply a reduction equivalent to about 9–11% of GDP in the size of measured general government expenditures.

Source: Dervis and Condon (1992).

6   Poland: glass half full

Stanislaw Gomulka

The primary purpose of this paper is to offer a policy-oriented overview of the current state of Poland's economic transformation, taking into account its starting point, the progress of reforms so far, policy errors in 1990-1, major economic, social and political problems in 1991 and 1992, and policy aims for 1993. The economic issues and policies are considered in their own right as well as in the broad social and political context. The paper has the following structure: section 1 - broad interactions between politics and economics in the process of transition; section 2 - macro stabilization; section 3 - micro liberalization; section 4 - privatization and other structural changes; and section 5 - major problems in 1991-2 and aims in 1993.

1   Broad Interactions Between Politics and Economics in the Process of Transition

It may be useful to address immediately the question of the mutual interplay between economic reforms and their political environment. In the case of Poland, the following sequence of powerful interactions has been at work:

(1) The pre-reform economic crisis of 1979-81, renewed in 1988-9 (crisis no. 1), led to the rise and survival of Solidarity, to the collapse of the limited reforms of the communist-led governments and, in the spring of 1989, to Round Table negotiations on power sharing and gradual dismantling of communist rule in Poland.

(2) These revolutionary political changes in Poland and the parallel political changes in the USSR in turn led, in September 1989, to the assumption of extraordinary power over the economy by radical liberal reformers, Solidarity experts, and the launching by them of economic reforms aimed at rapidly creating a mixed capitalist economy of the West European type.

(3) These historical reforms have brought large improvements, but also inflicted large costs - the transition-related economic crisis (crisis no. 2).

(4) This economic crisis has changed attitudes to reforms and reformers and has shaped the new political parties and their transition politics.

(5) This transition political process has gradually imposed a degree of control over the liberal reformers, forcing changes to the pace and substance of reforms, while maintaining their overall direction.

Sociological studies appear to suggest that, in the decade 1979–89, rejection of the political system was widespread and intense. Rejection of the state-dominated economic system, however, was still uncertain. In 1982–8, while some 60–80% of adults were in favour of introducing the laws of the market and free competition into the economy, the attitude to medium- and large-scale private business remained hostile (Kolarska-Bobinska, 1990, p. 163). Pre-1989 Poland was a country in which, according to Kolarska-Bobinska, only the myth of the free market developed. The institution itself was accepted only insofar as it was a rejection of the existing misery and a symbol of good things to be found elsewhere; the necessary implications in terms of ownership, job insecurity and work attitudes were yet to be considered and absorbed. The 1989 crisis served to initiate and accelerate this learning process.

By the time the Solidarity-led government came to power, in September 1989, popular support for a variant of the capitalist system was apparently high. The Solidarity-led political coalition had only a vague idea of what to do with power in the economy. It therefore handed over the task of designing the reform programme and conducting the transition to a small group of experts. In the virtual absence of political parties and under the pressure of crisis circumstances, these experts, led by Leszek Balcerowicz, assumed an unusual degree of power. Its legitimacy came above all from the evident collapse of the old economic system and the proven performance of the system about to be introduced. It also came from the trust of the nation and the new political elite in the knowledge of the experts to lead the country out of the crisis through the transformation to a Western-type economy.

Many of the experts and probably most of the population were, however, unaware of the necessarily large social and economic costs of the transformation. Instead of the expected rapid improvement in the standard of living, there came a shocking realization that Poland was entering into a prolonged period of massive recession. Accordingly, in the course of the reforms popular support for the Balcerowicz Plan declined steadily, from about 45% in favour and 10% against in October 1989 to about 20% in favour and 40% against in October 1991 (CBOS, BS 457, November 1991). The reforms have also brought about large changes for the better, enough to sustain broad support for the continuation of the reform process, as evidenced in high popularity ratings of the top political leaders. This mixture of large economic changes for the worse in some respects and remarkable improvements for the better in other respects has given rise to confusion and anxiety among the population, including the political elite, and a loss of confidence as regards what the next reform steps should be. This manifests itself in the 'withdrawal syndrome' of the electorate (42% participation in parliamentary elections in October 1991) and the split of the reform movement into a large number of political parties and factions within parties. This situation produced statements such as President Walesa's 'I am in favour of this reform but also against it' or, by a Solidarity union leader in January 1992, 'We strike not against the government but against the situation'.

These reform-related economic difficulties produced, in 1991 and 1992, a state of political near paralysis in the parliament, a weak presidency and governments unable to get most of their proposed legislation through parliament. In the meantime, a large budget deficit developed and the danger arose that this deficit would lead to a return of hyperinflation.

An effective government with a strong political base in parliament, one capable of taking unpopular decisions, was clearly needed to deal with these grave threats. On its transition path Poland arrived, in early 1992, at a crossroads of sorts. After a turbulent first half of the year, when Poland saw a government and two prime ministers appointed and dismissed, the fairly strong government of Miss Suchocka, which was committed to reform, came to power in the summer of 1992.

2 Macro Stabilization

2.1 Initial Conditions

The domestic credibility of the Polish government's macroeconomic policies was severely eroded in 1989 when massive subsidies led to a large budget deficit in the first half and resulted in near hyperinflation in the second half. External credibility was low and declining further with the rapid rise of international debts. International reserves were low, but the dollar deposits were so high that the share of zloty-denominated money in total money was, in December 1989, a mere 28%. The inflation rate of some 30% a month served two useful purposes: it eliminated the monetary overhang and it reduced drastically the real debt of the enterprise sector. A system of extensive price indexation of wages and benefits, however, worked to reproduce excessive purchasing power and high inflation. Food prices were already liberalized, but otherwise the quality of the price system was poor. In particular, interest rates were highly negative, energy prices were about a tenth of world prices, and the official exchange rate was, in September 1989, a seventh of the market exchange rate. Polish industry was highly material-intensive, and the whole economy was strongly dependent on supplies of energy and other inputs from the USSR, obtained largely in exchange for poor-quality Polish manufactured goods.

2.2   Sequencing

This has been discussed in a number of papers, e.g. Fischer and Gelb (1991), Dornbusch (1991), Gomulka (1990, 1992a), Nuti (1991), Portes (1992), and Wellisz et al. (1991). Here it suffices to note that the immediate steps, made in preparation for the 'Big Bang' of 1 January 1990, were designed above all to eliminate the budget deficit and to reduce drastically, through a series of devaluations, the gap between the market and the official exchange rates.

2.3   The 'Big Bang'

The operation aimed above all to improve radically and permanently the quality of prices, including the interest rate and the exchange rate, and to stabilize the liberalized prices gradually through the application of three anchors: the money supply, the exchange rate and an incomes policy. Given the initial conditions, achieving price stability was, in 1990, secondary to two other aims: a substantial increase in international reserves (which required a large up-front devaluation) and a major improvement in the quality of the price system (price liberalization and drastic increases of some administered prices during 1990 and early 1991). Large induced inflation justified in turn large monetary expansion, which helped to achieve the third aim: a severe reduction in the share of dollar currency in the total money supply.

Macroeconomic concerns dictated a course of action that resulted in a large initial price increase and hence a large fall in (statistical) real wages. Low wages helped to maintain high profitability of enterprises despite recession. This in turn ensured high revenue for the government budget and low expenditure on salaries in the budget-funded sector of the economy. High profitability was also helped, in 1990, by a large up-front devaluation of the zloty, designed to promote net exports and maintain stability of the exchange rate. This exchange rate policy sharply improved the external position of the country. The policy was inflationary in two ways, by increasing the cost of imports and by contributing to monetary expansion through the balance of trade surplus; but it also contributed to the budget and helped reduce recession. The microeconomic outcome of this macro policy was, however, that inefficient enterprises continued to be profitable, and therefore were not faced with the immediate necessity of undertaking any harsh cost-cutting measures.

The strategy itself was deliberate, even if it went too far in the first half of 1990. It was motivated by the desire to avoid a catastrophe of the East German type – large-scale bankruptcies and large-scale unemployment at the start of the reform. The implicit choice of sequencing was after all to deal first with macro problems, such as the budget deficit, inflation, international reserves and foreign debt, and only later with the more fundamental, difficult and time-consuming problem of microeconomic inefficiency.

2.4 The Stop–Go Sequence of Macroeconomic Policies

The initial aims were achieved fairly quickly; in particular, the near hyperinflation that was raging in 1989 was eliminated by the spring of 1990. Nonetheless, inflationary pressures were still high throughout 1990 and 1991. In the second half of 1990, the inflationary pressures increased. This was linked to the unintended stop–go sequence of policies adopted in Poland.

In the first half of 1990, policies were highly contractionary, in fact much more so than originally intended. Particularly restrictive were fiscal and monetary policies. The combined budget surplus of the total government sector, including special parabudgetary funds, was of the order of 8% of GDP in the first half of 1990. Since the budget was in deficit for a similar amount in 1989, the change in the fiscal position was unprecedented in magnitude, and it was achieved within a very short period of time. Monetary policy was also highly contractionary. Output immediately declined a great deal, especially in the sector producing non-essential consumer goods.

By the middle of 1990, the government had introduced policies intended to promote economic activity and to open domestic markets to foreign competition. In order to stimulate activity, the authorities reduced interest rates, increased credit to enterprises and increased government expenditure, but on a scale larger than initially intended. In the second half of 1990, wage increases were consequently large, nearly 10% a month, and inflation increased to about 5% per month. After a fairly sharp fall in the purchasing power of household incomes in the first half of 1990, by about 35–40%, there was thus a very rapid recovery in real incomes and consumption in the second half of 1990. Real wages in fact reached levels that began to undermine the international competitiveness of Polish exports as, in dollar terms, they exceeded the levels then prevailing in Czechoslovakia and Hungary. The level of economic activity did increase, especially in branches producing food products and consumer durables. There was also, however, an exceptionally large increase in consumer imports, turning a healthy trade surplus during the first three quarters of 1990 into a deficit in the fourth quarter of 1990. In response to all this, by the end of 1990 the central authorities modified monetary policy with a view to regaining macroeconomic control. This led to a new phase of 'stop' policies in the first half of 1991.

In early 1991, Poland was thus in a 'stop' phase of its reform path. The two dominant developments were: a continuing effort to regain macroeconomic control after it was seriously eroded during the last months of 1990, and a new supply-side shock in the form of the switchover to dollar prices within the CMEA area from 1 January 1991 and the consequent sharp fall in Polish exports to this area. The impact of the dollarization on Poland's inflation, terms of trade and recession was larger than anticipated. The price index increased by 15% in January, and industrial output declined by 15%. A further decline by about 10%

from April 1991 brought the level of industrial activity in 1991 down to about 65% of its pre-reform level. I estimate the overall (direct and indirect) impact of the CMEA collapse to be about 5% of GDP in 1991. The terms-of-trade losses during 1990–1 amounted to a further 3% of GDP.

2.5   The Nominal Anchors: Money, Incomes and the Exchange Rate

A highly restrictive monetary policy during the first quarter of 1990 and the general uncertainty about future sales had the result that during the first half of 1990 wages remained significantly below the ceiling levels specified by the tax-based incomes policy. The policy started to be binding only towards the end of 1990 and has since been the principal nominal anchor. In 1990 the policy restricted the growth rate of the wage fund in nearly all enterprises and, since January 1991, it has restricted the growth rate of average nominal wages in state-owned enterprises.

The basic problem with the Polish stabilization effort was that two nominal anchors, money and incomes, were too flexible during the second half of 1990 and most of 1991 to serve as proper anchors. In 1990 and 1991 monetary policy, with the exception of a few short periods (in particular, the beginning of 1990 and the turn of 1990 and 1991), accommodated price increases and, with the exception of the first four months of the year, the effective price indexation of wage norms was nearly 100%. The excessive and financially unsustainable wage indexation of benefits was in operation throughout this period.

There was already a clear need in the summer of 1990 to introduce an incomes policy with little or no price indexation of wage norms. The judgement was made, however, that for political reasons this was not possible. What the authorities did instead was to keep the exchange rate fixed in 1990, despite the 250% price increase, and continue to appreciate it in real terms in 1991 (when the rate of appreciation against the dollar was 28%). In this way the exchange rate became a major nominal anchor from the latter part of 1990. The result of this combination of a soft incomes policy, an accommodating monetary policy and a hard exchange rate policy was a sharp increase in imports, especially of consumer goods, and the disappearance of the trade surplus starting in the fourth quarter of 1990. This in turn led to a fall in international reserves and possibly excessive recession.

The economic policy implemented in 1992 and intended for 1993 aims to restore policy coordination by substantially changing the incomes policy, hardening the monetary policy and allowing some depreciation of the real exchange rate (Council of Ministers [CM], 1992a). The new incomes policy for wages in state enterprises is designed to meet the following criteria: allow a small increase in real wages when inflation is low and a fall in real wages when inflation is high; help managers of loss-making enterprises to reduce wage costs significantly; provide an incentive for exports, commercialization and privatization; and define a path for the gradual withdrawal of the policy along with the progress of privatization and the rise in unemployment. Moreover, the policy discontinued the practice of automatically linking wages in the government sector to other wages. It also aims to reduce the ratio of pensions to wages.

2.6 Public Finances: Deterioration in 1991 and Crisis in 1992

Whatever the health of public finances just before the start of transition reforms, post-socialist economies appear invariably to develop a fiscal crisis in the course of transition. The causes of this tendency are well understood, and I shall discuss them only briefly. Less clear but vital for policy-makers are the implications of such deficits for the inflation path, given the servicing requirements of the accumulating public debt and the credit requirements of the economy.

In the first year of reform, the budget deficit is typically low but the inflation rate is high, much of it due to corrective price increases. In the second and third years of reform, the deficit/GDP ratio tends to increase sharply, while the inflation rate declines. There comes a point, however, when the deficit is large enough to arrest and then to reverse the downward trend of inflation.

2.6.1 Causes of the Fiscal Problem

In Poland, fiscal developments in aggregate terms have been and are expected to be as shown in Table 6.1. Inspection of the table shows that the share of general government expenditure in GDP has been reasonably stable. The primary cause of the newly emerging fiscal gap has been on the revenue side. The central government was even able to reduce its expenditures by some 4% of GDP in 1991-2, compared with the levels in the years 1987-90. State revenues, however, fell by about 10% of GDP in 1991 and have remained low. This fall can be traced mainly to the collapse of enterprise profits, but also in part to a fall in turnover taxes as industrial output fell much more than the GDP. This suggests that the primary remedy for the budget deficit problem must be found also on the revenue side, probably through an increase in indirect taxes.

However, the expenditure side is also interesting to look at because of large shifts in its composition. Perhaps the most reform-related expenditure items are subsidies. Their pre-reform composition – about two-thirds of the total going to the household sector and about one-third to the enterprise sector – has remained virtually unchanged. But their total sum has fallen dramatically, from about 16% of GDP in 1987-8 to 12.9% in 1989, 8.2% in 1990 and 4.8% in 1991. On the other hand, the budgetary transfer to pension funds and the Labour Fund increased from 4% of GDP in 1987 to about 8% in 1990-1. The cost of unemployment benefits is still a relatively minor burden, less than 1% of GDP in 1991.

Table 6.1   Fiscal Indicators in Poland, 1987–93 (as % of GDP)

Indicator	Pre-reform			Transition				
	1987	1988	1989	1990	1991	1992[1]	1992[2]	1993[3]
State budget:								
Revenues	34.2	35.5	30.8	37.4	26.5	26.7	25.0	27.2
Expenditures[4]	37.7	37.0	36.9	36.7	33.0	32.8	35.0	32.3
Balance[4]	-3.5	-1.4	-6.1	0.7	-6.5	-6.1	-10.0	-5.1
General government:								
Revenues	47.0	48.0	41.4	48.3	42.3	42.0	41.0	42.5
Expenditure	47.8	48.0	48.8	44.8	48.5	48.2	50.0	47.5
Balance[4]	-0.8	0.0	-7.4	3.5	-6.2	-5.8	-10.0	-5.0

Notes:
1 Expected outcome as of December 1992 (CM, 1992b).
2 Expected outcome in the absence of corrective measures.
3 Expected outcome if measures proposed in the state budget for 1993 (CM, 1992b) are adopted.
4 On a commitment basis, except external interest which is on a cash basis.

Definitions: 'State budget' is the budget of the central government. 'General government' includes central government, local authorities and extra-budgetary funds.

Sources: IMF (1992b) for 1987–91, Polish Ministry of Finance for 1992–3.

The main problem on the expenditure side has been the meteoric rise of expenditure on pensions and other social insurance items. This occasioned the need to transfer resources from the state budget to the main three extra-budgetary funds: FUS (mainly workers' pensions), KRUS (mainly farmers' pensions) and the Labour Fund (mainly unemployment benefits) (see Table 6.2). Total expenditures of the three funds increased from 11% of GDP in 1987 to 18% in 1991, and were expected to reach 21.6% in 1992. Pensions alone accounted for 6.6% of GDP in 1987, but 11.1% in 1991 and 13.5% in 1992. As subsidies to the household sector were reduced, the authorities apparently felt compelled to increase the ratio of the average pension to the average wage rate from about half before the reform to about two-thirds in 1992.

A fortunate aspect of the Polish fiscal position so far has been the light burden, about 1% of GDP, of servicing the external debt. The agreement with the Paris Club of March 1991 on about US$30 billion of sovereign debt gave Poland three years during which 80% of interest payments due would be forgiven. Poland also continues not to service the bulk of the US$13 billion of commercial debt. It may therefore be expected that in 1994 and thereafter the burden of servicing the external debt will greatly increase, possibly to about 4% of GDP. This will still be lower than the Hungarian burden now, which, at some 6–8% of GDP, is a major cause of the weak fiscal position in that country.

Table 6.2 Transfers to Social Insurance Funds in Poland, 1988-92

	1988	1989	1990	1991	1992
To FUS:					
% of state budget	2.0	4.2	4.5	10.5	15.8
% of FUS's expenditures	8.0	12.5	16.3	9.2	26.2
To KRUS:					
% of state budget	1.9	3.5	3.8	6.5	7.9
% of KRUS's expenditures	75.0	99.7	96.8	87.3	94.2

Source: Polish Ministry of Finance.

About 90-100% of the deficit is financed by the banking sector, and about half to two-thirds of this is financed by the central bank. The difficulties in reducing the budget deficit are related to insufficient political cooperation between the government and the parliament, reflecting in part the rising national concern over the social costs of the transition.

The situation has arisen in part because of inadequate understanding of the reasons for a large budget improvement at the beginning of the reform, in the fourth quarter of 1989 and the first quarter of 1990. During that period of very high inflation, the nominal (zloty) value of two capital assets of the enterprise sector, foreign exchange deposits and inventories of materials, semi-finished and finished goods, increased rapidly. In line with the Polish accounting system, the consequent capital gains were counted as profits. However, insofar as they do not reflect any change in the volume of these two assets, the gains are 'paper profits'. The existence of these profits was well known, but their large impact on total profit and corporate income tax was never properly estimated. An attempt at such an estimate was made recently by Mark Schaffer (1992a). It appears that these paper profits significantly exceeded 'true profits' in the periods in question (fourth quarter of 1989 and first quarter of 1990), increasing the tax burden of the enterprise sector by a factor of 3.

This automatic anti-inflationary stabilizer had already helped to eliminate the budget deficit in November and December 1989. It also accounts for the fact that, in 1990, corporate income tax and dividend tax represented about 16% of GDP and half of the total budget expenditure, compared with about 11% in (say) 1985 and 7.8% in 1982, which was less than one-third of the total expenditure.

It is now clear that the government made two major errors in the fiscal field. It overestimated the size of the corporate and dividend taxes for 1991 by 6.5% of GDP, and it failed to increase indirect taxes sufficiently to compensate quickly for the shortfall in the direct enterprise taxes. In view of the technical difficulties in introducing the VAT system, the government could and should have sharply increased the turnover tax by broadening its base and raising tax rates. The fiscal situation would also have been helped by a stricter wage policy. Such a policy would have increased profits and therefore budget revenue, and it would have reduced wages in the budget sphere as well as wage-indexed welfare benefits, and therefore budget expenditure. These income measures would have required, however, close cooperation between the government and parliament, and this was singularly lacking in 1991 and continued to be insufficient in 1992.

Table 6.3   Budgetary Costs of Pensions and Unemployment Benefits, 1989–93

	1989	1990	1991	1992	1993
Pensions:					
No. (million)	6.8	7.4	8.0	8.5	8.9
Cost (% of GDP)	7.2	9.4	11.4	12.8	13.3
Unemployment benefits:					
No. (million)	0.0	0.5	1.4	1.4	1.2
Cost (% of GDP)	0.0	0.5	1.0	1.1	1.0
Total cost (% of GDP)	7.2	9.9	12.4	13.8	14.3

Note: Cost is net of personal taxes; numbers are averages for the year. Pensions are of three categories: old age, early retirement and disability. The first two categories represent about 60% of the total. The average unemployment benefit is about 32% of the average wage and about 50% of the average pension, the latter now being equal to about 65% of the average wage.

Sources: Author's estimates based on Poland's Ministry of Finance data for 1989–92 and projections for 1993.

Cooperation was and continues to be vital in implementing a programme of budget savings. These are necessary in view of the development portrayed in Table 6.2. Underlying that table are the data shown in Table 6.3. Inspection of these figures and of Table 6.2 above shows that the crisis of public finances is also the result of a sharp increase in welfare expenditures. The cost of unemployment benefits is as yet insignificant compared with the cost of pensions, which is the result of a large increase in both the number of pensioners and the real value of the average pension.

To conclude this discussion of public finances, it is worth noting two circumstances that are important and common to nearly all transition economies and that complicate the policy-makers' task of reducing the budget deficit. One is the poor quality of bank assets and the other is widespread private sector evasion of taxes. The two factors influence public finance policy in the following way.

The banking sector seeks to improve its portfolio of assets by lending more to the government and less to economic units. Given that, in Poland, about 50–60% of all enterprise debt is not being serviced, and that the government debt is fully serviced, the ability of the banking system to pay reasonable interest on deposits is enhanced with the persistence of a large budget deficit. The deficit is thus a way of providing a safety net for the banking system. In the course of time, the poor-quality debt will be a declining share of all banking assets, and therefore the significance of this factor should also decline.

The tax collection problem is in turn inducing the members of parliament representing taxpayers (who are the majority of the electorate) to impose an inflation tax in preference to other taxes. The reason is that, because it is difficult to evade, inflation tax is paid by those operating in the black economy.

3   Micro Liberalization

Liberalization applies not only to prices but also to regulations and policies concerning the private sector, foreign trade and foreign investment; demonopolization and competition; labour mobility and wage-bargaining; financial institutions and intermediation. There are few issues in this area that arouse controversy. Those that do include: the speed at which to increase administered prices to either world levels or subsidy-free levels; the extent of price regulation through subsidies for agricultural produce; the level of protection of domestic producers through tariffs, quotas and/or the exchange rate; and privileged treatment of the private sector.

Table 6.4   Percentage of Transactions at Free Prices, by Market Sector, 1989–92[1]

	1989	1990	1991	1992
Agricultural produce	41	100	100	100
Intermediate inputs	65	77	88	88[2]
Market supplies	26	73	85	85[3]

Notes:
1   Shares at 1 January of each year.
2   The share is 97% if prices whose changes are subject to reporting restrictions and can be delayed by up to three months are included as free. The 3% share of administered prices applies only to natural gas and electricity.
3   89% if prices whose changes must be reported and can be delayed by up to three months are included. The 11% share of administered prices applies to basic medicines and health services, household gas and electricity, alcoholic beverages (except imports), housing rents and passenger mass transportation tariffs.

Source: Economic Committee of the Council of Ministers (1991b), pp. 51–2.

3.1   Price Liberalization and the New Price Structure

From the beginning of 1990, foreign exchange and intermediate inputs were no longer subject to any central allocation.

The policy on most administered prices is governed by an agreement with the World Bank in connection with its Structural Adjustment Loan. The agreement committed Poland to freeze nominal subsidies to coal mines and liberalize domestic coal prices by 1 July 1990; to eliminate subsidies and the export tax on coal by the end of 1992; to bring prices of other forms of energy to industrial consumers into the same relationship with domestic coal prices as is typically observed in the West European economies by the end of 1991; to increase energy prices to household consumers to 50% of prices paid by industrial users by the end of 1990 and to 100% by the end of 1991; and to reduce substantially housing and transportation subsidies in the years 1991-3 (Memorandum of Development Policy, No. 16, June 1990). Poland has remained faithful to the terms of this agreement.

Budget outlays on price-related subsidies are expected still to be about 5% of GDP in 1992, of which nearly 4% of GDP are housing subsidies (on operation and maintenance, rents, central heating and hot water, gas and electricity and interest payments). These housing subsidies and increased household bills have absorbed not only the original coal subsidy, but also a part of the Soviet subsidy implicit in the originally extremely low prices of natural gas and oil. The share of household expenditure on energy increased from about 3% of total household expenditure in 1989 to about 15% in 1992.

To conclude, it would appear that the extent of price liberalization and the quality of the price structure have already more or less reached EC standards.

3.2   Demonopolization, Competition Policy and Foreign Investment

Progress so far has been substantial in increasing competition, marked in demonopolization and negligible in attracting foreign investment. The decentralization of foreign trade, a five-fold increase in the dollar purchasing power of the average wage (compared with 1985-8) and low tariffs have combined to expose domestic producers of tradables to foreign competition on a really large scale. Domestic competition has also been enhanced by a rapid expansion of the private sector, the breaking up, in 1989-91, of 290 large state enterprises into 996 enterprises, and the activities of the Anti-Monopoly Office and its eight regional offices. The industrial landscape still continues to be dominated by large-scale enterprises. Employment (and output) of these enterprises is tending to decline rapidly, however, while the number of small and medium-sized businesses, employing 5-200, is increasing fast.

The scale of foreign direct investment in Poland in the period January 1989 to October 1991 has been put by a government source at US$684 million

(ECCM, 1991b, p. 43). Foreign capital had also invested about US$100 million in privatization ventures and about US$50 million in the financial sector in the years 1990-1 (ibid., p. 43). To promote such investment, in June 1991 parliament passed a new foreign investment law, described by the OECD as 'quite liberal and comparable to FDI regimes in most OECD countries' (Schaffer, 1992c, p. 25). However, to make an impact commensurate with restructuring needs, foreign direct investment would have to be much larger, of the order of US$50 billion within the next 10 years. To achieve this objective Poland would have to reduce substantially the risk of political and economic destabilization. A second important condition is to reach an agreement with the London Club on the reduction and full servicing of the post-reduction commercial debt.

The World Bank is the largest and most enthusiastic institutional investor in Poland, committing about US$1 billion per year in support of the post-1990 reform. The absorption of this and other institutional and government credit lines has been: US$226 million in 1989, US$428 million in 1990 and US$800 million in 1991 (ECCM, 1991b, p. 22).

3.3 The Banking Sector

The state banking sector – the central bank, nine commercial banks and six specialized banks – accounts for about 95% of all banking operations. In October 1991, the nine commercial banks were transformed into joint stock companies in preparation for their privatization in 1992-5. There also operate or are about to operate some 70 private domestic and foreign banks.

In 1990 the financial health of banks improved, as bad debts were few and interest margins exceptionally high. This position changed radically for the worse in 1991. The main cause of the change was a sharp increase in the proportion of loans regarded as under- or non-performing (loans doubtful or lost). About one-third of all state enterprises are no longer considered creditworthy by banks (as of end 1991), and loans to state enterprises represent about 90% of the loan portfolio of the commercial banks. Profit margins also fell with the general decline of interest rates and increased competition among banks.

The privatization programme of the banking sector is now in danger of collapsing unless the financial position of the banks is clarified and improved. A particular threat is the so-called old debts, which were extended to state enterprises before February 1989 by the central bank, and for which the commercial banks, financially independent only since then, do not feel responsible.

The Ministry of Finance and the central bank have recently proposed a 'Programme for Restructuring the Banking Sector in Poland' (MF, 1992a), the primary initial purpose of which is to deal with the bad debts problem.

The implementation of the programme will lead to the closure of some of the state enterprises, compensation of some bank losses by the Treasury, and greater involvement of banks, including through the acquisition of shares, in the restructuring of enterprises regarded as still viable. The programme has been influenced by the strong criticism of and proposed remedies for the financial relations between state banks and state enterprises by Beksiak et al. (1991).

4   Privatization and Other Structural Changes

At the end of 1989, 8.3 million people, 47% of the workforce, were active in the non-state sector. However, about half of this employment was in private agriculture and much of the other half was in the semi-state 'cooperative sector'. In industry and services, state sector domination was overwhelming.

It is useful to distinguish the following routes to privatization (for recent extensive discussions of techniques, dilemmas, problems and results, consult Frydman et al, 1993, and Gomulka and Jdsinski, 1993):

(1)   Self-transformation of the cooperative sector by the removal both of central bureaucracy and of central allocation of inputs.
(2)   'Small privatization', through the sale or leasing of small portions of state-owned assets, e.g shops.
(3)   Medium-sized privatizations of small and medium state enterprises employing typically 100–500 people, using either:
   (a)   the Act of Privatization of State Enterprises – essentially employee and/or management buy-outs, a popular means of 'privatization from below', or
   (b)   the liquidation process under the State Enterprise Act, the enterprises being closed and their assets auctioned off.
(4)   'Classical privatization' along Western lines – auctions of enterprise shares, with special purchase rights reserved for the employees, and sales to foreign investors.
(5)   'Mass privatization', in Poland through the allocation of 60% of shares of large-scale enterprises to some 20–50 'National Investment Funds', which are essentially investment trusts, and then the sale to, or free distribution of the shares of these funds among, a large number of small investors. The remaining 40% of shares would be divided between the Treasury (30%) and employees (10%).
(6)   'Organic' or 'growth privatization', through the natural contraction of the state sector and the organic growth of the private sector under the new competitive conditions.

In Poland, routes (1) and (2) were put into effect immediately after the Solidarity-led coalition assumed power in September 1989, and became the most effective means of privatization in 1990. Route (3) was the main channel of privatization in 1991, involving about 400 enterprises through subroute (a) and about 500 enterprises through subroute (b). The total pool of enterprises of this medium-sized category is still about 6,000, out of a total of about 8,000. The organizational and other transaction costs are small with routes (1) and (2) and moderate with route (3). Only 22 enterprises were privatized, in 1990–1, through the classical method (4). These privatizations led, however, to the emergence of the share market and the establishment of the Stock Exchange in April 1991. Mass privatization is not to be in full swing until 1994. The necessary institutional preparations are under way and expected to be completed in 1993. Organic privatization has been taking place all along. Although there are no reliable measures of its progress and importance, the spectacular growth of the private sector has elevated this form of privatization.

A separate programme has been set up to privatize the state agricultural sector, which comprises 2,300 farms (about 20% of the country's total agricultural land), about 0.6 million households. The programme is run by a financially independent Agency for State-Owned Agriculture. The intention is to privatize 600–800 farms in 1992 (Ministry of Ownership Changes, 1992, p. 21).

4.1 Restitution

This problem is still unsolved, and continues to represent a considerable obstacle to privatization. A new draft Law on Re-privatization is to be presented to parliament before summer 1993. The intention was legally to separate the two processes of privatization and restitution by the device of the Treasury taking over any claims of previous owners, and settling such claims through the use of shares generated by the mass privatization programme.

4.2 Commercialization of State Enterprises

The commercialization programme started in autumn 1990 in response to a perceived large-scale shift of power in enterprises from managements to unions and workers' councils. The shift was thought to be capable of paralysing management efforts to initiate and implement cost-cutting restructuring programmes. In 1991, 350 enterprises were given supervisory boards with powers to act on behalf of the state owner. In 1992 an additional 400 such boards were to be created. Progress has been slow partly because the Ministry of Ownership Changes was not enthusiastic about the programme. Moreover, there is apparently no compelling evidence of an improvement in performance following commercialization.

4.3   Privatization and the Composition of Employment

Inspection of Table 6.5 reveals a spectacular growth during 1990–2 of the non-cooperative private sector outside agriculture, where the increase in employment was 2.3 million. Nearly all of this growth took place in the trade sector, however, largely at the expense of the cooperative sector. Still, private activity in industry did not shrink, and it positively expanded in construction and transport. On the other hand, there has been a very rapid decline in unemployment in the state sector, mainly under the impact of severe supply and demand shocks.

Table 6.5   Poland: Employment by Economic Sector and Ownership
Category, 1989–92

	1989	1990	1991	1992
(a) Levels (millions, end-year)				
Non-agriculture	12.8	11.8	11.3	11.3
State	8.9	7.6	6.5	6.0
Private	3.9	4.2	4.8	5.3
Old private	1.8	2.3	3.0	4.1
Cooperatives, etc.	2.1	1.9	1.8	1.2
Agriculture	4.8	4.7	4.6	4.5
State	0.6	0.5	0.4	0.4
Private	4.1	4.1	4.1	4.1
(b) Private sector (old private and cooperatives) share of employment (%, end-year)				
Trade	72.7	82.2	88.3	90.5
Industry	29.1	31.2	35.8	41.9
Construction	37.4	42.1	59.5	71.8
Transport	14.3	15.2	26.0	23.1
Communal services	29.9	30.0	40.3	44.4
Total economy outside private agriculture	31.2	33.6	40.3	44.4
Total economy	45.5	50.3	56.0	59.1

Source: Central Statistical Office, *Informacja o Sytuacji Spoleczno-Gospodarczej Kraju: Rok 1992*, Warsaw, 28 January 1993, p. 51.

In 1992 the output growth trends seen recently have changed. The shocks had already been absorbed, and therefore the recession-related contraction of the state sector should have slowed down, at least in terms of output. The privatization of the trade sector was nearly completed, and therefore the spectacular growth of the private trade sector should also have come to a halt.

4.4   Labour Market, Housing and Social Safety Net

During transition there is a distinct discontinuity in the demand for labour: large falls for most skill categories and sharp increases for some others. Although the influence of workers' councils has increased, and their primary concern is probably the preservation of employment, it is interesting that the sharp increase in overall unemployment has been caused by heavy shedding of employment across the entire mass of state enterprises and budget-funded institutions rather than through the closure of enterprises or a large influx of new labour. It is apparent that neither the traditional softness of the state enterprise budget constraint nor the shift of power to labour are factors strong enough to slow down considerably, let alone prevent, fairly rapid adjustment of employment to the demand for output. The unemployment increase has been uneven within the country. Lehmann et al. (1991) distinguish three types of regions: *modern*, where heavy industry is not dominant, the service sector is strong, and the supply of and the demand for labour are highly diversified with respect to skill; *heavily industrialized*, where large firms dominate, the service sector is weak and the private sector not substantial; and *agricultural*, where services and technical infrastructure are poorly developed and skill levels are low. The authors show that the unemployment/vacancy ratios are increasing to reach 'long-term levels' that vary between the three types in proportions 1:2:3.

The wage rate has long been perceived to be determined by political rather than market forces. To change this perception, the post-communist governments have tried to withdraw from wage negotiations completely. These negotiations are now decentralized to the enterprise level, where typically two enterprise-specific unions operate. The unions have a hierarchical structure, but there are no industry-wide or country-wide wage settlements. Despite unemployment, upward pressure on wages remains high. Management is in a weak position to resist the pressure. It also has no strong incentive to do so, since the prospect of commercialization and privatization has increased uncertainty for managers as well.

The government has taken a number of policy initiatives to provide a social safety net and to combat unemployment. Effective active labour policies, however, such as public works and large-scale retraining, are costly and have therefore been put on ice. The main function of the government has been to provide money: unemployment benefits, housing subsidies, 'free soup' for the poor, early retirement pensions, family support benefit, etc. The programme appears to have been successful in containing the growth of extreme poverty, and this containment has been and continues to be the overriding concern of the government's social policy.

To facilitate labour mobility, stronger policy action is needed to establish a properly functioning housing market. One possible move would be to impose a legal obligation on local authorities to sell or give away their housing stock to its present occupiers within a short period of time. Another move would be to release more land for housing construction. The result of the policy would be an increased release to the market of under-used accommodation, a faster market-driven reallocation of accommodation, and increased housing construction.

4.5   Major Income Redistribution

Who are the losers and who are the winners during the transformation so far? Considerable light is shed on this question by the household surveys of the Polish Central Statistical Office. A summary table has recently been compiled by Bywalec (1993).

Table 6. 6   The Level and Composition of Personal Real Incomes in Poland, 1985-91

Source of income	Level (1985=100)			Composition (%)		
	1988	1990	1991	1988	1990	1991
All income	113.6	102.7	108.8	100.0	100.0	100.0
Wages	111.5	75.5	73.4	46.3	38.2	35.1
Private agriculture	124.4	70.7	57.5	12.7	6.6	5.1
Other private activity	118.8	157.4	170.0	25.6	37.9	38.6
Welfare payments	111.5	95.6	124.0	15.4	17.3	21.2

Source: Bywalec (1993)

Table 6.6 provides startling evidence of a large-scale redistribution of incomes away from workers and farmers and in favour of pensioners and entrepreneurs. The original aim of the reformers was indeed to protect the poor and the rich. This policy aim has been clearly implemented. It may well be that the redistribution has been even larger than intended and desirable. The table also indicates that the overall level of real personal incomes has been quite stable. The propensity to save out of this income did increase sharply, contributing to a fall in the level of personal consumption. It is also to be noted that the fall in wage incomes is in part explained by a fall in the number of wage-earners. Some of the former wage-earners have become pensioners, unemployed or entrepreneurs.

5   Major Problems in 1991-2 and Aims in 1993

Before discussing the serious problems that developed in 1991-2 and are confronting Poland in 1993, it is important not to lose sight of the major achievements of the transition process so far. A selection of these, not necessarily in the order of importance, would be as follows.

Despite the high cost of the reform in terms of GDP, consumption and unemployment, extreme poverty has been largely avoided, and both the democratic process and respect for law have been preserved. Choice, accessibility and quality of goods and services have improved vastly. The costly readjustment of foreign trade away from the former CMEA area mainly to the EC area has been completed. International reserves have increased substantially, and a fifth of the total international debt has been cancelled, with the prospect of a further fifth of the debt being cancelled within the next three years. Consequently, confidence in the zloty has been established and maintained, and its internal convertibility at a unified rate has been preserved without difficulty. The inflation rate has been brought down substantially, from about 30% a month in the second half of 1989 to about 3% a month now. The quality of the price system has been improved radically, and small-scale privatization has been nearly completed.

At the end of 1991, the first post-Balcerowicz government came to power in Poland. It had the difficult task of counteracting the continuing recessionary tendency and promoting the privatization reform while at the same time defending the substantial stabilization gains of the previous two years – all this in circumstances of rising concern among the population over the social costs of the transition and a highly divided parliament.

In January and February 1992, the government took stock of the situation and considered policy corrections for 1992. The starting point was to note the adverse developments in 1991, which I have discussed already in section 2 of the paper, and which may be summed up as follows:

(1) High price indexation of wage norms and wage indexation of welfare benefits, and an accommodating monetary policy, led to the inflation rate continuing to be very high, despite a big appreciation of the real exchange rate and high unemployment.

(2) Delays in increasing indirect taxes and excessive rises in pensions and other benefits led to a crisis of public finances.

(3) The use of the exchange rate as a key nominal anchor, while incomes policy and monetary policy were lax, and delays in introducing higher import tariffs have led – through the large appreciation of the real exchange rate – to a spectacular rise in consumer imports and the disappearance of the trade surplus.

(4) While the collapse of CMEA markets was the main cause of recession in 1991, the influx of imports was also a factor in a rapid increase in the number of enterprises that became loss-making and ceased to service debt. This development has threatened a financial crisis in the banking sector.

(5) Despite a large fall in GDP, private consumption, especially of imported luxury goods, has increased significantly, while investment in fixed capital declined further.

(6)   The financial support of the IMF for the Polish programme was suspended in autumn 1991, after Poland failed to meet the performance criteria on the budget deficit and the expansion of credit for the second and third quarters. This support is crucial for the debt reduction programme and the flow of Western credit and direct private investment.

Excessive criticism of the policies in 1990-1, often for the wrong reasons, was unfortunately the intellectual starting point of the new parliament and the new government of Mr Jan Olszewski. It soon became apparent, however, that the necessary policy corrections would be costly in social and political terms, and that the scope for safe anti-recessionary policies, both macro and micro, is extremely limited. The government guidelines (CM, 1992a) were an attempt to meet the problems (1) to (6) by calling for a tougher incomes policy (I have already noted this in section 2 with respect to wages in state enterprises), a larger turnover tax, a real depreciation of the exchange rate and large reductions in some welfare benefits. Specific tax increases and benefit reductions were proposed in the state budget for 1992.

The broad macroeconomic aims of the new programme were to limit the budget deficit to 5% of GDP, to reduce the inflation rate from 60% in 1991 to about 45% in 1992, and to initiate a modest recovery (or to limit a further fall in GDP) through a trade surplus and possibly higher investment.

Since the new government inherited the prospect of a budget deficit of some 10-13% of GDP, the guidelines in effect called for a package of tax increases and spending cuts equivalent to about 5-8% of GDP. The increases had to be concentrated on indirect taxes and the cuts on material expenditure in the budget sphere and on pensions and other welfare benefits. Meeting the 5% limit on the budget deficit in 1992 was also an essential part of the government's anti-inflationary policy.

The Olszewski government did not have sufficient parliamentary support to implement its proposed welfare cuts. Where it could have acted, as in the case of indirect taxes, it moved slowly. Its fall in June 1992 created an opportunity to form a new government, headed by Miss Hanna Suchocka, with a stronger parliamentary base and a stronger commitment to the original reform principles.

The Suchocka government, while still a minority one, was prepared to accept the political risk associated with taking the measures needed to deal with the crisis of public finances. A package of such measures was proposed in August 1992, and incorporated in the state budget for 1993, which was submitted to parliament for approval in November 1992.

The measures include imposing a temporary import surcharge of 6% in 1993 and 3% in 1994, freezing thresholds in personal income tax and depreciation allowances in corporate income tax (for investments made before 1990), reducing the ratio of pensions to wages and, above all, increasing indirect taxes. The combined size of the measures is about 5% of GDP. Despite these measures, the projected budget deficit for 1993 is also about 5% of GDP. Armed with these budget proposals, the government was able to negotiate a standby agreement with the IMF, the implementation of which is linked with the second phase of the Paris Club debt reduction agreement.

By the beginning of 1993, the following four important pieces of the Polish reform jigsaw had therefore fallen into place: (1) the government's political base in parliament enlarged, (2) the crisis of public finances brought under control, (3) an agreement with the IMF reached, and (4) a new (temporary) Constitution adopted, clarifying the division of power between the government, the president and parliament. Moreover, in the course of 1992, a considerable recovery in industrial activity got under way (see Table 6.7). This recovery appears to be driven mainly by exports and the private sector, so it is probably part of a sustainable upward trend.

Table 6.7 Poland's Post-Reform Recession 1990-91 and Recovery 1992 (1990 = 100)

	Pre-reform 1989	1991 H1	1991 H2	1992 Q1	1992 Q2	1992 Q3	1992 Q4
Industry	131.9	92.1	84.1	85.0	85.1	88.9	96.4
Mining	135.1	96.6	92.6	99.5	89.7	92.4	92.4
Fuel & power	128.4	92.9	90.5	102.4	82.3	87.7	94.8
Metallurgical	124.6	86.8	68.4	72.7	77.7	68.1	77.4
Electro-engineering	128.2	84.9	70.5	67.1	72.9	74.1	89.9
Chemical	132.6	91.2	81.8	85.5	84.9	89.1	97.0
Mineral	127.5	100.5	94.5	79.7	100.4	113.3	106.2
Wood & paper	132.2	100.7	96.5	103.0	101.3	111.7	125.5
Light	151.0	95.6	78.4	78.1	75.5	81.9	91.4
Food processing	131.1	98.8	102.8	94.5	106.1	115.2	112.5
Construction	121.3	108.9		83.9	93.2	100.2	111.3

Note: The activity indexes are those of gross output. Data seasonally unadjusted.

Source: *Statistical Bulletin*, Central Statistical Office, Warsaw, January 1993, p. 21.

Looking ahead, the risks of political and economic instability are still high. These risks will be much reduced only when a new election law is adopted and a new less politically fragmented parliament is returned by a more mature electorate. Until this happens, a good working relationship between the government and parliament will remain a problem capable of seriously disrupting the economic transformation at almost any time.

Note

The author has been and continues to be Economic Adviser to Poland's successive Finance Ministers since September 1989. As a member of the Balcerowicz Group he advised the Polish government on the elaboration and implementation of the 1990–1 reform. He takes sole responsibility for the contents of the paper. Research support funded by the Leverhulme Trust is gratefully acknowledged.

Bibliography

Bednarski, M. (1991) 'Small Privatization in Poland', Polish Policy Research Group, Discussion Paper No. 7.

Beksiak, J. et al. (1991) 'Open Letter to the President of Poland on the question of the economy', Warsaw, 12 October, published (in Polish) in *Rzeczpospolita*.

Brada, J. C. and A. E. King (1992) 'Is There a J-Curve for the Economic Transition from Socialism to Capitalism', *Economics of Planning* 25.

Bywalec, C. (1993) 'Transformcja w portfelach', *Zycie Gospodarcze*, No. 2 (2750), 10 January, p. 7.

CBOS (Centre for the Study of Social Opinions) (1991), various reports (in Polish), Warsaw.

Central Planning Office (CPO) (1992) 'Information on Economic Situation in 1991 and Elements of a Forecast for 1992', Warsaw, 31 January, mimeo.

Commission of the European Communities (1992) 'Poland – Country Study', Brussels, September, mimeo.

Council of Ministers (CM) (1991) 'Poland's Budget, January 1 to March 31, 1992', December, mimeo.

(1992a) 'Guidelines for the Social and Economic Policy in 1992', Warsaw, 14 February, mimeo.

(1992b) 'State Budget of 1993', November, mimeo.

Dabrowski, J. et al. (1991) 'Report on Polish State Enterprises in 1990', Warsaw: The Research Centre for Marketization and Property Reform, February, mimeo.

Dabrowski, M. (1992) 'The Polish Stabilization 1990-1991', *Journal of International Comparative Economics* 1, 295-327.

Dornbusch, R. (1991) 'Experiences with Extreme Monetary Instability', in S. Commander (ed.), *Managing Inflation in Socialist Economies in Transition*, Washington DC: The World Bank.

Economic Bulletin for Europe (1991) Geneva: Secretariat of the UN Economic Commission for Europe, Vol. 43.

Economic Committee of the Council of Ministers (ECCM) (1991a), 'Guidelines for the Social and Economic Policy in 1992', Warsaw, 1 November, mimeo.

(1991b) 'Report on the State of the Economy', Warsaw, 21 December, mimeo.

(1991c) 'The Position of the Economic Council Regarding Main Directions of Economic Policy during Transformation', Warsaw, November, mimeo.

Frydman, R. and S. Wellisz (1991) 'The Ownership–Control Structure and the Behaviour of Polish Enterprises During the 1990 Reform: Macroeconomic Measures and Microeconomic Responses', in V. Corbo, F. Coricelli and J. Bossak, *Reforming Central and Eastern European Economies*, Washington, DC: The World Bank.

Frydman, R., A. Rapaczinski, J. S. Earle et al. (1993) 'The Price Verification Process in Central Europe', London: Central European University Press.

Fischer, S. and A. Gelb (1991) 'Issues in the Reform of Socialist Economies', in V. Corbo et al., *Reforming Central and Eastern European Economies*, Washington, DC: The World Bank,

Gomulka, S. (1990) 'Reform and Budgetary Policies in Poland, 1989–1990', *European Economy* 43, March.

(1991) 'The Causes of Recession Following Stabilization', *Comparative Economic Studies* 33(2), 71–89.

(1992a), 'Polish Economic Reform, 1990–1: Principles, Policies and Outcomes', *Cambridge Journal of Economics*, September.

(1992b), 'How to Create a Capital Market in a Socialist Country for the Purpose of Privatization', in Andreas R. Prindl, *Banking and Finance in Eastern Europe*, London: Woodhead-Faulkner; Polish original, (1989).

(1993a), 'Economic and Political Constraints during Transition', LSE, mimeo.

(1993b) 'The Size and Distribution of Bad Debt, and Macroeconomic Policy', LSE, mimeo.

Gomulka, S. and P. Jdsinski (1993) 'Privatization in Poland', LSE, mimeo.

Gomulka, S. and J. Lane (1993) 'Recession Dynamics in a Transition Economy Following an External Price Shock', LSE, mimeo.

Gontarek, W. (1991) 'Proposals for Financial Institutions Privatization Programmes', a report to Poland's Ministry of Ownership Changes, Warsaw, 3 September, mimeo.

Hare, P. and G. Hughes (1991) 'Competitiveness and Industrial Restructuring in Czechoslovakia, Hungary and Poland', *European Economy*, Special Edition No. 2.

IMF (1991) 'Concluding Statement of Mission', Warsaw, 18 November, mimeo.

(1992a), 'Concluding Statement of Mission', Warsaw, 12 February, mimeo.

(1992b) 'Poland – Annual Review', Washington DC, 9 July.

Kharas, H. J. (1991) 'Restructuring Socialist Industry: Poland's Experience in 1990', World Bank Discussion Paper No. 142.

Kolarska-Bobinska, L. (1990) 'The Myth of the Market and the Reality of Reform', in S. Gomulka and A. Polonsky (eds.), *Polish Paradoxes*, London and New York: Routledge.

Lehmann, H., E. Kwiatkowski and M. E. Schaffer (1991) 'Polish Regional U/V ratios and the Regional Pre-Reform Employment Structure', Centre for Economic Performance, Working Paper No. 149, London School of Economics, mimeo.

Lubbe, A. (1991) 'Transforming Poland's Industry', Polish Policy Research Group, Discussion Paper No. 13.

Ministry of Finance (MF) (1992a), 'Restructuring the Polish Banking System', Warsaw, 7 January, mimeo.

(1992b) 'State Budget for 1992: Assumptions and Early Estimates of Revenues and Expenditures', Warsaw, February, mimeo.

Ministry of Ownership Changes (MOC) (1992) 'The Government Programme of Privatization', Warsaw, 11 February, mimeo.

Nuti, D. M. (1991) 'Stabilisation and Sequencing in the Reform of Socialist Economies', in S. Commander (ed.), *Managing Inflation in Socialist Economies in Transition*, Washington, DC: The World Bank.

Portes, R. (1992) 'From Central Planning to a Market Economy', forthcoming in S. Islam and M. Mandelbaum (eds.), *Making Markets*, New York Council on Foreign Relations.

Rosati, D. (1991) 'Sequencing the Reforms in Poland', in P. Marer and S. Zecchini (eds.), *The Transition to a Market Economy*, Vol. 1, Paris: OECD.

Republic of Poland (1992) 'Memorandum of the Government of Poland on Economic Policies' (Letter of Intent), December, mimeo.

Schaffer, M. E. (1992a) 'The Polish State-owned Enterprise Sector and the Recession in 1990', *Comparative Economic Studies*, 34(1), Spring, 58–85.

(1992b) 'The Enterprise Sector and Emergence of the Polish Fiscal Crisis 1990–1991', Centre for Economic Performance Working Paper No. 280, September.

(1992c) 'Poland', Centre for Economic Performance Working Paper No. 183; in D. Dyker (ed.), *National Economies of Europe*, London: Longman, 239–77.

Tymowska, K. and M. Wisniewski (1991) 'Social Security and Health Care in Poland', Polish Policy Research Group, Discussion Paper No. 16.

Wellisz, S., H. Kierzkowski and M. Okólski (1991) 'Macroeconomic Policies in Poland in 1990 and 1991', Polish Policy Research Group, Discussion Paper No. 1.

Winiecki, J. (1991) 'The Polish Transition Programme at Mid-1991: Stabilization under Threat', Kiel: Institut für Weltwirtschaft, September.

World Bank and others (1991), 'Special Report on the State of the Polish Reform', December, mimeo.

7 Poland: glass half empty

Dariusz K. Rosati

1 Introduction

The comprehensive reform programme initiated in Poland in January 1990 aimed at replacing the socialist central planning system by a modern market mechanism. The launching of the programme was marked by overwhelming popular support and hopes that market-oriented reforms would soon bring about a significant improvement in the standard of living. The programme has also been highly praised by the international community for its boldness and determination (see IMF, 1990).

Three years later, it has become clear that the programme does not deliver on many of its important promises. The economic results of the first stage of transformation are at best ambiguous and at worst disappointing. Although some opinions claim almost complete success (e.g. Sachs, 1990, 1991; IMF, 1991; PlanEcon, 1990), many more authors are less sanguine (Nuti, 1991; Portes, 1991b, 1992; Laski and Levcik, 1992), and some even speak about of failure (see Kolodko, 1991a, b; Kurowski, 1991; Podkaminer, 1992).

Contrary to earlier expectations, the deep recession in 1990 was not followed by a recovery. Low levels of domestic demand, structural rigidities, and unfavourable external shocks pulled the Polish economy into an unprecedented depression in 1991. The sharp contraction in output and investment led to a cumulative fall in GDP by 20% over two years, and steadily growing unemployment rates were accompanied by persistent inflation, a high budget deficit and a deteriorating trade balance. On the positive side, one should note the fast expansion of the private sector, the further strengthening of monetary stability, and the significant relief in the external debt position, resulting from the successful debt reduction agreement signed with the Paris Club creditor governments in March 1991. On balance, however, these positive developments could not offset the negative impact of the deep recession in the state sector. Most of the key economic performance targets assumed for 1991 have not been fulfilled, and the unexpected depth of the crisis has shaken the political stability of the country.

The purpose of this study is to give a critical evaluation of the economic transformation process to date, with due attention also to the political and social aspects. The paper has five main sections. The next two sections review the reform results to date at the macroeconomic and institutional levels. In section 4, the main causes of the failure of reforms to achieve the expected results are examined, while the last section discusses the sociopolitical dilemmas of the reforms.

Throughout the study, the achievements of the programme (some of which are indeed remarkable) are given less attention than the failures, the main reason for this deliberate asymmetry being the need to focus on the problems and their possible solutions rather than on offering yet another record of successes. I believe that there is no alternative to market reforms in Poland, and that the general policy approach adopted – combining comprehensiveness, speed and overall financial discipline – has been essentially correct. Specific policy measures, however, were in many cases inefficient, misplaced, or simply erroneous. The economic, social and political costs of transformation could have been lower, and the overall results better, had some different measures been applied.

The current situation in Poland calls for innovative policy actions that would strengthen the emerging recovery and establish a framework for stable growth. These actions may best be formulated in the course of open and responsible discussion. The sense of urgency dictated the critical character of this study.

2   Reform Results to Date: More Pain than Gain?

2.1   Economic Performance in 1990–2: Financial Stabilization and Economic Recession

The stabilization programme brought about some undisputed achievements between 1990 and 1992. These include the marked slowdown in the inflation rate, the elimination of shortages and the restoration of general equilibrium in the goods market, the stabilization of the foreign currency market under conditions of internal convertibility, and the initiation of many institutional changes.[1] But the price of these achievements proved to be high in terms of output and employment losses, as well as in terms of social and political costs.

Right from the start of the programme, the Polish economy entered a deep recession, which had been expected, and remained in the recession for more than two years, which had not been expected. The sharp initial contraction in output and investment led to a fall in GDP by 11.6% in 1990. Unemployment rose from negligible levels to 1.1 million people, i.e. 6.5% of the total workforce, and industrial output fell by 24.2% in 1990 (see Table 7.1 for the main macroeconomic indicators).

Table 7.1   Poland: Main Economic Indicators, 1990–1.

Year, month	Index, preceding month = 100 Consumer price index	Net average wage[1]	Nominal incomes	Nominal expenditures	Monthly interest rate on refinancing credit	Industrial output[2]	Unemployment '000
1990							
Jan	179.6	101.8	137.5	119.2	36.0	69.5	55.8
Feb	123.8	115.2	103.7	90.6	20.0	69.7	152.2
Mar	104.3	137.4	120.1	123.0	10.0	69.3	266.6
Apr	107.5	95.0	101.7	118.7	8.0	71.5	351.1
May	104.6	97.0	100.8	102.5	5.5	72.0	443.2
Jun	103.4	102.3	109.2	105.0	4.0	72.7	568.2
Jul	103.6	110.8	111.1	110.4	2.5	76.5	699.3
Aug	101.8	105.0	107.6	115.4	2.5	82.1	820.3
Sep	104.6	107.6	106.7	103.7	2.5	79.0	926.4
Oct	105.7	113.6	118.9	126.4	3.0	80.5	1,008.4
Nov	104.9	112.0	104.8	102.5	3.7	81.7	1,089.1
Dec	105.9	103.1	115.4	116.6	3.7	76.1	1,124.8
1991							
Jan	112.7	99.8	89.6	88.5	3.7	92.0	1,195.7
Feb	106.7	112.5	105.1	92.6	4.6	93.9	1,265.0
Mar	104.5	103.8	112.2	122.6	4.6	95.1	1,322.1
Apr	102.7	98.8	100.8	101.8	4.6	87.4	1,370.1
May	102.7	97.9	92.0	93.6	3.9	85.1	1,434.5
Jun	104.9	102.0	104.9	98.0	3.9	83.8	1,574.1
Jul	100.1	104.8	106.5	108.8	3.4	81.6	1,749.9
Aug	100.6	99.7	102.3	103.6	3.1	80.8	1,854.0
Sep	104.3	102.9	101.9	104.1	2.9	77.0	1,970.9
Oct	103.2	108.8	105.5	114.6	2.9	78.4	2,040.4
Nov	103.2	105.0	99.1[3]	90.2[3]	2.9	82.2	2,108.3
Dec	103.1	108.7	–	–	2.9	75.3	2,155.6
1992							
Jan	107.5	90.9	–	–	2.9	84.6	2,211.8
Feb	101.8	101.1	–	–	2.9	90.8	2,245.6
Mar	102.0	109.4	–	–	2.9	99.2	2,216.4
Apr	103.7	104.1	–	–	2.9	103.5	2,218.4
May	104.0	94.6	–	–	2.9	102.6	2,228.6
Jun	101.6	102.7	–	–	2.9	107.9	2,296.7
Jul	101.4	105.5	–	–	2.7	109.7	2,409.1
Aug	102.7	100.6	–	–	2.7	107.6	2,457.1
Sep	105.3	104.9	–	–	2.7	113.3	2,498.5
Oct	103.0	105.8	–	–	2.7	108.6	2,477.3
Nov	102.3	106.9	–	–	2.7	112.9	2,490.1
Dec	102.9[4]	–	–	–	2.7	–	–

Notes:
1   Including bonuses.
2   'Socialized' sector only for 1990, corresponding month of previous year = 100
3   Series discontinued in 1992.
4   Preliminary.

Source: Compiled from Central Statistical Office data and National Bank of Poland data.

The feeble recovery registered in the second half of 1990, when output was growing at an average monthly rate of 1-2%, came to an abrupt halt in early 1991. Industrial output sank again in 1991 by 11.9% as compared with 1990, thus bringing the cumulative fall to 35%, and unemployment increased almost twofold, reaching 2.15 million people at end-1991 (11.5% of the total workforce). 'Mass' lay-offs, however, accounted for only 23% of the total figure (18% in January 1991), so that a major part of the increase was 'voluntary' unemployment and some across-the-board reductions in overemployment. The lack of mass lay-offs means that bankruptcies are still rather exceptional and no major reallocation of manpower has taken place in the industrial sector. Furthermore, changes in industrial employment levels have not been correlated with fluctuations in industrial output (see Figure 7.1), which confirms the relative inflexibility of employment in the state-owned, labour-managed firms that dominate the Polish industrial sector.[2]

Investment expenditures declined in 1991 by 4.1% in real terms as compared with 1990, thus falling 16% below the peak level in 1988. The fall in investment demand mainly affected domestic producers of capital goods (fall by 19%), whereas imports of machinery and equipment actually increased by 10%. For 1992, a further fall in investment was expected.

Private consumption declined by 15% in 1990 in real terms, but increased by 1-2% in 1991, in a somewhat surprising contrast to the steep fall in output and investment. The increase in consumption in 1991 was primarily the result of higher social transfer payments (pensions), credits and other incomes (increase

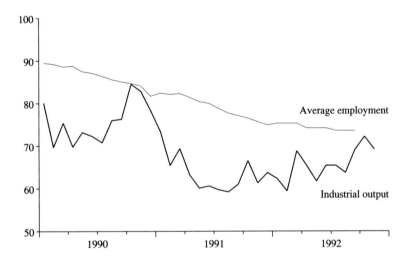

Figure 7.1   Industry: Output and Employment, 1989-92
(Monthly Average, 1989=100)

of 23% in real terms); by contrast, real wages declined by 8%, and individual farmers' incomes by 39%. The key component of the increased consumption was probably soaring consumer imports (twice as high as in 1990), financed by private transfers. Their share in total retail sales increased from 6.4% in 1990 to 15.2% in 1991.

Inflation fell sharply during the early months of the stabilization, but then stabilized at monthly levels of 3–4% and fluctuated around this level in response to policy changes and seasonal factors. In contrast with earlier periods, external shocks did not play a significant role in explaining price movements in the second half of 1991 and in 1992. It should be noted that the underlying inflationary trend during 1991 and 1992 was mainly caused by cost-push factors (increases in energy prices, transport and telecommunication tariffs, increase in depreciation charges due to the revaluation of fixed assets, discrete devaluation of the zloty in May and then continuous devaluation after October 1991, an increase in customs duties in August 1991, repeated increases in turnover taxes). This combination of factors explains the persistence of inflation, which runs at 3–4% per month (42–60% p.a.) despite continuous drastic monetary and fiscal restrictions. As a result, the price level in December 1992 was 45% higher than in December 1991, and 173% higher than in December 1990. The inflation index on a year-to-year basis was also around 45% in 1992, down from 70.3% in 1991 and 618% in 1990.

The external balance significantly deteriorated in 1991, after the remarkable improvement a year earlier. The overall trade balance turned from a huge surplus in 1990 (US$3.8 billion and 4.4 billion transferable roubles (TR)) to a deficit of some US$600 million in 1991, with a small surplus with Western countries being more than offset by a deficit with the former Soviet Union. Convertible currency exports reached some US$14.6 billion (an increase of 22% from 1990), while convertible currency imports jumped to US$15.5 billion (an increase of 87%).[3] The trade balance improved again in the first half of 1992, mainly owing to a favourable export performance boosted by real depreciation of the zloty and a large-scale reduction in trade barriers in exports to the EC. This tendency was, however, reversed in the summer because of higher domestic wage and price inflation, and only a small surplus was expected for the whole of 1992.[4]

While recession and inflation remained the two central worries in 1990, in 1991 some new problems emerged. From the beginning of 1991 there was a significant deterioration in the central budget position. The budget deficit grew rapidly from Zl 5 trillion at end-March to Zl 13.1 trillion at end-June, Zl 22.4 trillion at end-September, and Zl 30.6 trillion at end-December (some 12% of budget expenditures and 3.5% of GDP). The main reason for the high deficit was much lower than anticipated tax revenues from the enterprise sector.

One of the few bright spots in the otherwise depressed picture of the Polish economy was the remarkable expansion of the private sector in 1991. The growth in industrial output in the private sector was 25.4% in 1991, and its share in total industrial output sold increased from 17.4% in 1990 to 24.2% in 1991.[5] The value of 'private' exports increased five times compared with 1990 and amounted to 19.8% of total exports; the value of imports (statistically registered) increased 5.6 times and amounted to 46.1% of total imports. The share of private shops in total retail trade grew to over 80%, and nearly 40% of the total non-agricultural workforce was employed in the private sector. The expansion continued in 1992: at end-September the private sector employed 57.7% of the total Polish workforce, and 43.1% of the total workforce outside agriculture. The share of the private sector in industrial output in January–September 1992 was 28.6% (up from 23.1% in 1991), 76.8% in construction (61.2% in 1991)[6] and 32.7% in transport (24.3% in 1991).

Table 7.2   Economic Performance of the Public and Private Sectors in Poland, January–August 1992

Sector	Firms operating at a loss (% of total)	Share in total sales (%)	Profits Gross (Zl tr.)	Profits Net (Zl tr.)	Gross profit/ costs ratio (%)	Net profit/ sales ratio (%)
All sectors						
A	40.8	73.1	34.2	–7.0	4.3	–0.8
B	44.1	26.9	1.4	–1.9	0.5	–0.6
Industry						
A	40.6	44.5	14.4	–14.8	3.0	–2.9
B	41.8	6.8	1.3	0.2	1.8	0.3
Construction						
A	39.0	3.0	1.8	–0.4	5.6	–1.0
B	35.7	2.5	1.9	1.1	7.0	3.8
Transport						
A	49.7	4.3	0.9	–0.8	2.0	–1.6
B	59.6	0.6	0.2	0.5	2.7	0.8
Trade						
A	34.2	14.7	5.7	2.3	3.5	1.4
B	41.7	13.6	0.3	–0.7	0.2	–0.4

Note: A – public sector; B – private sector.

Source: Central Statistical Office, *'Informacja o sytuacji spoleczno-gospodarczej kraju*, I-III kwartal 1992r', Warsaw, 22 October 1992, pp. 18–19.

These optimistic trends were, however, partly contradicted by the apparently poor economic performance of the private sector. Table 7.2 illustrates the somewhat puzzling discrepancy in financial results reported by the public and private sectors in Poland.

The private sector shows much lower profitability, especially in industry and trade. Moreover, the share of firms operating at a loss is higher in all sectors for the private sector than for the public sector. One possible explanation of this paradox relates to the common practice of underreporting for tax reasons; another points to more intensive restructuring in the private sector, which may worsen current profitability.

In sum, the overall economic performance of the Polish economy in 1991 turned out to be much worse than expected only a year earlier.[7] It was not until 1992 that the situation started to improve, especially in industry, construction and foreign trade. But the recovery is still very weak and the basis for growth very fragile.[8]

Poland is on its way to restoring regular cooperation with the IMF. The growing budget deficit led to an excessive domestic credit expansion in 1991, and Poland failed to meet the performance criteria required for releasing the second tranche of the IMF credits under the Extended Facility Arrangement signed only in April 1991. The negotiations with the IMF on possible corrections of policy targets were postponed several times from the summer of 1991 and were eventually resumed in February 1992. It should be remembered that the fulfilment of targets negotiated with the Fund is necessary for the completion of the debt relief agreement signed with Paris Club creditor governments in March 1991. During negotiations in 1992 the Fund displayed remarkable flexibility in accepting Polish proposals for the 1992 budget deficit, which were revised upwards several times.

2.2 Planned Targets and Actual Results

The economic results of 1990 and 1991 remained in striking contrast with the targets formulated only several months earlier. The Polish stabilization-cum-reform programme failed to meet the macroeconomic targets forecast by successive governments and specified in the agreements with the IMF. In the Letters of Intent, submitted to the IMF in December 1989, August 1990 and March 1991 much more optimistic scenarios had been foreseen; specifically, a recovery was planned already for the second half of 1990, and then again for the second half of 1991. Not only did economic growth not resume after the initial shock, however, but the recession deepened. Observers are divided on whether these forecasts were too optimistic, or the realization of goals encountered some obstacles that could not have been foreseen, or some important mistakes were made in the design and implementation of the programme. Table 7.3 illustrates the gaps between targets and results of the first two years of stabilization.

Table 7.3   Reform-cum-Stabilization in Poland: Planned Targets and Actual Results (% Change Relative to Previous Period)

Macroeconomic variable	1990 Targets	1990 Results	1991 Targets	1991 Results
GDP	-3.1	-11.6	+3.5	-7.0[1]
Inflation:				
CPI, 1st quarter	75	132	23	26
CPI, whole year[2]	95	249	36	60
Unemployment:				
as %	2.0	6.3	–	11.4
in '000	400	1123	–	2155
Industrial output	-5.0	-23.4	–	-14.2
Budget balance:				
in money terms (Zl tr.)	–	+2.4	-5.5	-31.0
as % of GDP	-0.5	+0.5	-0.5	-3.5
Trade balance:				
in US$bn.	-0.8	+3.8	0	-0.6
in TR bn.	+0.5	+4.4	0	+0.4
Change in international reserves (US$bn.)	–	+2.4	+0.7	-1.3[1]

Notes:
1   Preliminary.
2   December–December.

Sources: The 'targets' were compiled from the Letters of Intent submitted by Polish governments to the IMF in December 1989 and March 1991, and the 'results' were taken from national statistics and various press publications.

Judging from aggregate macroeconomic figures, the first phase of stabilization was moderately successful on the financial side, and rather disappointing on the real side. The 'shock' therapy proved to be relatively effective in bringing down inflation within a few months of the initial price liberalization, although the sustainability of these results is questionable. The underlying inflation rooted in various cost and inertial factors turned out to be much more persistent, and after the initial deceleration from the monthly rates of 20–30% in the last quarter of 1989 and of almost 80% in January 1990, inflation continued at 3–5% per month from April 1990.

Price liberalization under strong monetary and fiscal restraint proved to be very effective in restoring a fundamental market balance in the Polish economy, which had suffered from endemic shortages for decades. Likewise, the policies applied worked surprisingly well in stabilizing the foreign exchange market: the black market premium, averaging 400–500% during the 1980s, was brought down to negligible levels almost instantaneously, and demand for foreign exchange stabilized, responding to the fall in real incomes and wealth, and to altered expectations.

The programme also appears to have had a strong positive impact on the fiscal balance and the external balance. The budget position improved remarkably during the first half year of programme implementation, mainly in reaction to the temporary boost to enterprise profitability from price liberalization and resulting capital gains on current assets (inventories and foreign exchange holdings). Once these short-term effects disappeared, however, the fiscal balance deteriorated because of continued demand depression and the subsequent fall in tax revenues. The improvement in the external position lasted longer because of the large initial undervaluation of the domestic currency. A substantial trade surplus was built up during the first year of stabilization, a rather unexpected result of the steep initial devaluation of the zloty and the sharp contraction in domestic demand; but it gradually dissipated during 1991 because of the continuous real appreciation of the domestic currency.

The impact of the external environment worked in favour of the Polish economy at the outset of stabilization, but against it in late 1990 and in 1991. When Poland launched its comprehensive reform in late 1989, not only did it receive strong support from the international community as the first country from the former Soviet bloc to pioneer market reforms (support that culminated in the debt reduction agreement in March 1991, and has faded away since then), but it also benefited from a relatively favourable situation on international markets. High (though stagnating) levels of domestic demand in Western countries in 1990 allowed Polish firms significantly to increase their convertible currency exports, thus cushioning the depressing impact of the sharp fall in domestic demand. Moreover, the majority of CMEA imports were still paid for in 'cheap' transferable roubles, and the Gulf War was something nobody expected. External conditions deteriorated in 1991, when the dismantling of the CMEA trade and payments system and the disintegration of the Soviet Union sharply reduced import demand in East European and CIS countries, while the recession in industrialized countries reduced the possibilities for shifting sales to Western markets.

The deterioration in external conditions is often given as an explanation for the worse than expected economic results of the reform programme. But, for all its convenience, this can account for only part of the domestic recession.[9] The data for 1991 point to a major miscalculation in economic policy in Poland. The error of -10 percentage points in forecasting the 1991 GDP is indeed striking and can by no means be explained only by unfavourable 'exogenous' developments. It seems plausible that in addition to adverse external shocks some more fundamental flaws marred the strategy, and that some policy errors were also made during its implementation.

2.3 The Enterprise Sector

The sharp increase in the profitability of enterprises in the first half of 1990 was a combined, one-time effect of large capital gains due to the price liberalization, low labour costs and high protection levels because of the undervalued zloty. The capital gains were obtained through the liquidation of excessive inventories and foreign exchange holdings, while upward rigidity of wages resulted from a combination of low indexation coefficients, the 'implicit' collective contract between Solidarity and Mazowiecki's government, and generally high uncertainty. These were purely short-term phenomena and disappeared towards the end of 1990; but the government's policy apparently failed to take into account the temporary character of the jump in enterprises' profitability, and continued its restrictive course into 1991 and 1992.

After the tightening of monetary and fiscal policies in the last quarter of 1990 and first quarter of 1991, the financial situation of state-owned enterprises deteriorated sharply. The 'easy' reserves were largely exhausted (excess inventories, foreign exchange deposits), and the contraction in output levels necessarily increased production costs per unit of output. The collapse of the post-Soviet market, the sharp increase in prices of energy and inputs imported from ex-CMEA markets, combined with the policy of a fixed exchange rate, contributed to a further reduction in sales revenues and profits. The proportion of aggregate before-tax profits of state enterprises to total sales revenues fell from 23.1% in 1990, to 9.0% in the first half of 1991, and to 6.9% for the whole of 1991. Similarly, the proportion of net after-tax profits to total sales diminished from 10.6% in 1990 to 0.2% and -2.0% in the corresponding periods of 1991. Figure 7.2 shows the ratios of gross and net profit to costs for enterprises during 1990-2.

The financial situation of enterprises in 1992 continued to be very precarious. The gross profit/sales ratio for January-October fell further to 3.0%, while the net profit/sales ratio remained negative (-0.6%).

Declining profits and the depletion of their financial reserves forced enterprises to resort to credit financing, in spite of generally high interest rates and with no prospects of immediate recovery. This policy necessarily further worsened their liquidity position. The level of (gross) indebtedness of enterprises, measured by the ratio of total debt outstanding to monthly sales, after a fall in the second half of 1990, systematically increased in 1991 (see Figure 7.3 and Table 7.4). As a result, the number of firms rated by banks as ineligible for credit increased from 88 in December 1989, to 548 in December 1990, to 2,880 at end-December 1991, and to 4,474 at end-August 1992. When confronted by the increasing credit squeeze in late 1990 and in 1991, enterprises again resorted to inter-enterprise credit, thus largely neutralizing the government's efforts to impose stricter financial discipline. The inevitable result was an increasing level of indebtedness of enterprises, a lack of funds for

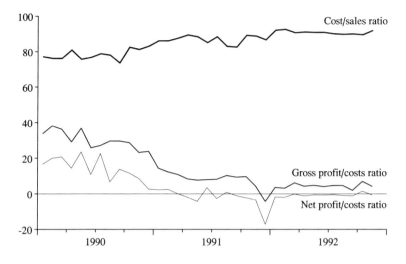

Figure 7.2 Profitability of Enterprises, January 1990 – November 1992 (%)

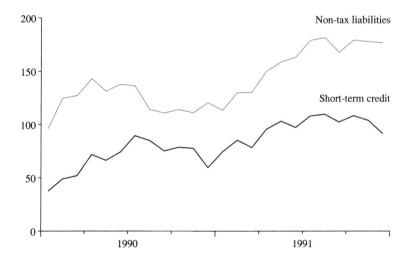

Figure 7.3 Bank Credit and Liabilities in Enterprises, 1990 and 1991
(as % of Monthly Sales)

Table 7.4   Indebtedness of Enterprises, 1989–92, end of period (Zl trillion)

Year, quarter	Total debt	Of which short-term credit	As % of sales Total debt	Short-term credit
1989				
Q4	26.3	20.2	75.0	57.7
1990				
Q1	39.0	30.7	66.0	51.9
Q2	57.8	43.9	97.6	74.2
Q3	74.6	52.5	106.9	75.2
Q4	95.1	50.8	111.1	59.3
1991				
Q1	104.3	65.6	124.5	78.3
Q2	117.7	78.2	146.2	97.1
Q3	132.8	87.3	155.5	102.2
Q4	145.2	92.9	142.5	91.2
1992				
Q1	162.2	101.2	117.2	73.1
Q2	169.5	99.2	116.6	68.2
Q3	176.8	99.6	114.0	64.2

Note: 1992 data are not comparable with 1991 data because of changed reporting rules.

Source: Central Statistical Office, *Statistical Bulletin*, various issues.

restructuring, and the accumulation of bad loans in commercial banks.

The growing trend in relative and absolute indebtedness of enterprises was clearly visible in 1991. The fall in the debt burden in 1992 was at least partly due to changed rules of calculation (debts to local governments and debts in the process of forced collection are now excluded from the total debt aggregate) and cannot be taken as a symptom of a radical improvement.

Polish experts are divided over the possible reasons for this dramatic deterioration in the financial position of enterprises in 1991. Three main causes are commonly cited: (1) the collapse of exports to the Soviet market, (2) the conservative behaviour of state firms' managers, who fail to undertake adjustment programmes aimed at reducing costs and improving competitiveness, (3) the excessive restrictiveness of macroeconomic policies. I comment below on points (2) and (3), leaving point (1) to be discussed in section 4.4.

The government's complaints about the conservative strategies pursued by state enterprises cannot be taken too seriously. They at best demonstrate the inability of the government (and of parliament) to apply the policy measures that would be effective in forcing enterprises into a desired behaviour pattern. The misjudgement of the adjustment potential of the enterprise sector was probably rooted in the free-market orthodoxy dominating the government's policies.

Managers of state-owned enterprises, when faced by liquidity problems, behave in a manner determined by the existing incentive structure; typically, they apply to the government to bail them out and try to put pressure on commercial banks to secure more credit financing, rather than lay off workers, change production programmes, or look for new markets and business partners abroad. In short, continuation and 'inertia' appear to be a safer strategy than restructuring under volatile conditions. Under the inefficient banking system and backed by strong labour unions, firms may still succeed in avoiding the crash. The specific institutional set-up established in 1981, under which workers' councils exert large real powers in enterprises, means that the conflict over income distribution has not been brought down to enterprise level, and still bears on the shoulders of the government. In fact, under the existing incentive structure, management and labour are encouraged to work hand in hand against the government, asking for tax reliefs, soft credits, subsidies and various protection schemes.

This behaviour pattern is sometimes criticized, especially by government officials, as being traditional or 'conservative'; but in fact it is perfectly rational given the existing incentives. The inertia should not be blamed on managers *in toto*; rather, the authorities failed to change the structure of incentives at the microeconomic level. If the threat of bankruptcy is not enforceable in practice, and if workers preserve their leverage over management, firms are likely to delay payments, maximize wages and disobey financial discipline rules. The uncertainty factor should not be disregarded either: unclear privatization plans, occasional campaigns against former *nomenklatura* managers, and constantly changing financial and tax regulations all favour the 'wait-and-see' strategy rather than a more entrepreneurial approach.

Central to the problem therefore seems to be the restrictive financial policy pursued by the government in late 1990 and in 1991, which was not accompanied by the necessary institutional changes at micro levels. Although correctly aimed at eliminating inefficient units through imposing a 'hard budget constraint', the policy failed to do so because of some conceptual and implementation mistakes. Excessive fiscal charges (with the so-called 'dividend' being particularly deleterious), a lack of investment incentives, and very expensive credit have squeezed enterprises out of liquidity and in effect reduced business confidence. While the budget constraint proved to be 'hard' for investment, it is still rather 'soft' for wage payments.

There are several reasons for the government's failure to enforce the closing down of inefficient units and to stimulate the reallocation of resources to expanding sectors. First, bankruptcy proceedings in practice proved very cumbersome, lengthy and inefficient. Second, enterprises managed to 'soften' their budget constraint by borrowing on the interest-free 'curb' credit market in the form of inter-enterprise credits. Third, they delayed – legally or illegally – payment of their tax liabilities (except for the 'dividend' tax, which was the trigger for initiating bankruptcy proceedings).[10] Fourth, the excess-wage tax system helped some of them to keep wage increases within limits.

The result is that, in present circumstances, the number of companies that in one way or another would qualify for bankruptcy has grown to levels that may be economically and politically unacceptable. The proportion of loss-making enterprises increased from 39% at end-1991 to 43% at end-August 1992 (against 1.9% at end-1990). Closures on such a massive scale can hardly be contemplated; besides, many of them would also be economically unjustified, because it is not at all clear what proportion of that number may result from inconsistent financial policies rather than from microeconomic inefficiency.[11] None the less, tolerating a large pool of inefficient companies in the economy is not only a bad policy but also carries a significant 'moral hazard' risk.

The inability to initiate and stimulate industrial restructuring on a larger scale should be regarded as a serious drawback of the government's policies in 1991. It is now clear that in this particular area macroeconomic restraint alone does not suffice. State enterprises are reluctant to embark on major restructuring programmes, not only because new credits are expensive and demand prospects are gloomy, but also because their managements lack job security and clear prospects about their future.

According to many Polish commentators (e.g. Lipinski, Nasilowski, Sadowski, and Zienkowski), the economic policy in 1991 was one-sided: macroeconomic restrictions should have been supplemented by a variety of industrial policies aimed at helping those enterprises and branches that had prospects of successful development and swiftly eliminating those that could not possibly be rescued.[12] For the time being, all enterprises, both efficient and inefficient, have suffered acute financial stress, and the lack of investment credits at acceptable interest rates and conditions makes the restructuring task difficult and risky.

2.4   Economic Recession: Mirage or Reality?

The scale of the economic recession in Poland is frequently disputed on the grounds that official statistics overestimate the actual fall in output. Three main arguments are typically raised in this context.

First, official macroeconomic statistics are considered as rather unreliable, as regards both the quality of the data as well as the methodologies used. Some of these problems have existed for years (e.g. reporting on the notorious 'overfulfilment' of planned targets by enterprises), but many are a direct consequence of the transition process itself. For instance, national accounts statistics are based on incomplete data (they do not cover a large part of private sector activities), quarterly data for GNP or NMP series are not computed, the activities of the service sector are monitored only partially, trade statistics are plagued by a combination of conversion, aggregation and classification problems. Perhaps the most important deficiency is that the official statistics fail to take full account of thriving private sector activities, including the 'shadow' economy (imports of consumer goods, retail trade and non-material services, in particular). For that reason it may be assumed that officially reported data on the most important macroeconomic variables (such as GDP, output, employment, individual consumption) should be revised upwards, although the scale of the revision is unclear.[13]

The second argument emphasizes the process of industrial restructuring that is taking place in the transition period. Some observers point out that in fact the recession is not as deep as it appears, the reason being that many activities have been discontinued because under the newly established set of market prices and more realistic exchange rates these activities turned out to yield negative (or very low) value added.[14] In this case, the disappearance of uneconomic output should not be welfare-decreasing. While the existence of value-added 'subtractors' in formerly centrally planned economies can hardly be disputed (especially in energy-intensive sectors, because of ridiculously low energy prices under central planning), the actual scale of the distortion remains problematic,[15] and it is unclear how the problem should be addressed by economic policy (whether and which of these activities should be temporarily protected, and by what measures). But the most important caveat to this argument is that, if negative value-added activities are indeed shed, the overall level of welfare should increase rather than decrease. It is quite difficult to demonstrate that this happens.

In a similar vein, it is sometimes argued that the observed recession simply reflects the elimination of uncompetitive production, which cannot find outlets under new conditions (Beksiak et al., 1991). That certainly happens, but the reasons for this 'revealed' low competitiveness may vary from microeconomic inefficiency of a basically structural character, to macroeconomic restrictions imposed on domestic demand and/or to market imperfections. In such cases, some activities that could possibly become competitive after some restructuring will have to disappear because macroeconomic policy is excessively restrictive and capital markets are underdeveloped. This line of reasoning also seems to ignore the presumption that the market-oriented transformation was undertaken with the aim not only of eliminating inefficient activities, but also of stimulating the expansion of those that are efficient.

It seems, therefore, that, while there is certainly a grain of truth in the proposition that the actual recession is not as acute as it may appear from official statistics, the difference is probably not as large as some observers claim. Moreover, the positive supply response is not as vigorous and forthcoming as initially expected. This may in turn mean that either the 'destruction' takes place at a disproportionately faster pace than the 'creation', or there are some important obstacles on the supply side. In any event, it would definitely be misleading and even dangerous to regard the present recession as something like a statistical 'mirage'. The deep contraction in output and employment is a matter of fact, which may or may not be disputed by academics but should not be ignored or belittled by policy-makers. Even if the real levels of living standards are indeed less affected than the statistics may suggest, a gap has none the less emerged between the reality and what was initially expected, no matter how naive or overly optimistic those expectations were.

Gomulka (1991b) argues that the fall in output following stabilization was inevitable for both supply and demand reasons. Supply fell because forced substitution (existing under shortage) was eliminated after price liberalization. But in this case the level of output in the deficit sectors would have increased or at least remained unchanged, which obviously was not the case in 1990.[16] It seems therefore that demand-side factors may have played the dominant role in the recession.

3   The Slow Pace of Institutional Reform

Many changes were expected in 1991 in the area of institutional and systemic reforms. The delay in introducing them in an efficient and workable form is seen by many observers as an important cause of the recession (Winiecki, 1992). Government plans for the immediate future included, *inter alia*, privatization and restructuring of the state enterprise sector, promotion of internal and external competition, further liberalization of the few remaining price controls, removal of barriers to foreign investors, restructuring of the banking sector, establishing capital markets and comprehensive fiscal reform.[17] Lengthy and cumbersome parliamentary procedures, a lack of political consensus over the pace and scope of the necessary changes, and a deteriorating political climate in the country did not allow for these ambitious plans to be realized. Although many of the initiatives are already fairly advanced, some of them have not yet reached the legislative stage. Among the most important reforms are the new foreign investment law, passed in June 1991, establishing the Warsaw stock exchange in April 1991, and the introduction of individual income taxation from January 1992.[18] By contrast, the introduction of the value-added tax has been repeatedly delayed and is now planned for 1 July 1993. Also postponed have been plans to integrate the parallel foreign exchange market for individuals with the official market, scheduled originally for the second half of 1991. Perhaps the most urgent task still pending is, however, the reform of the banking system, which is considered by many to be the main obstacle to speeding up the market transformation process in Poland.

3.1 Markets and Competition

Poland entered the reform programme with substantially liberalized market-access regulations. The Law on Entrepreneurship (already passed in December 1988) eliminated most of the previous administrative obstacles to commercial activities and put the public and private sectors on an equal footing. Entry and exit barriers in most branches were lifted, and licensing is required in only very few areas (e.g. production and trade in military goods).

In 1990, the foreign trade regime was one of the most liberal by international standards: the abolition of quantitative restrictions on imports and a very low tariff incidence (3-4%) made Poland one of the most open markets in the world. The continuous real appreciation of the zloty in 1991, however, wiped out the competitive edge of the Polish tradable sector, and the government decided to increase customs tariff protection in August 1991 (by an average of 10 percentage points).

The monopolistic structure of Polish industry and domestic trade, inherited from the central planning era, was a source of concern for economists and policy-makers, who feared that the monopolies might effectively block the functioning of emerging market mechanisms. The government policy was to break monopolies into smaller units in such areas as food processing, road transport and distribution, and to monitor monopolistic firms closely for unfair market behaviour. But only few monopolistic practices were actually registered: of 83 cases investigated by the Antimonopoly Board in 1991, only 20 were ruled to be illegal.[19] Nevertheless, the chronic lack of capital and continuously depressed demand clearly work against the establishment of competitive structures in some monopolized sectors, such as agricultural procurement or heavy industry.

On the other hand, the competitive pressure from imports was strong in 1991 because of the appreciated exchange rate and low tariff protection, and in some areas Polish firms may have been driven out of the domestic market. The competitive advantage of foreign suppliers was in many cases so large that only long-term restructuring programmes could help Polish firms in such sectors as light industry or agriculture.

The increasing pressure of foreign competition seriously undermined the initial support for trade liberalism, and calls for more protectionism are becoming widespread. In fact, since July 1992 the government has introduced a number of protective measures, ranging from a new, higher customs tariff, to restoring the state monopoly in trade in alcoholic beverages and tobacco products, to extending the range of trading activities requiring licensing. Protectionist tendencies, articulated in a particularly strong way by agricultural and industrial lobbies, may endanger the process of opening up the Polish economy.

3.2   Privatization and the Restructuring of the Enterprise Sector

The privatization process had already started in 1989 with some 'spontaneous' transfers of state-owned property in services and the housing sector to private hands. Later, in 1990, the Law on Privatization was enacted by parliament, establishing a legal framework for large-scale privatization of state-owned enterprises. But the early results of the process are at best mixed (Hare and Grosfeld, 1991; Dabrowski, 1991). Not only is privatization advancing at a much slower pace than expected, but its costs are high and the economic effects by no means impressive. The process became involved in endless political debates and is encountering growing social resistance. On the other hand, and in view of the protracted recession, rapid privatization seems to be increasingly regarded by many as a panacea for rapidly compounding economic and social problems in Poland (see e.g. Lipton and Sachs, 1990b). The discussion sometimes fails, however, to recognize the difference between the transfer of ownership and establishing a correct incentive structure; moreover, the goals of privatization have been specified vaguely and are excessively politicized.

3.2.1   The Objectives of Privatization: Speed versus Quality

The objectives of privatization in Poland have not been clearly and unambiguously specified. While for the majority of economists privatization is the means of upgrading economic efficiency at microeconomic levels, for many politicians it is mainly an important vehicle of fundamental sociopolitical change. Some people think of privatization as the most decisive and spectacular instrument of breaking with the communist past, while others look at it in terms of purely managerial goals. The confusion is frequently reflected in statements by Polish government officials.[20]

This apparent lack of clarity with respect to the key objectives of privatization probably not only derives from naive thinking on how to move instantaneously from central planning to a market economy, and from the concomitant excessive expectations so characteristic of early stages of the transformation, but, more importantly, it also reflects conflicting views on privatization and the role it should play in systemic transformation. It seems that in public debates the idea of privatization has gradually 'overreached' itself, and has been transformed into a universal instrument of systemic transformation, with far too many functions and goals attached.

As a result, economic, sociopolitical and ideological objectives seem to intermingle in public debates on privatization, adding to the inherent complexity of the whole issue. The government has made efforts to combine these different and clearly not always compatible objectives and considerations into a coherent privatization programme, but with little success. The institutional and legal framework established so far displays many contradictions, reflecting both conceptual errors and the excessive politicization of the issue.

The economic objectives of improving efficiency through a new structure of incentives seem to have shaped the government's thinking in the initial stages, but they were soon overwhelmed by more politicized considerations of treating privatization as an essential element in the process of creating a competitive market economy (Hare and Grosfeld, 1991). The direct consequence of this approach was the emphasis on wholesale privatization, with the *speed* of the process gaining more importance than its *quality*. This philosophy led to the formulation of fast-track policy proposals involving various 'give-away' schemes, such as voucher or certificate systems.

But this option was immediately attacked from two opposite sides. On the one hand, strong self-management and labour union lobbies argued in favour of 'employee privatization', involving the free distribution of shares in state-owned enterprises to workers, in order to create a system of employee shareholding or ESOPs ('akcjonariat pracowniczy'). Interesting enough, this concept proves the vitality of socialist-style ideas in Polish society, even though the term itself (socialism) is anathematized. On the other hand, liberals and more market-oriented economists strongly criticized any kind of free distribution scheme on the grounds of economic efficiency, 'fairness' and technical feasibility, and argued for a more gradual approach, allowing for better preparation and implementation of privatization decisions. Within this group, however, different opinions were expressed as to the desired size of the public (government) sector and the degree of state interventionism in the privatization process.

3.2.2 Problems Inherent to Privatization

At the outset of privatization, a number of legal, economic and social problems immediately emerged. First, issues pertaining to legal ownership and property rights proved to be more complex than expected, with restitution claims and the demarcation between state property and property of state-owned entities being most difficult to delineate. Property rights in state-owned enterprises are dispersed among managers, workers' councils and the so-called 'founding organs', and the relationship between these agents is not always transparent. The process of identifying and determining the real and legal owners of state property involves lengthy procedures and investigations, thus hampering the privatization process and adding to already high uncertainty. It should also be noted that no law on re-privatization or restitution has so far been adopted in Poland.[21]

Second, the lack of capital in the hands of private domestic investors has been regarded as the main obstacle to speedy privatization and served as one of the strongest arguments in favour of adopting some kind of free distribution of state-owned assets among the population at large (e.g. Lewandowski and Szomburg, 1989; Lipton and Sachs, 1990a). This argument, however, lost much of its significance after being criticized by many analysts, who proposed a variety of methods intended to circumvent the shortage of investment capital in Poland (see e.g. Kornai, 1990; Rosati, 1990; van Brabant, 1991; Nuti, 1991). One of the possible solutions could be based on 'non-monetary' credits extended by the State Treasury for the purpose of purchasing state assets.

The case for free distribution was additionally boosted by the apparently insurmountable problem of valuing state-owned assets. The absence of a stock exchange meant that an equilibrium price for assets could not be established, while distorted relative prices of inputs and outputs prevented the straightforward use of one of the well-known methods of financial analysis (e.g. discounted cash-flow techniques). This latter difficulty has been partly overcome by the sweeping price liberalization in 1990, accompanied by a significant opening up of the Polish economy to imports. While difficulties with proper valuations indeed remain, they should not, however, justify the waste of state-owned assets.

Fourth, privatization may not materialize quickly because of the lack of the institutional environment necessary for the private sector to operate properly. In this context, the role of competition and efficient financial markets is frequently seen as crucial (van Brabant, 1991). Sometimes, however, this dependence is seen from an opposite perspective: privatization is considered as an essential element in the process of creating a competitive market environment (Grosfeld, 1990).

More debatable is the view that one of the important obstacles in the privatization process is the acute shortage of managerial capabilities and skills in the state sector in Poland (van Brabant, 1991). It is true that managers of state-owned enterprises had to be cleared in the past by the political authorities, but this does not necessarily mean that they lacked experience and managerial talents. While being less experienced in market activities than their Western counterparts, Polish managers have generally been successful when doing business with Western companies or competing in international markets, as suggested by available, albeit mostly anecdotal, evidence. It seems that, in particular, those operating in the tradable sector are generally underrated by public opinion.

Lastly, as Nuti (1991) points out, the privatization process in Poland is bound to clash with strong self-management traditions. Powerful workers' councils had to be compensated or otherwise neutralized if privatization was to proceed fast, and not get bogged down in as yet unspecified employee ownership schemes.

3.2.3 The Privatization Strategy: The Initial Stages

Initially, the government envisaged the privatization process being shaped along the lines of the British experience with the privatization of individual companies in the early 1980s. Enterprises were to be privatized on commercial terms on the basis of careful valuation analysis. This concept came under criticism both from workers' organizations, which were strongly attached to the idea of 'employee ownership', as well as from proponents of free distribution schemes. The government, coming under strong political pressure, decided to withdraw the draft Act on the Transformation of State-Owned Enterprises from parliament in late 1989, and started working on a more eclectic strategy, which would allow for the conflicting interests of various political groups to be accommodated.

Indeed, it soon turned out that in the Polish conditions a much faster and broader programme would be preferable. The eventual adoption of the multi-path approach, reflected in the legal acts from 1990, was prompted by the desire to proceed with privatization as fast as possible, and took account of the almost complete lack of experience with mass privatization. It should be remembered that in 1990 in Poland there were a total of 8,500 state-owned enterprises, most of them in the material production sector, and more than 55,000 other state-owned entities, operating mostly in non-productive sectors (education, health care, finance, insurance, etc.). While obviously not all of them are to be privatized, it is nevertheless clear that the task of privatizing a sufficiently large chunk of the enterprise sector within several years is a monumental undertaking that requires a much more innovative approach.

The first, and rather spectacular, example of large privatization was the case of Universal, a large foreign trade enterprise. The Minister of Foreign Economic Relations decided in early 1990 to convert the limited liability company Universal, owned partly by the Treasury and partly by several industrial enterprises, into a joint stock company and to issue additional shares to be sold to the domestic public and to foreign trading partners. It was decided not to follow this example of privatization, which involved an increase in the initial capital rather than selling shares owned by the state. The critics argued that it was liable to facilitate the 'enfranchisement' of the former *nomenklatura*, who dominated big foreign trade enterprises.[22] Further privatizations were suspended until the new law was enacted.

The conflicting views on the scope, pace and methods of privatization led to prolonged debates on subsequent drafts of the privatization law and inevitably affected the final product itself. The law was adopted, after a long delay, only in July 1990, and only in rather general terms, requiring further elaboration and specification of practical procedures and rules. An important consequence of the multitude of views is the multi-track approach adopted in the government's privatization strategy.

The results of the early stages of privatization were not encouraging. First, the so-called large-scale privatization, relating mostly to big state-owned enterprises, was substantially delayed, not just because it took so long for parliament to pass the law, but also because subsequent steps concentrated on creating an organizational structure within the government to supervise the privatization process, rather than on privatization itself (Dabrowski, 1991). It was not until the Ministry of Ownership Transformation had been established in early autumn 1990 that the privatization programme took off, with the conversion of seven state-owned enterprises into joint stock companies wholly owned by the Polish Treasury on 27 September 1990. Five of these companies were sold through public offering in December 1990 and January 1991.

Second, the adopted method of selling enterprises one by one on the general market proved very time consuming, costly and inefficient. It took several months for consulting firms under contract to the Ministry of Ownership Transformation to prepare privatization plans and prospectuses. The cost of these services turned out to be unexpectedly high, reaching 22.3% of the value of issued shares (the total value of the issue was Zl 300 billion), and 13.4% of the total value of these five companies (Zl 500 billion).[23] These handsome fees were immediately questioned by many experts and officials on legal and economic grounds. Furthermore, the privatization of five companies of very good reputation and good financial standing over a period of four months cannot be regarded as a success, especially if one takes into account that they represent less than 1% of the total assets to be privatized.

Third, the sale itself was not without problems. Shares in two of the companies could not be sold in the originally planned period of six weeks because demand was too limited. This clearly demonstrated how narrow is the market for common stock among the general public in Poland, and that this method of privatization may be of only limited use.

Against this experience, the so-called 'small' privatization can be seen as much more successful. Already initiated in 1989, it was intended to transfer small and medium-sized companies, firms and shops, which were generally under the control of regional and local authorities, into private hands. The emphasis was on the service sector, especially retail and wholesale trade, housing, hotels and catering, and road haulage. The main method used in small privatization was leasing of assets by employees, liquidation and sale of parts of an enterprise against payments in instalments, or auctions. Because of the relatively small amounts of capital needed to take control of assets in the service sector, it was possible to transfer certain property rights (*ius utendi et fruendi*, in particular) quickly and on a relatively large scale. The process was particularly visible in the retail trade sector where, out of approximately 100,000 small and medium-sized shops located all over the country, some 80% were already 'privatized' (i.e. leased in most cases) by the end of 1990 (Bandyk, 1991).

3.2.4 The 1991 Privatization Programme
Slow progress in privatization and the unexpectedly deep and prolonged recession in Poland in 1990-1 induced the Ministry of Ownership Transformation to prepare a new programme, based on revised assumptions and aimed at the radical acceleration of the privatization process.

The main purpose of the new programme was to allow for massive privatization despite the obvious problems with the lack of capital and deficiencies of the existing institutional infrastructure. The new element in the programme was that it envisaged different privatization methods for different categories of enterprises. Specifically, with the aim of creating a 'critical mass' of ownership changes as soon as possible and to minimize the risk of the process being halted for political reasons, two separate programmes were formulated: a programme of 'mass' privatization, addressed essentially to several hundred of the biggest state-owned enterprises, and a programme of 'sectoral' privatization.

The 'mass' privatization plan included the following essential elements:

(1) a two-stage procedure, involving 'commercialization' first and privatization after;
(2) the 'non-capital' transfer of ownership, involving the free distribution among Polish citizens of claims on state-owned assets in the form of 'participation certificates', the offer of shares to employees on preferential terms (or free), and the allocation of shares to pension funds, insurance companies and commercial banks;
(3) the creation of financial intermediaries in the form of National Investment Funds (NIFs);
(4) management contracts for running individual enterprises and investment funds, to be auctioned among specialized management firms.

Initially, 500 of the biggest enterprises were selected for 'mass' privatization, but later during 1991 the number was reduced to some 200, because not all the enterprises qualified for the programme in terms of financial and structural criteria.

The principal advantage of the 'mass' privatization programme is, according to government officials and experts, the possibility of transferring property rights and establishing reasonably efficient corporate governance within a relatively short period, and with relatively little capital required. Moreover, the method avoids the ineluctable valuation problem, at least in the initial stages. Another advantage, which is particularly important for the general public, who are largely unfamiliar with the peculiarities of financial investments, is that investing in the shares of NIFs involves less risk than investing in the shares of particular companies.

But there were also some problems with this proposal. First, new legislation on privatization is required, and it may take a long time for it to be passed by parliament. Second, some observers seem to be uneasy with the large-scale reliance on foreign managers and consultants, expressing doubts whether their loyalty can indeed be guaranteed.[24] It is also doubtful whether these foreign firms can become familiarized in a reasonable time with the specific conditions of the Polish market, whether they will be interested in participating in the plan and on what conditions, and what will be the quality and integrity of their services. Third, conflicts with workers' councils are expected to intensify and may slow down the whole process.

The second component of the new strategy is 'sectoral' privatization. The government selected 34 industrial sectors (at sub-branch level) and commissioned sectoral restructuring and privatization studies from various consulting firms. The analysis is aimed at answering the question about the long-term economic and financial viability of a given sector under new market conditions. Individual enterprises, mostly medium scale, will be privatized through 'commercialization', or liquidation, or direct sale to large individual investors.

While the main economic slogan in 1990 in Poland was 'stabilization', in 1991 the emphasis shifted to 'privatization'. This changed again in 1992, after Mr Olszewski's government halted the privatization process for political reasons. Only after the change of government in the summer was the 'mass' privatization programme reactivated, but it still faces strong opposition in parliament. As a result of these stops and starts, the effects so far are not impressive. Out of a total of some 8,500 state-owned enterprises operating in the material sphere at end-1990, 2,100 enterprises (i.e. some 25%) had been or were still in the process of being 'transformed' (though not necessarily privatized) during 1990–2, but only 52 of them had been effectively privatized through individual sales or take-overs involving actual ownership transfer to private agents.

Experience so far indicates that all 'instant' privatization schemes should be treated with a measure of scepticism. No matter what method is selected, the formal transfer of ownership will not establish an efficient system of corporate governance, nor will it radically change incentives in the short run. Therefore, other measures should urgently be undertaken, parallel to privatization, like a massive conversion of state enterprises into joint stock companies, governed by managerial boards and not by workers' councils. On the other hand, privatization should proceed at a pace that would correspond to the rate of growth of an entrepreneurial class and capabilities. This could be considerably accelerated by opening up special (non-monetary) credit lines for privatization purposes, with privatized state assets as collateral (Rosati, 1990). The de-politicization of the privatization process is essential: fears that the whole reform might be halted and even reversed because of a possible return of communists to power became largely irrelevant after the disintegration of the Soviet Union and the collapse of communist parties in the region (even though self-management sentiments and growing populist tendencies may still impede the privatization process). This should allow for a more orderly implementation of reforms, thus avoiding hasty and ill-considered measures dictated by immediate political needs.

3.3 Reforming the Financial Sector

The inefficient commercial banking system in Poland has increasingly emerged as one of the main obstacles in the reform process. Major problems include:

(1) the poor quality of loan portfolios, making banks financially vulnerable and reducing their potential for financing sound projects;
(2) low capitalization, which makes banks unwilling to recognize non-performing loans;
(3) understaffing and limited professional capability, inhibiting sound credit policy and portfolio selection (notably between good and bad clients);
(4) the inability to resist pressures from local governments or big state enterprises for continuous financing ('credit automatism');
(5) poor legislation, low financial discipline and inefficient supervision by the central bank, making commercial banks vulnerable to corruption and frauds, as demonstrated by many scandals in 1991.

The need to overhaul the banking system has been fully recognized only recently; earlier, the issue had been rather neglected.[25] The efforts by the government to strengthen central bank controls over commercial banks and to help the banks to adjust to a competitive environment have, however, been erratic and largely unsuccessful: parliament and the president have long been split over the draft of a new banking law, and a new governor of the central bank (NBP) could not be appointed for more than six months because of bitter disputes among the main political forces.

To improve the situation in the banking sector, the government must quickly find a solution to the 'bad loans' problem. Several remedies can be envisaged. One possibility would be their consolidation and subsequent transfer to a new, state-owned financial institution, which would be empowered to impose some measure of direct controls over indebted firms. A more sophisticated solution would be to convert the overdue liabilities into short-term commercial paper, convertible into equity shares and issued by indebted firms, and then sold at a discount to commercial banks. Either the banks would impose stricter financial discipline on firms to speed up the necessary adjustment (e.g. through acquiring an equity stake in the troubled enterprise), or they would initiate bankruptcy. This would, however, further worsen the already overburdened balance-sheets of commercial banks. A recapitalization of banks might provide some relief, but it would require additional funds from the budget. These should, however, be provided, because fiscal revenues may be expected to increase as a result of the operation. A third option would be to write off some of the debts. An inevitable moral hazard problem could be minimized by making a credible policy commitment that this cleaning of balance-sheets was a one-time operation not to be repeated in the future.

Whatever method is selected, it must be followed by measures preventing the bad loans problem from re-emerging. This could be ensured by the 'commercialization' of banks, improved legal regulation of financial flows, including triggering provisions for initiating bankruptcy proceedings, and fast-track rules for closing down inefficient firms. Furthermore, principles of prudent lending policies and portfolio selection should be formulated and enforced to prevent banks from continuing to accumulate new non-performing loans. Technical assistance from Western countries would seem to play an essential role in these reforms.[26]

The Warsaw Stock Exchange was opened in April 1991; while having a positive demonstration and educational effect, it as yet has only a marginal role in stimulating full-fledged capital market operations in Poland. What is needed is an efficient mechanism of mergers, buy-outs and acquisitions among state enterprises, and between the public and private sectors.

4   Economic Lessons: What Went Wrong?

4.1   How Much Recession is Needed for Transformation?

Possible explanations of the extreme recession in Poland range over a large variety of exogenous and endogenous factors. Some of them are of a strictly economic character, others are dominated by bitter political disputes and internal conflicts. But the question that should perhaps be asked in the first place is whether the transition from central planning to market must inevitably be associated with a deep recession? After all, it was a common belief that the traditional communist system was so extremely inefficient and inactive that the very change of government and removal of odious communist powers would make a substantial difference in terms of economic efficiency and, consequently, in living standards. As one observer put it, 'if the initial situation was anywhere near so bad as it appeared – if the distortions were so great and these economies so mismanaged – there must be some programmes that would clearly make everyone better off' (Portes, 1991b, p. 3).

Three years' experience of the transition demonstrate that this view was probably overly optimistic and that some recession is indeed unavoidable. But this recognition should not obliterate whatever human errors and mistakes might have been made in the process of planning and implementing the transformation. Ample evidence exists to support the view that the inevitable costs of transition have been exacerbated and amplified in Poland by a combination of unfounded assumptions, wrong estimates, inconsistent policies, and simple inaction.

To be sure, *some* recession is most probably inevitable. For one thing, the shift from central planning to a market mechanism requires laying off labour to open the way for restructuring and to establish a pool of unemployed workers commensurate with the natural rate of unemployment (Laski, 1991). For another, the transformation implies a massive change in relative prices: some activities become inefficient, while others turn out to be more competitive. But destruction is easier and faster than creation: it takes less time to discontinue inefficient activities than to move resources to efficient uses, because in the latter case typically some investment is needed, and new technology cannot be put in place overnight. This loss of output and employment is, however, only temporary and should disappear after the initial reallocation of resources is completed; moreover, these losses should be partly offset by the efficiency gains that are likely to appear after the communist system has been dismantled.[27] On the other hand, the losses will probably be higher under the 'Big Bang', because the asymmetry between destruction and creation effects will be larger. Lastly, some short-term losses appear to be unavoidable because of the exhaustion of some resources, which were overexploited under central planning; for example, depleting natural resources without protecting or replenishing them, or lowering health standards.

But it is doubtful whether these factors can fully account for the massive and protracted downturn in economic activity that was observed in Poland over 1990-1. Other explanations have therefore to be sought. Among those deriving from economic considerations, three main groups of factors seem to be of major importance: (a) errors in the initial design of the stabilization-cum-reform programme, (b) policy mistakes during the programme implementation, and (c) external shocks, especially the demise of the CMEA and the collapse of the Soviet market.

4.2 The Initial Programme Structure: Too Much Stabilization?

4.2.1 Overestimation of Inflationary Overhang

Part of the blame for the striking lack of success could be put on the initial design of the reform programme implemented in Poland. Here, criticism falls into several categories. Some commentators indicate that the stabilization package was generally too restrictive, and that the monetary and fiscal squeeze led to an excessive fall in domestic absorption. The ensuing recession was thus caused by a combination of demand-side (reduced real incomes and wealth) and supply-side (credit squeeze, price shocks, monopolistic behaviour) factors (see e.g. Blanchard et al., 1991; Calvo and Coricelli, 1992; Gomulka, 1991b; Kolodko, 1991a, b; Nuti, 1992; Rosati, 1991b).

It may be argued that the main reason behind the excessive restrictiveness of the stabilization policies was the overestimation of the size of the inflationary overhang in the Polish economy in late 1989. The notorious shortage syndrome, so characteristic of the central planning system, could have led the programme authors (both the national policy-makers and foreign advisers) to believe that only very drastic deflationary measures could effectively mop up the excess liquidity and maintain the flow equilibrium afterwards. There were also considerable doubts as to the effectiveness of standard policy tools in restoring macroeconomic stability in a post-socialist economy. As a result, probably too many instruments aimed at demand reduction were put in place,[28] which not only wiped out the inflationary overhang but also sharply reduced 'normal' demand through the impact on real incomes and wealth. The cause of this miscalculation was the failure to take into account the sharp change in the demand for money, which was a natural outcome of price stabilization and reversed expectations.

A variant of this argument refers to the observed stock adjustment. Faced by the sudden change in relative prices and a liquidity squeeze, Polish firms reduced their inventory stocks and other liquid assets (e.g. foreign exchange holdings) accumulated in the past. The resulting fall in the demand for production inputs may indeed have been contractionary, but its impact was temporary and it could not have been responsible for a prolonged contraction, especially in 1991 (see Figure 7.4).[29]

Another line of criticism (but partly connected with the previous one) points to the one-sidedness of the programme, where the focus was primarily on stabilization goals, presumably with not enough attention given to the supply side and, especially, to institution building. The theoretical framework applied in designing the transformation was perhaps too much influenced by the IMF experience with stabilization and structural adjustment programmes in

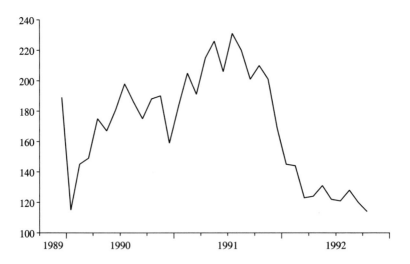

Figure 7.4   Changes in Inventories, December 1989 – October 1992
(Inventories as % of Monthly Sales)

developing countries, with too little attention given to the specific conditions of post-socialist economies (which are characterized by a lack of market institutions, the domination of the state sector, structural rigidities, unstable demand for money and financial assets, etc.).

This standard approach may need substantial revision in the light of the Polish experience in 1990-1 (confirmed by developments in other economies in transition). Perhaps the most important observation is that the pattern of reaction of economic agents to standard monetary and fiscal restrictions in the predominantly state-owned and monopolized economies is different from that in market economies. Exposed to financial squeeze, Polish firms tended first to reduce output and raise prices, then to suspend payments to their suppliers, negotiate various concessions from the banks and the budget, send workers on unpaid leave, and only having exhausted other possibilities did they start to reduce employment. Restructuring programmes, mergers and joint ventures, even if contemplated, rarely materialize in the form of concrete projects in the absence of the immediate threat of bankruptcy.

The (implicit) assumption of behavioural patterns similar to those observed in the West ignores the fact that enterprises in the East have been faced with a different structure of incentives.[30] The lack of genuine owners and an unclear allocation of property rights, the lack of a threat of takeover or acquisition, the excessive powers of workers' councils and/or labour unions, and little competitive pressure from outside make the behaviour of state firms very unresponsive and conservative. The critics of the stabilization programme argue that it actually neglected the need for an immediate and radical overhaul of the existing incentive structure, and thus failed to elicit a positive supply response from the enterprise sector.

4.2.2 Nominal Anchors

Lastly, the Polish stabilization plan was also criticized for its internal structure and design. Most controversial was probably the concept of nominal anchoring, which is one of the key elements in all 'shock' programmes. Experience from stabilization episodes in developing countries indicated that nominal anchors can serve as effective brakes on domestic inflation provided that they are accompanied by monetary and fiscal restraint. When applied in an economy in transition, however, this concept becomes more controversial and vulnerable.

Two main nominal anchors have been used in the Polish stabilization: nominal wages and the nominal exchange rate.[31] The policy of a fixed exchange rate, aimed at holding down the inflation rate, proved to be very costly in terms of output and employment losses. The initial devaluation, intended to anticipate the corrective inflation following the price liberalization and to prevent capital flight, turned out to be excessive because of the greatly overestimated zloty overhang in the hands of households.

Tax-based wage controls, used in Poland as the second nominal anchor, while failing to bring down inflation to single figures, have also had deleterious side-effects. The main theoretical argument for a tax-based incomes policy is that it alleviates wage pressure on prices and reduces the unemployment costs of stabilization (see Dornbusch, 1990). Moreover, the restrictive wage policy seemed even more appropriate in the economies in transition, where state firms are labour managed and thus tend to pay higher wages at the expense of profits (Coricelli and Rocha, 1991).

While the second argument is valid but should be addressed by direct measures (to remove the distortions faced by state enterprises), the first argument clearly misses the point in the context of the Polish economy. Keeping wages low to encourage labour hoarding and avoid excessive unemployment may be the right policy during the recession stage of a regular business cycle in a market-based economy, where necessary restructuring is marginal, but it is a highly dubious policy during a fundamental transformation, when a massive reallocation of resources is both desired and necessary. The specific wage policy actually applied in Poland, which led to a substantial fall in real wages, has proved socially unfair, economically counterproductive and politically dangerous.[32] Falling real wages reduce the incentives to reallocate labour, allow overmanning to be maintained in inefficient sectors and inhibit productivity growth. The flat wage structure inherited from the past is preserved, the labour market mechanism remains distorted and migration abroad is encouraged. The unfavourable redistribution effects of wage controls may also be pro-inflationary (due to declining savings ratios). While some form of incomes policy was probably desirable in the initial stages of stabilization (albeit mostly as a safeguard device), the indexation mechanism should have been discontinued as soon as possible.

The Polish experience suggests that nominal anchors can be useful instruments of anti-inflationary policies only within a specific policy package and only for a short period of time. If used simultaneously with sweeping price liberalization, then they are bound to produce severe distortions and welfare losses. If extended beyond the period of rapid initial disinflation following price liberalization (probably between four and six months), they are bound to delay the necessary restructuring, and eventually they may 'anchor' the economic recovery. Real anchors may therefore be more suitable at a later stage, once the initial disinflation has been successfully completed.[33]

4.2.3 Was the Devaluation Excessive?

Some degree of initial 'overdevaluation' of the zloty was certainly necessary because the subsequent 'corrective' inflation would quickly erode this margin, and because the credibility of the programme required the fixed rate to be maintained for some time. It could be argued that, without the initial 'overshooting', inflationary expectations would not change. This argument is developed formally in the Appendix.

The margin proved to be too large, however, and the fixed rate, once established, was maintained for too long. The exchange rate was fixed at a level twice the official rate in December 1989, and almost one-third above the black market rate. That could be justified theoretically only if the monetary policy were fully accommodative. But in circumstances of monetary and fiscal restrictions, coupled with a tight incomes policy, the devaluation was clearly excessive. The overshooting of the exchange rate had a strong inflationary impact through a sharp increase in input prices, and was also contractionary in the initial period because of the reduced real incomes of wage-earners and producers, especially in the non-tradable sector. Maintained for too long under high domestic inflation (the government switched to a crawling peg only in October 1991), the fixed exchange rate policy led to a substantial real appreciation of the zloty, heavy loss of competitiveness in the tradable sector, and a depletion of international reserves in 1991.

It has been argued that the initial devaluation could not be contractionary because the imports/GDP ratio was smaller than the share of dollar deposits in the total money supply, and hence the devaluation increased the nominal money stock more than the price level (Gomulka, 1991b). This argument is debatable. First, it was not just import prices that were affected by devaluation, but more generally the prices of all tradables. Second, the argument ignores the fact that households used to assess their dollar holdings with a black market rate rather than the official rate. In fact, the official devaluation by more than 200% over the last four weeks of 1989 had very little effect on the nominal money stock, because the black market rate changed only marginally; on the other hand, it had a very strong impact on prices. This asymmetry led to a sharp drop in the real money supply from the households' point of view. In this way, devaluation proved to be strongly contractionary, and hence excessive.

4.2.4 Social Safety Net too Generous

The stronger-than-expected recession also called for an urgent revision of the original social safety programmes, which had been based on more optimistic scenarios of economic recovery. Generous unemployment benefits and relatively high pension payments, connected with both the low retirement age and various indexation schemes, have proved unsustainable under recessionary conditions and in view of falling fiscal revenues. Shifting redundant labour to retirement may be politically more acceptable than tolerating massive unemployment or under-employment, but in the longer run it proves to be very costly in terms of budget expenditures.

The system of unemployment compensation adopted also gave rise to numerous abuses and significantly increased the moral hazard of reforms.[34] The changes in unemployment compensation schemes introduced in October 1991 and in March 1992 reduced the level of benefits received to 36% of average wages and limited the duration of benefits to 12 months.

4.3   Current Economic Policies: Anti-inflation Bias and no Learning-by-doing

An important reason for the excessive recession may be the misguided economic policies followed during the transition. The central objective of the Polish stabilization plan was to dampen inflation and restore macroeconomic equilibrium. That was indeed the most urgent task and no further progress could have been made in the direction of reforms, unless inflation was brought down to 'civilized' levels and kept under strict control. This is probably why the applied policy package was so concentrated on demand-reducing instruments and included so many austerity measures.

4.3.1 Policy Swings in 1990: From Relaxation in the Summer to Tightening in the Autumn

While the mistakes made in the initial design of the stabilization programme at end-1989 were to some extent both inevitable and understandable, mainly because of a lack of experience, great uncertainty and a political climate conducive to making bold and radical (sometimes too radical) decisions, the policy errors made later in the course of the programme's implementation could have been largely avoided. The biggest mistake was probably the wrong interpretation of the sources of inflationary pressures and the frustrating inability to cope with the deepening recession.

When the Polish economy showed signs of a modest recovery in the second half of 1990, inflation simultaneously accelerated, and the government decided to tighten monetary policies in an attempt to bring inflation under control. Financial restrictions were further strengthened in 1991 and maintained throughout the year. That policy can hardly be considered successful. While the monthly inflation rate diminished from some 5% in the last quarter of 1990 to 3% in the last quarter of 1991, industrial output dropped over the same period by 12%, and unemployment almost doubled to 2.1 million people. Clearly, the macroeconomic cost of reducing the monthly inflation rate by 2 percentage points over one year proved to be rather high. In what follows I will try to demonstrate that the main reason for this was the erroneous interpretation of the *sources* of inflationary pressures in the second half of 1990 and in 1991.

The government's reaction to the acceleration of inflation in the autumn of 1990 had far-reaching economic and political implications. The government assumed that inflation had been spurred by the relaxation of incomes policies in July (the one-time increase in the monthly indexation coefficient for wages from 0.6 to 1.0) and of monetary policies (a reduction in the monthly refinancing rate from 4% to 2.5%). It was also assumed that the relatively good financial position of enterprises might be behind the price increase. Thus, the tightening of financial restrictions seemed to be a logical response to this ostensibly demand-pulled inflation. Consequently, the National Bank of Poland (the central bank) raised the annual refinancing rate from 34% at end-September, to 43% at end-October, and to 55% at end-November 1990; also in November the NBP raised the reserve requirement ratio for deposits held by commercial banks.

Behind the accelerating inflation in the second half of 1990 the government therefore saw a causal relationship running from bank credit expansion to increasing wages and to growing aggregate demand. This view is shared by many authors (see e.g. Calvo and Coricelli, 1992; Dabrowski, 1992). They argue that the relaxation of bank credit did not lead to any output recovery, but was instead inflationary, because firms used the extra funds to raise wages and to repay inter-enterprise debts.

That interpretation was most probably wrong. While the relaxation of financial policies in July 1990 could indeed have been received by enterprises as a green light for cautious expansion, it had only a very limited impact on inflation. First of all, the declining trend in output was reversed and a slow growth in material production was observed. Second, statistics do not confirm the substitution of bank credits for inter-enterprise credits on any significant scale; on the contrary, both stocks have been moving together since July 1990, as illustrated by Figure 7.3. In fact, the second half of 1990 witnessed a substantial improvement in the structure of enterprises' balance-sheets (a reduction in both types of debt), probably a necessary step before healthy expansion can start. Third, the wage expansion in the second half of 1990 was not a result of more and easier borrowing, but was an inevitable 'catching-up' reaction after the sharp decline in real wages in the first half year. It should be noted that the enterprises' liquidity position improved initially because of sizeable capital gains; their restraint in paying higher wages was not therefore a result of lack of funds, but simply reflected high uncertainty, risk aversion and the political consensus reached (implicitly) between the Solidarity labour union and the Solidarity-backed government over a temporary fall in real wages. One should not forget that the official propaganda warned that mass bankruptcies and huge unemployment would come after a few months, and that only financial restraint could save firms from closing down. Moreover, the political climate was supportive of austerity measures, and the labour unions did not push for wage increases, hoping for a recovery in the second half of the year.

However, bankruptcies did not come by the hundreds, nor was the recovery in sight. Slowly growing unemployment, mostly voluntary, did not exert a moderating pressure on wage demands, the real value of savings was eroding rapidly, and patience was gradually exhausted. Wages started to grow faster, first within the limits prescribed by *'popiwek'*, and then beyond these limits (after October 1990). But this growth could hardly have been caused by credit expansion, because the ratio of credit for working capital to sales revenues of enterprises systematically declined between July and December 1990.[35] Moreover, the hypothesis that raising wages led to higher inflation through an increase in aggregate demand is not confirmed by statistical evidence.

To verify this proposition, a simple statistical exercise was performed. First, a regression of monthly inflation rates with respect to monthly changes in the average wage (including bonuses) and incomes of the population was tested for the period from March 1990 to December 1991. The relationship obtained between inflation and the explanatory variables (for both simultaneous and lagged values) proved to be insignificant; thus, other factors must have been at work.[36] I shall return to this point in the next section.

The policy course applied in 1990 has remained a matter of a considerable controversy. The prevailing opinion has been that the relaxation in the summer resulted in the acceleration of inflation, and hence the tightening was unavoidable. I do not share this view. Neither the one-time change in the wage indexation coefficient nor the monetary policy could primarily have accounted for higher inflation. On the other hand, fiscal policy was most probably much more deleterious: the fiscal adjustment from the surplus of Zl 6.5 trillion at end-June to less than Zl 1 trillion at end-December 1990 must have had a strong inflationary impulse, mostly because the fiscal expansion boosted the incomes of lower-income groups. With the benefit of hindsight it may be concluded that precisely the opposite combination was needed: it was not monetary policy that should have been tightened, but fiscal policy, in order to keep consumer expenditure under control and to stimulate restructuring and investment.

4.3.2 Sources of Inflation

More plausible in explaining the persistence of inflation seems to be the cost-push hypothesis. The sharp increase in energy prices in the wake of the Gulf War in the summer of 1990 and the gradual shift to dollar prices for CMEA imports exacerbated earlier corrective increases in some domestic prices (coal, transport tariffs, turnover taxes), and temporarily boosted inflationary expectations.[37] Moreover, the seasonal increase in food prices in the autumn of 1990 was mistakenly taken as another symptom of inflation getting out of control, and the government tightened monetary policy. Hence, macroeconomic demand-reducing measures were used to attack cost-push inflation, the inevitable result being that the economy slid further into recession, with no significant gain on the inflation front.

The cost-push interpretation is sometimes questioned on the grounds that 'cost push' would not materialize unless the monetary policy was accommodative, and hence the government was essentially right in focusing on macroeconomic restrictions. But this view ignores the substitution effect. It is true that monetary restraint always reduces inflationary tendencies, but it is more effective under demand-pull inflation than under cost-push; more importantly, under cost-push inflation it also exerts a strong recessionary impact because of the resulting demand shift from less to more essential products. Faced with steeply rising energy and input costs, many Polish producers had no choice but to increase their selling prices; but the cuts in the real money supply left many of them with rapidly slackening demand. The result was the continued recession-cum-inflation.

The lesson that may be drawn is that after the first phase of the programme, when the price level goes up following price liberalization and then inflation comes down due to restrictive stabilization measures, inflation may continue at an underlying rate determined mainly by cost and supply factors. This type of inflation requires clearly different anti-inflation policies than the initial, demand-pulled inflation. Another lesson is that anti-inflation policy targets should not be overly ambitious, and should be weighed against output/ employment costs: the rewards from reducing inflation from 100% to 10% are much greater than those from reducing it further from 10% to 1%. In this context, the 1% monthly inflation rates already aimed at in Poland in the second half year after the launching of the programme proved both costly and hardly feasible.

4.3.3 The Exchange Rate

Another reason for the excessive recession may have been the fixed exchange rate. Starting with the deeply undervalued zloty after the initial devaluation, the government maintained the level of the nominal exchange rate for more than 16 months, despite rapidly growing domestic prices (by more than 340% between January 1990 and May 1991), apparently being more concerned about the inflationary repercussions of devaluation and about the credibility of its exchange rate policy than about the deepening recession. But this turned out to be bad economics. Imports increased sharply in 1991, while exports stagnated, international reserves declined and interest rates continued to be high, contributing to the recession. Under conditions of fiscal and monetary restraint, a recovery would require an offsetting mechanism for 'crowding-in', e.g. in the tradable sector. A competitive real exchange would provide such a mechanism, at least in the medium run (Dornbusch, 1990).

This experience demonstrates (once again) that, after the initial large devaluation, the currency should not be allowed to appreciate too much in real terms, and that the anti-inflation target should not dominate the exchange rate policy beyond the period of rapid disinflation. Rather, it should gradually be supplemented by other targets, most notably maintaining high competitiveness in tradable sectors.

Eventually, the government devalued the zloty by 17% in May 1991, only a few weeks after declaring its firm intention to keep the exchange rate level unchanged.[38] The move, which was quite surprising in the context of earlier statements but otherwise long overdue, was probably spurred by a sudden deterioration in the foreign trade results in April (a monthly deficit of US$250 million). The devaluation was, however, too small to restore the lost competitiveness of the tradable sector,[39] and resulted in only a limited and short-lived improvement in the trade balance.

In October 1991, the National Bank of Poland switched to a crawling peg against a basket of major convertible currencies, with the monthly rate of devaluation set at 1.8%. While the abandonment of the dogma of the fixed rate was welcome, the switch to a crawling peg had not been preceded by any corrective devaluation of the zloty, thus probably leaving the Polish currency still overvalued in real terms. This led to another devaluation on 28 February 1992 by some 12%.[40]

4.3.4 Monetary Policy

According to official data, monetary policy in Poland was generally restrictive in 1991 and 1992 (see Figure 7.5). The broad money supply (M2 - including foreign currency deposits) declined in 1990 by 44% in real terms, reflecting a drastic fall in the real value of foreign currency deposits (their share in the total money stock declined from 72% at end-1989 to 32% at end-1991[41]), while the domestic money stock increased by 40% in real terms. The monetary squeeze continued in 1991: the real value of M2 dropped by a further 10%, while the domestic money stock declined by 1%. The rationale behind this austere money supply policy was apparently quite straightforward: it reflected the key assumption of the existence of a sizeable 'inflationary overhang', and the consequent conviction that inflation should basically be tackled with monetary and credit restrictions. While it was true that in late 1989 inflation was indeed fuelled by demand factors, the assumption of large 'excess liquidity' in the Polish economy was most probably wrong.

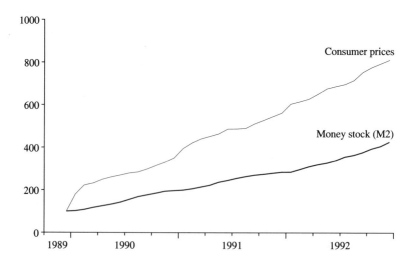

Figure 7.5 Money Supply and Inflation, December 1989 – December 1992
(December 1989 = 100)

It should be noted that the monetary disequilibrium in the late 1980s was rooted in growing inflation and widespread shortages, which reduced the demand for transaction money because of strong inflationary expectations – quite a typical development in an inflationary environment. As a result, the ratio of money stock to GDP fell well below long-term equilibrium values.[42] The stabilization operation, the elimination of shortages and the significant slowdown in price inflation after January–February 1990 all reversed expectations and increased demand for cash balances (a slowdown in velocity). After the initial squeeze, monetary policy should therefore have been less restrictive, responding to the increase in the demand for money. With a contracting money supply, however, the only result could be a sharp decline in the demand for goods and economic recession.

Another implication was that further restrictions in the money supply in late 1990 and at the beginning of 1991 must have led to even deeper recession. While some reduction in the real money stock at the beginning of the programme was indeed necessary to reverse expectations and eliminate the market panic characteristic of high inflation periods, the operation probably went too far and was not followed by a gradual growth in the money supply to meet the increase in demand for cash balances.

The main conclusion that can be drawn is that monetary policy should not be too restrictive for too long. While considered correctly to be the most powerful tool in dampening demand-pull inflation, the monetary policies adopted during stabilization proved to be both more contractionary and less efficient than expected. The policy of a positive real central bank interest rate under high and volatile inflation and a fixed exchange rate led to high nominal rates, sharp fluctuations in the real rates (*ex ante*), and sometimes excessively high real rates, as illustrated by Figure 7.6. Therefore this policy should be modified as soon as inflationary expectations have been reversed. While the principle of a non-negative real rate should be observed by the central bank (otherwise domestic savings would be discouraged), under falling inflation long-term interest rates (on investment credits) should be lower than short-term rates. Otherwise the recession is likely to continue beyond the initial period of extinguishing high inflation.

The excessive restrictiveness at the macroeconomic level was accompanied by a lack of discipline at the microeconomic level. The credit policy proved to be largely helpless in curbing bank lending to loss-making units. In fact, credit was released across the board, and banks' lending policy did not reflect the financial position of particular enterprises. The monetary authorities tried to focus on controlling the level of net domestic assets; but this approach, while theoretically correct, was largely inefficient in practice. The weaknesses of the credit policy led to an accumulation of bad loans in banks and to a general credit squeeze. Good firms would not borrow, either because bank rates were generally very high or because credit ceilings were binding, while bad firms

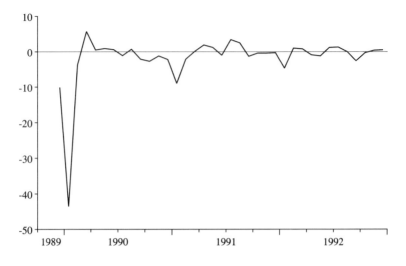

Figure 7.6   The Real Interest Rate, December 1989 – December 1992
(NBP Refinancing Rate Deflated by CPI)

were becoming more and more indebted. Monetary policy proved to be unable to 'fine-tune'.

In the specific circumstances of the Polish economy (an inefficient and rigid banking sector, a distorted incentive structure in enterprises), the monetary and credit policy instruments transplanted from industrialized economies did not work properly. The tight credit policy of commercial banks made enterprises resort to other sources of financing, most notably inter-enterprise credits. A sharp increase in inter-enterprise credits was observed in the Polish economy in the first phase of transition, when firms tried to escape the financial squeeze imposed by restrictive stabilization policies. After a temporary decline in the summer of 1990, the level of inter-enterprise credits started to grow again in the fourth quarter of 1990, probably in response to a tightening of credit policy. The ratio of inter-enterprise credit to total short-term credit extended by commercial banks increased from 68% at end-1989 to 170% at end-1991; this is an emphatic illustration of how limited the 'official' banking system's possibilities of imposing financial discipline on enterprises in fact are, without an accompanying reform of the whole financial sector in the country.

The economic consequences of excessive inter-enterprise credits may be very damaging. First, they in effect neutralize monetary policy at the macroeconomic level by allowing firms to borrow on the zero-interest 'curb' market and thus circumvent credit restrictions. Second, they distort microeconomic adjustment, because the allocation of inter-enterprise credit is typically across the board and efficiency neutral. Thus, good and bad firms end up in a similar position. Third, financial discipline is weakened, as no interest is charged on inter-enterprise credits.[43]

4.3.5 Fiscal Policies

Falling output and sales of enterprises led to a dramatic deterioration in the central budget position. Since February 1991, government revenues have consistently lagged behind expenditures, and as a result a budget deficit emerged, growing steadily to Zl 14.2 trillion at end-June 1991, and Zl 30.6 trillion at end-December (about US$2.7 billion and about 3.5% of GDP).[44]

The main reason for the budget collapse in the first half of 1991 was much lower than planned tax revenues, connected with the declining profitability of enterprises (lower income tax revenues and 'dividend' payments) and the general recession (lower revenues from turnover taxes). The two main sources of budgetary revenues – income tax and turnover tax (planned to secure more than 70% of all revenues in the initial budget) – produced only 30% of planned receipts up to June. The resulting gap was only partly offset by higher than planned revenues from customs duties and especially from the excess-wage tax. (Incidentally, the much higher than expected revenues from the excess-wage tax provide yet another illustration of the 'perverse' objective function of state-owned enterprises: they are ready to protect labour at the expense of diminished profits and capital depletion.) On the other hand, the budget expenditures proved to be unsustainably high, especially social security payments, unemployment benefits and some other transfer payments.

The Polish fiscal system is outdated and inefficient. The lion's share of budget revenues used to come from the state enterprise sector in the form of income tax (40% on taxable profits), turnover tax (rates varying from 0% to 80% of sales revenues), and other taxes like the wage tax, the excess-wage tax and the 'dividend'. Excessive fiscal charges coupled with a sharp fall in enterprise sales inevitably led to a sharp fall in government revenues.[45] The difficult position of the budget was further weakened by the laxity of tax collection.[46]

Confronted with rapidly shrinking tax revenues and with a deficit looming large, the government had to cut current expenditures. This immediately provoked strong criticism of the government's policy in parliament. The budget crisis undermined the political position of Mr Bielecki's government, and was probably the key issue behind his failure to be nominated as Prime Minister again after the parliamentary elections. Nevertheless, from a strictly economic point of view, and contrary to prevailing opinions in Poland, the 1991 deficit may have been beneficial for the economy after all. As is well known, a deficit *per se* does not need to be inflationary: it depends on the structure of expenditures and on the ways by which it is financed. Under the conditions of deep recession in 1991, the deficit probably served as an 'automatic stabilizer', increasing effective demand while apparently not adding too much fuel to inflationary pressures.

The fiscal problem, however, became much more difficult in 1992. The initial government plan to limit the budget deficit to Zl 65 trillion, or 5% of GDP, had to be revised upwards in view of rapidly shrinking revenues. It was estimated that the deficit would probably reach Zl 73–75 trillion in 1992, and would not diminish in 1993. Two-thirds of the deficit is secured by the sale of Treasury bills to the banking system, which crowds out other borrowers and inflates public debt to dangerous levels. Another problem is keeping the deficit under control: the higher the deficit, the higher interest rates have to be to keep inflation at bay, but this, in turn, would further depress the economy and reduce the tax base of the budget. Lastly, the sharp curtailment of public investment contributes to depressed business confidence. This vicious circle can probably be broken only through a cautious but sensible stimulation of investment demand and exports.

One of the necessary measures would be to shift from taxing production to taxing consumption. It should be noted that the increase in individual consumption in 1991 by 6–8% under conditions of falling output signals a major distortion in the existing tax structure. The corporate income tax system should provide sufficient incentives for output expansion, while budget revenues can better be protected with increased taxes on consumption (sales tax, turnover tax, excise tax). Consumption taxes are less dependent on fluctuations in profitability, and could restore the balance between consumption and savings. While inflationary in the initial stages, they would be anti-inflationary in the longer run (through their impact on consumer expenditures and savings). Other measures could include a tax credit on reinvested profits and accelerated depreciation schemes. But their impact on investment would depend mostly on general business confidence and the investment climate in the economy.

4.3.6 Incomes Policy

As already mentioned, the excess-wage tax was considered as the main instrument of wage restraint and as a protective measure against excessive unemployment. It was (implicitly?) meant to protect employment levels at the expense of real wages. But this is a bad instrument. Surprisingly, despite all kinds of critical opinions about the deficiency of this instrument, it was planned to apply the '*popiwek*' in 1992 and in 1993.

To be sure, it is, in a sense, a very convenient policy tool. It is conceptually simple and easily enforceable. On the other hand, it is also very inefficient and has harmful side-effects. To begin with, total wages (and, since 1991, only wages in the socialized sector) constitute only a fraction of the total incomes of the population. Their share declined from 45.7% in 1989 to 30% in the last quarter of 1991, and the share of wages paid in the material goods sector is even lower. The policy of controlling incomes with the help of a tax imposed on only a small and declining fraction of total incomes (and thus aggregate demand) cannot be terribly effective (even if some other incomes are fully or partly indexed to wage incomes). But the side-effect is that wages in the state sector lag behind all other incomes, and this creates a potentially explosive social situation among workers in state-owned enterprises. Second, the '*popiwek*' does not prevent firms from raising wages, as demonstrated by the 1991 data: the increase in total wages above the limits can be estimated at 4–5%. Under pressure from workers' councils and labour unions, enterprises prefer to pay '*popiwek*' and pay higher wages, at the expense of profits. Third, labour lay-offs are not avoided as expected, but at best delayed; and unemployment is systematically rising anyway.

The negative side-effects of the '*popiwek*-cum-indexation' system include the preservation of the distorted and egalitarian wage structure from the past, mass migration abroad, discrimination between public and private sector companies, the depletion of the capital stock (profits are given up for taxes and wages), delayed industrial restructuring, restrictions on the labour market mechanism, falling work discipline and moral hazard. It would be much better therefore to address the problem at source: if labour-managed firms are prone to pay higher wages at the expense of profits, their 'commercialization' and restructuring would be both more efficient and less socially dangerous. If fiscal instruments are to be used at all, wages should be taxed at a rate essentially close the rate charged on profits, thus leaving the budget revenues insensitive to income distribution.

4.3.7 The Need to Shift from Stabilization to Growth

Two general conclusions can be drawn. First, the mistake that was probably made during the first phase of transition was the failure to recognize in time the changing macroeconomic conditions in the Polish economy, and to make the necessary policy adjustment. Emerging unemployment, the elimination of shortages and the restoration of basic monetary equilibrium are all symptoms of transforming the Kornai-type, supply-constrained economy into a Keynesian-type, demand-constrained one. While the transformation is still far from being completed, the change in macroeconomic balance should not be ignored. A gradual shift in macroeconomic targets from anti-inflation to anti-recession, and in economic policies from demand reduction to supply support measures, is therefore required, thus opening the way for a transition from stabilization to recovery and growth.

Subsequent Polish governments, preoccupied mainly with the inflation demon, and apparently unable to move beyond the initial policy design (which worked so well in the initial stages of transformation), were largely helpless when confronted with emerging new problems, such as the growth in inter-enterprise credits and bad loans in the banking system, the collapse of exports to the Soviet market, the inefficiency of bankruptcy procedures, diminishing fiscal discipline, and inertia in the state sector.

Therefore, the focus on macro stabilization, which dominated the first phase of transition, should be quickly balanced by more emphasis on extensive institutional reforms, especially in the banking sector and financial regulation, as well as structural policies. The frustrating inertia observed in the Polish enterprise sector should probably not be taken as a proof of the inability of *all* state firms to adjust; it rather demonstrates that correct and strong enough incentives have not yet been put in place.[47] Privatization is probably the most important instrument of structural change; but it is necessarily slow and costly. Other possibilities should not be neglected in dealing with the large state sector. Corporatization, 'commercialization' and other institutional measures designed to establish a correct incentive structure (e.g. managerial contracts) can be carried out relatively fast and at low cost, and yet they can substantially increase the flexibility of the state enterprises in responding to market signals. If not accompanied by the necessary institutional change, macroeconomic restrictions are destructive, and stabilization effort can be largely wasted.

4.4 Adverse External Shocks

There is no doubt that 1990-1 was a period of unprecedented shocks for the Polish economy. The recessionary impact of domestic reforms was further exacerbated in Poland by a series of unfavourable external developments, including the Gulf War, the dismantling of the CMEA and the political and economic disintegration of the Soviet Union. The increase in energy prices, followed by the shift to convertible currency payments and world market prices in mutual trade, adversely affected Polish terms-of-trade: while forced to pay higher prices for imported fuels and raw materials, Polish producers at the same time faced a sharp decline in demand for their traditional exports of manufactured goods. The most important export market in the region – the Soviet Union – collapsed in 1991, partly because of the shortage of convertible currencies, partly because of increasingly inefficient and chaotic foreign trade and foreign exchange controls, and partly because of sheer political disintegration. As a result, Polish exports to the ex-Soviet market and other ex-CMEA countries declined in 1991 by 35-40% in volume terms. Moreover, because of the shortage of convertible currencies, a considerable proportion of deliveries were in effect not paid for by Soviet importers, adding to the financial difficulties of Polish enterprises.

While the adverse impact of the Eastern trade collapse on the Polish economy is undisputed, it is not yet clear to what extent it has contributed to the observed drop in industrial output. Available evidence suggests that this factor, while providing a convenient opportunity for shifting responsibility for the present recession to external, largely exogenous developments, may in fact be overstated in official statements. It is true that the *volume* of exports to ex-CMEA markets in 1991 declined by some 40% as compared with 1990 (with the ex-Soviet market accounting for the bulk of the fall); but at the same time *export prices* increased by more than 50% owing to the dollarization of trade (and the high implicit dollar/rouble rate), thus partly compensating Polish firms for the loss of export volumes and leaving the *level* of export revenues much less affected.[48]

If, under these conditions, the *share* of CMEA-oriented exports in total industrial output sold diminished by 3 percentage points in 1991, it was not just because of falling export volumes, but also because of the policy of a fixed exchange rate, which provided less and less incentives for exporters, who were facing rapidly rising prices at home. It should be noted that, although industrial exports to all non-CMEA countries increased by 30%, their share in total industrial output also declined by 2.5 percentage points. It appears, therefore, that a stronger recessionary impulse may have come from the appreciated exchange rate and the resulting relative decline in export revenues in general than from the collapse of ex-CMEA markets.[49]

4.5 Short-term Prospects: Is the Recovery Sustainable?

According to many observers, the systematic growth in industrial output after April 1992, as well as the good performance of the construction and export sectors, are signs that the recovery is coming at last. A closer examination of the underlying causes of the output expansion, however, casts doubt on this optimistic assessment.

Since both consumption and investment stagnated or declined during 1992, the only factor behind the growth of industrial output must have been the growth of exports, especially to Western markets. Trade statistics are not yet available, but, according to balance of payments data, export earnings in January–September 1992 totalled US$10,368 million, 11.8% more than in the corresponding period of 1991, while imports grew by only 2.5% to US$9,349 million. Export expansion in the first half of 1992 was, however, boosted by some short-term, temporary factors, which will largely lose their significance in the second half and in 1993. Part of the effect of the elimination of tariffs and non-tariff barriers on a large proportion of Polish exports to the EC on the basis of the Association Agreement since March has already faded; also, the commodity structure of Polish exports (dominated by resource-based and simple labour-intensive goods) does not offer prospects for a long-term expansion. Moreover, exports were encouraged and imports discouraged by a real depreciation of the zloty in the first half of 1992; but this changed in the second half, when wages and producer prices increased at a faster pace than nominal devaluation of the zloty (see Figure 7.7). As a result, export expansion slowed down in the second half of 1992, and the trade surplus diminished to some US$700 million at end-November. The current account may deteriorate further in 1993 because of increased imports of grain (the result of the 1992

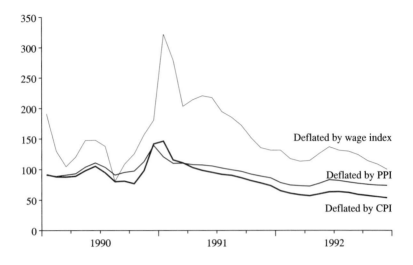

Figure 7.7   The Real Exchange Rate in Poland, 1989-92
(December 1988 = 100)

drought) and higher debt service payments.

The key condition, however, for any sustainable recovery is investment expansion. And yet investment in 1992 was probably lower by 3-4% than in 1991, the reason being high interest rates, the poor financial condition of enterprises and limited business confidence. While the unstable political situation makes any change in the business climate very difficult, change in credit and financial policies seems more feasible. To boost investment opportunities and prospects, interest rates have to be reduced and credit conditions for investment projects relaxed. This should be accompanied by faster devaluation (or a corrective one-time realignment of the exchange rate) to prevent the increase in demand from translating into higher imports and to maintain the profitability of exports. Otherwise the basis for growth will remain very fragile and uncertain.

It is quite certain that inflation will be present in the Polish economy for some time to come, not only because of the likely relaxation of some financial restrictions, but also because of the new round of increases in the few prices that still remain under government control (prices for energy, gas and heating, transport and telecommunication tariffs, housing rents), the increase in indirect taxes (VAT) and the necessary devaluation of the zloty.[50] But inflation may eventually settle down around monthly levels of 1-2%, provided that the government succeeds in keeping the fiscal deficit within limits, no major external shock occurs, and the sociopolitical situation remains under control.

Even if the economy continues to grow in 1993, responding positively to the easing of macroeconomic policies and to intensified privatization efforts, unemployment may in the meantime grow to 2.8-3.0 million people (14-15% of the total labour force), and inflation will persist. GDP is expected to grow by 2% in 1993. But things could get much worse if the populist and excessively interventionist approach gets the upper hand and a wage-price spiral is set in motion, with a rapidly deteriorating external balance.

5   The Social and Political Aspects of Reform

5.1   The Evolution of the Political Situation

The political situation in Poland in 1990-1 evolved from almost total national unity in support of the market reforms launched by the first non-communist government of Mr Mazowiecki, to intensified political conflicts and social protests over the costs of reforms at end-1992.[51] Central to this rapidly changing sociopolitical climate in Poland is the deep economic recession: the country's GDP has dropped by some 20%, and unemployment has been rising steadily, reaching levels that may be potentially explosive in a society accustomed to job security for decades. The recession added fuel to the unfolding political struggle, which was triggered by the presidential elections in 1990 and further inflamed by the parliamentary elections in 1991. Both campaigns, together with the local government elections in April 1990, were supposed to end the transitional period of 'dual power', thus completing the peaceful process of political transformation.

But the outcome, contrary to earlier hopes, proved to be rather disappointing. In the political sphere, the loose coalition of political forces that, under the banner of the Solidarity labour union, had removed the Communist Party from power in 1989, disintegrated rapidly during 1990-1, becoming deeply divided over the distribution of transition costs and the speed and scope of the reform process. This political dispersion manifested itself in the emergence of a mosaic of political parties, most of them quite new on the political scene, largely unknown to the general public, and small in terms of the number of members. Together with a rather unfortunate electoral procedure that favoured small parties, this dispersion resulted in the election of a highly fragmented parliament, with 29 political parties represented, and no single political organization strong enough to win an absolute majority.[52] In the economic sphere, the continuous campaigning, abounding with populist slogans and outright demagogy, led to excessive and often unfair criticism of the government's economic policies. The inevitable result was waning support for austerity measures, and calls for a more interventionist and less restrictive approach.

The new government led by Ms Suchocka was formed on the basis of an ad hoc coalition of the main Christian Democratic and liberal parties. But, with several major parties remaining outside the government coalition, with widely dispersed political forces in parliament, and with the sometimes ambiguous policy of the President, the political position of the new government remains precarious. The fragility of the government's political base was demonstrated during the autumn parliamentary debates on the 1992 budget revision, and further confirmed by the recent wave of strikes in the coal mines. Conflicting economic interests, diverging views on the required policies, and differing concepts of political reform among the coalition parties indicate that the present government's political base may not be sustainable in the longer run.

5.2   The Political Economy of the Transition

The nub of economic and political transformation in Poland (as in other Central and East European countries) consists of replacing inefficient totalitarian central planning by a market democracy. But long-term benefits require some sacrifices in the short run. Who gains and who loses in the transformation? What is the political economy of this process? It is interesting to examine to what extent those social groups that have supported the transformation in the hope of gaining better living standards may actually count on it. As can be seen from the Polish experience, the distribution of the transition costs follows a specific pattern, which may become an important source of frustration and instability in the young democracies.

In *The Road to a Free Economy* (1990), János Kornai addresses his free market manifesto to various social groups. He not only maintains that capitalists will benefit from the market-oriented transformation but seeks to reassure the reader that so too will many other groups: liberals will be happy to see their ideas implemented, young people will be offered exciting new opportunities, consumers will enjoy the elimination of shortages, and pensioners will welcome the halt of inflation. This seems to be an overly optimistic view. The most likely outcome is that in the short run only two categories are likely to gain: entrepreneurs (actual and would-be) and owners of property. With the latter category practically extinct under communist rule, and with the so-called middle class confined to a rudimentary private sector, this leaves a rather narrow social base to support the transformation process consistently. The contrast between the large majority coalition *before* the transformation and the small minority reaping immediate benefits *after* the transformation is indeed baffling.

A closer look at the distribution of costs and benefits among various social groups reveals that the economic burdens fall mostly on wage-earners and farmers. In Table 7.5 changes in the level of real incomes are shown, while Table 7.6 illustrates changes in the income structure.

While the figures presented also reflect changes in sectoral manpower allocation (with large shifts from the public to the private sector), the observed

Table 7.5   Changes in the Real Incomes of the Population, 1990–1
(Previous Year = 100)

Item	1990	1991
Total incomes[1]	73.4	103.0
of which:		
Wages	62.8	91.6
Social transfers	81.8	126.2
Incomes of individual farmers	37.6	60.7
Incomes of private sector (non-agric)	133.5	101.0
Other incomes[2]	94.0	105.2

Notes:
1   Nominal incomes deflated by consumer price index (1990 – 717.8, 1991 – 170.3).
2   Including consumer credits (net), interest on deposits, insurance payments and foreign transfers.

Source: Compiled from Central Statistical Office statistics.

Table 7.6   Changes in the Structure of Incomes of the Population, 1989–91
(Shares in the Total Incomes of the Population, %)

Item	1989	1990	1991
Wages	45.7	39.1	32.4
Social transfers	15.9	17.7	21.7
Agriculture	13.5	6.9	4.8
Private sector	8.2	14.9	14.8
Other incomes[1]	16.7	21.4	26.3

Note:
1   Including consumer credits (net), interest on deposits, insurance payments and foreign transfers.

Source: Compiled from Central Statistical Office statistics.

pattern of income distribution during the first year of stabilization is very illuminating. Total real incomes plummeted by 26%, with the most dramatic fall for incomes of wage-earners (by more than one-third) and especially those of individual farmers (by more than half). The two pivotal social groups were therefore hit hardest in the first period of transformation. The private non-agricultural sector, which was the main gainer in 1990, saw its income position stagnate in 1991.

By contrast, recipients of transfer payments seem to have been best protected; their share in total incomes increased substantially. But the unusually high ratio of pensions and other social transfers to wages, reaching almost 70% in 1991, is something of a curiosity for a country in a deep crisis.[53] In sum, it is hardly surprising that successive governments in Poland struggle for political survival only a few months after being brought to power by an overwhelming majority of the population. Such a policy of income distribution in a Western country would probably be politically suicidal for any government.

It should be noted, however, that the analysis of changes in real incomes and savings in the economies in transition from one system to another is obstructed by statistical and measurement problems. The key issue is how to measure the real wage (savings level) in a shortage economy. It is well known that the statistical real wage (defined as a nominal wage deflated by the price index) does not reflect real purchasing power. On this premise, some authors claim that, even though the statistical real wage has fallen in Poland, the people may actually be better off because of the elimination of shortages (Lipton and Sachs, 1990a).[54]

This is, however, a debatable view. Nobody denies that the elimination of shortages is a good thing. But how this relates to the real wage is a more complex story. First of all, we do not have a clear picture of the scale of shortages in a centrally planned economy; experts' opinions differ in this respect. It may be that they are largely induced by excess demand for goods caused by the high velocity of money in an inflationary environment, and would disappear in a stable-price, no-shortage environment.[55]

More importantly, this view ignores the income distribution aspect. Shortages imply rationing by queuing, which clearly benefits low-income groups. After liberalization, prices reach market-clearing levels, no rationing is required, and queuing is no longer necessary. While high-income groups can afford to pay higher prices, low-income groups are no longer able to trade leisure time for goods, and may be forced to reduce their consumption because some categories of goods have simply become too expensive and thus unaffordable. Whether society as a whole is better off (in the short run) cannot now be determined for sure, as the social utility function is in principle unknown.

An important cost of transformation is connected with unemployment. As mentioned earlier, the shift to a market system must lead to unemployment, not only because the market economy operates with a 'natural' level of unemployment, but also because the asymmetry effect between the destruction and supply-side response during the transformation leads initially to frictional lay-offs. Not only has unemployment risen in Poland, but its level has gone far beyond the limit that was originally envisaged. Both unemployment and reduced job security hit primarily wage-earners.

5.3 Political Lessons

Market-oriented transformation involves some recession in the initial stages and entails a significant redistribution of income and wealth. These reforms affect the living standards of the population and therefore cannot be credibly carried out by governments that lack political legitimacy (Nuti, 1992). *Political approval* for reforms is thus indispensable for successful transformation (Russia may be an example of a country where the reform-minded government is unable to carry out radical reforms because of the fragility of its political base). The political space required for transformation can in principle be obtained either through a democratic upheaval (as in Poland, Hungary or Czechoslovakia), or through a kind of 'social pact', or (exceptionally) through authoritarian rule.

Political support will, however, be *short lived*. The social costs of transition, resulting from the necessary stabilization policies, are bound to erode popular support for the reforms. That is why governments should avoid making overly optimistic statements about reform prospects and should undertake unpopular measures early in the reform programme. On the other hand, the programme should be able to bring about some improvement in living standards soon after its introduction; if it fails to do so, a dangerous expectations gap emerges. In Poland, this critical period lasted for only about nine months; perhaps it would have been longer had the presidential campaign in the autumn of 1990 not split society into a mosaic of political parties fighting each other with astonishing hostility. In Romania, workers' protests and the lack of consensus over the required path of reform led to the fall of Mr Roman's government less than a year after the beginning of the stabilization programme. In Czechoslovakia, the 'grace' period was longer, probably because of relatively better initial conditions, but the much-praised social stability weakened when the election campaign started in May 1992. The split between the Czech and Slovak republics was clearly prompted by deteriorating living conditions, especially in Slovakia. In Hungary, where the fall in living standards appears to be the smallest, society is demonstrating more patience.

The apparently systematic overoptimism in setting policy targets in all countries in transition may suggest that policy-makers tend to ignore the *time factor*. The time-lags between policy actions and expected outcomes were largely unknown when the reforms were started, but generally they seem to be longer than was expected. When the Polish government launched its economic programme in January 1990, it promised that the economic recovery would begin in the second half of 1990; but the recession continued throughout 1990 and 1991, and it was predicted that GDP would not start to recover before 1993. This means that pre-transformation levels of per capita GDP in Poland may not be reached before the year 2000. Not surprisingly, people feel bewildered or even deceived. This frustration is likely to result in calls for increased social and economic protectionism during the transition, and, if not addressed properly, may give rise to frequent changes of government. The tendency to make overoptimistic predictions and to shorten the time horizon – a phenomenon that may be called the *'zoom' effect* – is quite common in all transition countries.

The main social groups (wage-earners and farmers) are likely to be the *main losers* in the first stage of transformation. Their incomes should therefore be protected to some extent, in order to preserve their support for reforms and to prevent the reform process from being derailed. But the methods adopted should not interfere with emerging market mechanisms; direct labour subsidies or (selective) consumption subsidies would thus be superior to price controls or wage indexation.

An efficient mechanism for solving *social conflicts* has to be established, allowing a consensus on vital policy issues to be reached between the main social groups, without impeding current policies. Parliamentary institutions may be too weak and unstable to perform this task; so it may be necessary to establish an institutional framework for direct negotiations between unions, farmers, business groups and the government for solving immediate conflicts. This social-pact type of solution should be designed not to circumvent parliament, but to speed up formal procedures and allow for more efficient bargaining.

Frequent elections at the national level should be avoided, for they induce needless political conflicts and make people believe that a simple change of government may radically improve the situation. The inherent conflict between the restoration of democratic mechanisms of decision-making on the one hand, and the need to apply unpopular economic policies on the other hand, should be solved through making general elections as early as possible and then giving as much time as possible to the elected government. Poland's constant electoral campaigns with their disastrous effects on economic policies should serve as a clear warning in this respect: all the campaigns have been dominated by highly critical (and at times even unfair) anti-government propaganda and by irresponsible promises made by very minor parties and unknown politicians.

This leads us to the danger of *populism*, which looms large in the course of transformation. Whereas imaginative economic policies may reduce this danger up to a point, in no case should populist demagogy be left unanswered. An efficient information policy and popular economic education should be high on the list of priority actions for governments starting the transformation process.

If the first stage of transformation fails to meet popular expectations, necessary market reforms may be delayed because of a lack of social actors with a strong interest in the transition to the market economy. If the middle class is weak and dispersed (and this is the case in transition countries), the reform-oriented government will have to represent the interests of a 'phantom' class, thus acting in the interests of future generations rather than of any existing social group.

This leads to *political instability*. The clash of various interests may be too violent to be solved through parliamentary procedures – as would probably happen in Western Europe. Democratic institutions and practices are still rudimentary, the new political elites lack experience in solving conflicts and accommodating different positions, and no patterns of negotiation and cooperation among the various political parties have yet been established. The parties themselves are weak and lack credibility, and their constituencies are unstable and mistrustful. In such circumstances every government committed to genuine market reforms may expect to come under early popular pressure to ease economic policy or to resign. One implication is that frequent changes of government in East and Central European countries are quite likely. Another is that economic policies may become less and less restrictive over time. The most ominous threat is that political instability will endanger democratic rule and lead to authoritarian government.

5.4   Conclusion: The Need for Political Stabilization

The process of reform in Poland is probably entering a critical stage. Economic recovery must come soon in order to alleviate social tensions; otherwise the government will sooner or later be forced to give in to demands for more economic interventionism and social protection, thereby obstructing the market mechanism and slowing down the necessary restructuring. As a result, irreparable damage may be inflicted on Polish society in terms of loss of confidence in market systems and democratic institutions. In this sense, the economic recovery is a necessary condition for maintaining political stability.

   On the other hand, political stability is also an essential prerequisite for the continuation of economic reforms in these countries. Free markets require political democracy, but for them to be firmly established, time and patience are needed as well. Reforming governments should be offered both – not just to prepare and implement decisions, but to see the first positive results. Democracy cannot paralyse executive powers (Balcerowicz, 1992). Otherwise no structural reform can succeed. At present, however, no economic upturn can be seen in the immediate future, whereas time and patience are quickly running out. How can this vicious circle can be halted and reversed?

   It seems that relief could come from a concerted effort to support recovery through a combination of domestic and international measures. First of all, a gradual shift in economic priorities from stabilization to growth has to take place, with a broad range of policy instruments assigned to deal with structural changes and institutional reforms. The role of the state in overcoming recession and enhancing smooth and vigorous restructuring will probably have to be greater than originally envisaged. Although the danger of excessive and distortionary government intervention cannot be excluded, it would be unreasonable to assume that this type of intervention will always be welfare reducing, as it was under central planning. The emerging market mechanism should not be inhibited by state intervention; rather, government actions should strengthen and amplify the market forces in all those areas where they are weak, underdeveloped or distorted.

The change in economic policies would not, however, be sufficient. It is clear that the domestic potential for economic recovery in Poland is limited, at least in the short and medium run. Investment levels are low and falling, capital resources are meagre, and production is not competitive. These constraints can probably only be overcome with the help of a comprehensive external assistance programme, consisting of three key elements: financial assistance for industrial restructuring, technical assistance for institutional remoulding, and enlarged market access to industrialized countries.

APPENDIX: Devaluation overshooting in the transition to convertibility and free prices

Transition to a market economy requires a comprehensive stabilization programme, which typically includes two critical components: price liberalization and internal convertibility. One of the problems that has to be confronted concerns devaluation. The question arises: how much should the government devalue the domestic currency to secure convertibility under widespread liberalization? The problem will be discussed with the help of Figure 7.A1, where the exchange rate, measured on the vertical axis (in units of domestic currency per unit of foreign currency), is shown to be dependent on the supply of and demand for foreign currency (measured on the horizontal axis).

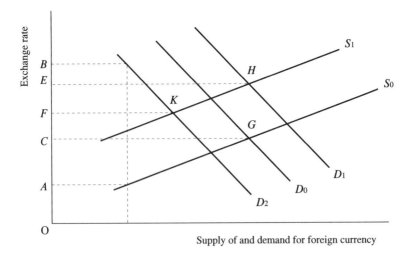

Figure 7.A1   Devaluation Overshooting in the Transition to Convertibility and Free Prices

If the initial official rate is OA and the black market rate is OB, the equilibrium rate would be OC, corresponding to the point G of intersection of the initial demand and supply schedules, D_0 and S_0. But this may be interpreted as a 'static' equilibrium; if prices are liberalized, both schedules may be expected to shift upwards to D_1 and S_1, and the equilibrium exchange rate would rise to OE, corresponding to H. Hence, if the government assumes that the effects of price liberalization affect the demand and supply schedules, it should aim at rate OE. In fact, this was most probably the reasoning behind the sharp devaluation of the Polish zloty in January 1990.

It can, however, be demonstrated that this level of exchange rate would certainly be too high, and thus the devaluation of EA/OA would be excessive. The 'overshooting' would have several causes. First, it is by no means certain that price liberalization has to result in shifting both the demand and supply curves upwards. The shift will certainly take place to the extent that wages are allowed to grow; but at the beginning of stabilization strict incomes polices are normally applied, preventing wages from increasing proportionately to the exchange rate. On the other hand, an increase in goods prices may be expected to produce a demand shift from goods to other assets, including foreign exchange, thus leading to some increase in the equilibrium exchange rate. But this effect is unlikely to assume significant proportions in countries in transition (CITs), because the degree of dollarization prior to stabilization was typically quite substantial in these countries. Hence, the upward shift of the demand and supply schedules will be limited.

More important, it can be expected that the demand for foreign exchange will actually decline as a result of the fall in real incomes and of the reversal in expectations. If it may be assumed that the demand for foreign exchange in CITs is a function of real income (the 'shortage' component) and the 'interest parity' (the portfolio component), then the demand function can be analytically expressed as follows:

$$D = a(Y/p) + b(d^e - i)\Phi \qquad (A1)$$

where d^e is the expected rate of depreciation of the domestic currency and i is the domestic interest rate on zloty holdings. d^e can be expressed as being dependent on the current difference between the black market rate Φ_B and the official rate Φ_O (black market premium):

$$d^e = c(\Phi_B - \Phi_O) \qquad (A2)$$

Substituting and differentiating yields:

$$dD = -a(dp/p)(y/p) - bc(d\Phi_O/\Phi_O)(\Phi_B/\Phi_O) - bdi \qquad (A3)$$

As can easily be seen, all three components of the equation – the real income effect, the expectation effect, and the interest rate effect – are unambiguously negative, therefore dD < 0. It means that the demand schedule shifts downward, and the equilibrium exchange rate will definitely be below OE, and probably also below OC. In Figure 7.A1, the new demand schedule D_2 intersects the supply schedule S_1 at point K, corresponding to the equilibrium exchange rate OF, which is lower than OE.

What happens if the exchange rate is fixed at a higher level, e.g. OE? An excess supply of foreign exchange (or a trade surplus) is expected to emerge soon, and, depending on the degree of monetary accommodation, the demand and supply schedules will drift upwards, thus driving the equilibrium rate towards OE, and the initial 'undervaluation' of the domestic currency will gradually disappear. This scenario was observed in Poland in 1990 and 1991.

The mechanism described relies crucially on the assumption on how expectations are actually formed. If a continuous function (A2) is assumed, the 'proper' equilibrium rate could in principle be established *a priori*, provided other parameters are known. But if expectations follow a non-continuous pattern, a 'ratchet' effect would require the initial devaluation to be sufficiently high to reverse expectations, and then overshooting is inevitable.

Notes

Helpful comments on the first draft by Daniel Cohen, Mario Nuti and Richard Portes are gratefully acknowledged. The revised draft was completed in December 1992.

1 Detailed discussion of the Polish stabilization and reform programme of January 1990 can be found in Rosati (1991a, b), Dabrowski (1992), Kolodko (1991a), Gomulka (1992).
2 Throughout 1990 and 1991 Polish firms hoarded labour while reducing output. Two central factors can be identified behind this behaviour. First, since labour costs increased less than other production costs because of the less-than-proportional indexation scheme and the punitive excess-wage tax, firms were encouraged to substitute labour for other production inputs (capital). Second, labour hoarding is typical of labour-managed firms: the strong position of workers' councils in state-owned enterprises enabled them to protect employment levels under falling output.
3 The increase in convertible currency trade in 1991 resulted partly from the switch from transferable rouble to convertible currency settlements in trade with former CMEA member countries.
4 Because of technical problems connected with the introduction of the new system of statistical reporting modelled on EC rules, trade data from customs statistics for 1992 are not yet available except for the first quarter. According to payments statistics, the trade surplus of US$1 billion registered during January–July shrank to US$734 million at end-November 1992. It is, however, expected that trade data obtained from customs statistics will show a much smaller surplus for the year.
5 It should be noted, however, that a significant part of this increase resulted from the

privatization process, and not from a genuine expansion in output in the private sector.

6 Including cooperatives.

7 In March 1991, the IMF's Managing Director, Mr Camdessus, was still calling the Polish experience an 'encouraging one' (IMF, 1991, p. 127).

8 The systematic growth of industrial output since April 1992 has been driven mainly by export expansion to OECD countries, while other components of final demand either stagnated (consumption) or declined further (investment).

9 Some recent estimates suggest that the impact of the 'Soviet trade shock' may have been responsible for 3–6 percentage points of the 7.2% GDP fall in 1991, depending on the exchange rate used for conversion of rouble trade flows (Rosati, 1992).

10 Tax arrears at end-August 1992 were Zl 28.4 trillion (15% of all budget revenues over January–August), up by 9% since January 1992.

11 One of the inconsistencies relates to the so-called 'dividend' tax, which is charged on companies in proportion to the book value of their assets. Enterprises in capital-intensive sectors, or those endowed with relatively modern capital stock, have to pay very high dividends, amounting sometimes to 80% of gross profits, while old enterprises, with largely depreciated capital assets, pay only symbolic dividend amounts. As a result, net after-tax profit ratios in the former group are lower than in the latter group, thus penalizing modern, technologically advanced and ecologically 'clean' companies. Moreover, the way the 'dividend' is calculated is obviously flawed: not only is its base (i.e. capital assets) periodically revalued to take account of inflation, but the interest rate applied is a 'nominal' rate, thus including the inflation factor. As a result, enterprises pay the inflation 'premium' twice. Despite overwhelming criticism of the obvious absurdities of the 'dividend' tax, it was extended for 1992.

12 See press reports of the second conference of economists convened by President Walesa in September (e.g. *Zycie Gospodarcze*, No. 39, 29 September 1991).

13 All its merits notwithstanding, the 'statistical' recession argument is sometimes overdone when it relates to the reporting practices of state-owned enterprises (see e.g. Beksiak et al., 1991). While under central planning enterprises had incentives to cheat on the degree of fulfilment of planned targets, these incentives largely disappeared with the abolition of central command planning in 1982. Moreover, there was also a tendency to hide reserves and to underreport productive capacities under socialism, to avoid higher planned targets.

14 For a full and succinct development of this argument, see McKinnon (1991).

15 Attempts to estimate the proportion of negative value-added industries in Poland have been undertaken by some authors (e.g. Konovalov, 1989; Hare and Hughes, 1991), but the results obtained depend heavily on certain critical assumptions that may be problematic. First, the official exchange rate applied in both studies for the valuation of tradables clearly distorts the results, because the dollar values are systematically underestimated. If a more realistic dollar rate were applied, then the 'dividing line' of domestic resource cost = 1.0 would be shifted upwards, thus making more activities competitive. Second, the generally poor performance of the food-processing industries may to a considerable extent be due to the application of distorted world prices, which are depressed because of massive subsidies on agricultural and food exports paid by the most important exporters (the EC, the

USA). Third, contrary to what is claimed in the study, the applied world/domestic price ratios do not have to overestimate the magnitude of value added, because exported goods, while indeed being generally of better quality than domestically sold output, also require better material inputs, better packaging, after-sales service and guarantees, i.e additional costs. Besides, the 'quality' argument is of lesser importance in the case of commodities, which account for a considerable proportion of Western-oriented exports. Fourth, the static character of the analysis and the reliance on 1988 data limit the usefulness of the results. To give one example, contrary to what might have been expected, the food-processing industries registered remarkable export expansion in 1990 under the new price–cost structure. In sum, the generally pessimistic conclusions may have to be revised.

16   All industrial sectors contracted in Poland in 1990 by 10–30%, with energy (–9.7%), precision instruments (–16.1%), iron and steel (–17.1%), engineering (–19.6%) and metallurgy (–19.7%) being least affected. Consumer sectors generally contracted more in 1990 (light industry by 33.8%, food processing by 23.7%, wood and paper by 24.9%). This across-the-board decline and its specific structural pattern do not seem to fit Gomulka's hypothesis of the supply side being constrained by forced substitution.

17   See *Rzeczpospolita*, 14 March 1991.

18   The personal income tax (PIT) will be a progressive tax on earned income with three rates (20%, 30% and 40%), but low-level incomes within some range will be excluded through tax allowances. Dividends will be subject to 20% of PIT withheld at source, while capital gains will be exempt from tax until end-1992. There are no plans, however, to subject agricultural incomes and personal interest receipts to income tax. This solution may discourage investment in stocks, favouring savings deposits held with banks. Moreover, the ability of fiscal authorities to collect the PIT on time and to prevent tax evasion seems to be very limited at the moment. Thus individual income taxation may be very inefficient, at least initially.

19   *Rzeczpospolita*, 8 January 1992.

20   For instance, the list of objectives of privatization presented by Bandyk (1991) includes both short- and longer-term objectives, economic and sociopolitical ones; in addition, it combines in a rather loose manner the ultimate goals with various ways and means of privatization. In sum, it covers almost all essential aspects of the transformation.

21   Private property was taken over by the state following nationalization acts issued in the 1940s and 1950s. Altogether, 20,740 private enterprises belonging to Polish and foreign nationals were nationalized in 1945–59. Since 1986, the former owners or their legal successors have been able to apply for compensation or restitution of their property.

22   Only two years later (December 1991) the privatization of another foreign trade company, Elektrim, was eventually approved, and the method applied was a combination of employee buy-out, public offering and invitation for selected institutional partners. Privatization of foreign trade enterprises has become a highly sensitive issue since the Universal case, when it turned out that these companies have a very large cash-generation potential due to their quasi-monopolistic position in foreign trade, which was not always reflected in their valuation.

23   *Zycie Gospodarcze*, No. 42, 1991.

24 See the report prepared by the Polish Academy of Science, *Zycie Gospodarcze*, No. 45, 1991.

25 As one prominent government adviser noted not so long ago: 'The experience [of Poland] suggests that the reform of the banking system, although important, can wait until a later stage of the reform process' (Gomulka, 1991a, p. 67).

26 Some steps have recently been taken to improve the situation. The plan that was adopted in autumn 1992 calls for the consolidation of 'bad loans' in special departments to be established in commercial banks, and for large-scale recapitalization of banks. The 'dormant' stabilization fund of US$1 billion, offered to Poland by the G-24 group at the outset of the stabilization programme in January 1990, will most likely be used for that purpose. On the other hand, indebted enterprises will have to issue bonds against overdue debts, which, at least in theory, will enable banks to initiate bankruptcy procedures.

27 Some commentators insist that the economic structures bequeathed by communist regimes are so hopelessly inefficient, their human and physical capital stock so obsolete and worn out, that once exposed to international prices and competition they cannot possibly survive. But this view does not explain the scale and persistence of the depression, at least in terms of general equilibrium analysis. First, the change in relative prices, while worsening conditions in some industries, has (by definition) to improve conditions in other industries. Second, the absolute level of competitiveness is determined by the real exchange rate: theoretically, there should be a sufficient rate of devaluation to reduce the share of uncompetitive industries to a minimum. The only exception to this rule is the negative value-added case, but it is unlikely to assume significant proportions in the Polish economy.

28 One of the examples of 'excessive' measures was the sharp increase in interest rates on *old* debts of enterprises in January 1990, a move that amounted to a tax on enterprises' assets. As Nuti (1990) points out, a capital gains tax should have been used instead.

29 The ratio of inventories to monthly sales fell sharply in January 1990 to 1.15 from the 1989 average of 1.89, but then increased again, and by the third quarter of 1990 exceeded its level in 1989. In 1991 the ratio fluctuated between 2.0 and 2.2, but it fell to 1.2–1.3 in March 1992 and has remained at that low level since then. Inventories in the enterprise sector in September 1992 were only 7% higher than in September 1991, but monthly sales were 80% higher (in nominal terms).

30 This view has also been shared by some IMF officials. In an interview, the IMF representative in Poland (speaking in his personal capacity) admitted that it had been a mistake to assume that state enterprises and banks would behave according to market principles (*Rzeczpospolita*, 4–5 April 1992).

31 Sometimes the nominal money supply is mentioned as the third nominal anchor, as bank-specific credit limits imposed a constraint on the growth of monetary aggregates.

32 The excess-wage tax, called '*popiwek*', links the growth of wages in individual enterprises with an average inflation rate for the country, thus breaking the relation between individual wage and individual work performance. Moreover, the concept of '*popiwek*' is flawed by a more fundamental contradiction: the assumption that the lack of genuine owners would lead to excessive wage payments at the expense of profits is at odds with the idea of preventing excessive wage payments through

taxing profits. If nobody is interested in profit maximization, penalizing profits for excess wages does not appear to be very effective. Indeed, this is confirmed by Polish enterprises' behaviour in 1991 and 1992.

33 The economy 'anchored' with the fixed exchange rate is bound to defend this rate with high nominal interest rates, which is necessarily contractionary. Adopting a policy of constant real money supply following market stabilization would probably be less recessionary.

34 Ample evidence exists (albeit mostly anecdotal) that many unemployed people, while registering for unemployment compensation, work in the black economy in the private sector or start their own commercial activities (this phenomenon is particularly strong in large urban areas).

35 Dabrowski (1992) claims that the 'relaxation' of monetary policy in mid-1990 was a 'serious economic and political mistake'. But even his own data do not support this view (leaving aside the political implications). According to his Table 1, net domestic assets (NDA) grew at the monthly rate of 4.6% in March–July 1990, when inflation was falling and output stagnated, and at 3.0% in August–December 1990, when inflation was rising and output was expanding. Regressing his data on NDA against monthly inflation rates (CPI), the following equations have been obtained for simultaneous and lagged NDA values (standard errors in parentheses):

$$CPI = 118.4 - 0.132\,NDA \qquad R^2 = 0.2158$$
$$(0.089)$$

$$CPI = 149.2 - 0.421\,NDA(-1) \quad R^2 = 0.5988$$
$$(0.122)$$

$$CPI = 104.7 + 0.006\,NDA(-2) \quad R^2 = 0.0001$$
$$(0.189)$$

$$CPI = 89.6 + 0.152\,NDA(-3) \quad R^2 = 0.0808$$
$$(0.182)$$

$$CPI = 92.7 + 0.121\,NDA(-4) \quad R^2 = 0.0491$$
$$(0.189)$$

The first two specifications show a negative correlation between NDA and CPI, while the other three display a very weak positive correlation. Hence, no relationship can be demonstrated between the changes in NDA and the changes in the inflation rate, and the Dabrowski's hypothesis on the impact of 'relaxation' is not supported. By contrast, Dabrowski is right to criticize the excessive shift in the budget policy.

36 The following equations were obtained (*t*-statistics in parentheses):

$$CPI = 111.665 + 0.068\,WAGE - 0.138\,INCOME \qquad R^2 = 0.0753$$
$$(0.732) \qquad (-1.201)$$

$$CPI = 93.906 + 0.023\ WAGE(-1) + 0.075\ INCOME(-1) \qquad R^2 = 0.716$$
$$(0.245)(0.654)$$

$$CPI = 91.524 + 0.040\ WAGE(-2) + 0.080\ INCOME(-2) \qquad R^2 = 0.1130$$
$$(0.430)(0.687)$$

where CPI is Consumer Price Index. The following equation was obtained for net domestic assets (NDA) of the banking system for the period from March 1990 to December 1990:

$$CPI = 106.406 - 0.017\ NDA \qquad\qquad\qquad R^2 = 0.0072$$
$$(-0.076)$$

37 The share of dollar transactions in Polish imports from the Soviet Union (the main supplier of fuels and raw materials) increased from 35% in the second quarter of 1990, to 64% in the third quarter of 1990, and to 76% at the end of 1990, even though the formal abolition of rouble trade was planned for 1 January 1991. This important fact seems to be ignored by many observers in explaining the acceleration of inflation in Poland in the second half of 1990.

38 See: Letter of Intent to the IMF, *Rzeczpospolita,* 18 April 1991.

39 Since the May devaluation was coupled with the abandonment of the dollar-pegging and the shift to basket-pegging, the rate of devaluation against other currencies (mostly EMS currencies) was merely sufficient to offset their relative appreciation against the dollar, leaving their zloty rates practically unchanged.

40 In fact, the government decision might have been motivated primarily by much worse than initially anticipated foreign trade results in 1991. While preliminary trade figures for 1991 showed a surplus of some US$200 million, the revised data (available at end-February) revealed a deficit of some US$600 million. Official international reserves declined from US$4,850 million in January 1991 to US$4,300 in January 1992.

41 The initial ratio of hard currency accounts to the total money stock was definitely inflated, because it was converted at the depreciated exchange rate of Zl 9,500 per US$.

42 This is demonstrated by the following table, where M1/GDP and M2/GDP ratios are shown for Poland, 1985-91.

Year	1985	1986	1987	1988	1989	1990	1991
M1/GDP[1]	0.192	0.192	0.179	0.142	0.081	0.065	0.124
M2/GDP[1]	0.375	0.372	0.368	0.311	0.249	0.195	0.271
M2/GDP[2]	0.212	0.209	0.199	0.157	0.091	0.074	0.133

Note: M-values computed as geometric averages of beginning- and end-of-period values.
Sources:
1 Central Statistical Office statistics for M1 and GDP
2 *International Financial Statistics*, line 34 for M2.

43   Some authors tend to disregard these costs, arguing that inter-enterprise credit is an illiquid monetary asset and is, therefore, of limited danger to the overall effectiveness of monetary policy (e.g. Gomulka, 1991a, p. 67). This is simply not true. If firms are not restricted in spending categories, they can increase or continue to pay wages through inter-enterprise 'borrowing', even though the commercial banks refuse to provide financing. Less liquid assets (bank deposits of 'creditor' enterprises, inventory stocks, foreign currency holdings) are converted into highly liquid assets (wages paid in cash), and the structure of the total money stock changes in favour of more liquid assets. Furthermore, if many firms behave in a similar manner, it is very likely that, at some point in the resulting chain-reaction, inter-enterprise credit gets monetized (when the banks extend additional credits to their more creditworthy clients). Both effects, the 'substitution' effect (substitution of more for less liquid monetary assets) and the 'monetization' effect (the increase in the money supply through additional lending), work together to strengthen the inflationary impact through an increase in demand, and to slow down the necessary restructuring process by allowing inefficient firms to escape bankruptcy.

44   In view of the much smaller revenues than planned at the beginning of 1991, the central budget was revised in November 1991. That was essentially an accounting operation, aimed at realigning the main budget positions with the expected outcome for the whole year. Total planned revenues were reduced from Zl 289 trillion to 217 trillion, total expenditures were cut from Zl 293 trillion to 243 trillion, with the deficit increasing from Zl 4 trillion to 26 trillion (*Rzeczpospolita*, 13 November 1991).

45   The excessive 'fiscality' in the enterprise sector can be seen from Figure 7.2. While the ratio of costs to sales revenues increased by 8 percentage points from 1990 to 1991 (from 79% to 87%), gross profitability dropped by 21 percentage points (from 29.4% to 8%) and net (after-tax profitability) dropped by 16 percentage points (from 13.4% to -2.3%).

46   Arrears in tax payments and various ad hoc tax credit allowances amounted at end-November to 11% of total budget revenues earmarked for 1991 (*Rzeczpospolita*, 6 February 1992, p. IV).

47   That Polish state firms can adjust, provided incentives are strong enough, is demonstrated by the remarkable expansion of convertible currency exports in 1990 (by 40%), or by the sharp reduction in inventories in the first few months of stabilization.

48   The level of export volumes must fall under sharply rising prices, unless the price elasticity of demand is zero. But the *ex post* price elasticity of demand for Polish exports in the ex-CMEA markets was close to unity.

49   The situation, however, may look different at the microeconomic level. The fall in ex-CMEA demand was not proportional for all categories of goods; some Polish exporters faced a total disruption of *all* their exports, with no immediate possibility of shifting sales to other markets.

50   According to some observers, some two-thirds of price inflation in Poland in 1991-2 can be considered to have been caused by government decisions (see e.g. Zienkowski, 1993).

51   According to public opinion polls, Mr Mazowiecki's government, after announcing its bold programme of market-oriented reforms, enjoyed 90% support in December 1989; only two years later, support for market reforms had fallen below 50% (*Gazeta*

Wyborcza, 4 February 1992).
52 The strongest party, the Democratic Union (led by former Prime Minister T. Mazowiecki), won only 11.9% of votes, taking 62 out of 460 seats in the Sejm; on the other hand, left-wing parties linked to the former communist-led coalition won almost a quarter of all seats.
53 This is not just connected with the very low retirement age limit in Poland, but may also be a symptom of excessive social safety programmes, including overly generous unemployment compensation schemes (on this issue, see Holzmann, 1991).
54 Some prominent authors pushed this line of reasoning to extremes, arguing that workers are in fact better off because their wages, expressed in dollars, increased substantially (Sachs, 1990). But this is simply false. One cannot speak of an improvement on the grounds that the statistical wage increased from US$108 to US$131, because the purchasing power of the dollar declined over the same period by more than half.
55 The real money stock (M2) in Poland declined only by 3% between November 1989 and June 1990; but GDP declined over this period by some 10%, and the economy moved over this period from endemic shortages to general financial equilibrium.

Bibliography

Balcerowicz, L. (1992) 'Demokracja nie zastapi kapitalizmu' [Democracy is not a substitute for capitalism], *Rzeczpospolita*, 9 October.
Bandyk, C. (1991) 'Privatization in Poland. Problems, Achievements and Foreign Investment Policy', Warsaw: Ministry of Ownership Changes, June, mimeo.
Beksiak, J., U. Grzelonska, T. M. Rybczynski, and J. Winiecki (1991) 'List otwarty w sprawie gospodarki', *Rzeczpospolita*, 15 and 16 October.
Blanchard, O., R. Dornbusch, P. Krugman, R. Layard and L. Summers (1991) 'Reform in Eastern Europe (the WIDER Report)', Helsinki: World Institute for Development Economics Research.
Brabant, J. M. van (1991) 'Property Rights Reform, Macroeconomic Performance, and Welfare', in H. Blommestein and M. Marrese (eds.), *Transformation of Planned Economies: Property Rights Reform and Macroeconomic Stability*, Paris: OECD.
Calvo, G. and F. Coricelli (1992) 'Stabilizing a Previously-Centrally-Planned Economy: Poland 1990', *Economic Policy* 14, pp. 208-25.
Caselli, G. P. and G. Pastrello (1990) 'Poland 1990: From Plan to Market Through Crash?', *WIIW Forschungsberichte*, No. 166, Vienna, August.
Coricelli, F. and R. R. Rocha (1991) 'A Comparative Analysis of the Polish and Yugoslav Programmes of 1990', in P. Marer and S. Zecchini (eds.), *Transition to a Market Economy*, Paris: OECD, pp. 189-243.
Dabrowski, M. (1991) 'Privatization in Poland', Warsaw, mimeo.
   (1992) 'The Polish Stabilization 1990-1991', *Journal of International and Comparative Economics*, No. 1.
Dornbusch, R. (1990) 'Policies to Move from Stabilization to Growth', London: CEPR Discussion Paper No. 456.
   (1991) 'Strategies and Priorities for Reform', in P. Marer and S. Zecchini (eds.), *The Transition to a Market Economy*, Paris: OECD, pp. 169-83.

Gabrisch, H., K. Laski, et al. (1990) 'Transition from the Command to a Market Economy', *WIIW Forschungsberichte*, No. 163, Vienna.

Grosfeld, I. (1990) 'Prospects for Privatization in Poland', in *Economic Transformation in Hungary and Poland, European Economy* 43, Brussels: Commission of the European Communities.

Gomulka, S. (1991a) 'Poland', in P. Marer and S. Zecchini (eds.), *The Transition to a Market Economy*, Paris: OECD, vol. I.

(1991b) 'The Causes of Recession Following Stabilization', *Comparative Economic Studies*, 33(2), Summer.

(1992) 'Polish Economic Reform 1990-1991: Principles, Policies and Outcomes', *Cambridge Journal of Economics*, September.

Hare, P. G. and I. Grosfeld (1991) 'Privatization in Hungary, Poland and Czechoslovakia', London: CEPR Discussion Paper No. 544.

Hare, P. and G. Hughes (1991) 'Competitiveness and Industrial Restructuring in Czechoslovakia, Hungary and Poland', London: CEPR Discussion Paper No. 543.

Holzmann, R. (1991) 'Safety Nets in Transition: Concepts, Recent Developments, Recommendations', in P. Marer and S. Zecchini (eds.), *The Transition to a Market Economy*, Paris: OECD, vol. II, pp. 155-80.

IMF (1990), *IMF Survey*, 19 February.

(1991), *IMF Survey*, 15 April.

Kolodko, G. W. (1991a) 'Inflation Stabilization in Poland: A Year After', 1st International Economic Conference, Università di Roma, 'La Sapienza', Rome, 7-9 January, mimeo.

(1991b) 'Transition from Socialism and Stabilization Policies', *Rivista di Economica Politica*, June, pp. 289-330.

Konovalov, V. (1989) 'Poland: Competitiveness of Industrial Activities, 1961-1986', Washington DC: The World Bank.

Kornai, J. (1990) *The Road to a Free Economy. Shifting from the Socialist System*, New York: Norton.

Kurowski, S. (1991) 'Anatomia stabilizacji', *Zycie Gospodarcze*, No. 47.

Laski, K. (1991) 'Transition from Command to Market Economies in Central and Eastern Europe: First Experience and Questions', The Vienna Institute for Comparative Economic Studies, mimeo.

Laski, K. and F. Levcik (1992) 'Alternative Strategies for Overcoming the Current Output Decline of Economies in Transition', Vienna: Österreichische Nationalbank, Working Papers, No. 9.

Lewandowski, J. and J. Szomburg (1989) 'Property Reform as a Basis for Social and Economic Reform', *Communist Economies*, No. 3.

Lipton, D. and J. Sachs (1990a) 'Creating a Market Economy in Eastern Europe: The Case of Poland', *Brookings Papers on Economic Activity*, No. 1.

(1990b) 'Privatization in Eastern Europe: The Case of Poland', *Brookings Papers on Economic Activity*, No. 2.

McKinnon, R. (1991) *The Order of Economic Liberalization: Financial Control in the Transition to a Market Economy*, Baltimore, MD: Johns Hopkins University Press.

Nuti, D. M. (1990) 'Stabilization and Sequencing in the Reform of Socialist Countries', World Bank-IIASA Seminar, March, mimeo.

(1991) 'Privatisation in Socialist Economies: General Issues and the Polish Case', in H. Blommestein and M. Marrese (eds.), *Transformation of Planned Economies: Property Rights Reform and Macroeconomic Stability*, Paris: OECD.

(1992) 'Lessons from the Stabilisation Programmes of Central and Eastern European Countries, 1989-1991', Commission of the European Communities, Economic Papers, No. 92, May.

PlanEcon (1990) *PlanEcon Report*, No. 38-39, 28 September.

Podkaminer, L. (1992) 'Inflacja hiperrecesyjna' [Hyper-recessionary inflation], *Zycie Gospodarcze*, No. 19.

Portes, R. (1991a) 'The Transition to Convertibility for Eastern Europe and the USSR', in A. Atkinson and R. Brunetta (eds.), *Economies for a New Europe*, London: Macmillan.

(1991b) 'The Path of Reform in Central and Eastern Europe: Introduction', *European Economy*, Special edition No. 2, Brussels: Commission of the European Communities.

(1992) 'The Contraction of Eastern Europe's Economies', Discussion at IMF-World Bank conference, Washington DC, 3-5 June.

Rosati, D. K. (1990) 'Pulapki prywatyzacji' [Privatization traps], *Zarzadzanie*, No. 10.

(1991a) 'The Sequencing of Reforms and Policy Measures in the Transition from Central Planning to a Market Economy', in P. Marer and S. Zecchini (eds.), *The Transition to a Market Economy*, Paris: OECD, vol. I.

(1991b) 'The Polish Road to Capitalism. A Critical Appraisal of the Balcerowicz Plan', Thames Polytechnic Papers in Political Economy, New Series No. 2, Spring.

(1992) 'The Impact of the Soviet Trade Shock on Central and East European Countries', Geneva: UN ECE, mimeo.

Sachs, J. (1990) 'A Tremor, Not Necessarily a Quake, for Poland', *International Herald Tribune*, 30 November.

(1991) 'Sachs on Poland', *The Economist*, 19 January.

UN ECE (1991) *Economic Survey of Europe 1990-1991*, New York: United Nations Economic Commission for Europe.

Winiecki, J. (1992) 'The Polish Transition Programme: Stabilization Under Threat', *Communist Economies and Economic Transformation*, 4 (2).

Zienkowski, L. (1993) 'Z hamulca - na gaz?', *Polityka*, No. 1, p. 4.

Appendix*   Central Europe: recent economic developments

Czech and Slovak Republics

Some indications have become available that the economic stabilization which seemed to occur in mid-1992 (production in traditional sectors was stabilizing at its depressed level, and output and employment growth in new sectors, e.g. the private service sector, was gaining momentum) was only short-lived. First provisional estimates show a decline of GDP by almost 10% in 1992 compared to 1991 (GDP dropped by 16% in 1991), implying a significant deterioration in economic performance in the second half of the year (minus 5% compared to the first half). Furthermore, inflation, which came down to a single-digit figure between May and August 1992, accelerated again to a monthly rate of 2% from September, before the introduction of VAT led to another surge in prices in January 1993. The acceleration of inflationary pressure forced the central bank to tighten monetary policy through increasing its key interest rates by 1.5% to 9.5% (discount rate) and to 14% (lombard rate) from 30 December. The general government budget remained by and large balanced, although its underlying trend was not very favourable. The allocation of shares for the first wave of large-scale privatization was completed by the end of 1992. In April/May ownership rights will be transferred, and new shareholders will be able to exercise their voting rights as from June 1993.

Uncertainty about the procedures and effects of the separation of Czechoslovakia into two independent states may have been the major cause of the surprising further decline in economic activity in the course of the year. Indeed, the 'divorce' dominated political discussion and political action throughout 1992, unsettling potential domestic and foreign investors.

*   This Appendix is an excerpt from the January/February 1993 issue of *Economic Reform Monitor*, prepared by the Directorate-General for Economic and Financial Affairs of the European Commission.

Furthermore, investment and modernization of the capital stock were also hampered by large-scale voucher privatization, as new owners were not yet installed, while old owners and managers were not seriously interested in restructuring. In consequence, under-investment has continued in both republics (except in the Slovak housing sector). Unemployment rates continued to come down in the course of 1992. Labour productivity, however, has not yet picked up. This indicates that large-scale adjustment in the labour market is still to be accomplished.

The balance of payments was very strong in 1992, although the trade performance weakened in the course of the year. The overall balance of payments is estimated to have recorded a surplus of US$2.2 bn (US$1.2 bn in 1991). The trade balance is estimated to have registered a small deficit, although exports to the West have been growing strongly. Inflows of foreign direct

Czech and Slovak Republics – Main Economic Indicators

	1990	1991	1992	latest
GDP at constant prices[1]	0	-16	-10	Q1-Q3
Czech Republic[1]			-8	Q1-Q3
Slovak Republic[1]			-10	Q1-Q3
Agricultural production[1]	-2	-14		
Industrial production	-4	-21	-17	Q1-Q3
Czech Republic[1]	-3	-25	-17	Q1-Q3
Slovak Republic[1]	-4	-25	-17	Dec
Consumer price index[1]	10	58	12	Dec
Czech Republic[1]	10	57	13	Dec
Slovak Republic[1]	11	61	9	Dec
Unemployment rate (%)[2]	1	7	5	Dec
Czech Republic[2]	1	4	3	Dec
Slovak Republic[2]	1	12	10	Dec
Budget balance (% of GDP)[3]	0	-2	-2	Dec
Czech Republic[3]			-1	Dec
Slovak Republic[3]			-4	Dec
Trade balance (US$bn)[4]	-0.8	0.9	-0.3	Jan-Nov
Current account (US$bn)[4]	-1.1	1.0	0.9	Q1-Q3
Gross foreign debt (US$bn)[2]	8.1	9.3		
Debt/export ratio (%)[5]	135	91		

Notes:
1 Percentage increase over (the same period of) the previous year.
2 End of period.
3 Consolidated state budget deficit, accrual basis.
4 In convertible currencies.
5 Gross hard-currency debt as percentage of hard-currency exports.

investment, initially very strong, were dampened during the second half of 1992 by the impending dissolution of the federation. Official reserves were reaching the equivalent of 2.8 months of imports by year-end (1.3 months in 1991). In view of the strength of the reserves, the authorities decided not to draw on IMF resources under the stand-by arrangement during the latter part of the year, although the performance criteria were met and the review of the programme was successfully completed. At end-1992, gross external debt in convertible currencies stood at US$9.9 bn, and debt service at 13% of exports (down from 15% in 1991). The exchange rate, which is pegged to a basket of five currencies, remained stable.

The separation of the two republics has been managed in a peaceful way. The two republics agreed to divide assets and liabilities in the general ratio of 2 (for the Czech Republic) to 1 (for Slovakia). Furthermore, a customs union was established and monetary union was initially maintained, until separate currencies were introduced on 8 February.

Both the Czech and the Slovak economies are suffering from the transformation problems typical of all formerly centrally planned economies. Slovak industry is concentrated on heavy industry and arms manufacturing, which is not in itself a disadvantage in the short run, as long as competitiveness at present exchange rates is achieved and international market access is not impeded by foreign governments for political reasons. However, with respect to attracting foreign direct investment, with its potential to create jobs, the structure of manufacturing industry in the Czech republic may give it a significant advantage over Slovakia.

Available information on the relative economic performance of the two republics indicates that Slovakia is performing better in terms of inflationary pressure while the Czech republic has a better record in output and public finances, and the labour market. Slovak inflation is expected to have reached 9% in 1992, compared to 13% in the Czech Republic. Also, average nominal wages in Slovakia increased more slowly than in the Czech Republic. On the other hand, Slovakia's GDP fell by about 10% in the first three quarters compared to a decline of about 8% in the Czech Republic. With respect to the structure of domestic demand, Czech consumption and investment declined at about a similar pace, while a strong recovery in (construction) investment in Slovakia was more than offset by a sharp slump in consumption. Slovakia's public finance deficit is approaching 4% of its GDP while the respective Czech deficit has been contained below 1% of the Czech GDP.

So far, the Czech Republic's labour market seems to have digested economic shocks, both external (collapse of CMEA trade) and internal (transformation process), more easily than Slovakia. Although output and employment in agriculture, industry and construction, which employed about 60% of the total labour force, dropped roughly similarly in both republics (which, incidentally, means that the negative output shock for Slovakia has not been as disastrous as expected), unemployment is much higher in Slovakia than in Bohemia and Moravia. By end-1992 the Czech unemployment rate stood at below 3%, while Slovakia's unemployment rate came down from almost 13% in early 1992 to slightly above 10% by the end of the year.

Hungary

1992 was the third consecutive year of severe contraction in the Hungarian economy. With the breakdown of the CMEA trading system, the transition to a market economy has been more painful than expected. The positive effects of the reform are starting to be felt, however, with the development of the private sector and the emergence of market mechanisms. A mild recovery, or at least a stagnation, is expected in 1993.

After declining by 10.2% in 1991, GDP is estimated to have fallen by 5% in 1992. Although export growth was sustained, with an expected growth rate in volume of between 5 and 8% in 1992, private consumption fell by more than expected, as a result of the decline in purchasing power and the still high propensity of households to save. But the main factor in 1992 was the reduction in stocks, which took place in response to the tightening of financial constraints. These trends were attenuated in the last part of the year, opening the way for a recovery in 1993.

In the first eleven months of 1992, industrial production stagnated around the

Hungary - Main Economic Indicators

	1990	1991	1992	latest
GDP at constant prices[1]	-5.0	-10.2		
Agricultural production[1]	-4.0	-3.0		
Industrial production[1]	-10.5	-19.1	-11.0	Jan–Nov
Consumer price index[1]	28.9	35.0	23.0	Dec
Unemployment rate (%)[2]	1.7	8.5	12.2	Dec
Budget balance (% of GDP)[3]	0.8	4.6		
Trade balance (US$bn)[4]	0.3	0.2	0.3	Jan–Nov
Current account (US$bn)[4]	0.1	0.3	0.5	Jan–Nov
Gross foreign debt (US$bn)[2]	21.3	22.7	22.1	Nov
Debt/export ratio (%)[5]	335	245		

Notes:
1 Percentage increase over (the same period of) the previous year.
2 End of period.
3 Consolidated state budget deficit, accrual basis.
4 In convertible currencies.
5 Gross hard-currency debt as percentage of hard-currency exports.

low level prevailing at the end of 1991. The recession affected all sectors, but particularly metallurgy and engineering, which were producing at about one third of their 1985 level of output. The official statistics, which do not fully take into account the expanding private sector, overestimate the recession. In 1991, industrial companies employing fewer than 50 employees, the category where the private sector is concentrated, increased their production by 50.1%, compared to a fall of 21.5% for companies with more than 50 employees. In 1992, the contribution of the private sector to GDP is estimated to have increased from 25% to around 30%.

The number of registered unemployed reached 663,000 by the end of the year, corresponding to 12.2% of the workforce. The Ministry of Labour has predicted that unemployment will reach a peak close to 20% in 1993, even if a recovery materializes. Real per capita income shrank by 3.6% in 1991, and by 2.4% over the first eleven months of 1992 compared to the same period of 1991. Hungarians have responded to the deterioration in their living conditions by increasing savings: the savings ratio increased from 9.8% in 1990 to 15.3% in 1991. Data on households' savings for the first three quarters of 1992 indicate that this trend continued throughout 1992, although a slowdown in the savings growth was recorded at the end of October.

Since January 1991, when consumer prices increased by 7.5%, monthly price increases have overall decelerated, resulting in an inflation rate of 35% in 1991. Inflation slowed down further in 1992, with an annual rate of 23%. This trend is projected to continue with an inflation target of 14–17% for 1993, in spite of large price increases in January related to the switch to a two-tier VAT system.

For the second consecutive year, the recession undermined the fiscal stabilization undertaken by the Hungarian government. In 1991, the deficit target was overshot by one percentage point of GDP. In 1992, the central government fiscal deficit amounted to Ft 197.1 bn, exceeding its original target of Ft 70 bn. Spending was kept within budgetary limits. But all the components of fiscal revenue yielded less than expected and had to be revised downwards. A special effort was made to improve the collection of companies' arrears in the payment of social security contributions and taxes, in particular customs and excise duties. The deficit was financed by domestic savings and bank liquidity. In 1992, the government started to issue long-term bonds and from the end of November allowed foreigners to buy such bonds as a step towards liberalizing capital markets. However, government debt is rapidly increasing and its service is becoming an increasing burden for the government: in 1993, debt service will amount to about 16% of total expenditures. The worse than expected fiscal performance led to the suspension, in summer 1992, of the IMF three-year extended financing facility which became effective early in 1991. With the approval of the 1993 budget, based on a budget deficit of Ft 185.4 bn, Hungary will comply with the target of a public deficit below 6% of GDP, and the IMF is likely to resume assistance.

The positive external performance is an unexpected feature of the Hungarian transition. In 1991, the current account in convertible currency recorded a surplus of $267 million, a result in sharp contrast with the original forecast of a deficit of $1.2 bn. In 1992, a similar outturn occurred with a trade surplus of $272 million and a current account surplus of $520 million at the end of November against a forecast of a trade deficit of between $300 and $500 million. In spite of an increase in the travel allowance from US$50 to US$300 in July, the tourism account improved. The trends are, however, not as favourable as the overall results for the year suggest. Since mid-1992, the monthly trade balance has been in deficit, with export growth levelling off and import contraction coming to a halt. This is also reflected by customs data, which, for the period January–November, show a trade deficit of $423 million, a decline in imports of 2.9% compared to the same period last year, and an increase in exports of 9.8%. Corresponding figures for the period January–July were, respectively, $60 million, -8.8% and 14.1%. Hungary is progressing further in reorienting its trade towards the EC, which from January to October 1992 represented 50.5% of Hungarian exports, against 46.1% in the same period of 1991. Trade with the ex-CMEA partners is slowly recovering: in the first ten months of last year, Hungarian exports to the zone increased by 14.3% and imports by 10.1%.

International reserves in foreign currencies expanded from $1.1 bn at end-1990 to $ 4.8 bn at the end of November 1992. They now cover more than 5 months' imports. Gross external debt in convertible currencies is stabilizing, reaching $22.1 bn at the end of November 1992. Fluctuations around this level are mainly related to the changes in the D-Mark/US$ exchange rate. Foreign direct investment, which reached $1.45 bn in 1991, well above the expected $550m, progressed but at a slower rate in 1992: by the end of October, $1.14 billion had come into the country.

The Forint was devalued three times in 1992, in March by 1.9% against the dollar-ECU basket, in June by 1.6% and in November by 1.9%. This devaluation by 5.5% does not make up for the inflation gap between Hungary and its main trading partners. But, given the good balance-of-payments performance and the sustained inflow of foreign capital, the Hungarian government thinks that the economy can cope with an appreciation of the Forint. On 1 July 1992, an inter-bank market was set up and the foreign exchange regulations were further liberalized. To begin with, the fluctuations of the Forint vis-à-vis the main currencies will be limited to 0.25%.

In 1992, the changes affecting the productive sector accelerated. In 1991, 11% of state assets were sold, yielding total income close to Ft 40 bn, of which 85% was hard-currency cash. In 1992, it is estimated that 16 to 17% of state assets were privatized and privatization income amounted to Ft 72.1 bn, with a lower foreign participation. Transformation of enterprises into companies has been slower than expected and the deadline for completion of transformation had to be postponed until mid-1993. The enforcement of the bankruptcy law in 1992 has been a very active channel of restructuring: between January and November 1992, 3.2% of economic organizations, i.e. 2145 cases, declared bankruptcy. The legislation mainly affected agriculture and, within the sector, the co-operatives. It also significantly affected large companies with more than 300 employees. The development of the private sector was sustained with the continuous expansion of small and medium-sized enterprises and joint ventures. Overall, the number of companies increased from 29,400 at end-1990 to 52,700 at end-1991, to reach 67,400 in November 1992. However, all these positive developments are mainly concentrated in the industrial and trade sectors. Restructuring has hardly begun in large sectors of the economy, such as the financial sector or the large monopolies of infrastructure and public utilities, and to some extent agriculture. In 1993, the government intends to extend the reform to these sectors. A major step was made with the approval of a credit consolidation scheme in December 1992, which will enable about Ft 153.1 bn of bad debts to be cleared from the banks' balance sheets. The banks will then be on a sound basis to be privatized. In the short term, the recapitalization of the banks should also free some resources for more profitable segments of the economy and result in lower interest rates. This should ultimately foster the expected recovery in investment.

The programme of structural reform proceeds. In 1991, efforts were concentrated on the completion of the legal and regulatory framework for a market-based business environment and the launching of the privatization process. In 1992, the government focused on ways to speed up privatization and prepared the ground for a reform of public finance and social sectors. In 1993, these efforts will be continued with the reform of the transfer and social security systems and the privatization of the banks. No major change in the macroeconomic policy stance is seen as necessary for the time being, since the government considers that past stabilization policies and the present degree of development of the private sector provide adequate conditions for a recovery.

Poland

The declining trends which were strongly evident in the Polish economy during 1989 were exacerbated by the radical stabilization measures introduced by the 'big bang' of 1 January 1990. The stabilization programme was supported by the $1 bn Polish Stabilization Fund, comprising contributions from a number of Western donors. The programme helped to reduce inflation from 640% in 1989 to 45.6% in 1992. The effect of the drought on food prices in the second half of 1992 prevented inflation from falling faster (non-food price inflation stabilized at about 36% towards the end of the year)

GDP declined by 12% in 1990, 7% in 1991 and an estimated 1% in 1992. The decline in 1992, however, conceals an improvement in industrial output, which increased by 3.5% compared to 1991, mainly through increased exports. Moreover, had it not been for the large fall in agricultural output (estimated to be 14%) because of the drought, GDP would have shown some growth in 1992. Privatization and the restructuring of state enterprises have resulted in an increase in the contribution of the private sector to total GDP. This rose from 28.4% in 1989 to 45.3% in 1992. However, the combination of the recession and the restructuring process has resulted in increased unemployment, which rose from negligible levels at the start of 1990 to 2.5 million in December 1992 (13.6% of the work force). Moreover, the effects of restructuring on the many areas dependent on single large plants or sectors has led to substantial regional variations in unemployment. The rate ranges from 5.9% in Warsaw to over 20% in some northern and eastern regions. The overall rate of growth in unemployment has, however, slowed down in recent months, reflecting the recovery in industrial output.

Poland – Main Economic Indicators

	1990	1991	1992 latest	
GDP at constant prices[1]	-11.6	-7.2	-1.0	Jan–Dec
Agricultural production[1]	-2.2	-0.9	-14.0	Jan–Dec
Industrial production[1]	-21.3	-14.0	3.5	Jan–Dec
Consumer price index[1]	249.3	60.4	45.6	Jan–Dec
Unemployment rate (%)[2]	6.3	11.8	13.6	Dec
Budget balance (% of GDP)[3]	3.1	-5.6	-6.0	Jan–Dec
Trade balance (US$bn)[4]	2.2	0.1	0.7	Jan–Dec
Current account (US$bn)[4]	0.7	-2.2	-0.2	Jan–Dec
Gross foreign debt (US$bn)[2]	49.0	48.4	50.9	Sep
Debt/export ratio (%)[5]	400	340	300	Jan–Sep

Notes:
1 Percentage increase over (the same period of) the previous year.
2 End of period.
3 Consolidated state budget deficit, accrual basis.
4 In convertible currencies.
5 Gross hard-currency debt as percentage of hard-currency exports.

The pronounced decline in economic activity has had an adverse impact on the public finances. In both 1991 and 1992 the budget deficit overshot its targeted limit. This was mostly due to the poor financial condition of many state enterprises, which resulted in the accumulation of tax arrears amounting to 43 trillion zloty (about $3.2 bn) by March 1992. Moreover, the upturn in activity during 1992 was mostly concentrated in the growing private sector, from which the government is experiencing difficulties in gathering taxes. The financial position of state enterprises did not improve, so tax receipts from them did not recover.

The 1992 budget originally envisaged a deficit of 65.5 trillion zloty ($4.8bn), keeping the deficit within the limit agreed with the IMF, of 5% of GDP. However, this target was revised to 82 trillion zloty (about 7% of GDP), in agreement with the IMF, following lower than expected revenues and the refusal of parliament to sanction cuts in pensions and benefits designed to compensate for the shortfall. The eventual outturn is now thought to be 69.3 trillion zloty (about 6% of GDP), substantially lower than the revised ceiling. The 1993 budget envisages a deficit of 5.1% of GDP, and will form one of the performance criteria for a new IMF stand-by loan. This package includes the introduction of a temporary 6% import surcharge. The budget has been agreed by the cabinet and is under discussion in parliament, where it has met with strong opposition, particularly to the proposals to limit expenditure on pensions.

Pressure to raise expenditures is coming from trade unions. Although the government did not concede to pay demands in the wave of strikes during the summer, unrest continues, stemming from both wage demands and workers' concerns about privatization and unemployment. In an effort to ease workers' concerns and prevent further disputes, the government has proposed a raft of measures under a new 'Pact on State Enterprises'.

The introduction of convertibility and the adoption of a liberal trade regime in 1990 were aimed at importing the world price structure and promoting trade with the west. To a large extent this has been successful, although in 1991 the rapid breakdown of CMEA trade, the rise in energy prices and the real appreciation of the zloty resulted in a weak trade balance. The first 11 months of 1992 saw a trade surplus of $734m. However, this conceals a markedly different performance between the first and second halves of the year. The first half saw exports rising above imports, which remained steady, but after mid-year imports rose sharply to match export levels. This is thought mainly to reflect the effects of the drought on agricultural trade.

Two recently negotiated trade accords are to come into effect in 1993. An agreement with Hungary, the Czech republic and Slovakia providing for free trade in a limited group of industrial goods will come into effect on 1 March 1993, the ultimate aim being a customs union by 1 January 2000. A trade agreement with EFTA was initialled in November, to come into force on the same day.

The convertibility of the zloty was established in January 1990, in conjunction with a devaluation. Since then, two further discrete devaluations have been required, in order to maintain competitiveness and offset the effects of domestic inflation. In addition, a 'crawling peg' policy has been in operation since October 1991, which entails a 1.8% devaluation of the zloty each month against a basket of five Western currencies.

Poland had been unable since 1981 to service fully its external debt, which in February 1991 stood at around $48.5bn, of which about $32bn was owed to 17 of the Paris Club of government creditors. In March 1991 Poland reached an agreement with the Paris Club, which envisages an ultimate reduction of the net present value of the debt by 50%. The first 30% reduction is to be achieved by March 1994, the remaining 20% is contingent upon an IMF-supported programme being in place. The government and the IMF have reached an agreement in principle on a stand-by loan that would release the second debt-reduction tranche, but its adoption hinges on the Polish parliament accepting the agreed budget deficit limit for 1993. The Paris Club deal is an umbrella agreement, requiring each creditor to negotiate a separate bilateral agreement with the Polish authorities. By end-November 1992, some 14 bilateral arrangements had been reached with the western creditors. The Polish government is seeking a similar deal on the $10.6bn owed to commercial banks, plus $1.5bn of overdue interest. Total foreign debt amounted to $50.9 bn at the end of September 1992.

The stabilization of the Polish economy has been broadly successful, but the unanticipated weakness of the supply response has led to a shift in the focus of attention towards structural reform and institution-building: in particular, privatization and the reform of the financial system. A large number of small and medium-sized enterprises have already been privatized through a system of direct sales by auction, but the privatization programme for large enterprises has progressed at a slow pace. The privatization laws provide for two methods of case-by-case privatization, either through commercialization, i.e. the transformation of a state-owned enterprise into a joint stock or limited liability company, or through liquidation, i.e. the dissolution of an enterprise and the privatization of its assets.

The laws also envisage a mass privatization scheme, which is currently under parliamentary scrutiny. Under this scheme 600 state enterprises, to be managed by 20 National Investment Funds, would be transferred to private ownership. To encourage fund managers to maximize the value of the companies for which they were responsible, they would receive both a flat-rate payment and further payment on the basis of the enterprises' performance. Participation certificates would be sold to Polish citizens for a fee equal to not more than 10% of the average monthly wage.

By the end of September 1992, some form of ownership transformation had taken place in 1,875 enterprises, leaving 6,305 still under state ownership and control. The so-called 'Pact on State Enterprises' is intended to accelerate the progress of privatization. Certain specified groups of state enterprises would be given six months to decide upon their preferred privatization method and to submit a plan for restructuring. Acceptable plans would then receive favourable terms for debt rescheduling, tax arrears and workers' equity and representation. Failure to submit a suitable plan would result in commercialization on less favourable terms. This scheme would exclude those enterprises covered by the mass privatization programme and certain sensitive sectors.

The privatization process is complicated by the absence of a sound commercial banking system. A two-tier banking system has been created, by the removal of the 'big nine' state commercial banks from the control of the National Bank of Poland (NBP). In addition, a liberal licensing policy has resulted in the creation of about sixty new private banks, half of which are privately owned while the rest belong to state enterprises. However, about 90% of commercial credit is managed by the nine state commercial banks, the large majority of which goes to state enterprises. These banks inherited portfolios beset with problems of bad loans, which have subsequently been exacerbated by the recession. The government is examining proposals for the recapitalization of the banks using the Polish Stabilization Fund. During the course of 1993 the NBP aims to abandon direct credit ceilings in favour of greater use of interest rates and open-market operations to control credit. Treasury bill sales proceeded in 1992, attracting some foreign interest. The Treasury debt to the NBP increased by 42 trillion zloty in 1992.

A thorough reform of the country's public finances is under way. The tax system is being overhauled, with the aim of increasing tax revenues from the rapidly expanding private sector in order to make up for falling revenues from unprofitable state enterprises. Personal income tax was introduced from 1 January 1992, and value added tax is scheduled to be introduced in mid-1993.

Index